SCARLETT
FEVER

FEATURING

The Collection of
HERB BRIDGES

SCARLETT FEVER

The Ultimate Pictorial Treasury
of *Gone With the Wind*

by **WILLIAM PRATT**

Macmillan Publishing Co., Inc.

NEW YORK

Collier Macmillan Publishers

LONDON

Macmillan Publishing Co., Inc.
866 Third Avenue, New York, N.Y. 10022
Collier Macmillan Canada, Ltd.

Library of Congress Cataloging in Publication Data
Pratt, William, 1939-
Scarlett fever.
 1. Gone with the wind. [Motion picture]
2. Mitchell, Margaret. 1900-1949. Gone with the wind.
3. Mitchell, Margaret, 1900-1949—Film adaptations.
I. Title.
PN1997.G59P7   791.43′7   77-13825
ISBN 0-02-598560-4

First Printing 1977

Printed in the United States of America

Sincere thanks is extended to:

The New York Daily News for permission to reproduce the photograph of Vivien Leigh on the cover of this book, which appeared in its Coloroto section in the December 17, 1939 edition.

The *Atlanta Journal* and the *Atlanta Constitution* for permission to reproduce photographs of Margaret Mitchell, Clark Gable and Vivien Leigh.

The Academy of Motion Picture Arts and Sciences for permission to reproduce photographs of its awards statuettes, plaques and scrolls (© A. M. P. A. S.).

The Book-of-the-Month Club for permission to reproduce the cover and inside pages of its June 1936 bulletin to members.

The New York Times for permission to reproduce the first page of its May 4, 1937, edition and to quote lengthy excerpts from its August 1, 1976, story by Joseph Morgenstern concerning the proposed sequel to *Gone with the Wind* (copyright © 1976 The New York Times Company).

Photoplay magazine for permission to reproduce pages from its October 1937 and November 1937 issues and the *Photoplay* Gold Medal Award for 1939 (which was voted to *GWTW*).

RCA Victor for permission to reproduce the jacket cover of original recording of *GWTW*'s score (copyright © 1954 Radio Corporation of America).

Time magazine for permission to quote lengthy excerpts from its May 5, 1961 review of *GWTW* (copyright © 1961 Time, Inc.).

TV Guide for permission to reproduce the cover of its November 6, 1976, edition with artwork by Richard Amsell (copyright © 1976 Triangle Publications, Inc.).

Variety for permission to quote lengthy excerpts from its June 9, 1976, issue concerning the proposed sequel to *GWTW* (copyright © 1976 Variety, Inc.).

Underwood and Underwood for permission to use the photograph of the time capsule on page 77.

*To Margaret Mitchell and her feverish Scarlett,
who gave the world a tomorrow filled with hope . . . and dreams*

Contents

THE BOOK

THE MOVIE

3

THE PHENOMENON

1976 AND THE FUTURE

Acknowledgments

The author expresses his thanks for these essential contributions:

To
MARGARET RYAN PRATT,
ROGER ELLIS BLUNCK,
JAMES REID PARIS
and WILLIAM PARIS
for their invaluable research and editorial assistance
and for the restoration of something almost lost.

To
ROBERT SUSSMAN
for his photography of Atlanta and the Herb Bridges Collection.

To
K. F. P.
who made it possible.

and to the following who unselfishly donated time, effort and encouragement to this project and in so doing caught *Scarlett Fever* themselves: Julia Anderson, Lynne Anderson, Anne Babatch, Dorothy C. Brennan and Stephen Wechter of the Fort Lee (New Jersey) Free Public Library, Patricia Buckley, Yvette Curran, Edmund Davidson, Paulette Frank, Patricia Goff, Douglas Gorab, Kathy Goss, William Griffin, Richard Harwell, Robert H. Hausladen, Jr., of the Southern Comfort Corporation, L. Lee Helsby, Ellen Houlihan, Donald E. Jones, Paula and Jack Kramer of Movie Star News, Peter Lenihan, Susan Leslie, the Libby Family, Rose Lillian, John Malanga, Mary Catherine McGrane, Michael Mentone, Francis R. Meyer, Jr., Erica Miles, Fred Miles, Virginia Miles, Helen Mills, Janet Musgrove, Kathleen Napoli, Barbara Novack, Joel Novack, Fred W. Oser of the Monmouth County (New Jersey) Library, Carole Owen, Michael Owen, Adeline Pagliughi, R. A. Roberts, Diane Romano, Fred Romary, Agnes C. Ryan, Richard Siegel and Roy Friedlander of Illustrators, Inc., Thomas Snyder, Eric Spilker, Syril Stavitsky, Phyllis Sussman, Richard Walton, Rosalind Wallace, Caryn Watkins, Robert Wille and Rebecca Winter.

Introduction

Why *Gone with the Wind*? I had never really thought about it. In my younger days I just assumed that *everyone* regarded it as the ultimate phenomenon and didn't wonder why I had accepted it in that way myself. Until I began this project my own connections with it were limited to the movie version, which I had viewed more times than I prefer to admit during each of its theatrical reissues. Even before being exposed to the film I had heard about its marvels from my godmother, who loved the book and had seen the picture repeated times herself. She told me that a woman named Margaret Mitchell had written a story based on the life of her grandmother and that it had later become "the best movie ever made."

After what seemed an eternity (doesn't it always in childhood?) the picture returned and my brother and I trotted off to see it at a local theatre. In those days children's morals were carefully protected in theatres by women called matrons, who saw to it that no unaccompanied youngster remained after six o'clock. So, just as Scarlett was hiring convicts for her lumber mill, that stern lady in white escorted us from the auditorium—leaving us to wonder how the story ended. The following evening one very irate mother returned with sons in tow, demanding to know why tickets were sold to children for such a long movie if they couldn't see it all. The embarrassed manager quickly admitted us all—this time free of charge. (Years later my concentration would be broken during that same scene—courtesy of the National Broadcasting Company—and again I would have to wait twenty-four hours to see the conclusion.)

I had become fascinated with the lady who made a dress from her drapes, although, admittedly, the story was a little over my head at that age. But when the picture returned seven years later I was able to grasp the poignancy and importance of it all and saw it eight times within five months. It was then that I also attempted to read the book but soon put it aside because, I feared, the vast differences between the two might spoil something that had become quite special in my life. I almost resented Margaret Mitchell's novel for that reason and vowed never to try reading it again. But fate has a way of changing things. I have now read the book several times and have added a rich new treasure to my life which I look forward to revisiting on future occasions.

Drawing the assignment to write a book on the history of *Gone with the Wind* did not seem as challenging at first as it soon became. I told friends it would take me about "three months." Instead it involved a full year of dawns through midnights, seven days every week, and

even then I felt I had only scratched the surface. It would be impossible to tell the *whole* story of *Gone with the Wind* in a single book or possibly even in a shelf-full. But, like David O. Selznick, who gave the illusion of presenting the complete novel on screen, I determined to present all the highlights—and some of the more amusing trivia—of that phenomenal "event" which had grasped America's attention for more than forty years.

The quest brought me to Herb Bridges, who owns what is probably the world's largest collection of *GWTW* memorabilia, highlights of which were used to illustrate this book. Herb's path had crossed *Gone with the Wind*'s even before he realized it, since he once worked as an usher at Loew's Grand Theatre, where the picture had premiered. Years later, when that theatre's management discovered original displays from that 1939 engagement stored in its attic, Mr. Bridges was able to rescue them just before their scheduled destruction. In the intervening time Herb's collection had grown from what, it would seem, was an almost trivial beginning. In the early 1960's, while attending a holiday party, he became involved in a debate as to what actress had played Belle Watling on screen. Herb was sure it was Ona Munson but purchased an old copy of *GWTW*'s movie edition a few days later to prove it to his disbelieving friend. At the time the used-book dealer had offered him a first edition of the novel but Herb turned it down. Upon reflection he decided it would be a nice thing to have and returned to the store, but found the book had already been sold.

Herb Bridges eventually found another first edition, purchased it (the first of many he would own, quite a few autographed by the author), and a challenging avocation began. Within a dozen years he had accumulated hundreds of editions of the book from virtually every country it was printed in, several of them autographed by heads of state. Herb's voluminous collection of books became, he was later informed, the third largest in the world—exceeded only by those in the Margaret Mitchell Estate and the Atlanta Public Library.

The pursuit of collectibles next led Herb Bridges to those connected with the movie version, and through the years he acquired thousands of photographs related to the film, as well as posters, dolls, trinkets and other fascinating memorabilia. A high point in his life occurred when he produced an exquisite display featuring his collection for Rich's department store in Atlanta to tie in with the festivities surrounding the 1967 "premiere" of *GWTW* in that city. Most remarkably, the Herb Bridges collection was amassed basically through the gentleman's correspondence with other *GWTW* followers throughout the world, since he only infrequently leaves his home town of Sharpsburg, Georgia, where he lives comfortably with his wife, Eleanor, and their three children.

Herb Bridges was far from alone in devotion to *Gone with the Wind*. In my research, conversations and personal encounters I received only a hint of the vastness of it all—which was fairly overpowering and more than a little frightening to someone trying to set the "whole" story down on paper. There was the charming Yvette Curran of New York, who first read *Gone with the Wind* in its French translation at age ten when she was living in Egypt. According to her own description, she was "shaken beyond words" and "started to reread it an hour after finishing the last page—the hour in between was spent in loud sobs mourning Melanie's death and Rhett's departure." Yvette's continuing love affair with *GWTW* impelled her to learn English in order to read the book in its original language and she would eventually lose count of the number of times she had read it in its entirety. After seeing the film, Yvette—an impressionable eleven—began collecting every picture and clipping from it she could find. After twenty-five years of searching, she has assembled what she feels is the most comprehensive collection of pictures from *GWTW* in existence—more than twenty-five hundred—which she keeps in forty-five custom-made leather albums. Each picture has been captioned with matching lines from the book or movie script.

But there were still others I encountered whose lives were touched, if even in small ways, by the total phenomenon of Margaret Mitchell's story and its film: Kathryn Libby of Connecticut, who reserved a place of honor in her home for a Scarlett O'Hara doll; Michael Owen, who devoted an entire wall of his Brooklyn Heights apartment to framed photographs of "Rhett Butler"; Anne Campbell of Montreal, who wrote to tell me that the television showing of *GWTW* marked her eighty-first viewing of the film; and the youthful Henry and Gina Zerella, who selected "Tara's Theme" as *their* song to be played at the reception following their wedding.

Why *Gone with the Wind*? I couldn't get that question out of my mind. What was there about it that had so captured the imagination of millions decade after decade? I thought of its place in my own life and realized it had been there all along. I remembered that those reissues of the movie version had coincided with important milestones in my past—my high school graduation, the death of my father, and at another turning point which was to profoundly influence my personal future. It seemed to be there continually waiting throughout my life at moments of joy or decision, poignance and tragedy—even to two hours before its network television premiere.

It had been *Gone with the Wind*, indirectly, that led me to the longest association of my professional career and projects related to it that guided me through my most difficult time there. And it was *Gone with the Wind*, directly, that took me away from there to something far more important.

Even more significantly, I realized that *Gone with the Wind* had imparted a philosophy to me years ago that sustained me through all the crises and traumas of my life: to think about them tomorrow and to realize that tomorrow is indeed another day.

Why *Gone with the Wind*? I think I know now.

WILLIAM PRATT, 1977

THE BOOK
The Fever Begins

"I just lifted the phrase from its context because it had the far away, faintly sad sound I wanted."

—Margaret Mitchell

Margaret Mitchell and the Remington portable typewriter she used to write her book.

1926-1934: The Legend Years

Nineteen hundred and twenty-six . . . Americans were celebrating a very special birthday and a triumphant flight over the North Pole . . . Republican leadership had dominated the country for five years, while older generations despaired for the future of wild youth in an era called "The Jazz Age" . . . commercial aviation, sound movies and television were much-discussed novelties not taken too seriously by the sophisticated public . . . the National Broadcasting Company inaugurated network radio programming from New York City to as far west as Kansas City, delighting over two million listeners . . . a method was introduced to bring published literature to customers through their mailboxes . . . and a young Atlanta newlywed quietly busied herself with pleasure-writing a romantic novel of the Civil War . . .

The mystery surrounding her would never be solved and that was what the lady wanted. When she died, all private papers were destroyed in accordance with her wishes, ending any possibility of future probing into her personal life. What remained were her business correspondence, loving remembrances from those who knew her and one published book. Yet that single work, never originally intended for the world to see, had brought her international renown, destroyed the harmony of her life and provided the basis for the most enduring phenomenon of the twentieth century.

Like many other born authors, Margaret Munnerlyn Mitchell never quite understood why she *had* to write. But she was decidedly a victim, like those before her, of that obsession to set down on paper certain events, thoughts, or fancies, and of that ability to do it with a seeming lack of effort. Her life had started—of course, in Atlanta—on November 8, 1900, the eighth anniversary of her parents' wedding. With her brother Stephens, who was five years older, Margaret enjoyed a normally placid childhood—but one which yielded enough imaginative background to enthuse any eager young girl with a pronounced literary flair.

Many of Margaret's early traits would continue to manifest themselves well into her adult life. Even before she had been able to write, she enchanted friends with her ability to tell a story and these tales often showed a strong fascination for the supernatural. As soon as she acquired the basic skills, Margaret became an avid reader and started writing her stories, initially in the form of dramas, which were occasionally performed with help from her playmates. But even though she could act in these for her family and friends, Margaret Mitchell possessed an innate shyness with strangers which her

mother sternly tried to correct lest it be mistaken for lack of manners.

A bit of a tomboy, young Miss Mitchell's favorite pursuit was pony riding, a pastime destined to work a profound and doublefold effect upon her future. From the age of six, Margaret had found the most available riding companions to be aged Southern veterans who still boasted of their Confederate campaigns, argued about Sherman and relived the Civil War and its aftermath. Before she was completely certain as to when it had all occurred, she was surrounded by legends of the War Between the States. But it was fairly impossible to grow up in the South in the early part of the century and not be exposed to stories and anecdotes concerning that conflict. Among Margaret's earliest memories were Sunday gatherings where she listened quietly as family and friends spent afternoon hours recounting adventures of the South's tragic and bitter loss. But, as she would later tell, her imagination was most vividly stimulated on country rides with her mother when they would see solitary chimneys in the forest, remnants of homes burned by Sherman's forces. Maybelle Mitchell used these as examples to remind her daughter how urgent it was to be prepared for life's obstacles and how imperative it could be to rise above defeat, as Mrs. Mitchell's own parents had after the war. Young Margaret took serious heed of this grim lesson in survival.

Maybelle Stephens Mitchell instilled in both her children the need for education, even bribing Margaret with money to read the classics. By adolescence, a willingly compulsive reading habit had become part of Margaret's everyday life. By then she could well appreciate the value of education as well as the proud ancestry of her family's history. Her father, Eugene Mitchell, was a prominent lawyer, an organizer of the Atlanta Bar Association, and had been a member of the Board of Education of the City of Atlanta. Eugene had married Maybelle Stephens in 1892, and his wife became one of the founders of the women's suffrage movement in Atlanta and was prominent in the affairs of the Sacred Heart Catholic Church. Margaret's ancestry on her father's side was Old American of Scotch, Irish and Huguenot French descent. Her mother's heritage was also American, traceable to primarily Irish beginnings. Both sides of her family tree had lived in the Carolinas and Georgia since the Revolution and were in Atlanta for over a hundred years. Margaret Mitchell was of the fifth generation in her family to live in that city of which she would remain proud throughout her lifetime.

Margaret had been born in Atlanta's substantial

Jackson Hill neighborhood but the family moved to long-famous Peachtree Street in 1912. She had stopped riding her pony in 1911 in exchange for a full-grown horse, but the animal fell while she was riding him that year and she sustained a badly injured leg. Still, in addition to riding, Margaret also went to dancing school where she became quite adept, played baseball energetically and loved swimming.

From early plays such as *The Fall of Ralph the Rover* and *In My Harem,* Margaret's proficiency in writing expanded to stories, which she set down in school copybooks. As the volume of these increased, Mrs. Mitchell devised an ingenious method of storage for her daughter's handiwork in large white enameled bread boxes. After an elementary education at several of Atlanta's public schools, Margaret entered Washington Seminary, a private girls' high school. While there, at age sixteen, she finished her first novel, entitled *The Big Four,* which consisted of fourteen chapters and was handwritten on over four hundred manuscript pages. Then, at the end of her junior year, one of her short stories, "Little Sister," was published in the school annual.

An early photographic portrait of Miss Mitchell that was later used by her publisher to publicize her novel.

Shortly after her graduation from Washington Seminary in June 1918, Miss Mitchell became engaged to Lieutenant Clifford Henry, but the couple was parted that September when Clifford sailed to Europe to serve in the World War and Margaret left for Smith College in Northampton, Massachusetts. A month later, Clifford Henry was killed in France.

In addition to that tragedy, Margaret's introduction to college life coincided with a worldwide epidemic of influenza, which eventually infected both her parents. While her father survived, Margaret was summoned home from Smith in January 1919 when it had become apparent that her mother was dangerously ill. Sadly, Mrs. Mitchell had died before her daughter arrived. After the funeral, Margaret returned to finish her freshman year but came back to Atlanta in June to manage her father's home, forever ending her formal education.

Miss Margaret Mitchell made her official "debut" in Atlanta society in September 1920 and about that time began calling herself "Peggy," a nickname which would be quickly adopted by all but her oldest friends and family. In that same year, while riding with friends in Athens, Georgia, her horse slipped and fell, further injuring the leg she had damaged nine years before. Her limb would never be completely the same again and she was forced to give up riding permanently.

The following year, a stir among Atlanta's older citizens following Peggy's expert performance of a French "apache dance" during a debutante's ball resulted in her future exclusion from Atlanta's Junior League. This slight, however, did not affect her popularity with suitors, among whom John Robert Marsh, a copy editor for one of the local newspapers, made a favorable impression upon the family.

But it was Berrien Kinnard Upshaw, a college student at the University of Georgia, to whom Margaret became engaged and whom she married on September 2, 1922. Meanwhile, Berrien Upshaw had cultivated the friendship of John Marsh, and Mr. Marsh was best man at their wedding. The newlyweds returned from their honeymoon to settle, for the time being, in the Mitchell family home. But Mr. Upshaw was not an emotionally stable man and the marriage ended after only a few months when he left the Mitchell house and did not return.

Economic conditions in the South had been declining for several years and even the Mitchells were adversely affected. With a broken marriage to forget, Peggy decided she could help out the family by getting a job and felt newspaper work might be suited to her abilities. She approached Harllee Branch, city editor of the *Atlanta Journal,* showing him some written material from her college days. Impressed by the young lady's earnestness, Mr. Branch would have employed her, but at the time there were no women reporters on his regular staff.

Some of her sex were working on that paper's *Sunday Magazine*, however, which was but ten years old and employed only five people. Peggy learned about an open position on it and was interviewed by the distinguished editor Angus Perkerson, who hired her. She began a professional journalism career on December 20, 1922, at a salary of $25 a week.

The independent Atlanta-owned *Journal* was a daily, evening and Sunday publication produced in a grimy five-story red-brick building infested with rats and roaches and encompassed by the acrid smoke and bellowing noises of an adjacent railroad. The *Sunday Magazine*'s own quarters—one dark, gloomy room on the third floor—inspired Peggy to call it "The Black Hole of Calcutta."

Journalism was very much a man's enterprise then with its rowdy, hard-drinking reporters whose crude language and vulgar jokes were an accepted part of their business temperament. The men on the *Journal* worked a six-day, forty-eight-hour week, not including night assignments, for meager pay, but they enthusiastically loved their profession. It wouldn't have seemed predictable that they could accept a well-bred girl, not quite five feet tall, as one of their team, yet they soon did. Peggy's wry sense of humor and conversational talents initially attracted her new colleagues' attention. But the little lady's aptitude and ability to work hard were what won their lasting esteem as she displayed a willingness to cover any assignment and became particularly adept at interviewing.

The new reporter first used the byline "Peggy Upshaw" over a story in the *Magazine*'s December 31, 1922, issue. She soon changed that to "Peggy Mitchell" and, under it, became quite popular with Atlanta's Sunday readers as she proceeded to write what would eventually total 128 feature articles in the next three and a half years. Her stories were characterized by a lively wit and engaging style, and in her assignments she found herself involved in a wide variety of experiences from swinging in a chair sixteen floors above the ground to riding a circus elephant. Whether interviewing Rudolph Valentino or discussing the pros and cons of bobbed hair, Margaret Mitchell conveyed news items entertainingly, but had also found the means to act as spokesperson for her younger generation.

Angus Perkerson and his wife Medora Field Perkerson, who also wrote for the *Sunday Magazine*, were to become lifelong friends of Margaret Mitchell. Mrs. Perkerson would later comment on Peggy's capabilities as a reporter, remembering that she didn't make excuses, never fell down on a story nor felt superior to her assignments. Her work showed "that something extra" even in the simplest story and, since she genuinely liked people, those she talked to were honest in return. Peggy was an excellent interviewer, a difficult task, because she made

her subjects feel relaxed and showed she was interested in anything they said. In so doing, she got the facts the paper really wanted.

In addition to writing features for the *Sunday Magazine*, Peggy took on extra duties such as proofreading, worked her charm in the composing room, escorted visiting dignitaries around Atlanta and eventually drew assignments for "hard" news reporting on the daily *Atlanta Journal*. Her job fulfilled that born need to set down what she wanted to say on paper and, in doing it, also satisfied her patriotic love for the city of Atlanta. She began privately to write fiction again and one of her unfinished stories concerned a character named "Pansy Hamilton," a young Atlanta girl of the 1920s era. Then, she completed a novella entitled *Ropa Carmagin*, detailing the adventures of a young girl's love for a mulatto man. Peggy did not intend for any of this writing to be seen by the public and, indeed, it never would be.

The loneliness Margaret suffered immediately after the breakup of her marriage was relieved through a bonus from her new profession. She now had a new circle of acquaintances to entertain at her family home, along with some of her older friends like John Marsh. He was more than just a party guest, however, and within a year and a half friends recognized a serious relationship between them. John had recently given up his copy editor's position on the *Atlanta Georgian* to take a job with the Georgia Power Company in the advertising and publicity division. Meanwhile, Peggy sought and was granted a divorce from Berrien Upshaw and she married John at a Unitarian ceremony on July 4, 1925. The couple secured a modest three-room apartment on Crescent Avenue in Atlanta which Margaret wittily christened "The Dump." Major surgery and hospital expenses incurred by John shortly before their marriage had left the couple somewhat in debt but they were determined to live within their means and pay back what was owed as soon as it was feasible.

Career-minded, liberated Peggy did not let marriage smother her identity and their apartment door featured separate calling cards, one in John's name and another proudly proclaiming "Miss Margaret Munnerlyn Mitchell." John and Peggy were a sociable couple and their circle enjoyed many entertaining evenings at "The Dump." A quick and satisfying wit punctuated her clever relating of stories, that childhood talent which had developed even more through the years. Sometimes, as in the holiday season, the Marshes might entertain a hundred friends and relatives. But Margaret, who loved to listen as well as talk, really preferred small groups wherein conversations could be savored to the fullest.

Since she was a charming, fun-filled hostess and a warm friend, few in Peggy's group suspected how introspective a person she could really be. The demands of newspaper work had somewhat conquered her innate shyness but even the thought of immersion into a large crowd of total strangers still terrified her.

In early 1926 the Marshes had considerably repaid most of their debts, and wanting to encourage her husband's career ambitions, Peggy decided one salary would be sufficient for the present. She resigned from the *Journal* in May of that year and settled into the freedom of unemployment. Peggy found herself reading more than ever, feeding an insatiable appetite for information on the Civil War. What was once a hobby spurred by the conversations she heard in childhood became by then a devoted pursuit. Research was alternately frustrating and rewarding since accounts varied in great degree, depending on the source material. Her father Eugene, a founder of the Atlanta Historical Society, was a comforting referee in settling such disputable reports. Also useful were old newspaper files, and there were vintage library books, which she borrowed by the stackful. It was a carefree time of following one's own selected pursuits that was annoyingly interrupted in the early fall when she sprained an ankle. It proved to be an injury to that same area previously damaged in her two riding accidents, and when the doctors diagnosed arthritis, she was forced to undergo the unpleasantness of traction. Afterward, Peggy found herself a virtual prisoner on crutches in the confines of her tiny apartment. For an intelligent, vibrant and knowledge-hungry young woman, this long recuperation seemed like a sentence of doom. Especially in that year, 1926, when the entire nation was filled with the excitement of recent accomplishments, with a promise of even more in the future. No, Peggy Marsh was not about to remain hobbling around a small set of rooms when everyone else was involved in a contagious surge of progress.

This was America's Sesquicentennial Year and primary focus was on Philadelphia, where an exposition commemorating the one hundred and fiftieth anniversary of the signing of the Declaration of Independence had opened at the beginning of June, continuing through the end of November. The impressive spectacle had cost over $18,000,000 to erect and operate, which showed in buildings called "Palaces," dedicated to manufacturers, agriculture or the arts. Among the six million attendees were European royalty and America's President.

Calvin Coolidge, a Republican, had ascended to the presidency in 1923, succeeding Warren G. Harding, who died in office just as a scandal within his administration was being unearthed. Mr. Coolidge was elected to a full term in 1924 to preside over a country that, content and progressive, saw no reason for a change in leadership. And "progress" was certainly the slogan of 1926, when Richard E. Byrd's exciting flight to the mysterious North Pole claimed a milestone triumph for the United States.

Commander Byrd was not alone in eyeing the skies, as the Ford Motor Company detailed to the President its recent progress in the development of commercial aviation, which, the company felt, had a profitable future. And although some observers ridiculed the thought, experiments in Paris for the instantaneous transmission of moving images by wireless were hailed by Americans as establishing the discovery of a method of "television."

It was difficult for some to accept that possibility when radio was still such a novelty, but the New York radio station WEAF boosted its own medium in regard when, on November 15, 1926, it demonstrated, before a thousand guests, the first national transmission of a program —to affiliated stations in twenty-one cities, as far west as Kansas City. More than two million listeners heard opera singers, vaudeville performers and humorist Will Rogers contributing to an event which marked the end of rural isolation. From then on, small-town Americans were able to experience first hand many major city events they otherwise could only have read about. Significantly, the National Broadcasting Company had been born. A type of radio programming that became rapidly popular after its introduction that year was the "continuing series," usually heard in daytime hours and affectionately called "soap opera" because of its sponsorship.

The death of Rudolph Valentino in August saddened Margaret since her *Atlanta Journal* interview with him had been among the highlights of her journalistic career. Even at that time she had thought of him as a courteous but sadly wearied man. She had learned a valuable lesson by observing that vast success had brought the actor little personal happiness and that he could not comprehend the reason for the adulation he received.

Peggy loved the movies, and it was remarkable to her that Warner Brothers had introduced "sound" to films during the year in *Don Juan*. Although this was still only the synchronization of music and sound effects, the prophecy of "talking films" seemed like even more fun to look forward to. She could not have avoided noting the remarkable progress made by the fledgling Metro-Goldwyn-Mayer studio, only two years after its formation through a merger of two older companies. This new combine was dominating the nation's attention with three major films which had opened in 1925 but were still attracting large crowds. *The Big Parade* had broken all previous long-run records in its engagement at New York's famous Astor Theatre, while the spectacular *Ben Hur* was rumored to be the most expensive motion picture ever made, costing almost $4,000,000. *The Merry Widow* was a delightful picture which starred the highly popular John Gilbert and Mae Murray. Margaret had no way of knowing it then but two young men who had taken "extra" roles in that film, Clark Gable and Walter Plunkett, would significantly become involved in her future. Although she was aware of M-G-M's new star Greta Garbo, whose 1926 debut was greeted with quick enthusiasm, Peggy did not know that another young man, David O. Selznick, would soon join that studio as a minor producer and would eventually become a major creative force in the movie industry.

Her lifelong interest in writing directed Margaret's attention to the newly formed enterprise which introduced a method of bringing published literature to customers through their mailboxes rather than stores. Among that Book-of-the-Month Club's initial offerings were Edna Ferber's *Show Boat* and Ellen Glasgow's *The Romantic Comedians*. Miss Ferber, born in Michigan, had been producing novels and short stories for fifteen years which leaned strongly on the struggles of contemporary women. Her novel *So Big* had been awarded the Pulitzer Prize for fiction in 1925, and *Show Boat,* set in the South's late nineteenth century, had created modern fiction's most popular team of lovers, Magnolia Hawkes and Gaylord Ravenal. Although she was born of an aristocratic Virginia family, Ellen Glasgow's work revolted from the genteel Southern fiction of the past and etched social portraits of class conflict and women betrayed by an outdated code of chivalry.

Across the ocean in England another woman writer, Agatha Christie, had just produced a fourth mystery, *The Murder of Roger Ackroyd*, which would became the most famous of over eighty such novels written in her lifetime. As the daughter of a suffragette, Margaret was as proud of these accomplishments by her sex as she was when nineteen-year-old Gertrude Ederle became, that year, the first woman to swim the English Channel, breaking former speed records set by men. However, it seemed that unless a woman enjoyed success in athletics, writing or performing, she would find equality an elusive privilege in a world dominated by men.

Liberated Peggy must have laughed at the cautious observers who direly predicted that the permissiveness of Hollywood's films would lead to social disintegration. She herself was tired of the profanity she found in books but knew the movies were still relatively innocent. She had often written, during her *Journal* career, about women of the era who revolted against suppression by adopting the freedom displayed by actress "flappers," a term the older generation thought synonymous with a total abandonment of morals.

It both surprised and amused Margaret to note that Sinclair Lewis declined the 1926 Pulitzer Prize for fiction awarded to his novel *Arrowsmith*. Mr. Lewis commented that such honors tended to make writers "safe, polite, obedient and sterile" and advised fellow novelists to refuse such prizes if they wished to remain free from constricting standards. A dozen years later *Arrowsmith* would be sent on an eerie voyage into the future with a work written by Miss Mitchell herself.

As a journalist, Margaret noted with interest the intriguing six-week disappearance of evangelist Aimee Semple McPherson, which left a debatable "kidnapping" mystery unsolved. And it certainly seemed a frustrating limit of freedom when Atlanta's Board of Education prohibited the teaching of evolution in the city's public schools. But she was not surprised, as others were, that Prohibition had not halted the tragedies of alcoholism. Her own circle enjoyed moderate social drinking and she knew that to forbid something was a predictable means of encouraging the growth of organized crime. Yet Peggy was forced to acknowledge the futility of several famed entertainers whose success did not prevent them from being among those led to addiction or death by indulgence in narcotics.

As a Southerner, Margaret Mitchell was deeply concerned when a resurgence of the Ku Klux Klan threatened a future with continued racial strife. But progress toward a richer "tomorrow," not the human concerns of the present, was what thrilled Americans in a year crowded with such innovations as the institution of airmail service and the first successful transatlantic telephone conversation.

Peggy had to get involved in something that year and she turned to the foremost talent she had always possessed. She began to write a novel, using her Remington portable to type on yellow copy paper, which had been a gift from John to encourage her to do exactly that. As with some of her other stories, Peggy had no idea at first if she would finish this one or not, but it soon seemed different and more involving and she liked that feeling. Margaret devoted some entire days to the project, breaking only for meals; at other times, feeling unproductive or bored, she got away from it completely. Since she had envisioned the entire narrative beforehand, she could write in whatever sequence she pleased, and she did, in fact, write the last chapter first. Thus she was able to bring all her themes and characters toward an eventual destination which she had already mentally laid out for them.

Although she kept the nature of her constant typing a secret, it was impossible to conceal from visitors the fact that she was engaged in something. But since she had done some form of writing all her life and had recently worked at it professionally, there was no real surprise or anticipation generated among her friends. As soon as she felt able to hobble out into the world again, Peggy gave a clue to her secret project when her friends learned she was again researching the Civil War era in the Atlanta library's old newspaper files. At least, they surmised, it was fairly evident what the background of her "piece of writing" was. This could not have startled anyone since, while on the *Journal*, Peggy had written a series on the bravery of several Confederate generals that had been so well received by the paper's subscribers that it was expanded to four Sunday articles instead of the two originally planned. She was marvelously adept at bringing these Civil War heroes to vivid life in print, as she relived for her reading audience their courage in various battle campaigns, including Gettysburg.

When she had researched these articles, Peggy had found herself equally intrigued by another type of Confederate hero—the women behind the front who had nursed the wounded, run plantations, gathered crops, woven cloth for uniforms and valiantly carried on even when their men were maimed or killed. It would be these women, two in particular, to whom Margaret would devote most of her story. Her leading female character, however, would bear little resemblance to the patriotic wives and widows the South was fond of recalling in the tales of the Confederacy. In fact, Peggy's entire story would be quite different from anything her curious friends might have imagined.

Almost twenty years after she began work on her novel Margaret Mitchell's biographer, Finis Farr, would —with the cooperation of her estate—reveal many little-known facts of her early life and family history. Although Mr. Farr drew some parallels between the author's own life and her story, there were many more sources of motivation quite evident through a closer scrutiny. However, Miss Mitchell and her survivors feared misinterpretation and would tend to discourage what was never a difficult analysis.

Margaret's thorough familiarity with the Civil War provided her with ready access to her story's historical background. But what of the fictional characters she was creating? She had dug back into her own family ancestry and found remarkable inspiration. Margaret's maternal great-grandfather, Philip Fitzgerald, had been taken from Ireland by his family while he was still a child during that country's rebellion against England. Philip had later settled in Fayetteville, Georgia, after the American Indians ceded that area to the federal government. A short and boisterous fellow, he married Eleanor McGhan, a young Catholic girl from Maryland, and brought her to Georgia's Clayton County, where they managed a plantation worked by scores of black slaves. The Fitzgeralds had three daughters, one of whom, Annie, was to be Margaret Mitchell's grandmother. Annie was born on the Clayton County plantation in the 1840s and later attended the Fayetteville Academy. Her parents' home and lands were devastated by Union soldiers during the Civil War, although the family overcame its misfortunes and eventually regained its former stature in later times of peace.

At the time of Sherman's siege Annie Fitzgerald had been in Atlanta, where she met and married a soldier, John Stephens. They were parted as Atlanta fell when Annie was forced to evacuate with other civilians and her new husband left with the army to fight in the last futile campaigns of the war. When they were later reunited, the couple settled in Atlanta and their home at 296 Cain Street was one of the few locations which had escaped Sherman's torches in November 1864. (It would be in that very house that Margaret Mitchell would be born, thirty-four years after the Civil War officially ended.) Annie Fitzgerald Stephens was a strong, fearless and self-willed woman who had seen the South crumble while she was still a teenager, had been an eyewitness to the destruction wrought in Atlanta and on her family's plantation and had persevered with her husband, despite setbacks, throughout the Reconstruction era. Her strong character traits, even in old age, produced several conflicts with her equally independent granddaughter, but Margaret nevertheless held the lady in great respect.

As she wrote her story, Peggy Marsh devised a family not unlike the Fitzgeralds, giving them another Irish name —"O'Hara." Although Gerald O'Hara, the patriarch she created, came to America after running afoul of the British himself, he was also a short man who settled in Georgia and acquired a plantation, in the Clayton County area ceded by the Indians in 1821, much as Philip Fitzgerald had. Gerald, like Philip, married a young Catholic girl, although Eleanor D'Antignac was from South Carolina, not Maryland. The O'Haras had three daughters also and their eldest, Pansy, was schooled at the Fayetteville Academy where Annie Fitzgerald had received her education.

Pansy was about Annie Fitzgerald's age when war broke out and Margaret placed her in Atlanta during the siege, where she would also be parted when Atlanta fell, from a man who left to fight the Yankees. But this character, whom the author called "Rhett Butler," was far different in background and moral fiber from her own grandfather, John Stephens. Margaret, in fact, created in Butler one of the future's most beloved fictional rogues.

Margaret reached into her own personal experiences to conceive that Pansy would marry a young Confederate, Charles Hamilton, shortly before he died in the early days of the war, as Clifford Henry had died soon after his engagement to her in 1918. Again, the qualities of these two men would not be comparable, only the framework of their relationships to the young ladies. It was also a personal note that Margaret's parents had lost a child, Russell, in infancy, as would Gerald and Eleanor O'Hara lose three sons shortly after their births. Whereas Margaret had scandalized Atlanta's Junior League with her apache dance, Pansy O'Hara outraged the Old Guard Confederacy by dancing with Rhett Butler while she was still in mourning. Pansy and other Atlanta women were called upon to nurse wounded soldiers after each battle, and the flow of wounded hit its peak, in Margaret Mitchell's story, amid the chaos of civilian exodus as Atlanta fell. Peggy remembered all too well the effects of Atlanta's 1917 fire when she volunteered to help stricken refugees in a scene of panic and confusion not unlike the one she was writing about.

But while Atlanta still stood strong, Pansy entertained

many a soldier, just as Margaret herself engaged in social affairs to help the morale of soldiers during the World War. The famed Cyclorama, an impressive work of art designed and developed by German artists in the late nineteenth century, had become one of Atlanta's major attractions, as it depicted the Civil War battle waged outside that city in the summer of 1864. It undoubtedly had stirred Margaret's imagination even in girlhood, and she, not surprisingly, highlighted that battle in her story, with Pansy and other women watching its progress from the city's rooftops. Pansy's Atlanta residence, home of her "Aunt Pittypat Hamilton," was one of the few buildings to survive Sherman's ruthlessness as was, in reality, Annie Fitzgerald Stephens' house in Atlanta.

As there had been three men in Margaret Mitchell's own life—Clifford Henry, Berrien Upshaw and John Marsh—so would there be three husbands for Pansy O'Hara. It would become evident early in the written narrative that Rhett Butler loved Pansy from the start, and continued to love her throughout her second marriage to a man named Frank Kennedy. Margaret had later become aware that she had really cared for John Marsh all along, even before she married Berrien Upshaw, though she had not realized it at the time. After Mr. Upshaw's departure, a story would persist that Margaret slept with a gun near her bedside for years until she learned of the man's apparent suicide. It may have been this short-lived marriage which gave her memories of violence transferred to Rhett Butler's drunken behavior or his threat to kill Pansy after their child's death.

Margaret had received a second chance for happiness when she and John Marsh finally got together. Although she gave Pansy that same chance with Rhett, it was not to be permanent, for Margaret had devised as her ending—which she wrote first—the unsettled question of whether or not these lovers would ever find peace together. While Rhett had waited for Pansy, as John had for Margaret, he could not believe she would ever change enough to ever be the woman he wanted and eventually he left her. Herein was the key to what made Margaret Mitchell's heroine different. What was it about Pansy that Rhett had hoped would change? Miss O'Hara was a stubbornly selfish girl whose childlike mind remained devoid of adult emotions. She was not, in any way, like the nineteenth-century fictional heroines usually depicted in the South. Education and upbringing had brought her neither the sophistication nor knowledge necessary to compete with the idealism and intellectuality around her. Yet her stubborn will had provided the impetus for an ability to rise above defeat throughout and after the war, while her selfish streak allowed rationalization for a determined survival instinct—even at the expense of others' well-being or of violations in the strict Southern code of ethics.

Survival!—an important lesson inspired by her mother's early lectures and reinforced in her own years of Civil War research—became the major theme of Margaret Mitchell's story. Maybelle Mitchell had referred to those woodside chimney remnants as "Sherman's Sentinels," and Margaret even included them in a key scene where Pansy, returning home from besieged Atlanta, viewed the ruins of the neighboring MacIntosh plantation. Although Pansy would find her own home had been spared, she lost the innocence of her girlhood when she saw the Yankees' destruction of her once-peaceful surroundings. Calling upon God to witness, Pansy swore to survive at any price. And Margaret Mitchell thus immortalized the first fact of life taught to her.

That tragic train ride home from Smith College to the bedside of her mother was faithfully integrated into Margaret's story as Pansy drove a wagon from Atlanta for a day and a half to reach her mother, who had been stricken with typhoid. Both Mrs. Mitchell and Mrs. O'Hara expired before their daughters arrived, and they had both died of a disease complicated by exhaustion from tending the sick. Eugene Mitchell had sunk into a condition of deep shock at the news of his wife's death, although he eventually recovered. Gerald O'Hara's resulting instability mirrored Mr. Mitchell's, but he was not to regain his faculties. Pansy found it necessary, at nineteen, to take charge of her plantation just as Margaret took over the affairs of her family's home at almost that age. It would be a long time before Pansy returned to Atlanta. Margaret Mitchell never returned to Smith College after finishing her first year there.

Peggy's paternal grandfather, Russell Crawford Mitchell, fought in the Civil War, as did the story's Frank Kennedy, and like that character he set up a lumber business afterward. Although her grandfather died while she was still a child, Margaret undoubtedly learned details of such lumber concerns, which were so mandatory to Reconstruction Atlanta. Accordingly, Margaret made just such a mill business an essential part of Pansy O'Hara's postwar survival.

Peggy Mitchell Marsh would have no children and found writing about them quite elusive. But her heroine's selfish nature provided a handy escape. Although Pansy bore a son, Wade, and a daughter, Ella, these children would receive almost no characterization in the story. Pansy repeatedly brushed them aside, finding others to safeguard their welfare, and this allowed author Mitchell the license she needed to completely avoid their development. But, after marriage to Rhett Butler, Pansy's third child attained far more story prominence, as Margaret was able to infuse in her some of her own childhood characteristics. Bonnie Blue Butler became an individualistic little girl who loved her pony, and, as her own life had been altered by riding accidents, the author deigned that the child would be killed in such a fall. Earlier in the novel Gerald O'Hara had died in a similar mishap. Although Ella never materialized from the story's background, quiet little Wade Hamilton finally achieved some life after Bonnie's birth. Stephens Mitchell would have been about Wade's age when his sister's earliest memories of him formed, making it a bit easier for Margaret to develop the boy from that point on.

Pansy O'Hara had been raised, as Margaret was, by a devoutly Catholic mother. As she grew older, especially after Eleanor O'Hara's death, Pansy fell away from both her religion and its teachings. Although Margaret's own admirable and generous nature was not at all like that of selfish Pansy, she herself had undergone a similar drifting away from the faith of her youth. In this regard she imparted perhaps the story's closest personal sharing between author and created character. Similarly, Margaret bestowed her own sense of humor on Rhett Butler. His quick wit in retorts to Pansy's ignorance or in observances of Atlanta's pompous citizens gave the narrative another individual quality, contrasting it with the typical long-suffering fictional romances so popular at the time.

When Margaret was finally able to get out again, she attended a card party given by Medora Perkerson and met Lois Dwight Cole, a Smith graduate whose interest in book publishing had gained her employment at The Macmillan Company of New York City. Miss Cole had recently come to Atlanta to manage the general books division of that publisher's branch there, and from her first meeting with Peggy Marsh she realized she had met someone quite extraordinary.

Lois became a regular at the Marshes' "Dump" and after a while her new friend confided in her that she was working on a piece of fiction. Peggy was in the habit of covering both typewriter and copy pages with a large bath towel if company arrived, and this intrigued Lois, who had already been captivated by the Mitchell flair for sparkling, fun-filled conversation. Always on the lookout for potential Macmillan material, she asked Peggy to submit it to her company when it was finished. Margaret laughed the idea away since, she said, it was only something she was doing to pass the time and it would probably never be completed.

Privately, though, Margaret Mitchell did not regard her project lightly. She had, in fact, invested in it something even deeper than family history and personal experience. She had always loved and felt akin to Atlanta. As an individualist, she appreciated that city's unorthodox history and its position of prominence in the South, despite criticisms from other staid Southern locales. Her inspiration for Pansy O'Hara actually came from Atlanta itself. Pansy was as unorthodox for her time as that town and she was, in fact, given the same year of birth by her creator as that in which Atlanta received its final name. Margaret's heroine paralleled the city both in progres-

sive adaptability before the Civil War and in the ability to rise from the ashes and restore themselves afterward, without being trapped or deterred by past glories. Yes, Pansy *was* Atlanta! But Atlanta was not the entire South. Margaret provided the necessary artistic contrast in portraying the gracious dignity and steadfast commitment to a doomed way of life in the person of a secondary character, Melanie Hamilton. This gentle girl was the sister-in-law whom Pansy would hate until, at her death, she realized that it was women like Melanie who had formed the backbone of the Old South's civilization. Melanie's ideals were strong and her will to survive as dedicated as Pansy's but, like the prewar South, her physical attributes were too weak and she perished trying to propagate her breed.

A frustratingly large part of Pansy's life was devoted to the pursuit of Ashley Wilkes, the man Melanie married early in Margaret's story. He represented Old South romanticism, the nobility and heroism to fight a war he knew was hopeless to safeguard an institution—slavery—he thought was wrong. Afterward, completely unable to adjust to the new mercantile reality, he became anachronistic. Rhett Butler, on the other hand, was not only a realist but a totally amoral man who profited through the South's misfortune. After a rebellious youth, misunderstood by his Old Guard Southern family, Rhett seemed bent on revengeful success, feeling no loyalty to person, place or code. His character embodied both the rebel and the opportunist present in all societies.

Rhett Butler behaved chivalrously toward Melanie Hamilton, for he could not completely escape the nostalgic respect for Southern ideals. But he met his match in Pansy O'Hara, and although he loved her, he stepped aside and left her to a selfish, willful existence after Melanie's death. At the conclusion of Margaret's story Pansy realized that Ashley would cling forever to his vanished dreams, and that now that she could finally have him, it seemed he had never been what she really wanted. With Melanie gone, Pansy needed a now-respectable Rhett's encouragement to continue and vowed to win him back. Just as postwar Atlanta wanted assurance from the South that it really belonged to a culture it had once felt unnecessary.

Since Georgia had recently suffered from a plague of boll weevils—those insects which destroyed cotton crops and with them the financial well-being of the state—Margaret was able to see first hand the physical and mental anguish of a destroyed economy. It was not far different from the post–Civil War period she used to frame the second half of her novel. Without originally intending it to happen, her story had gradually taken on hints of family history, some personal recollections and characteristics and even her feelings for the city and state she loved. It had, in its own way, become a handily therapeutic means of unburdening herself of the tragedies she observed in current life and those she had learned of through years of studying the South's darkest era. Realizing this, Margaret seriously doubted if she would ever let anyone see it, although one person already had.

It would have been relatively impossible for gregarious Peggy to keep the entire plot development totally to herself and continue such disciplined work for several more years on such a long project. Those moments of doubt which would inevitably creep into any writer's mind might have discouraged her long before if she hadn't had John Marsh to boost her spirits.

Peggy had related the entire plot line to her husband at the very beginning of her undertaking and he was immediately receptive to it. John was able, through this, to read any portion of the nonsequential manuscript and understand how events fell into place. His copy-editing experience was invaluable in correcting inconsistencies even in the Georgian dialect of the blacks and his enthusiasm for the whole story was genuine. The relationship the Marshes shared was too honest for John to give his wife any false praise and that, in itself, would have violated his professional training. But John sincerely admired and was involved in the structure and development of what they may have jokingly referred to as "The Adventures of Pansy O'Hara."

Margaret worked on the story throughout 1927, and she felt herself emotionally involved in the continuing national excitement over such newsmaking events as Calvin Coolidge's decision not to seek a second Presidential term and Charles Lindbergh's nonstop flight across the Atlantic. Peggy would have laughed heartily if anyone had predicted then that she would, within a decade, become as prominent a public figure as Captain Lindbergh or that her phenomenal acclaim would be compared to his.

As a woman author and a Southerner, she took pride in the success which greeted Florenz Ziegfeld's musical stage production of Edna Ferber's *Show Boat* in New York. The play's score, composed by Jerome Kern and Oscar Hammerstein II, swept the country, especially the touching "Ol' Man River." And since the movies were such an everyday part of American life, Margaret couldn't have missed the journalistic coverage devoted to the founding of the Academy of Motion Picture Arts and Sciences in May. The idea of forming such a group to arbitrate industry disputes and recognize accomplishments was attributed to Louis B. Mayer, production chief of the M-G-M studios. That company's art director, Cedric Gibbons, designed a nude male statue which held a sword and stood on a reel of film as the symbolic token to be presented annually for meritorious film achievements. Previous forms of recognition for the motion-picture industry did already exist since both *Photoplay* magazine and The National Board of Review had ini-

tiated such yearly awards in 1920. Meanwhile, Warner Brothers created quite a stir when it kept its year-old promise and released a motion picture, *The Jazz Singer*, that contained portions of spoken dialogue and songs. The screen had learned to "talk"—and even sing!

As Margaret continued to write and the typed manuscript grew, she had to devise a means of filing it and, bound into the apartment's small area, she chose a quite rudimentary one. Each chapter, finished or not, was placed in a separate manila envelope which she stacked, in order, in a pile on the floor near her typewriter table. By the end of 1927 the stack became so high that she pushed them away and started another.

The year 1928 was no less stimulating to Margaret's creative abilities. When Amelia Earhart volunteered to be a passenger on the airplane *Friendship*, becoming the first woman to fly across the Atlantic, she encouraged the safety of future commercial aviation and scored a high point of courage for her sex. Prosperity continued throughout America and another Republican, Herbert Hoover, was elected President, heavily defeating New York's Democratic former governor Alfred E. Smith in an election marked by an unprecedented turnout of voters. New York State's own newly elected governor, who won by only a slight majority, was, however, a Democrat. Franklin D. Roosevelt, who had been an unsuccessful Vice-Presidential nominee in 1920, thus began what would be a rapid rise in national government.

Hollywood's first "Academy Awards" were revealed in February 1929 in a special booklet prepared by the two-year-old film organization. Three months later those tributes, in eleven categories, were officially presented at a banquet where Paramount Pictures' *Wings* was named "Best Picture" of the August 1927 through July 1928 season. Silent-screen acting honors were voted to America's Janet Gaynor for three performances and Germany's Emil Jannings for two. (In the future winning thespians would be selected for only one film.) One of Mr. Jannings' honored contributions was for *The Way of All Flesh*, directed by the respected Victor Fleming, whose work inspired *The New York Times* to describe the film as "a poignant character study that bristles with carefully thought out detail." Mr. Fleming's creation had also been nominated in the "Best Picture" category. A special award given by the Academy revealed, just through its wording, what had really happened to the movie business during the past year or so: "To Warner Bros. for producing *The Jazz Singer*, the pioneer outstanding talking picture which has revolutionized the industry." Significantly, this was the first and only Academy ceremony where the major honorees were silent films.

But even a Hollywood scenario couldn't have captured the drama that swept the country in mid-autumn of that year. America had enjoyed rising prosperity since the World War ended in 1918. But on October 29, 1929, a total crash in the value of financial securities on New York's stock market signaled the failure of America's economic system, and as the accumulated fortunes of the wealthy vanished, so did the everyday security of the working classes. Job losses were immense as businesses crumbled, life savings evaporated as banking establishments failed, and America's Great Depression began, bringing with it poverty, hunger and despair.

After this, Margaret Mitchell decided to abandon her writing project. It now seemed frivolous to her, with the entire country in serious doubt as to its survival, to continue the long narrative of one selfish girl's pursuits even though they were inspired by a survival theme. At that point there were still three chapters unwritten, including the opening, some undecided alternate versions of others, and the cumulative work had been given no title whatsoever.

In those tragic times Margaret and John Marsh, along with millions of other Americans, turned to movies more than ever for escape from surrounding problems of the Depression. Even though early "talkies" were often inane, their novelty couldn't have come at a better time. Musical films with mindless little plots that placed no burden on an audience flourished but another trend in movies was sociologically alarming. Crime—organized and individual—rose steadily during the Depression and 1930's gangsters became almost heroic symbols for taking what they wanted from the establishment, much as Jesse James and other legendary outlaws had done following the Civil War. Many of the most notorious types of that new era's lawbreakers were immortalized on film to amazingly wide public acceptance.

At the same time there was a noticeable resurgence of interest in historical novels. That type of fiction had never completely faded from popularity but showed reborn enthusiasm in certain periods. For almost two decades, beginning in 1930, such an era began as each year brought a new romance of the past which would become extremely popular. *Cimarron*, a story of pioneer Oklahoma by Edna Ferber, was 1930's best seller and the cornerstone of this revival, which involved not only book buyers but library borrowers as well. Perhaps in the turmoil of the Depression, which made it difficult to face the present or future, it was more rewarding to look backward and realize people of former times had survived even worse problems.

By late 1930, when Americans had accepted the fact that hard times were upon them for a while, Margaret's lengthy story no longer seemed so futile to her. For a few months, into 1931, she worked again at revisions and minor additions but realized, in doing so, she was mutilating her original copy and it would need complete retyping if anyone were ever to read it. The worked-over copy paper was already in danger of disintegration.

Back in Hollywood, even the new film Academy admitted their second annual awards, for the 1928–1929 season, had been delayed for eight months because the voters, like everyone else in America, were having a difficult time evaluating the merits of "talking" pictures. Rudimentary sound techniques, even in the finest efforts, had given this new art form the dubious categorization of a novelty. When results were finally announced in April 1930, the highest honor was voted, perhaps in desperation, to a picture that was at least pioneering—M-G-M's, and history's, first all-*musical* film, *The Broadway Melody*.

The "talking" screen had indeed revolutionized the industry. In its earliest days, since the menacing microphone could not be moved at great lengths, actors were forced to remain in fairly stationary positions and to clearly enunciate long passages of dialogue, something totally new to several silent-screen actors. That deadly recording mechanism did not always capture voices with fidelity and sometimes exaggerated speech impediments or foreign accents out of perspective. As a result, some movie stars were relegated to supporting roles or early retirement. Still, several "silent" luminaries like Norma Shearer, Joan Crawford, Ronald Colman, Gary Cooper, Janet Gaynor, W. C. Fields and even the Swedish Greta Garbo would experience equal success in the new medium. Others who had formerly not found first-class prominence, such as William Powell, Marie Dressler, Lionel Barrymore, Wallace Beery, Basil Rathbone or newcomers Claudette Colbert, Myrna Loy, Jean Arthur, Loretta Young, and Carole Lombard, used their voices as the needed asset to achieve absolute stardom.

But there was also an influx of completely new screen performers, many from the stage, who were to akin themselves nicely to the infant technical process and become Hollywood's new "royalty" for the entire decade of the Thirties and even longer. Names introduced in those first few years which were destined to become legendary included Leslie Howard, Bette Davis, Katharine Hepburn, James Cagney, Humphrey Bogart, Jean Harlow, Ginger Rogers, Mae West, Bing Crosby, Spencer Tracy, Edward G. Robinson, Barbara Stanwyck, Irene Dunne, Cary Grant, Paul Muni, Marlene Dietrich, Laurence Olivier, Jeanette MacDonald, Charles Laughton, Rosalind Russell, Helen Hayes, Fredric March, Margaret Sullavan, Miriam Hopkins, Ray Milland, Merle Oberon, Randolph Scott, Sylvia Sidney, Robert Montgomery, Robert Taylor and John Wayne.

Not surprisingly, a large percentage of those new stars were employed by Metro-Goldwyn-Mayer, a studio eager to maintain a position of supremacy in the industry and to live up to its motto: "More stars than there are in heaven." Louis B. Mayer and his young production chief, Irving Thalberg, also proudly advertised the firm's continuing accomplishments as evidenced by the six Academy Awards granted to M-G-M contract players within the initial seven such presentations. Nine of the studio's features were nominated as "Best Picture" in addition to the two that won the honor. *Grand Hotel*, based on Vicki Baum's 1931 best-selling novel, had earned M-G-M its second major trophy and initiated an "all-star" policy the studio would lean on heavily in the future wherein many famous players would join forces to make a certain picture a box-office triumph.

No new player, however, rose as quickly in the favor of both ticket buyers and studio chiefs as Clark Gable. After a few minor parts had stirred favorable "fan" reaction and earned him an M-G-M contract, Mr. Gable was cast as Norma Shearer's manhandling leading man in a 1931 version of Adela Rogers St. Johns' novel *A Free Soul*. Clark's romantic image, which so attracted women, also evoked empathetic admiration from male viewers. Within a year Clark had soared to "star" status in a succession of films with Greta Garbo, Joan Crawford, Marion Davies, Wallace Beery and Carole Lombard. Then, when he co-starred with the "platinum blonde" sensation Jean Harlow in Victor Fleming's *Red Dust*, it was evident that a new breed of realistic male screen actor had been publicly accepted and Mr. Gable's own position in M-G-M's "heavens" was seemingly permanent. For some scenes in 1932's experimental adaptation of Eugene O'Neill's *Strange Interlude*, Clark adapted a slight mustache which would, with a few exceptions, be retained for his future performances.

Lois Cole had continued all that time to encourage Margaret Mitchell to finish her manuscript and submit it to Macmillan, an idea the lady refused to take seriously. Lois was amused, but not discouraged, when after asking Peggy's opinion of it, she was told, "It stinks!" Nevertheless, Lois had provided Margaret with many interesting vignettes about the publishing industry at a time when there was fascinating progress being made by women authors. Edna Ferber's *Cimarron* had quickly been made into an Academy Award-winning "Best Picture," while Pearl S. Buck's *The Good Earth* had become a best-seller on its way to winning the Pulitzer Prize for fiction. That honor had also recently been bestowed on Julia Peterkin's *Scarlet Sister Mary* and Margaret Barnes' *Years of Grace*. Peggy Marsh also noted with considerable pride that all five of 1931's best-selling new authors were women, and she was totally aware that book buyers were newly intrigued by historical fiction.

After working all those years Margaret Mitchell would really have liked an outside appraisal of her novel, and Lois Cole would have been the most likely candidate to secure that for her—if the work had ever been finished, retyped and put into shape. Yet there were personal reasons which kept Peggy from doing just that. She had included too much of her own life and family history for framework purposes and wanted no misinterpretations as to where personal recall ended and fictional characteri-

M-G-M's A Free Soul *in 1931 starred Norma Shearer and featured Leslie Howard and newcomer Clark Gable.*

zation took over. There was still another fear—even greater—which had sent those yellow manuscript pages on their journey from a typewriter under a towel to exile in manila envelopes, which would eventually be placed in clothing closets, crammed amidst pots and pans or even pushed under a bed.

The childhood fascination Margaret had felt for the supernatural, which manifested itself in her early story-telling, later encouraged a strange dread within her after some extrasensory premonitions during her teenage years. During her senior high school term, in that fall when she turned seventeen, Peggy had written an untitled story in which the tragic news of a young soldier's wartime death was delivered in a message to his sweetheart. It was less than a year later that Margaret's fictional tragedy became painfully and personally true with the death of her young fiancé, Clifford Henry. Three months later Margaret experienced another sad premonition when the influenza epidemic struck her parents in Atlanta. On the train ride home from Smith College she suddenly and clearly knew that her mother would already be dead when she got there.

Although she didn't know it at the time, Margaret had

David O. Selznick and George Cukor came to M-G-M for Dinner at Eight *and were introduced to that studio's "star power."*

displayed psychic prophecy even in the writing of her novel. She had created a character who would be so closely identified with a film actor of the following decade that public demand would force him into an assignment he himself did not want. That man, destined to be called "King" of all motion picture stars, was totally unknown to moviegoers throughout the period when Margaret was writing, yet so uncanny was the parallel between character and actor to be that false legends would persist that she had written her story with him in mind.

Even in the last moments of her conscious life Margaret Mitchell would be inexplicably fated to take a step backward—rather than forward—into the path of a careening car as if to keep an unavoidable date with destiny. If the lady did indeed possess a form of extrasensory perception, it would certainly have been the deciding factor in withholding a manuscript that could drastically change her life. She had been a witness to the futility of success in Rudolph Valentino's life, and, as a journalist, had seen the ruthless prying into the personal affairs that become a fact of life to those in the public eye. The deep tragedy she saw in the March 1932 kid-

napping of Charles Lindbergh's infant son, who was found dead two months later, reinforced her knowledge about the risks of fame. Had she been single, Margaret might have taken the gamble just the same to help advance the prestige of women. But it was most important to her that John Marsh remain the breadwinner and that his career be the only point of professional focus in their relationship.

After Lois Cole moved to New York in 1932 to accept an associate editorship at Macmillan, the world of book publishing receded from Margaret's everyday Atlanta life. Without all those fascinating reports of that industry from a close friend, Peggy lost her enthusiasm for her writing project. Later in 1932 the manila envelopes disappeared into various hiding places in the Marsh apartment, where they were meant to remain indefinitely. But significantly, when the Marshes moved from "The Dump" that year to a larger apartment, the manuscript moved with them—if only to find newly secretive areas of repose in a second location. Those stacks of manila envelopes had undergone quite a serviceable history of their own, having been used at various times to seat company, support a sagging sofa, or, individually, as memo pads for grocery lists and telephone numbers.

Margaret Mitchell may not have been aware of young David O. Selznick's earlier career at Paramount Pictures but she certainly must have taken later notice of his name on screen credits and advertisements on such 1932 RKO films as *What Price Hollywood?* and *A Bill of Divorcement*, both directed by George Cukor. Mr. Selznick also received credit as the "executive producer" on *King Kong*, the popular novelty horror movie which received great publicity and box-office attention. Although David had nothing to do with the artistic aspects of that project, his clever management of its budget had allowed the creative team to achieve many of the marvelous effects acclaimed by critics and audiences. When, early in 1933, Mr. Selznick joined his father-in-law, Louis B. Mayer, at Metro-Goldwyn-Mayer, it seemed an advantageous move for both producer and studio. His first assignment there, an "all-star" version of George S. Kaufman and Edna Ferber's 1932 Broadway success *Dinner at Eight*, was an auspicious beginning. At his new location David had a far wider choice than before of properties, directors, contract actors and production teams to work with—an impressive lure for any industrious filmmaker dedicated to stressing quality in films.

Mr. Selznick's next two M-G-M projects, *Night Flight* and *Dancing Lady*, gave him the opportunity to work with Clark Gable, and the latter, a Joan Crawford musical, introduced Broadway's Fred Astaire to the screen. *Viva Villa*, a 1934 release, would be the very first Selznick production nominated by the film Academy as a "Best Picture," while his *Manhattan Melodrama* that year was destined to win a trophy for its original story by

Arthur Caesar. The screenwriters who adapted Mr. Caesar's ideas were Joseph L. Mankiewicz and Oliver H. P. Garrett, both destined to be significantly heard from again. *Manhattan Melodrama* paired William Powell and the young Myrna Loy for the first time (along with Clark Gable) and was also the film which notorious gangster John Dillinger had been watching just before he met his death from FBI bullets on a Chicago street. Immediately after that film's completion, Mr. Powell and Miss Loy began work in another M-G-M vehicle entitled *The Thin Man*.

Rapidly rising director George Cukor had traveled to M-G-M for *Dinner at Eight* but returned to RKO for that studio's *Little Women*, a project planned but not executed by David O. Selznick. The results, due largely to a fine cast headed by the brilliant Katharine Hepburn, enhanced Mr. Cukor's reputation even further. Soon he too would become a regular employee at Metro-Goldwyn-Mayer.

Margaret Mitchell would later beome involved in a controversy when she commented on how well she thought Miss Hepburn looked in *Little Women*'s hoop-skirts. What had really impressed her was the authenticity those period costumes had been endowed with by their creator, Walter Plunkett. That gentleman had by then abandoned his acting ambitions and carved a nice career for himself at the RKO studio as a costume designer.

David O. Selznick, during his tenure at RKO, had also encouraged a major film innovation when he commissioned composer Max Steiner to write full-length "background scores" for many of the films he was involved with. Filmmakers had previously doubted whether audiences would accept music played underneath the spoken dialogue if it did not originate from a visible source such as a radio or phonograph. But in films like *Bird of Paradise* Max Steiner proved his themes could enhance drama rather than detract from it. With his fascinatingly eerie score for *King Kong*, Mr. Steiner set a milestone in the future history of film composition. When Academy Awards were finally instituted for this field in 1935, two of the three nominated scores would be Max Steiner compositions.

As a writer and journalist, Peggy Marsh had certainly followed the career of playwright Sidney Howard whose *They Knew What They Wanted* had received the 1925 Pulitzer Prize for drama. That play had, within a few years, served as the basis for both a 1928 silent movie from Paramount called *The Secret Hour* and a 1930 talkie from M-G-M entitled *A Lady to Love*. Both versions had considerably diluted the major character's bootlegging profession, a discouraging factor to any writer. But *The Silver Cord*, his 1926 play, was transformed into a successful 1933 RKO film in which famed stage actress Laura Hope Crews recreated her brilliant performance as a domineering mother. Not too inci-

dentally, that film featured costumes designed by Walter Plunkett and music by Max Steiner.

It had been predictable, even in 1930 when a Democratic landslide swept the country, that Americans hoped a change of leadership would bring them out of the Depression. Franklin Roosevelt's record plurality reelection as New York's governor that year had made him a natural contender for the next Presidential contest. His securing of the Democratic nomination had been followed by a phenomenal victory over incumbent Herbert Hoover's Republican ticket and did, in fact, mark the beginning of a slow return to better times. Along the way there would be "New Deal" policies, including bank holidays, relief for the unemployed and a repeal of Prohibition.

Most Americans were far too busy with their own problems then or too involved with their pastimes to take much notice of foreign affairs. The imperialistic policies of Japan and its aggression against China coincided with the rise of Chancellor Adolf Hitler and his 1934 assumption of the presidency of Germany, a country that had withdrawn from both the League of Nations and the Disarmament Conference. Other countries, such as Spain and Italy, also suffered economic problems and fascism was on the rise.

But, despite storm clouds abroad, the Depression or even architectural wonders like the Empire State Building and the George Washington Bridge, "movie-crazy" Americans were more interested in "fan" magazines, Walt Disney's "Mickey Mouse" and the new Radio City Music Hall in New York. That champion of film palaces, designed to seat 6,200 people, had been conceived for stage spectacles but became much more practical as a motion-picture theatre. Within its first two years, after inaugurating the showing of movies in early 1933, the Music Hall's reputation for presenting the finest films available grew with its bookings of *King Kong*, *The Silver Cord*, *Morning Glory*, *The Private Life of Henry VIII*, *Little Women*, *Cavalcade*, *It Happened One Night* and *Of Human Bondage*. It was considered a major accomplishment for a producer to have one of his films play there.

Margaret Mitchell reasoned, by late 1934, that it was wiser to remain just Mrs. John R. Marsh, an identity that fulfilled her completely, and to enjoy the parade of American life from the inconspicuous vantage point of a private Atlanta citizen. For diversion, there were movies like *Of Human Bondage*, featuring the distinguished Leslie Howard and the exciting new star Bette Davis. It was amusing to note all the acclaim greeting that film when one realized that only 250 copies of W. Somerset Maugham's masterpiece had been sold in the two years following its 1915 publication. What a contrast to the hundreds of thousands of copies presently selling of that long new book *Anthony Adverse*!

The Macmillan Company

Appropriately, the publishing company destined for a rendezvous with Margaret Mitchell's novel traced its earliest American origins to the period immediately following the Civil War. A generation before that, in 1843, Alexander and David Macmillan had opened a bookshop on Aldergate Street in London, England. Then in 1869, an American agency for these brothers was established in a private residence on Bleecker Street in New York City under the management of George Edward Brett, who retained that post until his death in 1890. Mr. Brett's son, George Platt Brett, succeeded him, and in 1896, when Alexander Macmillan died, two distinct companies were organized—Macmillan & Co., Limited of London and The Macmillan Company of New York—with George Brett named president of the American division. Although its principal stockholders were then still in England, The Macmillan Company would afterward date its history as an American publishing enterprise from that year. (Coincidentally, it was also in 1896 that the first motion pictures were shown, spawning an industry that was to have a significant effect on the future of book publishing.) In 1931 Mr. Brett was named Macmillan's Chairman of the Board, a capacity he served in until his death in 1936, while his son, George Platt Brett, Jr., succeeded him as president.

Best-seller lists for works of fiction had appeared for the first time in 1895, only one year before Macmillan gained its American independence. By 1897, the new publisher had secured second and fourth positions in those annual tallies with James Lane Allen's *The Invisible Choir* and Flora Annie Steele's *On the Face of the Waters*, respectively. After the company enjoyed a similar success in 1898, the classic *Richard Carvell* by American novelist Winston Churchill—not to be confused with the famed British statesman—made appearances on best-seller charts for both 1899 and 1900, selling 200,000 copies within its first year in print. Macmillan's reputation for success with fiction grew over the next two decades, largely because of Mr. Churchill's efforts, and the company often attained number-one position in selling strength for an entire year. Those Winston Churchill novels which reached first sales positions on yearly compilations were *The Crisis* in 1901, *The Crossing* in 1904, *Coniston* in 1906, *Mr. Crewe's Career* in 1908 and *The Inside of the Cup* in 1913.

Macmillan also celebrated leading fiction sales of the year in 1902 with Owen Wister's *The Virginian*, and again in 1917 with H. G. Wells' *Mr. Britling Sees It Through*. Other authors who contributed to the publisher's success during that era were Maurice Hewlett, Charles Major, Ernest Poole, Mary Sinclair and Jack London. Mr. London's *The Call of the Wild* was successful, although not phenomenally so, following its 1903 publication. Through the years that followed it would become a literary classic, selling over a million and a half copies and eventually reaching the second-largest-selling position in Macmillan's fiction history. And when the first Pulitzer Prize for a novel was granted in 1918, it was a Macmillan book, *His Family* by Ernest Poole, that was selected for that honor.

The publisher also measured victories in the general nonfiction field, and achieved a highly respected reputation in the textbook market. Nevertheless, there were many other publishing companies and Doubleday, Harper, Scribner, Holt, Appleton, Houghton Mifflin, Bowen-Merrill (later Bobbs-Merrill), Putnam, Dodd-Mead, Lippincott, Dutton and Harcourt-Brace were names equally familiar to book buyers.

Maria Chapdelaine by Louis Hemon was a critical and financial success for Macmillan in 1922 but, unfortunately, the company's fast start in the competitive fiction field lapsed afterward with no annual best-selling totals being recorded for the next eight years. In a concentrated effort to regain the fiction market Macmillan decided to put a large promotional push behind promising new writers. This proved successful in 1932 with English novelist Phyllis Bentley's *The Inheritance*. An even larger advertising expenditure on *As the Earth Turns*, the work of young Maine author Gladys Hasty Carroll, resulted in second position in 1933's fiction sales. Another writer from Maine, Mary Ellen Chase, an English professor from Smith College, kept the Macmillan name popular in 1934 with her novel *Mary Peters*, and Rachel Field, who had formerly written children's books, strengthened the company's adult market in 1935 with *Time Out of Mind*.

Macmillan's editors were well aware in early 1935 of what regional women authors had done for the company. As they began to make plans for the coming year's acquisitions, they examined general trends that had proved successful for their competitors. They noted that Hervey Allen's extremely long novel, *Anthony Adverse*, had sold 476,000 copies for Farrar & Rinehart and remained the number-one best seller in both 1933 and 1934. In the midst of the Depression Americans had little money for diversion and seemed to feel the relatively modest price of a long book was a good investment. Also the renewed popularity of historical fiction was continuing, not only with *Anthony Adverse*, but in 1934's two runners-up sales champions. Caroline Miller's *Lamb in His Bosom*, published by Harper, and Stark Young's *So Red the Rose* by Scribner, were both novels of the Old South and Miss Miller's work had won the 1934 Pulitzer Prize.

The analysis indicated that the editors should be on the lookout for a long book about the South by a new author. Book publishers, in business for profit, would rarely make a major investment in a totally obscure or unrecommended writer, even if the manuscript were in line with current trends. A recommendation came at this time from Lois Cole, who was associate to Macmillan editor-in-chief Harold S. Latham. (Mr. Latham had joined Macmillan in 1909, working his way up from the advertising and accounting areas to become a director of the firm by 1935.)

Since the end of the World War public interest in novels had sharply increased, competition for authors had heightened and Macmillan editors went on yearly scouting trips to recruit necessary product. Harold Latham had been traveling to England for the past few years but decided that it might be advantageous instead to try a three-month tour of America in the spring of 1935. When Lois told him about Peggy Mitchell Marsh's unseen manuscript, she added that if Mrs. Marsh could write as well as she spoke, there might be a book there for Macmillan. Harold Latham decided to make Atlanta his first destination and Lois Taylor wrote to her old friends there asking that Mr. Latham be granted any possible help to make his visit worthwhile. Peggy Marsh attended several functions to which Mr. Latham was invited upon his arrival in Atlanta and—from the first—found herself being questioned by him about a possible manuscript. She politely denied having anything ready for submission to a publisher.

In a booklet published by Macmillan the following year, Mr. Latham recalled his first meeting with the lady. "Finally it was my good fortune to meet Peggy Mitchell," he wrote. "She proved to be a diminutive person with a very lively sense of humor and a proficiency in the art of conversation rarely encountered these days. We talked about a good many things at this first meeting, and more particularly about Southern literature, about which I found she had, as indeed about many things, positive ideas. Finally . . . I swung the conversation around to her own work. Imagine my surprise and disappointment when she informed me, very pleasantly but with firmness, that while she might have been playing around with the idea of doing a novel some time or other, she had nothing to show me.

"My interest in Miss Mitchell had been greatly stimulated by my meeting with her, and I made many inquiries of my Atlanta friends about her. . . . She was known to have a critical mind, an impatience with shams, an eager curiosity and a striking ability to get at the root of things. A librarian of Atlanta told me that when Peggy got started on the trail of something, the solution was as good as found. She is an indefatigable research worker. All of these reports made me the more regretful that no manuscript was forthcoming."

After the final reception given for Mr. Latham by Atlanta's literary circle, Margaret offered to drive several of the guests home. On that ride fate provided a catalyst in the form of a young rival who, unsuccessful in her own attempts at publication, chided Peggy's endeavors at writing and ridiculed Harold Latham's solicitations for her work. The young lady plainly said that she felt Margaret Mitchell wasn't serious enough about life to be a novelist. Outwardly, Peggy laughed the incident away. Temper has always been a motivator of actions and, luckily, sometimes the results are worthwhile. In a fighting mood Peggy Marsh returned home, gathered together whatever manila envelopes she could find and brought them to Mr. Latham's hotel shortly before his departure.

Mr. Latham later recalled what was probably the most unorthodox manuscript presentation in publishing history. "A few hours before I left Atlanta, the telephone in my hotel room rang and Miss Mitchell's voice came to me over it informing me that she was downstairs in the lobby and would like to see me. I went down, and I shall never forget the picture I have of Margaret Mitchell . . . a tiny woman sitting on a divan, and beside her the biggest manuscript I have ever seen, towering in two stacks almost up to her shoulders. 'If you really want it, you may take it, but it's incomplete, unrevised, there are several versions of some of the chapters, there is no first chapter,' Miss Mitchell went on hurriedly, as though there were danger of changing her mind if she stopped to think. 'I hadn't any intention of letting you or any publisher see it. I only wrote it for my own entertainment. . . . You can't possibly be as surprised at being given it as I am at letting you take it.' . . . My luggage accommodations were limited, and try as I would I could not make room for the manuscript. . . . But I had no intention of letting it get out of my hands, so before I left Atlanta I purchased a suitcase in which to carry it."

The next city on Harold Latham's itinerary was New Orleans and when he arrived there he found a telegram at his hotel with the brief, demanding, soon-to-be-legendary message: PLEASE SEND MANUSCRIPT BACK I'VE CHANGED MY MIND. But Mr. Latham had started reading it and thought otherwise.

1935: With a Lower-Case "w"

In late April 1935 Harold Latham's response arrived at the Marsh home asking that the Macmillan people in New York also be granted the opportunity to judge a project which he thought, from only a partial reading, to be totally worthwhile. Oh well, Margaret thought, at least she was keeping her old promise to Lois by letting that company see the manuscript. The publisher would probably be forced to return it unread because of its decrepit, unfinished condition, and Margaret felt she could accept that kind of rejection without feeling slighted in any way. Indeed, Lois Cole later told Margaret that it was one of the most battered manuscripts she had ever come across.

Meanwhile, although they were impressed by Mr. Latham's enthusiastic recommendation, Macmillan decision makers wanted another opinion as well and sought an appraisal from Charles Everett, professor of Columbia University's English department. The analysis which Professor Everett returned to Macmillan was highly favorable and it noted that Margaret's literary device of "using an unsympathetic character to arouse sympathetic emotions seems to me admirable." He called the story "really magnificent" with a "high degree of literary finish." The professor advised Macmillan: "By all means take the book. It can't possibly turn out badly." Nonetheless, he had strong reservations about the conclusion, disliking the finality of Rhett's decision to leave Pansy. "The end is slightly disappointing," he said and suggested that Macmillan ask Miss Mitchell to "strengthen the last page." As an afterthought, Professor Everett recommended *Another Day* as a possible title.

By late July a Macmillan contract was on its way to Atlanta offering Margaret Mitchell advance payment of $500 in exchange for permission to publish her untitled novel. The proposed royalties were the standard 10 percent of retail price with an escalation to 15 percent if the book sold more than ten thousand copies. Of course the company would have to regain that $500 before she would receive any further royalty payment.

Margaret's only reaction was honest puzzlement that anyone had been able to understand her unkempt manuscript, and she wondered how the publisher expected to market the first book of a completely unknown author. John Marsh assured her that their contacts in Georgia would probably guarantee a sale of several thousand books. She doubted that but, after letting her father and brother look over the document, signed the contract on August 6, 1935.

Although Margaret had forgotten to include some manila envelopes containing portions of the novel, she had inadvertently included the one containing *'Ropa Carmagin* among the many she gave to Harold Latham. Macmillan was equally enthusiastic about the novella but was not prepared to publish such a short book at that time. When the editors returned it to her, they proposed possible later publication of it, together with other stories Margaret might have. At a future date, however, she destroyed it. But a rumor that Macmillan possessed two additional chapters of Margaret Mitchell's novel would persist through later years, based on hearsay from someone's recollections of the *'Ropa Carmagin* manuscript.

Then came the tricky part. Margaret had incorporated much of her Civil War background material from early memory or from library research but without recording exact sources. She had no intention of letting the book see print without rechecking all that data and carefully cataloging backup references for every historical fact she mentioned. Macmillan had not scheduled publication until the following spring so she felt there would be ample time to renew that research, tie up loose ends, write bridges or missing material and conceive an opening chapter. But although she worked steadily the time flew by and at summer's end she felt no closer to completion than at its start. Margaret was optimistic though in feeling it would all come together at once.

The story, as it stood, began with seventeen-year-old Pansy fretting over the betrothal of Ashley Wilkes, the man she loved. Margaret devised a new opening—which she would revise many times—in which the girl learned that news from twin suitors. She used these brash Tarleton boys then to frame a description of the unpolished life in Georgia's Clayton County, the environs of the O'Hara's plantation. At the same time, she made her heroine one year younger and pinpointed the time element as mid-April of 1861, two days after the shelling of Fort Sumter. In a later decision as to the final disposition of Frank Kennedy, Pansy's second husband, Margaret chose a Ku Klux Klan raid as a more dramatic means to eliminate him.

In early September Margaret notified Macmillan that she expected to be through with her revisions in a few weeks. One thing still seemed wrong to her although it was rather late in the day to contemplate such a change. But "Pansy" was rather a frail name for the character who so determinedly fought her way through those hundreds of pages. Since she had already made arrangements to have the manuscript retyped, with outside help, Margaret knew a name change, which would affect almost every single piece of manuscript paper, would have

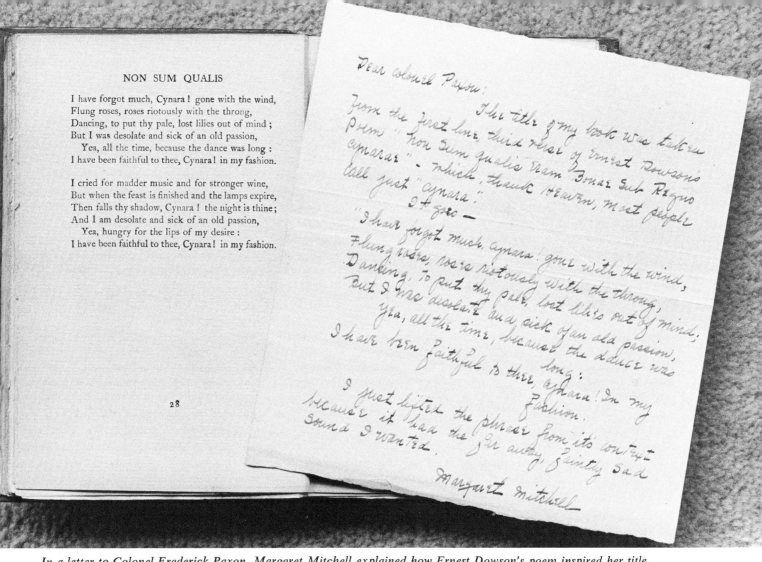

to be decided immediately, before that typing project began. She thought of many names during the next two weeks and almost accepted the idea that "Pansy" was at least a little different from the names of most fictional heroines of the day but decided nonetheless to turn to her story again for inspiration. One section, which would eventually form the major part of Chapter Twenty-four, had undergone no revisions since she first wrote it. It detailed Pansy's arrival at the ruined MacIntosh plantation and continued through her return home until she wearily fell asleep that night. Pansy had thought of her Irish ancestry and gotten some inspiration from their valiant fight to rise above misfortune. "There were the Scarletts who had fought with the Irish Volunteers for a free Ireland," Margaret had written, ". . . and the O'Haras who died at the Boyne." She read that line over and over again since something had caught her attention, although she couldn't at first comprehend what it was. Finally she realized—a new name for the girl in her story had existed all along.

Margaret, who often showed a tendency toward humorous exaggeration, would later say that Scarlett was among "hundreds" of names she submitted to Macmillan with a notation of her preference for it. In any case, Macmillan thoroughly approved and that little decision then meant weeks of searching the manuscript to change each reference from Pansy to Scarlett. At the same time she also changed the girl's mother's name from Eleanor D'Antignac O'Hara to Ellen Robillard O'Hara. Luckily, an alteration of the family home from Fontenoy Hall to Tara had been made long before Harold Latham left Atlanta with the manuscript.

Something else had bothered Margaret while rereading that section about her heroine's return home. In the early part of the chapter, after leaving Atlanta, Pansy—now Scarlett—had dreaded what she would find upon her arrival at Tara. Peggy had created a significant paragraph summing up the girl's fears but wanted a stronger phrase to emphasize the devastation that had spread through the Georgian countryside.

As she had grown older, Margaret acquired a fondness for poetry and often turned to it for relaxation in such moments of stress as these. Ernest Dowson was among her favorite poets and she was as moved by his work as she was by the knowledge that the tragic Englishman had realized so little of his potential when he died, at age thirty-two, only nine months before she was born. Like Margaret, Mr. Dowson had been shy, sensitive and proud. He had cared more for his prose than his verse, never realizing he would be best remembered for the latter.

The most famous Dowson lyric employed a title taken from the first poem in *The Odes of Horace, Book IV: "Non sum qualis eram bonae sub regno Cynarae,"* which translated as "I am not like I was [the kind of person I was] under the reign of the good Cynara." His work expressed the first-person longings for a lost love as each of its four verses repeated ". . . I was desolate and sick of an old passion . . . I have been faithful to thee, Cynara! in my fashion."

But it was the first line of the third verse that now caught Margaret's eye: "I have forgot much, Cynara! gone with the wind." Those last four words perfectly described the ravaged Georgia Scarlett saw on her sad trip to Tara and they also impressed Margaret enough to include them as a title possibility on a list sent to Macmillan along with several others. Professor Everett's original suggestion of *Another Day* had remained the book's "working title," although Macmillan editors had hoped a better idea might come along. They had briefly considered the story's concluding line of dialogue, "to-morrow is another day," until a search revealed there were far too many books in print with the word "tomorrow" in the title. Margaret's new letter included such offerings as *Baa, Baa Black Sheep, Bugles Sang True* and especially *Tote the Weary Load,* a line from Stephen Foster's "My Old Kentucky Home" which she had used numerous times throughout her text.

She expressed a preference for *Gone with the Wind* and carefully wrote it so the "w" in "with" was properly in a lower case. Macmillan enthusiastically concurred with her suggestion, although Peggy still held some reservations. She would admit later that while the expression moved her deeply, it wasn't until after publication that she realized how perfect a title it really was. At that time she explained the genesis of it to her friend Colonel Frederick J. Paxon, co-founder of Atlanta's Davison-Paxon department store.

"The title of my book," she wrote, "was taken from the first line, third verse of Ernest Dowson's poem . . . which, thank Heaven, most people call just 'Cynara.' " . . . I just lifted the phrase from its context because it had the far away, faintly sad sound I wanted."

Margaret still felt the need to shorten the book, and in eliminating material, Scarlett's youngest sister was among those who suffered. A lengthy passage in which, after her father's death, Scarlett lovingly remembered Carreen as a baby and tried to discourage the girl from entering a

Margaret Mitchell, Harold S. Latham of Macmillan and Medora Perkerson, at the April 1935 luncheon where it all began.

convent was totally deleted. In the new version Scarlett expressed little interest in either of her sisters, which was more in keeping with her unrelenting selfishness, and Carreen's vocation was mentioned only in passing.

At the same time, Margaret added a section in which Scarlett visited the Fontaine family after finding Tara ravished by Yankees. These neighbors generously offered to share their provisions with the O'Haras since they had been more fortunate in eluding Union destruction. Without this, Margaret felt, there was no acceptable explanation why all eleven of Tara's charges did not starve to death. Then Margaret moved Ashley's admission of love for Scarlett from the later lumber mill sequence, where they were observed by his sister, to a much earlier point in Tara's orchard during postwar days. The result added some fascinating irony to that mill scene because Scarlett would be accused there of something which, for once, she was innocent of.

As steadily as Margaret attempted to work, there were endless interruptions. Illness, problems, even death among close friends and family could certainly not be ignored, but she bore down as much as was humanly possible. In such a long work consistency was a prime concern and, again, John's copy-editing experience was of invaluable help. Nevertheless, later comments about Margaret's style of "reinforcing" facts might not have been made had she more time for tightening. In more than one instance she would repeat a statement in exactly the same fashion without realizing, from such close exposure, that it had already been said. In some other instances—as to exactly when Scarlett began drinking, for example—there would remain apparent contradictions.

By year-end Margaret's sight had become strained, her scalp had broken out from a nervous reaction, and she was physically, mentally and emotionally exhausted. There had, by then, come those moments of regret. If she hadn't signed that contract, she wouldn't be undergoing all these agonies which had torn her well-adjusted home life apart. All for something she had never wanted or sought at all. Why had she agreed to do it?

As Peggy Mitchell Marsh pressured herself with deadline assignments, events were occurring that year within industries and to personalities whose paths were destined to cross or parallel her own. In February Clark Gable and Claudette Colbert had become the first actor and actress to win top honors for the same film at the Academy Awards ceremonies, a feat that would remain unchallenged for forty-one years. There had been an earlier uproar when nomination lists excluded Bette Davis's striking performance in *Of Human Bondage,* so to soothe Bette's irate supporters the Academy threw the voting open to "write-in" ballots. At the time there were only three nominees in each acting category and the order of

runners-up was announced along with the winners but Miss Davis still placed fourth at the finish line. Even more fascinating was the substantial "write-in" vote received then by unnominated six-year-old Shirley Temple, who had recently been acclaimed one of the greatest box-office attractions on the screen. Accordingly, a miniature statuette was presented to Miss Temple "in grateful recognition of her outstanding contributions to screen entertainment."

With five awards Columbia Pictures' *It Happened One Night* established a new Academy Award record, for in addition to Clark's and Claudette's performances, the film was honored for Frank Capra's direction, for its screenplay and as "Best Picture of 1934" (the Awards now being on a calendar year basis). It would be future irony for Clark Gable that, although the major part of his acting career was to be spent under contract to Metro-Goldwyn-Mayer, his only Academy Award would come through a "loan-out" to another studio.

Earlier in 1935 M-G-M had premiered David O. Selznick's production of *David Copperfield*, directed by George Cukor. The speculation which started a year before when Mr. Selznick launched a "talent search" to find just the right child to play the title role ended with the selection of "unknown" Freddie Bartholomew. This was providential for both the producer and his studio since they immediately engaged the boy for *Anna Karenina* with Greta Garbo and Fredric March and then placed him under contract. David Selznick was thrilled to be filming versions of famous books and, in addition to those works of Dickens and Tolstoy, he began production on another Dickens classic *A Tale of Two Cities* with Ronald Colman. But his employment at Metro-Goldwyn-

Clark Gable and Claudette Colbert became the first acting team to win Academy Awards for the same motion picture, a feat not duplicated for forty-one years.

Mayer was not altogether rewarding. His assignment to supervise *Reckless* proved disappointing despite the best efforts of William Powell, Jean Harlow and director Victor Fleming and the picture's substantial profit. But art was more important than profit to Mr. Selznick and he did not wish to suffer any more indignities such as being assigned *Meet the Baron*, which featured a group of gentlemen known to film history as "the Three Stooges." His career at M-G-M, he felt, had reached an apparent impasse and, to better himself, David sought independence from his father-in-law to produce films on his own.

Meanwhile, history was being made in the motion-picture industry with the opening of Pioneer Pictures' *Becky Sharp* at the Radio City Music Hall. An adaptation of Langdon Mitchell's dramatization with Miriam Hopkins as William M. Thackeray's classic *Vanity Fair* heroine, it was the first feature filmed in a new three-color process developed by the Technicolor Company. A vast improvement over previous color presentations, the event was described by *The New York Times* as "incredibly thrilling" and a momentous experiment of historical importance that reproduced not the colors of nature but of a vividly artistic dream world. The reviewer's only reservation was the need for accustoming the eye to what he called a phenomenon, a prophecy and "the most significant event of the 1935 cinema."

Pioneer Pictures had been founded by Merian C. Cooper, former RKO co-worker and close friend of David Selznick, with financing provided by millionaire John Hay Whitney. While that company's second Technicolor production, *The Dancing Pirate*, was not scheduled for release until 1936, Mr. Cooper and Mr. Selznick persuaded Mr. Whitney to refinance Pioneer as part of a new company—Selznick International Pictures, Inc.—with David O. Selznick as president, Merian C. Cooper as vice president and not too surprisingly, John Hay Whitney as chairman of the board. Like its predecessor Pioneer Pictures, Selznick International was closely linked with the propagation of the Technicolor process in feature motion pictures since the principals owned a great deal of that color company's stock. David's brother, famed talent agent Myron Selznick, was another investor in Selznick International, along with members of the Whitney family and Irving Thalberg of M-G-M and his actress-wife, Norma Shearer. David O. Selznick contributed himself and his talents.

The new company was located in Culver City, on the same street and only a few blocks away from Metro-Goldwyn-Mayer. The studio it occupied had formerly been the headquarters of moviemaker Thomas H. Ince and its administration building was a replica of the Mount Vernon, Virginia, home of George Washington. The studio's "back lot," for outdoor set construction, encompassed an impressively spacious area called "Forty Acres" which had served as the filming site for many a noted movie, including *King Kong*.

For Selznick International's baptism into filmmaking, David Selznick chose a nineteenth-century book which had been a personal favorite in his youth. *Little Lord Fauntleroy*, published in 1886, was written by Frances Hodgson Burnett, an author who came to America from England at the close of the Civil War and settled in Tennessee. Miss Burnett was to produce best-selling novels for four more decades until her death in 1924. Mr. Selznick selected Hugh Walpole, who had scripted *David Copperfield*, as the picture's adaptor, and John Cromwell, noted for *The Silver Cord* and *Of Human Bondage*, as its director. Youthful actors Freddie Bartholomew and Mickey Rooney were borrowed from M-G-M, and the filming, which began in September 1935, was completed in six weeks at a cost of $560,000—a sum considered average for a first-class movie of the day.

Although *Little Lord Fauntleroy* was photographed in black and white, David started planning his first Technicolor film while it was still in production. This would be based on the 1905 best-seller *The Garden of Allah*, a novel with a religious theme that had been filmed as a silent in 1926 by M-G-M. He began negotiations to contract Marlene Dietrich and Charles Boyer as its stars. It had always been considered naive practice for a new film company to christen its first production as "number one." Accordingly, Selznick International Pictures assigned production numbers "S.I.P.—100" to *Little Lord Fauntleroy* and "S.I.P.—101" to *The Garden of Allah*.

Other Hollywood highlights in 1935 included Spencer Tracy ending his contractual obligations to Fox Films and enlisting in the ranks at Metro-Goldwyn-Mayer to begin a mutually strengthening relationship which would span two decades. The Marx Brothers in *A Night at the Opera* were a comedy triumph for M-G-M director Sam Wood, and a former Cecil B. DeMille actor, William Boyd, adopted a new identity to begin a series of "Hopalong Cassidy" films. Composer Max Steiner increased respect for motion-picture background music with his scores for *The Informer, She* and *Alice Adams*. Director Victor Fleming guided young Henry Fonda to a bright film debut in *The Farmer Takes a Wife*, and in the same year newcomers James Stewart, Errol Flynn, Olivia de Havilland, Rita Hayworth, Eleanor Powell, David Niven, Luise Rainer and Ann Rutherford were introduced to American moviegoers.

After another "exhaustive talent search" to produce a leading man for Norma Shearer in George Cukor's *Romeo and Juliet*, Irving Thalberg promptly cast Leslie Howard—to no one's real surprise! Mr. Howard was the current acting rage—on screen in Alexander Korda's *The Scarlet Pimpernel* and on the New York stage in Robert E. Sherwood's *The Petrified Forest*. Mr. Korda, who was England's counterpart to David O. Selznick, had recently contracted a beautiful young stage actress, Vivien Leigh, for future assignments in his London Films productions.

Clark Gable had an industrious year after acquiring his gold statuette. He appeared in four films, most notably *Mutiny on the Bounty*. This compelling drama, produced by Irving Thalberg, was adapted from Charles Nordhoff and James Norman Hall's best-selling 1932 novel with Charles Laughton impressively cast as the ruthless "Captain Bligh" and young socialite-actor Franchot Tone in support. When M-G-M's *China Seas*, with Mr. Gable, Jean Harlow, Wallace Beery and Rosalind Russell, was released, some of the film's notices mentioned a clever bit of comedy by an unidentified black actress. That lady's name was Hattie McDaniel.

Another "loan-out" assignment sent Clark to Darryl F. Zanuck's Twentieth Century Pictures for a film adapted from Jack London's 1903 Macmillan novel *The Call of the Wild*. At the time this film was being released to theatres, Mr. Zanuck was in the process of merging his enterprising young company with the historic Fox Films Corporation, a concern which had been saved from bankruptcy only by the strength of its leading players, humorist Will Rogers and diminutive Shirley Temple. The combined Twentieth Century-Fox studio shortly became one of the four leading motion-picture distributors in the country. Tragically, Will Rogers was killed in an Alaskan plane crash that August, before he had ever actually worked for the new institution. While Twentieth Century Pictures had previously been distributed by United Artists, that corporation was able to rationalize the loss of this unit since they signed an exclusive eight-picture contract in July 1935 to release the films of the new Selznick International establishment.

Although the 1934 Pulitzer Prize for fiction had been voted to Caroline Miller's Southern story *Lamb in His Bosom*, the financial value of the Civil War to the entertainment world suffered a severe blow when Paramount's film version of Stark Young's 1934 best seller *So Red the Rose* failed to excite ticket buyers. Although it was a beautifully photographed epic featuring Margaret Sullavan and Randolph Scott, *So Red the Rose* presented too grim and unrelenting an outcome for Depression audiences. For some time to come it would be cited as the cause of Hollywood's reluctance to pursue other Civil War stories.

Phenomenons of 1935 were the dance team of Fred Astaire and Ginger Rogers, celebrating their second year together with *Top Hat* and *Roberta*, and the singing team of Jeanette MacDonald and Nelson Eddy, seen on the screen for the first time in M-G-M's *Naughty Marietta*. America was more movie-struck than ever and no one provided the bonanza for studio and exhibitors or even manufacturers and retailers as had that remarkable sprite, Shirley Temple. Little Shirley's rapid rise had culminated

Clark Gable won his second Academy Award nomination for M-G-M's Mutiny on the Bounty.

in unprecedented acclaim the previous Christmas season when she sang "On the Good Ship Lollipop" in *Bright Eyes*. The caustic reviewer of *The New York Times* called her the most improbable child in the world and, defining her "slightly sinister emotional tricks" coupled with the studio's "ruthless exploitation" of her talents, feared that the optimism and cheerful determination of her films might cause "an epidemic of axe murders and grandmother beatings."

Miss Temple was an absolute delight to Americans who, even as they slowly recuperated from the Depression, wanted little association with stark reality. If shop-girl Joan Crawford could find a prince charming like Clark Gable or alluring Jean Harlow could seem attainable to the average man, nothing more profound was needed in a screenplay. Dramas or biographies were acceptable if they were plushly historical. "Screwball" comedies along with nonsense musicals were the new rage. Some grim little social documents were produced by Warner Brothers but they captured more attention from critics than audiences. M-G-M realized even their Greta Garbo tragedies would have been failures if they hadn't earned more money overseas than domestically, but her image contributed to the studio's star prestige and Irving Thalberg himself supervised her career. While moviegoers did enjoy a good cry, they preferred happy endings. Poking fun at the rich while glamorizing the

"So Red the Rose!"

The Flower of Southern Chivalry
Dewed with the Shining Glory
of a Woman's Tears . . .

The Girl He Left Behind Him

Slaves in the First Frenzy of Freedom

A Son of the South Goes Forth to War

A Daughter's Love Heals War's Wounds

A Last Sad Parting as the Bugles Sound

Women Await the Dreaded News

War's Axes Smash a Southern Home

"SO RED THE ROSE," starring MARGARET SULLAVAN and Walter Connolly with Randolph Scott. Directed by King Vidor. From Stark Young's novel. A Paramount Picture.

Paramount's So Red the Rose *gave the Civil War a bad reputation at the box office.*

lives of the working class seemed a guaranteed formula for studio profit.

The heart-tugging Shirley Temple sagas were also a godsend to the guardians of the newly formed Motion Picture Producers and Distributors' "Code of Ethics." Established in 1934 by necessity in answer to the outcries from women's groups and the Catholic Church which was outraged at the sexual innuendoes of Mae West, suggestive costuming and the gangster film trend, its tenets were strict and simple: "No picture shall be produced which will lower the moral standards of those who see it," and "law, natural or human, shall not be ridiculed nor shall sympathy be created for its violation. The Code absolutely forbade any picturization of nudity, sexual acts, unpunished crime, brutality, revenge, violence, narcotics addiction, attractive adultery, homosexuality, lustful kissing, venereal disease, childbirth, ridicule of religion, miscegenation or even hints of unacceptable language. This last was carefully spelled out in Section V, "Profanity": "Pointed profanity . . . Hell, S.O.B., Damn, Gawd, or every other profane or vulgar expression however used, is forbidden." Whether or not this forced protection had an actual effect on crime and morality in America was something even sociologists couldn't ascertain. But it was indisputable that Hollywood exerted a profound influence on American life as seen in its journalism, advertising, buying trends, fashion modes and even everyday conversations, which were saturated with the names of scores of film players.

Shirley Temple's phenomenal popularity brought her the top position in box-office and tie-in merchandise earnings in 1935. No less than four of her films received bookings at the Radio City Music Hall, and the last of these, *The Littlest Rebel,* was a Christmas present that even repaired some of the damage *So Red the Rose* had done to the film marketability of the Civil War. Shirley sang and danced with the great black entertainer Bill Robinson, then cooed her way onto Abraham Lincoln's lap to save her Confederate father's life, which caused *The New York Times* to note that Stark Young's portrait of ruin may have been mistaken and that the War Between the States might have been a chummy little affair after all.

The total phenomenon of this exceptional child was certainly a boon to the still depressed economy with her endorsements of jewelry, watches, dresses, music, soap, glassware and comic strips. The famous Ideal Toy series of dolls and accessories brought sales numbering in the millions while, as a bonus to her peer group, she was the inspiration for the "Shirley Temple Cocktail," a non-alcoholic mixture which made youngsters feel sophisticated while their parents were imbibing. Similar promotions for items related to the Walt Disney cartoon characters proved equally popular with the buying public and this direct relationship of the entertainment world to business would, predictably, inspire imitations many times in the near future.

Back in Atlanta Margaret Mitchell continued the struggle with her manuscript, even cutting and pasting pieces together when she made further eliminations. Peggy knew already that she would not submit it without her father, Eugene, reviewing every page for historical accuracy. But she sought further assurance from Wilbur Kurtz, a noted Civil War historian, whom she had previously met on an excursion sponsored by the Atlanta Historical Society. Margaret wrote to Mr. Kurtz in mid-November asking if he would check the war campaign backgrounds of two and a half chapters in her story. He gladly complied and soon returned those sections with his complete approval. Wilbur was later to find it necessary to deny that he had given the author any creative help and to insist that her excellent research had been above reproach.

Plans to film Edna Ferber's new historical best seller, *Come and Get It,* must have caught Margaret's attention that fall, as well as talk of translating two of James Hilton's 1935 pacemakers, *Good-Bye Mr. Chips* and *Lost Horizon,* to the screen in the near future. She may also have noticed some similarity between her own Scarlett O'Hara and Ada Fincastle, Southern heroine of Ellen Glasgow's *Vein of Iron,* the novel which captured second place in sales honors for the entire year. Miss Glasgow's determined heroine had been able to sustain her entire family through bleak poverty only by asserting the "vein of iron" in her willful character.

The New York Film Critics Awards were newly established by reviewers of that city's leading newspapers. The group selected *The Informer* and its director, John Ford, Greta Garbo in *Anna Karenina* and Charles Laughton for both *Mutiny on the Bounty* and *Ruggles of Red Gap* as its first honorees. Several published reports indicated this group had been formed because of dissatisfaction with the annual awards of the motion picture Academy. Soon the New York Film Critics Awards would be considered the second most important honors in the film industry, and although the allegations about the organization's founding purpose were repeatedly denied, there were destined to be few occasions during the next decades when Hollywood and New York would agree on their choices.

Meanwhile at Macmillan, heavy effort was being expended to complete the company's spring 1936 catalog for use by its salesmen to garner advance orders. A full page was devoted to Margaret Mitchell's upcoming novel, although the description of it was far from inspired: "The stirring drama of the Civil War and Reconstruction is brought vividly to life in this really magnificent novel." An April 21, 1936, publication date was promised with a tentative retail selling price of $2.50. In Macmillan's rush to meet the salesmen's selling tour deadlines, a typographical error occurred in a reference on the catalog's inside front cover, where the book was humorously misidentified as *Come with the Wind*!

Eugene Mitchell was the foremost historical authority on whom his daughter relied for the historical accuracy of her research.

1936: "To J. R. M."

Nineteen hundred and thirty-six . . . a Presidential election year, an Olympiad and a healthy outlook for the Depression's end . . . England's monarchy was never closer to America's hearts while threatening war clouds formed over Germany . . . the astounding best seller Anthony Adverse *came to the screen just as the last silent movie was released . . . Selznick International Pictures found success with its first production, then made a legendary purchase for $50,000 . . . and a new type of "Scarlett fever" spread rapidly throughout the country . . .*

It was not until late January of 1936 that Margaret had felt, with assurances from John and her father, that the manuscript was finally in order. She could then include a title page with *Gone with the Wind*, a phrase she had gotten quite used to, emblazing its identification. Copy for only one more page remained to be typed—that part of a book, it was joked in publishing circles, that no one but the author's family read: the dedication. This seemed to be, Margaret thought, the only part of her ordeal which required no second thought. As she typed "To J.R.M."—in initials indicative of her guarded privacy—she recalled the encouragement, thoughtfulness, patience and aid her husband, John Robert Marsh, had volunteered in those last seven grueling months.

The manuscript went off by airmail to Macmillan and the Marshes hoped for a return to their peaceful life with nothing more vexing than the pleasant anticipation of seeing the book in print. But on February 10 the initial galley proofs arrived (with many more to come) and the tedious work of proofreading was upon them for another month. Margaret worked scrupulously and mailed the galleys back in batches, the last of them being received in New York during the third week in March. Amazingly, bound copies of the book were delivered to Macmillan's editorial offices only one month later—quite a herculean job considering the novel's length.

By publishing standards, Macmillan's initial order for ten thousand copies of *Gone with the Wind* was considered optimistic and, when printed, they carried the legend "Published May 1936" on their copyright pages. As soon as there were books on hand, Macmillan's subsidiary rights department sought tie-in interest from the Book-of-the-Month Club, and with the assistance of an outside agent, Annie Laurie Williams, made it available for those possibly interested in film rights. In all, with those review copies dispatched to even regional publications throughout the country, one thousand of the ten thousand copies had been sent out free of charge.

With planned publication in sight, Harold Latham pre-pared a letter on Monday, April 13, 1936, for reviewers, clergymen, broadcasters, lecturers, authors and the like which was to be signed by George Brett, Jr., and sent simultaneously with copies of the book during the next few days. This read, in part: "We are about to publish a book the importance of which prompts me to break my long established rule of not writing to make a personal appeal with reference to any books . . . I promise you that I shall not make a habit of doing it, but at the same time I feel that I am justified in doing so now. The book about which I write is to be published on May 5. It is a first novel by Margaret Mitchell of Atlanta, Georgia, entitled *Gone with the Wind*, and an advance copy is being dispatched to you under separate cover. . . . [It] appeals to all of us here as being such an important novel that I am hoping I may persuade you personally to read it. . . . I believe it to be a significant and important novel of the American scene. . . . The author, a young Southern woman, has in my opinion created a great novel."

The balance of Mr. Latham's draft sounded even more like a form letter as it solicited reviews and comments but he attached to it a personal note for Mr. Brett's attention: "If the Book Club should select the book, *which it probably won't*, we would have to send around a correction of the date to everybody, but even so I do not think we ought to wait." Contradicting his pessimistic prediction, the Book-of-the-Month Club did decide, two days later, to make *Gone with the Wind* an "early selection." By the end of the month the organization confirmed Miss Mitchell's novel as its *feature* selection for July and it planned a forty-thousand-copy printing, which forced Macmillan to delay its official publication date until June 30. All that really meant was that advertisements would be delayed and reviewers would be asked to withhold their printed opinions until that date. Copies were released to bookstores on schedule in May and buyers received a bonus since a prepublication price was set at $2.75 (for a product that would later sell for $3.00).

The Book-of-the-Month Club had come a long way in the ten years since Harry Scherman founded it in 1926. Mr. Scherman's idea of sifting through all the new books he and his small staff could get from publishers to offer "the best" to American subscribers had been quite revolutionary. The notion of expecting American readers to buy a series of new, unacclaimed books through the mail had been ridiculed but Harry Scherman believed it would work if he utilized an impressive group of experts to recommend those monthly offerings. It succeeded enough to lure sixty thousand customers within its first two years and, within that first decade, two-thirds of the Club's main selections had become best sellers. Some of the most prominent titles recommended by the Book-of-the-Month Club in that period included *Elmer Gantry, Bambi, All Quiet on the Western Front, Grand Hotel, The Good Earth, Mutiny on the Bounty, National Velvet* and *Anthony Adverse.*

When *Gone with the Wind* came to the Club's attention there were some doubts about the characterization and the writing quality. One judge admitted that he found the book a "page turner" but wondered if other readers would. Nevertheless the panel of authorities agreed to adopt it as a main selection and devoted four and a half of the July pamphlet's sixteen pages to the novel and its author. Henry Seidel Canby began his unbiased review in that brochure by saying, "This book has been waiting to be written for many years," but then offered several reservations including his personal dislike for the Rhett Butler character. One could hardly have anticipated a heavy sales response from Mr. Canby's favorable but guarded opinion which, at best, granted that "if Miss Mitchell is not Tolstoi, she has certainly proved herself to be a very satisfying novelist, at a time when so much of our most skillful fiction is more brilliant than readable." However, through its adoption by the Book-of-the-Month Club, *Gone with the Wind* was granted the chance to reach further than mere bookstores —to every village and hamlet with a post office.

Macmillan became gradually aware that May of a rather strange occurrence. Without benefit of either advertisements or reviews (except for some regional report-

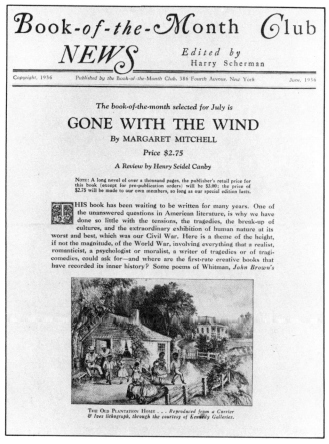

The June 1936 brochure issued by the Book-of-the-Month Club (above and below) highlighted Gone with the Wind as the feature selection.

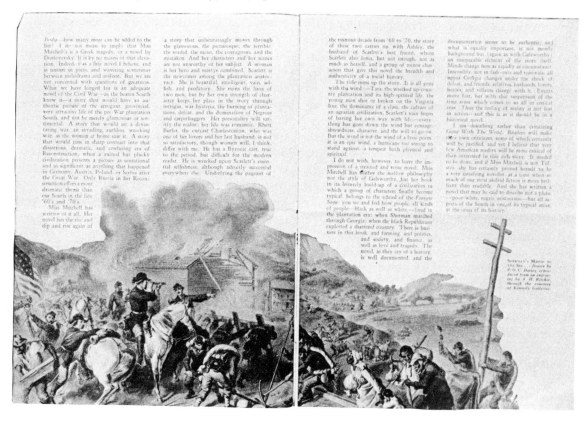

27

One of the early advertisements for Macmillan's best seller as it appeared in the Saturday Evening Post.

age), bookstores were placing early reorders for *Gone with the Wind*. Word-of-mouth, always the most valuable asset in marketing any commodity, seemed to be spreading rapidly about the new Civil War novel and its unconventional heroine. Customers were steadily asking storekeepers for *that* new book, occasionally without remembering the title or sometimes requesting it as "Scarlett O'Hara." Librarians, many who had not yet ordered it, found it heading their most-requested list. Macmillan quickly placed a second order for ten thousand copies and these carried a new legend, "Published June, 1936," without any reference whatsoever to the prepublication May printing. These new books were so quickly disposed of that the company realized its plans were too modest and ordered twenty thousand for the third press run. The wild enthusiasm raged even further and two weeks later an additional twenty thousand copies were printed. Before its official publication date had arrived, more than sixty thousand *Gone with the Wind*'s had been shipped to retailers which, together with the forty thousand Book-of-the-Month Club editions, brought a total of one hundred thousand copies into print. A dazed Margaret Mitchell accepted this news as having no more relation to reality than the two checks Macmillan had sent her in June for $5,000 apiece.

Even as reviews were finally breaking during the first week of July, public demand had multiplied. The twenty thousand copies which comprised a fifth printing, delivered for publication date had been instantly devoured a day later by an America suddenly infected with a strain of "Scarlett fever" totally unlike the one known to medical science. Stores were unable to satisfy demands or, indeed, to keep the novel in stock more than a day after shipments arrived. A July 13 Macmillan press release tried to soothe out-of-stock clients by promising, "a sixth printing, making a total of 140,000 copies to date, is being rushed through the press. It will be ready this week and orders now on hand can then be taken care of." A week later, after the lucky seventh run, the company announced "176,000 copies of Margaret Mitchell's *Gone with the Wind* have now been printed in an attempt to cope with the steady inrush of orders."

Still not enough! Bookstores reported their windows broken as copies of the novel were stolen, and since journalistic interest in this phenomenon had developed, the book became known in newspapers by its initials *GWTW*—a designation that spread as contagiously as talk of the story itself. The Macmillan Company of Canada, which had also published Miss Mitchell's work on June 30, noticed an outbreak of the fever in its own country, while the Book-of-the-Month Club found it necessary to order an additional twenty thousand copies for its subscribers.

By July 23, as they shipped their ninth printing to bookstores, Macmillan people informed the trade that "what is believed to be a record in recent years has been established. . . . Although it has been published only one month, printings total 201,000 copies." The following day they announced new book orders of over ten thousand more. "Scarlett fever" raged even further! The presummer appearance of lengthy *Gone with the Wind* had made it an ideal project for vacation reading and, throughout August, Macmillan engaged two separate printing plants and two binderies, working in three eight-hour shifts, to produce six more printings totaling another 130,000 copies. It was, by then, not only the best-selling book of the week or month but had already become the number-one sales leader of the year. With a fourteenth return to press in early September—and new totals of 370,000 copies in print—*Gone with the Wind* had made history as *the* fastest-selling book of all time. The fever had infected the nation and it seemed incredible that it was just the beginning!

Ironically, the initial copies of *Gone with the Wind* had arrived at Macmillan's New York office at almost the same time as the first Selznick International production premiered at that city's Radio City Music Hall. *The New York Times* commented, in reviewing *Little Lord Fauntleroy*, that David O. Selznick had carried with him from M-G-M "his ability to deal faithfully and tenderly with the classics of literature." That paper's critic thought the picture "a warm, sentimental and gently humorous film edition," called attention to "period settings which have been contrived so handsomely" and concluded that "it is a signally successful maiden venture from Mr. Selznick's new producing company."

And Katharine Brown, story editor at Selznick International's New York office, had been among the very first to catch "Scarlett fever" when, after reading the book, she sent an urgent wire to David O. Selznick in California on May 20, 1936: "WE HAVE JUST AIR-MAILED DETAILED SYNOPSIS OF GONE WITH THE WIND BY MARGARET MITCHELL, ALSO COPY OF BOOK. I BEG, URGE, COAX AND PLEAD WITH YOU TO READ THIS AT ONCE. I KNOW THAT AFTER YOU READ THE BOOK YOU WILL DROP EVERYTHING AND BUY IT."

Because he respected Miss Brown's judgment, David Selznick gave himself the weekend to consider the synopsis, but he declined her exhortation in a wire he sent the following Monday. While he courteously assured Kay that *Gone with the Wind* was "a fine story," he saw no reason to buy it since he did not have a major female star under contract. He did ask her, however, to carefully watch the book's sales trends in case it showed promise of becoming another *Anthony Adverse*—which was highly unlikely since Hervey Allen's best seller had just changed publishing history. Mr. Selznick offered to reconsider if the Mitchell novel should prove to be a runaway success but when he mentioned *So Red the Rose*, Kay realized there was little chance he would change his mind.

That night David felt his absolute refusal might have dampened Kay Brown's enthusiasm for bringing other stories to his attention so he wired her again the next day to suggest she mention *Gone with the Wind* to John Hay Whitney and Merian C. Cooper as a possible purchase for Pioneer Pictures, the Technicolor wing of Selznick International. As an afterthought, David hinted to Kay that were he still employed by M-G-M he would acquire it as a vehicle for such possible stars as Clark Gable and Joan Crawford.

The situation became a bit more complicated in the next two days when John Hay Whitney expressed real interest in the Mitchell book, at the same time Metro-Goldwyn-Mayer was beginning its own discussions concerning a purchase of it. After checking with insiders at M-G-M, David learned there was little genuine interest in the story among that studio's executives, but he knew that Irving Thalberg might very well gamble on the rights for a personal production there. After all, Irving's *Mutiny on the Bounty* had been adapted from another historical novel and it had won the Academy Award only two months before.

After examining early trends, Katharine Brown informed her employer of the amazing sales pace of Miss Mitchell's novel and David felt his chances of competing

financially with M-G-M or the other major studios growing remote. The film industry was acutely aware of how many recent best sellers had been converted into critically successful movies: *The Bridge of San Luis Rey, Bad Girl, Back Street, The Fountain, Little Man, What Now?, Magnificent Obsession, Private Worlds* and *Oil for the Lamps of China*. The "presold-audience" syndrome had also led Warner Brothers to invest $1,000,000 in the production of *Anthony Adverse*, which the studio was just then preparing to release. And *All Quiet on the Western Front, Cimarron, Grand Hotel* and *Mutiny on the Bounty* were film versions of foremost best sellers that had won four of the first eight "Best Picture" honors from the Hollywood Academy. And Irving Thalberg was at that very moment working on a much-delayed adaptation of *The Good Earth*, Pearl Buck's best seller and Pulitzer Prize winner.

Even though *So Red the Rose* was the current industry joke, David Selznick had not forgotten that D. W. Griffith's *The Birth of a Nation*, based on a 1905 Thomas Dixon best seller called *The Clansman*, was still the most profitable motion picture of all time, and its Civil War framework was somewhat comparable to that of *Gone with the Wind*. Although accurate financial returns had not been recorded in the years following *The Birth of a Nation*'s 1915 release, informed industry sources believed its showings had earned as much as $50,000,000!

If Irving Thalberg should remain his major competitor in purchasing the Margaret Mitchell novel for the screen, David had one thing in his favor. He knew that Irving was weakened and fatigued from filmmaking pressures and overwork with the completion, production or planning of nine major M-G-M films, all of which were draining his perfectionist strength. David wired Kay Brown with instructions that should Mr. Thalberg—and thus M-G-M—pass on *Gone with the Wind*, she must try to get a one-week option on the property, for which he authorized her to spend up to $1,000. In the meantime, Mr. Selznick and his studio forces devoted themselves to completing *The Garden of Allah*, and a *Gone with the Wind* film sale remained, for the time being, at an impasse.

In New York City, Macmillan had been undergoing its own *Gone with the Wind* problems. The novel had originally been promised in its catalog at a $2.50 retail price. After the company's book production experts had received the manuscript and estimated typesetting and printing costs, that price was no longer feasible. While a prepublication charge of $2.75 was set to lure advance interest, Macmillan decided that with its official release the book would have to cost its readers $3.00. While *Gone with the Wind*'s 1,037 pages of printed text were slightly under the 1,224 pages in *Anthony Adverse*, which had also carried a $3.00 price, book buyers received considerably more of a bargain than with the other prominent sales leaders that year. Macmillan's own *Sparkenbroke* cost $2.75 for only 551 pages, as did Scribner's *The Last Puritan* with 602 pages. The six other major 1936 sellers were priced at $2.50 for even less content: *It Can't Happen Here* (458 pages), *White Banners* (400 pages), *The Hurricane* (257 pages), *Drums Along the Mohawk* (592 pages), *The Thinking Reed* (431 pages) and *Eyeless in Gaza* (473 pages). And at a $2.75 charge from the Book-of-the-Month Club, *Gone with the Wind* was far from the most expensive book that organization offered its subscribers for July.

A quarter or fifty cents was still something to be considered in 1936, but *Anthony Adverse*'s huge success at $3.00 had provided Macmillan with enough optimism to feel the new book would recoup its expenditures. Not enough, though, to keep the company from asking Margaret Mitchell to surrender the escalating royalty clause in her contract and accept a straight 10 percent royalty on all copies sold. The publisher proposed this with the assurance that it would also be investing a considerable sum in advertising the novel at publication time. Miss Mitchell agreed and was surprised and delighted when, in the midst of the sales surge in late May, Macmillan reinstated the clause, assuring her royalties of 15 percent on all copies sold in the future. Margaret wrote to Harold Latham to thank him personally for what she felt sure was his hand in that dealing.

Most of the world had enjoyed peace for eighteen years but just as *Gone with the Wind* made its debut there appeared threatening new clouds of conflict. Germany's Chancellor Adolf Hitler had violated the World War I peace treaties in March by seizing the Rhineland, thereby challenging his European neighbors to war and leaving the world in a breathless state of dread. Shortly afterward bloody civil war erupted in Spain under the rebel leadership of General Francisco Franco while Fascist dictator Benito Mussolini's Italian combatants surged through Ethiopia. The curtain had ascended on the panorama of Scarlett O'Hara's wartime travails at a very apt time.

Margaret Mitchell's narrative of political confusion in the Reconstruction days found a mirror in the 1936 Presidential campaign as well. Just as publication of her book was dawning, Franklin D. Roosevelt was nominated for a second term and faced a bitter fight through Republican charges that he had violated American rights, the powers of Congress and the Supreme Court, threatened free enterprise and had contempt for the Constitution. Like Scarlett, Mr. Roosevelt emerged victorious after a bitter fight. A far more pleasant 1936 interlude surrounded a black man, Jesse Owens, who became an American hero with his personal championship at the summer Olympics in Berlin. However, the dominance of Germany at those games was an ominous warning of her militaristic ambitions. With their closing, no further Olympic meets would be held for the next twelve years.

For Margaret Mitchell there had been no interval of peace that spring. Even before official publication she had unknowingly begun the second phase of her literary career—letter writing. As clippings of early reviews from across the country came to her attention in May, Peggy's inbred Southern courtesy impelled her to send thankful acknowledgments to their originators. These lengthy letters, which often began, "I am Margaret Mitchell of Atlanta," were modest yet genteelly strict in correcting misimpressions. And while she freely admitted to lack of style, Margaret was quick to defend the accuracy of her book's historical facts. She had long dreaded possible Southern resentment toward the book's legend-destroying nature but early reviews from her native section were extraordinarily laudatory. Also to be answered, she felt, were the never-ending notes from strangers—some with copies of *Gone with the Wind* to be autographed. The new author tried to comply with such requests and strove to make her written replies interesting and cordial.

But by late June the sheer volume of incoming mail had bewildered her as much as the numerous invitations to attend—or worse, address—women's group meetings, literary societies and autographing parties. The press was already satisfying the curiosity of newspaper readers through continuous visits to the Marsh home. Peggy, as a former reporter, understood the journalists' motives but was alarmed to the point of overanxiety by their constant intrusion. Worst of all was the pressure to make speeches, a thought she abhorred.

As early as April Margaret's friend Susan Myrick of *The Macon Telegraph* had coerced her with the teasing blackmail of a bad press to address the Writers' Club of Macon. Although this initial experience at oratory delighted its audience, it drove crowd-shy Margaret into a state of frenzy. After another speech to the Atlanta Librarians, whose research aid she appreciated enormously, Margaret swore there would be no more. She couldn't courteously get out of two autographing sessions at Atlanta department stores but flatly refused to go to New York for more of them or related publicity appearances sponsored by The Macmillan Company. An almost mandatory reception given by the Atlanta Historical Association on June 27 couldn't be ignored but a flood of other invitations from every remote acquaintance in her own city—and elsewhere—had to be dealt with differently. With an undaunted spirit of fairness Margaret refused them all.

June 30, 1936—Publication Day! Matters immediately got worse. *GWTW* fever engulfed Atlanta and the Marshes had no private time, even to sleep. Countless uninvited callers freely arrived and an unending number of intruders telephoned around the clock. Some of these strangers had absolutely inane requests and questions. Others—in person or by mail—felt they deserved a share of Margaret's new "fortune." Those who sincerely appreciated the book didn't realize the additional strain they placed on its author with their perpetual question: "Did she get him back?" Even walking down an Atlanta street presented the hazard of attracting encounters with the curious, the well-wishing or the unbalanced. Outwardly Margaret seemed to be taking the phenomenon in her stride but inner turmoil and confusion were undermining her physical endurance.

After being coerced into a radio interview with Medora Perkerson on July 3, the very eve of her eleventh wedding anniversary, Margaret noticed the circuslike atmosphere heightening. Simultaneously, she was forced to deny rumors of fantastic cash inducements to sell movie rights since, as yet, she had not received *any* offer from Hollywood. Faced with all this furor, lacking the time to even read the major reviews (which were just appearing), much less to acknowledge them by letter, Peggy felt the need to flee. She drove in secret to the town of Gainesville, Georgia, where she calmed slightly from a state of anger and hysteria. Then, finally, she was able to study what the critics had written and to reply in turn.

The reviews seemed amazingly favorable even with the reservations which many of them included. The mixed or unfavorable notices did not engender any bad feelings since Margaret originally had little faith in the book herself. She did wonder, though, if those who complained about the lack of social significance had actually read the story *she* had written. From New York City, the center of publishing, came some comments which amazed her. The *Herald-Tribune* book supplement proclaimed in a first-page review that "the story, told with such sincerity and passion illuminated by such understanding, woven of the stuff of history and of disciplined imagination, is endlessly interesting." Amusingly, it referred to the author throughout as "Mrs. Mitchell."

The New York Times Book Review, which similarly honored *Gone with the Wind* on its first page for July 5, found the book more noteworthy as a first work than as a great one. J. Donald Adams thought, "This is beyond doubt one of the most remarkable first novels produced by an American writer. It is also one of the best." And, he observed, "although this is not a great novel, not one with any profound reading of life, it is nevertheless a book of uncommon quality, a superb piece of storytelling which nobody who finds pleasure in the art of fiction can afford to neglect." After stating that it was "the best Civil War novel that has yet been written," Mr. Adams provided a quote which Macmillan would soon place

Only a short time after seeing sample copies of her novel, Margaret Mitchell received her first royalty checks and heard news of interest from Hollywood.

atop every new front cover of the book's dust jacket: "In sheer readability, it is surpassed by nothing in American fiction."

Other sections of the country were more unreservedly enthusiastic. *The Chicago Daily News* termed *GWTW* "one of the great novels of our time" and *The Boston Herald* said "it will be hailed as The Great American Novel and it will deserve all the praise that it receives." Various magazines offered their opinions, with *The New Yorker* describing Margaret as "a staggeringly gifted storyteller" and calling her book "more than a novel, perhaps a whole library in itself." *Newsweek* observed, "this book contains a literary experience rare as a roc's egg: the full realization of characters," and *The Publishers' Weekly* predicted "*Gone with the Wind* is very possibly the greatest American novel."

Margaret's acknowledgments at this time (postmarked from Gainesville), initiated a trend toward apology for delay which, as her future time grew scarcer, would become a trademark in her letters. They were also filled with the loose exaggerations all good storytellers allow themselves. For this reason she dreaded that this correspondence would ever see print, but for the moment she randomly selected dates for having started or finished her manuscript, described recent weight losses varying from ten to seventeen pounds and lengthened her tenure on the *Atlanta Journal* to five, sometimes six years. Such carefree digressions from fact in conversation or letters would soon haunt Margaret to a point where she hesitated being open or animated with any outsider.

One statement she had made in careless jest concerned her youthful knowledge of the Civil War: "I heard everything in the world except that the Confederates lost the war. When I was ten years old, it was a violent shock to learn that General Lee had been licked." This quote would return to torment her again and again and, despite later denials and protests that she had always known the war's outcome, even her publisher forever used that phrase in biographical sketches. Years later, in an attempt to clarify another misunderstanding, John Marsh wrote to Macmillan, "She had the gift of exaggeration, like Gerald, and used it at times to make her statements more vivid. After her novel had made its big success, she lost the privilege of speaking lightly in her letters."

As Margaret secluded herself in that Gainesville hotel room, delighting in some of the more glowing clippings which favorably compared *Gone with the Wind* with *Vanity Fair* and even *War and Peace*, her attention was drawn to the fine review by Herschel Brickell in *The New York Evening Post*. Mr. Brickell, although a Connecticut resident, was originally from Mississippi and Lois Cole had already relayed a message to Margaret that he planned to travel South soon and wanted to meet the author of *GWTW*. In telling Mr. Brickell how delighted she would be to meet him, Peggy also frankly expressed her recent plight to this kindred soul. "I'm sure Scarlett O'Hara never struggled harder to get out of Atlanta," she wrote, ". . . than I have suffered during the siege that has been on since publication day. If I had known being an author was like this, I'd have thought several times before I let Harold Latham go off with my dog-eared manuscript."

While still in Gainesville Margaret also corresponded with George Brett of Macmillan to thank him for her royalties and for the faith the company had expressed with its massive advertising. Macmillan had indeed shown great confidence even before *Gone with the Wind*'s advance sales proved larger than those of any novel the company had published in the previous five years. The publisher had appropriated $10,000 for a countrywide campaign and taken full-page ads in *The Publishers' Weekly* on April 18, May 23 and June 13. Then, at publication time, its ads saturated the book-reviewing pages of New York newspapers as well as those of national magazines. Daily advertising was placed in all important Eastern cities and in the major West Coast ones as well. Very special attention was given to the South, where ads were run in virtually all cities and towns regardless of size.

One week after publication, on July 7 (the same day Margaret Mitchell had fled to Gainesville), David Selznick sent a wire to Kay Brown in New York instructing her to close negotiations for *Gone with the Wind* film rights, proposing a maximum of $50,000 for an outright sale or a guarantee of $5,500 for a sixty- to ninety-day option. In the month that had passed, neither M-G-M nor any other film studio had made a concrete offer, but, with the reviews, David realized sharp competitive bidding would soon ensue.

The following day Macmillan sent news of this movie sale to the Mitchell home in Atlanta and that bulletin was waiting for Margaret when she returned from Gainesville on July 9. This was all she needed on top of that hurricane of humanity that still engulfed her hometown existence. Peggy realized the sale would mean a trip to New York City at the end of the month for contract signing, a journey she did not relish in her present state of exhaustion.

Also awaiting her was an invitation to a writers' seminar about to begin in Blowing Rock, North Carolina, at which Herschel Brickell and various authors would be present. Although she had declined all other such offers, she decided to accept this one. More personally rewarding than anything the critics had written were the favorable comments Margaret had received by mail or had read in print from fellow authors, many of them Southerners, and the thought of being in the company of such people seemed therapeutically calming.

It had already cheered Peggy when Stephen Vincent

Benét, creator of *John Brown's Body*, and Thomas Dixon, whose *The Clansman* had inspired *The Birth of a Nation*, had sent her personal letters, as did Stark Young and Hervey Allen. Best of all were the comments from other Southern women authors. Pulitzer Prize–winning Julia Peterkin had written of *Gone with the Wind* in a *Washington Post* review: "I believe it is unsurpassed in the whole of American writing." And Ellen Glasgow offered that "It is a fearless portrayal, romantic yet not sentimental, of a lost tradition and a way of life." Although she could not yet comprehend it, Margaret Mitchell had joined a select group of prominent and best-selling authors in an age that included, in addition to those just mentioned, Edna Ferber, Sinclair Lewis, Booth Tarkington, Erich Maria Remarque, Thornton Wilder, Pearl S. Buck, James Hilton, Lloyd C. Douglas, Louis Bromfield and A. J. Cronin.

Her car trip to that Blowing Rock mountain resort provided Peggy Marsh with another short period of relief from the mania her book was presently inspiring. Even more important, it introduced her to Herschel Brickell, who would become a close and valued friend.

Shortly after returning from the North Carolina mountains Margaret journeyed to New York City with her lawyer-brother Stephens. On the following day, July 30, she signed a contract with Selznick International Pictures for $50,000. But she would not agree to it until the Selznick lawyers had rewritten the document to absolve her from any liability for damage suits and, more significantly, to exclude her from any future connection whatsoever with the film's production. Margaret had to explain this stand repeatedly to those who misunderstood her motives. More aware than anyone that the book's great length would present its screen adapters with severe problems, she was not about to officially sanction any cuts or changes which might infuriate its supporters—especially in the South. An even wiser reasoning was her fear that such changes might distort historical fact and irritate Southerners much further.

There had also been a temporary misunderstanding as to exactly who was representing Margaret's interest in that film sale. The Selznick people assumed that Annie Laurie Williams was Margaret Mitchell's agent. Margaret contended that Miss Williams had been retained by Macmillan only to *help* in these dealings and that her publisher was actually responsible. Miss Mitchell was indeed correct in her assumption, for the 10 percent agent's commission was split equally between Macmillan and Annie Laurie Williams, with the balance—$45,000 —going directly to the author.

Despite future stories to the contrary, the quick film sale was not a matter of other studios having turned the book down, but merely of which one got to Miss Williams and Macmillan first with the best offer. Less than a month had passed between the appearance of

On July 3, 1936, Miss Mitchell was coerced into a rare radio broadcast from Atlanta.

reviews and the finalization of the film sale, quite a feat even by Hollywood's "overnight" standards. It was generally agreed, at the time, that the sale involved the largest amount of money ever paid to an unknown author for a first novel. Nevertheless, for years afterward Margaret Mitchell was forced to deny that she had been taken advantage of by a premature movie sale of her book. Even before the contract signing, rumors had spread that the lady had innocently surrendered it to Selznick, while in galley proofs, for a ridiculously low sum. Actually, because of the tight production schedule, galleys had not been circulated to film companies and the book itself was used to arouse interest when printed copies were available in May. As Margaret would later say: "I finished reading galley proofs on *Gone with the Wind* in March 1936. It is highly doubtful that anyone in Hollywood read it in galley proof. If they did, no offer was made to me at that time. The book was published at the end of June 1936 and I had not disposed of the movie rights and would not dispose of them at that time. . . . As the prepublication sale was something between 50,000 and 90,000 copies, I knew my work would be fairly successful. *Gone with the Wind* had sold several hundred thousand copies by the time I disposed of the moving picture rights."

One of the most strangely persistent "movie-sale" fables, later printed in many sources, involved Bette Davis and her employer, Jack L. Warner. This myth, which would survive for many years, concerned Miss Davis's pioneering effort for actors' rights by a trip overseas to accept outside assignments, thereby escaping the banal scripts which Warner Brothers was contractually forcing upon her. Immediately before her departure, the story went, Mr. Warner supposedly tried to placate her with news that he was buying a new story, *Gone with the Wind*, with her in mind. Knowing nothing of such a book, Miss Davis scoffed at the idea and departed for England. Although such a conference may well have taken place in May of 1936, by August of that year, when Bette's trip actually took place, the entire film industry, and much of the country, was well aware of the Mitchell novel and that film rights had already been sold to Selznick International.

The contract signing in New York had provided Margaret Mitchell with an opportunity to meet Katharine Brown of the Selznick Company, a lady she would correspond with heavily over the next few years. She was also able to visit Herschel Brickell and his wife Norma, and to sanction his story about her that was to appear in *The New York Evening Post* on August 7. Margaret would later refer to that article as the kindest and most accurate one written about her. "What makes a book so popular," Mr. Brickell questioned in that story, "that everybody wishes to read it and, having read it, to tell everybody else about it in a desire to share the excitement? . . . why a historical novel of the Civil War should in this year of a national election and a threatened European conflict occupy the leisure of thousands of Americans in every part of the country. . . . I asked her [Margaret Mitchell] if she had any explanation of her own of the novel's widespread appeal, and she said she supposed it was because the book dealt in primitive emotions which moved in straight lines. . . . She is small, has red hair . . . is as amusing as she is good-looking, a first rate story-teller and mimic, speaks with a perfect Georgia accent." Mr. Brickell concluded by predicting: "I can see no competition to *Gone with the Wind* for this year's Pulitzer Prize in fiction."

Unhappily, Margaret's New York visit was cut short even before she was able to thank the people at Macmillan for their hand in her success. The dizzying frustrations of the past two months suddenly manifested themselves in the form of acute eyestrain, which forced the author home to a darkened bedroom where she lay immobile for several weeks. For even more weeks she was unable to use her eyes for anything really strenuous any longer than a few minutes each day.

Meanwhile, The Macmillan Company was encountering another unique *Gone with the Wind* phenomenon that summer. Book collectors—those primarily interested in "first editions"—were at odds as to how to identify such copies of Margaret Mitchell's novel. Those who had purchased it at publication time found the "Published in June" designation but saw there had been three printings in that month alone. Others who had earlier copies marked "Published in May" supposed theirs was the real first edition but wanted assurance. Many collectors wrote to the publisher in hopes of obtaining a valued first copy directly—something that had been impossible almost from the beginning. Another sought fact was the volume of the initial print run, since value would be determined by the number of copies which had been circulated. This last tidbit was considered privileged information by the publisher since rival authors might well complain that their books had been slighted.

In reply to such inquiries Macmillan prepared a form letter that read in part, "We originally intended to have this book published in May but the Book-of-the-Month Club read it and were anxious to issue it for their subscribers so in order to accommodate them we postponed the publication until June 30th. Their editions as well as our subsequent printings carried the lines 'Published in June' on the copyright page. The book bearing 'Published in May' on the copyright page is actually the first edition. We are sorry that we are completely out of stock of the first edition. . . . We make it a rule not to give definite information in regard to the number of copies printed in the first editions; so we are sorry that we cannot give you this information."

The publisher could hardly complain over such minor clerical burdens when the success of *Gone with the Wind* had brought floods of customers into still-depressed bookstores. These people often purchased other titles as well, and all publishers benefited from the surge, as did retailers, printers and paper suppliers. Macmillan's publicity staff was kept continually busy dispatching these breathless little items to the press:

"A single order from Macy's totalled 50,000 copies . . . entire freight cars were filled with paper outside the printer for use on *Gone with the Wind* orders. . . . Forty-five tons of boards and 34,000 yards of cloth have already been used as well as enough paper to fill twenty-four carloads . . . one day's order from Chicago book-dealers would fill a solid freight car, and was estimated to have a value of $12,000. . . . *Gone with the Wind* has been reported, as of September 11, 1936, the best-selling novel in every one of the seventy leading bookshops from coast to coast for six consecutive weeks."

At that time *Gone with the Wind*'s dust jackets began to carry its amazing sales totals on their bottommost portion, just as they carried *The New York Times* quote on the very top. After four September press runs the book's new covers announced that, with seventeen printings, 450,000 copies were in circulation. This figure included books distributed by The Macmillan Company of Canada, Limited, whose copies had been shipped simultaneously with New York orders from the Ferris Printing Company in America. That was the normal arrangement between the two affiliated companies, and Macmillan in New York kept track of all Canadian sales and royalties. Those jacket totals did not, however, include the Book-of-the-Month editions, and the Club was still placing constant reorders of its own.

The bond between Macmillan of New York and Macmillan & Co., Ltd. in London was then still close, and on September 29, 1936, *Gone with the Wind* was officially published in Great Britain utilizing the same format, pagination and dust jacket as the United States edition. From that company's St. Martin's Street offices orders would be shipped to Australia, India, South Africa and other countries of the British Commonwealth. Word had already traveled across the Atlantic, it seemed, for *Gone with the Wind* was sold out in England even before its official release date. The novel was returned to press in London in September and was quickly reprinted again in October and November. It was at that point, quite early in the book's English history, that Vivien Leigh first read it and became acquainted with the character of Scarlett O'Hara. More than two decades afterward she would recall for interviewers Lewis Funke and John E. Booth, "From the moment I read the book, I said 'I've got to play that' and I was laughed to scorn on it."

Six more American press runs in October and new totals to be reckoned with: twenty-three printings, 625,000 copies in the United States and Canada plus 75,000 taken for Book-of-the-Month Club subscribers. By mid-November publishing insiders were calling *Gone with the Wind* the fastest-selling book since 1900 (qualified with the reminder that some others had drawn larger sales, but only over a longer period of time). With 750,000 copies shipped, it seemed no other novel could compete with it for the Christmas trade.

The publication of her book in Braille in November cheered Margaret Mitchell. By then she had completely recovered from—but not forgotten—her perilous bout with eyestrain. Margaret was truly touched when Atlanta's Library for the Blind notified her that month that *Gone with the Wind* in Braille had arrived.

Three print orders from the Ferris Company in November and two more in early December showed Macmillan's good will to booksellers in allowing them ample *GWTW* stock for Christmas shoppers. With the last 1936 shipments on their way, Macmillan bookkeepers recorded that there had been twenty-eight printings of 975,000 books within six months after official publication and less than eight months since it had first appeared in stores. Meanwhile, serialization of *Gone with the Wind* was already under way in a Danish periodical, appearing sectionally there throughout the month of December.

On December 15, 1936, the millionth copy of the novel was printed and Macmillan publicly promised that—as soon as it was bound—the milestone book would be sent to Margaret Mitchell, who maintained that she didn't own a single edition, having given all her personal copies away to friends. Considering the mechanics of binding, shipping and stocking in stores—and the fact that Macmillan itself did not advertise the millionth sale until the thirty-first printing in January 1937—it would be inaccurate to claim that *Gone with the Wind* sold one million copies in 1936. Nevertheless, in the future most sources would.

After securing film rights to the year's best-selling book and with *The Garden of Allah* virtually completed, David O. Selznick indulged in a much-needed Hawaiian vacation, during which he finally read that book—infecting himself with an incurable case of "Scarlett fever." When he returned to Hollywood he thought to secure George Cukor as a probable *Gone with the Wind* director, inspired by their mutual success with *David Copperfield*. He found Mr. Cukor agreeable to the proposal but explained to him that there was at present absolutely no starting date planned. The facilities of Selznick International were still extremely limited, with no contract stars, little staff and, as yet, not even a trademark. Each film David made was carefully thought out in advance to keep it from being lost in the tidal wave of Hollywood product flooding the country each year.

The initial Selznick International productions had comprised only two of the sixteen films released by the United Artists organization in 1936. It was competing for attention even within that distribution company with films made by Samuel Goldwyn, Charles Chaplin, Mary Pickford and Alexander Korda. More significantly, there were forty-five feature presentations that year from Metro-Goldwyn-Mayer, fifty-six from Warner Brothers, sixty-eight from Paramount, thirty-nine from RKO, fifty-one from Columbia, fifty-seven from the new Twentieth Century-Fox Corporation and almost two hundred more from minor companies and foreign producers.

That extensive flow was, nevertheless, quickly devoured by the country's eighteen thousand movie houses, which were vying for business from eighty-eight million American ticket buyers each week. There had been even a greater upsurge in production recently since a new phenomenon, "double features," had found rapid acceptance in 85 percent of the nation's theatres, and the public then *expected* to see two pictures for each quarter admission they paid. As a result, producers faced problems of running time even with their major presentations. David's *Little Lord Fauntleroy* had run ninety-eight minutes and *The Garden of Allah* was eighty-five minutes long, in line with most "A"-type features of the day. He knew adapting *Gone with the Wind* to that brief a span was out of the question but he also realized that Warner's *Anthony Adverse*, at two hours and sixteen minutes, had covered little more than half of the story of the original novel. David noted that many reviews of that picture had discussed its length, and he paid careful attention to the printed reports that Warners were considering filming the remaining portion of the book as a sequel. But he was also wary, since some critical notices of *Anthony Adverse* had contained comments like "Because of the necessity for telling so much story in so little time, it sometimes seems a bit disjointed and episodic." To avoid such dangers, David Selznick knew that a careful adaptation of Margaret Mitchell's novel could take a year and would need the creativity of an expert. He foresaw no *Gone with the Wind* cameras rolling in 1937, or possibly even the following year.

Budget planning was another serious consideration before filming preparations could begin. M-G-M had been able to appropriate between $1,000,000 and $2,000,000 for *Mutiny on the Bounty, Romeo and Juliet, The Great Ziegfeld,* his own *A Tale of Two Cities,* or any Greta Garbo picture, while they spent $350,000 just on the earthquake sequence of *San Francisco.* David's facilities could not compare with those at his father-in-law's studio and he realized that for every "blockbuster" M-G-M produced, they made at least five moderately budgeted films to guarantee stockholders a healthy annual profit. Still, both David Selznick and John Hay Whitney believed in "spending to get," feeling such gambles on their few pictures were wiser investments if they wanted anything more than a "break-even" achievement at year's end. Unfortunately Selznick International noted signs of financial disappointment that autumn, following mixed reviews of *The Garden of Allah*—despite the novelty of Technicolor. Another such failure could put the new movie concern into bankruptcy.

While use of Technicolor had proved successful for Paramount with *The Trail of the Lonesome Pine* and for Fox on *Ramona,* the last Pioneer film, *Dancing Pirate,* had proved an outright money loser and Hollywood, in general, was approaching the color process with great hesitation. Nevertheless, David foresaw *Gone with the Wind* being filmed in Technicolor if public interest in that innovation had not faded altogether by the time he started. Meanwhile, he proceeded to utilize Technicolor in his third Selznick International/Pioneer film, *A Star Is Born.*

David Selznick was hardly unaware of another problem which *Gone with the Wind* presented—that of censorship! Strangely enough, there was a double standard of morality in 1936 America as to what was acceptable on the screen and what was commonplace in books or on the stage. All of Hollywood was aware of the power exerted by the Catholic Legion of Decency and of the 3,500-word "Encyclical" which had been issued by Pope Pius XI the very week *Gone with the Wind* had been published. In that statement, the longest ever issued by a Pontiff primarily to Americans, the Church leader had said, "everyone knows what damage is done to the soul by bad motion pictures." Rapid promises had been made in response by Will Hays, enforcer of Hollywood's Production Code, that even stricter allegiance would be paid to set standards of morality—and David Selznick had just enlisted his new studio in the obedient ranks of that Hays office! The producer realized the great danger in violating the code's tenets if he showed Scarlett offering herself to Rhett for tax money to save Tara or pictured the prostitute Belle Watling in any way whatsoever. So much to be considered! David began wondering if he had not made a mistake and if Margaret Mitchell had not been right after all when she said her book was not filmable. Delay seemed the only hope of circumventing those numerous impediments.

Meanwhile he proceeded with *A Star Is Born,* a project he had personally conceived, which contrasted the rise and fall of careers in the "make believe" world of Hollywood. In developing that idea, David found he was called upon to lay it out himself, although he gave story credit to William Wellman and Robert Carson. Even after employing Mr. Carson, Alan Campbell and the noted Dorothy Parker to develop the screenplay, David found he was rewriting (or refilming) various episodes and was soon proud of his previously unutilized abilities as a screen writer.

Unintentionally, *A Star Is Born* also began a period of filmed "auditions" for *Gone with the Wind.* David had considered, as others had, that Fredric March might portray Rhett Butler, and Janet Gaynor's screen image was ideally suited for Melanie Hamilton. Using both these players gave David Selznick the opportunity to judge a working relationship, while simultaneously observing how they photographed in Technicolor. He decided then, wherever it was feasible, to use *Gone with the Wind* candidates in his next few films.

In truth, casting wheels had been turning in David's head ever since he first read *Gone with the Wind,* and he couldn't very well ignore the "helpful" predictions offered by journalists in need of feature material. The popular Clark Gable seemed an early favorite all around for the Rhett Butler role, with speculative competition offered, especially by Southerners, by Ronald Colman and Basil Rathbone. That variance, it seemed, depended on whether readers interpreted Rhett in the romantic personification of Mr. Colman or in the villainous style of Mr. Rathbone. David Selznick had himself thought of Gary Cooper, since that actor's contractual obligations to Samuel Goldwyn fell in line with a common distribution company, United Artists.

For the role of Scarlett O'Hara, almost every lady who had walked before a camera seemed to have a following. David was quite in tune with the acclaim surrounding Bette Davis, who had just won the Academy Award, and Katharine Hepburn, who had been announced as her runner-up. There was also no ignoring their fellow nominee, Miriam Hopkins, who was originally from Georgia and who had strong Southern support. Interestingly, the Hopkins belle was just then successfully portraying an *English* girl in Alexander Korda's *Men Are Not Gods*. More surprisingly, the unique stage actress Tallulah Bankhead had many supporters—even, momentarily, David himself—who remembered her Alabama origins. But Tallulah's recent screen roles had far from mesmerized America's ticket buyers.

Still, David realized that the dominance of a well-known screen actress could easily turn *Gone with the Wind* into a personal vehicle rather than the "David O. Selznick Production" he was already foreseeing, and he was particularly anxious to leave his artistic mark in Hollywood. None of his films at other studios had as yet won him an Academy Award, nor did the first two releases of Selznick International seem likely to receive major Award consideration in 1936. Should the screen version of *Gone with the Wind* live up to the potential provided by the book, David wanted assurance that credit would go to him and that it would not be remembered as a Bette Davis, Miriam Hopkins or Katharine Hepburn picture.

He faced no such threat from the employment of even the most famous male stars. After all, he remembered, no one had called *Mutiny on the Bounty* a Clark Gable film. But, on the other hand, if he used a comparative "unknown" as Scarlett O'Hara, he would be presented with a particularly vexing problem. The prospect of nurturing an obscure actress through what could be the screen's most demanding role appealed to him, for she would be a future asset for his studio; but that actress would have to be exceptionally talented, almost certainly quite experienced, and capable of carrying the foremost demands of the entire screenplay. Could such a woman be found in time? There was here another good reason for delay. But, more importantly, the longer actual production could be postponed, the more feasible it was that the public would forget some sub-plots and characters in the lengthy story and thus accept a version shortened for theatrical practicality.

Mr. Selznick knew from past experience that a bogus "Hollywood search" could create marvelous publicity. He even sanctioned his publicity staff's suggestion of pretending to scour the South in hopes of finding Scarlett O'Hara or other characters. David delighted in the good will such an expedition might generate even though he knew from the outset that such a trip would not unearth a Scarlett and probably no one at all. Although some journalists would hint at specious motives, only Margaret Mitchell herself seemed to realize that the entire venture was a complete hoax. But meanwhile, David dutifully went through the motions of considering famous players as he screen-tested Tallulah Bankhead in December. The results of the effort of that indomitable actress, who had

Rare first editions of Gone with the Wind *would later vary in value according to the conditions of their dust jackets and whether they were autographed—or personally autographed—by the author.*

made her debut in silent films eighteen years before, to portray sixteen-year-old Scarlett spoke for themselves. Afterward, David very courteously informed Miss Bankhead that she was out of the question.

But beforehand, in attending to first things first, David had sent word in September to Margaret Mitchell inviting her to Hollywood for conferences on the *Gone with the Wind* screenplay. While Miss Mitchell declined the invitation, she did return the encouraging message, "please don't forget that I'd be glad to do all in my power to assist" if David should send a research staff to Atlanta. Later that month, Mr. Selznick asked Katharine Brown to approach playwright Sidney Howard to consider a script assignment at Selznick International—hopefully *Gone with the Wind*. David advised Kay to use the helpful influence of Merian C. Cooper, a friend of Mr. Howard's, and assured her that George Cukor thought Sidney a good choice for that challenging project. Mr. Howard's adaptation of Sinclair Lewis' *Dodsworth*, for the stage in 1934 and for Samuel Goldwyn's 1936 film version, had been critically successful, making him a prime candidate for difficult assignments.

Sidney Howard showed enthusiasm for the idea of adapting *Gone with the Wind* and David sent him careful instructions which advised him not to include Civil War battle sequences, since they had not occurred, in the first person, in Miss Mitchell's novel. Meanwhile, Margaret Mitchell, through her new friend Kay Brown, suggested that while Selznick International was on their Southern tour, they would benefit by contacting Wilbur Kurtz, the historian who had been so helpful to her the previous year. Peggy then wrote to Wilbur that she had "planted a seed" with the movie company that he was the *only* Civil War authority in their area. When the film people arrived, she would tell them she felt it essential for them to bring Mr. Kurtz to California to offer historical advice.

However, poor Margaret was still unable to relieve the added pressures that film version had wrought on her own life. A new deluge of letters offered suggestions for or oppositions to various Hollywood players, as she simultaneously tried to decline offers to write magazine articles without offending the requesters. But while she steadfastly refused to divulge her age and busily denied rumors of physical impairment, Americans continued to wonder exactly who the woman was who had written that big book. To better understand that lady, in a collage of her own words from the time:

"I am Margaret Mitchell of Atlanta . . . alas, I am the most normal of creatures. Sometimes when I reflect upon this, I realize I can never become truly great, not being abnormal and having no temperament . . . I do not like to write . . . I write slowly, rewrite twenty or thirty times, throw away what I've rewritten and start over again . . . I haven't any literary style and I know it but have never been able to do anything about it . . . I like best to listen to people talk about something that they know about . . . I wrote the book nearly ten years ago . . . it seemed, to be quite frank, pretty lousy . . . writing was a dreary dull job. You sweated and groaned and itched and broke out in rashes and then felt like you smelled bad . . . I wouldn't go through this again for anything . . . I thought I'd been several kinds of an ass to get myself into so vulnerable a position and if it hadn't been that I feared The Macmillan Company would have me certified as a lunatic, I'd have tried to get the manuscript back . . .

"Heaven knows I didn't foresee the Depression and try to write a novel paralleling it in another day . . . I wanted to picture in Melanie as in Ellen the true ladies of the Old South, gentle and dear, frail of body perhaps but never of courage . . . there was precious little obscenity in it, no adultery and not a single degenerate and I couldn't imagine a publisher being silly enough to buy it . . . I had gotten so tired of finding 'son of a bitch' on the first page of every novel I opened . . . had I pictured some of the more dreadful things I uncovered in my research, my book could never have been published . . . However lousy the book may be as far as style, subject, plot, characters, it's as accurate historically as I can get it . . . I am sending you the autograph with the greatest pleasure . . . I took the liberty of autographing a copy for you . . . just as we were going to press titleless, I picked *Gone with the Wind* . . . Oh, heavenly day! *A Day at the Races* is being advertised. When it comes we will abandon all work and visitors and spend the week at the movies. I can hardly wait . . .

"God knows, I didn't expect the book to sell like this . . . my husband and I had established a pattern of living that pleased us very much. It was a very quiet pattern, perhaps, but we liked it and we are determined to keep it . . . this period of my life has been my unhappiest one. And I resent this as I think it should be happy and exciting . . . God, what a life. There is really nowhere I can go . . . I thought I had learned most of the peculiarities of mankind while I was a reporter but this is an education. After all, when I was a reporter I only saw criminals, prize fighters, politicians, debutantes and fatigued celebrities. It was seldom that I met the sturdy middle classes. If I could just gain about fifteen pounds I could stand meeting them a bit better . . . well, life goes merrily on. The mail mounts and mounts. Special deliveries wake us at dawn demanding to know if Scarlett ever got him back . . . I do not have a notion of what happened to them and I left them to their ultimate fate . . . I know they are different from the usual Civil War characters. They aren't lavender-and-lace-moonlight-on-the-magnolias people.

"I haven't sold the movies rights for three to ten million dollars as rumor has it . . . I suppose you know that casting this picture is the favorite drawing room game these days . . . Can it be possible that I am the only woman in the world who doesn't want to be in the movies? . . . Several ladies wired me that their little daughters tap dance beautifully and do the 'splits' most elegantly and can't I get them into *Gone with the Wind*? (No, they haven't read the book, they admit) . . ."

And to that most-asked question of whether she would write another book, Margaret gave one of her most inspired replies: "Do I look like that kind of a fool?" Almost without fail Peggy Marsh kept her sense of humor, but underneath the sometimes hilarious recountals of her new topsy-turvy life was a poignant plea begging for relief from those endless intrusions. "The phone is going every minute," she told Herschel Brickell, ". . . and the door belching strangers who want autographs and want to see what I look like and want me to make speeches and go to parties and tell what I like for breakfast and if I wear lace on my panties and why I haven't any children . . . people boldly asking me my age, my royalties, can I get their cook in the movies in 'my' film, am I a Catholic? . . . It's only eleven A.M. and I've been going since dawn and feel as though it were midnight."

Public sympathies in America had never been closer to the British monarchy than when Edward VIII, King for less than a year, renounced his throne in December to marry an American divorcée, Wallis Simpson. David Selznick felt this touching event had given modern meaning to the age-old conflict of love between royalty and commoner. As a result, he set in motion a third film version of *The Prisoner of Zenda*. In the major male roles, David planned to "audition" leading *Gone with the Wind* candidate Ronald Colman, along with one of his own personal choices for either the Rhett or Ashley role, Douglas Fairbanks, Jr.

Additionally, while he knew that John Hay Whitney wanted a comedy produced, his own plans for a Technicolor production of *The Adventures of Tom Sawyer* were well under way. Still, as long as he was in control, Selznick International would produce only one picture at a time—enabling him to supervise every detail. David had no intention of following the tragic example of Irving Thalberg, who had succumbed to pneumonia that September after weakening himself from the strain of an all-too-consuming career. Mr. Thalberg's widow, Norma Shearer, immediately announced plans to retire, disappointing those who hoped she might play Scarlett O'Hara.

On a happier 1936 movie note, David Selznick carefully followed the progress of Olivia de Havilland, whom he considered a prime possibility for Melanie Hamilton. After only one year in films the twenty-year-old actress had played the lead in *Anthony Adverse* and was being teamed with Errol Flynn in a series of adventure films. Young Mr. Flynn was another actor whose name was being mentioned often by Hollywoodites as a Rhett Butler nominee. Both those players were, incidentally, contracted to Warner Brothers, home studio of the popular Bette Davis. And Miss Davis had won even more fans by appearing with Leslie Howard in *The Petrified Forest*.

Then Charles Chaplin set back the cinema clock several years by releasing a virtually silent film, *Modern Times*, in which former bit player Paulette Goddard made a nice impression as his leading lady. The first "full-sound" version of the Edna Ferber–Jerome Kern–Oscar Hammerstein II musical *Showboat* was a large critical success, boosting Irene Dunne's stock as a candidate for Scarlett or Melanie, while that film also provided Hattie McDaniel with excellent exposure—allowing her to sing with the noted Paul Robeson. And David's former RKO co-worker, Max Steiner, had justified the Selznick "innovations" in film scoring by winning an Academy Award for his music in *The Informer*. For Clark Gable, 1936 provided a romance with the brilliant comedienne Carole Lombard and a dynamic role in *San Francisco* with Jeanette MacDonald and Spencer Tracy.

David Selznick had been sincerely heartened to receive an autographed copy of *Gone with the Wind* and a personal message from its author. "I would like to take this opportunity," Margaret Mitchell had written, "to tell you how very happy I am that my book has fallen into your hands. I have seen the care and the patience which you have lavished on your other productions and so I know that my book will enjoy the same happy fate." David was grateful that Miss Mitchell expressed faith in both his own and Sidney Howard's abilities. He had no intention of allowing her novel to be distorted in the manner another very famous and beloved book had recently been.

Fredric March and Olivia de Havilland played the leads in Warner's Anthony Adverse *and both entered the* Gone with the Wind *casting competition.*

America's champion in best-selling fiction until that time had been *In His Steps* (subtitled: *What Would Jesus Do?*), the story of a minister who followed the example of Christ. The book had been written by Charles Monroe Sheldon, a Kansas pastor, and published in 1896. Although not a sensation at the moment of its emergence, the inspirational novel, which was released in paper covers by Advance Publishing Company, had gathered momentum through the years and eventually had sold more than six million copies. An additional two million hardcover copies distributed by Grosset and Dunlap had, in turn, made *In His Steps* not only the largest seller in fiction since such records were first kept in 1895, but the all-time best-selling American book of any kind next to the Bible. By 1936, it had been translated into twenty-three languages and become the basis of a film version released that October.

Unfortunately, as the first endeavor of the short-lived Grand National studio, the film was necessarily a low-budget production which retained the title of the book and emphasized its theme in terms of a modern corollary, concerning two wealthy young people who violated their parents' wishes by eloping and dedicating themselves to a life of farming. The act of filming this all-time best seller by thoroughly revising its story could not have been very encouraging to Margaret Mitchell, nor was the rumor that Hollywood originally considered changing the inspirational story's title to *Sins of the Children*!

For Margaret Mitchell, there was good and bad news that fall. On the brighter side was a booklet published by Macmillan "in response to a flood of requests from readers all over the country for information about the author and her book." It was hoped that this brochure, *Margaret Mitchell and Her Novel*, would relieve Peggy from some of her correspondence burden, as it detailed Harold Latham's account of finding the manuscript, reprinted Herschel Brickell's interview (Margaret's favorite) and included quotes from some of the best reviews. Margaret had even written a brief biographical sketch for inclusion which said, in part, "I am very small. . . . Like most small people I feel myself as big as anyone else and twice as strong. But I am only four feet, eleven inches tall. . . . If the novel has a theme, the theme is that of survival. What makes some people able to come through catastrophes and others, apparently just as able, strong and brave, go under? We've seen it in the present Depression. It happens in every upheaval. Some people survive; others don't." The souvenir booklet also told readers about an upcoming Selznick movie version and that "The picture will be released through United Artists." Then in a concluding section, Macmillan gave answers to the most asked *Gone with the Wind* questions. The most frequently requested one was: "Did Scarlett get Rhett back?" The response was: "Miss Mitchell says she simply doesn't know. To her, the book ended where it ended and she hasn't an idea of what happened after the last chapter."

The bad news came on October 22 when columnist Louella Parsons, journalistic champion of nonsense, distortion and filmland mythology, reported a "hot" news item concerning the *Gone with the Wind* casting: "No one has yet been chosen and will not be until the author, Margaret Mitchell, is consulted." To Peggy's further horror, Louella proclaimed that "For ten years Miss Mitchell wrote on this book, apparently a terrible toll, for she is now fighting blindness and so serious is her condition that her doctor will not permit her to come to Hollywood." Peggy turned on her Southern charm in a letter to Miss Parsons telling her she knew that "everyone in the world reads your column." Then she pleaded with Louella not to print any further rumors about the moviemakers consulting her, and made public her stand that when she sold the movie rights, she had ended association with it. In the context of her letter, Peggy also assured Miss Parsons, "I'm not going blind and have no intention of going blind!"

Then, as if a "Sears-Roebuck Hour" radio broadcast, arranged by Selznick International, which presented one scene from *Gone with the Wind* with Robert Montgomery as Rhett and Constance Bennett as Scarlett, weren't enough to broaden attention, Margaret felt the effects of Russell Birdwell. Mr. Birdwell, a former reporter, had been hired by David Selznick to publicize his studio's films and immediately achieved a reputation as master of the Hollywood "publicity stunt." Russell thought he was only doing his job when he informed the press that a contingent of Selznick people would be traveling to Atlanta to confer with Miss Mitchell about casting and producing *Gone with the Wind*. Margaret realized she had better straighten Mr. Birdwell out, and wrote him a little letter expressing her feelings—which were none too kind. She had previously offered to introduce the Selznick group to proper historical authorities, but had given no promise of any technical help herself, much less casting advice. "I will feed them fried chicken," Margaret promised, ". . . but all parts of the film job are on their hands and not on mine." She made it clear to Mr. Birdwell that if he planted any other such stories, she would refuse to even meet the movie crew. The film folk did arrive in December and, although Peggy Marsh was disappointed that David Selznick, George Cukor and Sidney Howard had not come, she was happy to reacquaint herself with Kay Brown of the New York office.

Margaret had corresponded with Sidney Howard since first hearing he would write the *Gone with the Wind* scenario, assuring him how pleased she was and how much she had enjoyed the William Wyler movie version of *Dodsworth* which Mr. Howard had scripted. Although tentative plans were made several times, Sidney Howard never would go to Atlanta and he never did meet Margaret Mitchell. Mr. Howard had been a bit startled at first when, after writing to Margaret in all innocence for help with dialogue problems of the black characters, he received a lovely reply from the author stating that she would be of no help to him whatsoever.

After months of deluge, Margaret steeled herself and made some important decisions in early December—no more photographs and no more autographs! The latter decision was especially difficult since once she made it a rule she would break it for no one, not even family or friends. Something had to be done, what with almost a million copies of her book in print. As each day brought more parcels containing books, Margaret could not afford to spend time wrapping, addressing and mailing them back, nor the money for return postage. The same lady who in July had written to a Pennsylvania man, "It means a lot to an author to know that her book pleases readers—pleases them enough to make them write long and kind letters. I will be glad to autograph your book. Just send it to me," was now forced to write notes of refusal. Yet those long, gracious letters of explanation produced the much-sought autograph after all. In certain important other cases, Margaret would autograph a blank card and suggest it could then be inserted into a copy of *Gone with the Wind.*

A new pictorial magazine, *Life,* was introduced to Americans in November 1936 and the weekly did not waste much time in turning to America's leading phenomenon. Although John and Peggy Marsh would not pose for *Life*'s staff, the magazine included a photograph of their apartment house along with some older pictures in a story which reprised the well-known facts but made a greatly exaggerated guess in stating Macmillan had realized a $600,000 profit from the book. Its most amusing vignettes involved the "Tara craze" which had erupted in the Atlanta and Jonesboro environs. Although Margaret had carefully described the locale so it could not be placed, certain Georgia plantation owners, *Life* reported, were making money showing off their houses. Even fun-

nier was the news that Atlanta area gasoline stations were readily locating Tara for tourists at a great distance away from their businesses.

As *Gone with the Wind* hats, birthday cards, poems, ads and jokes remained the vogue, Margaret Mitchell was left to wonder exactly what sort of monster she had created. She confided her doubts to Herschel Brickell: "Sometimes, when I have a minute, I ponder soberly upon this book. And I can not make heads or tails of the whole matter. . . . There is no fine writing, there are no grandiose thoughts, there are no hidden meanings, no symbolism, nothing sensational—nothing, nothing at all that have made other best sellers. . . . Then how to explain its appeal from the five-year-old to the ninety-five-year-old? I can't figure it out."

The mass appeal of *Gone with the Wind* was no less a puzzle to outside observers. Unlike other whims of the recent past, those four united words in Margaret Mitchell's title represented an unprecedented magic to many of its readers, who, in turn, felt the book, its heroine and even its author "belonged" to them. Something in this phenomenon was more vast and, as time would prove, more lasting than unusual characters or precise history in a well-written novel. Underneath lay an undeniable appeal to the very basics of human nature—a selfish struggle to survive and the hope for a better "tomorrow." Even in 1936, it seemed probable that an answer to the riddle of *Gone with the Wind*'s hypnotic infectiousness would never be satisfactorily explained The solution was hidden in the individual imaginations of its supporters, to each of whom those four words meant something preciously unique—to each of whom they inspired a separate dream.

Meanwhile, Margaret Mitchell continued to search for an answer somewhere in those 1,037 printed pages which began "Scarlett O'Hara was not beautiful" and ended—500,000 words later—with an optimistic promise that "tomorrow is another day."

The Story and Its Characters

"... he had never known such gallantry as the gallantry of Scarlett O'Hara going forth to conquer the world in her mother's velvet curtains and the tail feathers of a rooster."
—Margaret Mitchell, <u>Gone with the Wind</u>

PART ONE
Chapters 1–7, Pages 1–138
(SCARLETT O'HARA)

Sixteen-year-old Scarlett O'Hara was selfishly unaware in April 1861 that the comfortable Georgian existence surrounding her Tara plantation was undergoing tumultuous change. Bored with talk of war, Yankees or Mr. Lincoln, and jealously annoyed by the attention menfolk gave to these subjects, she busied herself with beaux, clothes and dreams of her fancied love for a handsome neighbor, Ashley Wilkes.

Although not conventionally beautiful, Scarlett's charm captured men's attention as it complemented her green eyes, white skin, black hair and seventeen-inch waistline, which she ascertained was the smallest in three counties. A recent two-year stay at the Fayetteville Female Academy nearby had done little to improve her sketchy education and she had not willingly opened a book since leaving there. Nevertheless, no girl in Clayton County danced more gracefully than she. Ellen O'Hara, her mother, had been raised in the tradition of great ladies but young Scarlett had found the road to ladyhood quite difficult. She possessed the eruptible passions of her Irish father and those green eyes were turbulent, willful and lusty with life.

Through the persistence of her mother and her black Mammy, Scarlett had become an apt pupil, although she learned only the outward signs of gentility. There was no real wish on her part to go beyond appearances for they, alone, seemed to bring her the popularity she wanted. If superficially she was sweet, charming and giddy, she was in reality self-willed, vain and obstinate. Scarlett could deceive her mother, but she had never been able to fool Mammy for long. Mammy, a huge old woman with small shrewd eyes, felt she owned the O'Haras body and soul and was devoted to the family with her last drop of blood. She had been raised in the bedroom of Ellen O'Hara's mother, had been Ellen's Mammy and had come with her from Savannah after she married Gerald O'Hara. Her love for and pride in the eldest O'Hara daughter were enormous but Scarlett dreaded Mammy's lectures on deportment.

Scarlett never had any women friends since she regarded them as enemies equally in pursuit of men. Her mother was the only woman she ever admired. But to be as truthful and unselfish as Ellen might, she feared, deprive her of most of the joys of life. And Scarlett O'Hara had no intention of missing anything. Perhaps "tomorrow"—when there was more time—she would try to be a great lady like her mother.

It had been two years since Scarlett had first become possessed by a secret and feverish passion for Ashley Wilkes, although he had never seemed especially attractive during her childhood. Yet when he rode to Tara to pay respects after a three-year Grand Tour of Europe, he had ridden into her heart as well. Afterward Ashley squired her to various county events and she became more certain that she loved and wanted this blond knight. He was aloof but courteous with an exasperating quality of reserve. Although Mr. Wilkes was proficient in the usual country diversions, his interests went even deeper —to books, music and writing poetry. Scarlett did not understand him but positively sensed that he loved her as well. He had never said this nor tried to show it physically. Still, she had often noticed him looking at her with a puzzling yearning and sadness. Scarlett expected him to propose, but when he did not, the fever within her rose higher and hotter. The very mystery of Ashley Wilkes excited her curiosity. He was a man who moved in an inner world more beautiful than Georgia, one from which he returned to reality with reluctance. He never more than politely involved himself in those things which were of vital interest to everyone else.

It was only two days after the Yankees had been shelled at Fort Sumter, on that sunny April afternoon, when Scarlett's pampered little world received its first unwelcome jolt. Her twin beaux, Brent and Stuart Tarleton, had extracted a promise from her of waltzes at the next day's ball in return for telling a secret they learned in Atlanta on their recent return home. It was an announcement to be made at that gala dance on Ashley's

Twelve Oaks plantation of his bethrothal to his cousin, Melanie Hamilton. The strapping Tarleton boys related the news nonchalantly since it was a Wilkes family tradition to marry cousins. In fact, Ashley's sister Honey was also expected to someday marry Melanie's brother, Charles Hamilton, whom Scarlett thought of as an awful sissy.

The nineteen-year-old twins had no idea what a shock they had given the vivacious young lady they were courting. There was no way their minds could have accepted Scarlett's preference for the dedicated Ashley Wilkes. The sons of the richest family in the county, they believed, along with other residents, that all that mattered in their North Georgia locale was raising good cotton, riding well, squiring ladies elegantly and holding one's liquor. Clayton County was relatively new and, according to older Southern standards, a bit crude. The Tarletons were fitting representations of the lifestyle there, as was their mother Beatrice, who managed the largest horse-breeding farm in the state. Mrs. Tarleton also rode herd on a husband, two older sons, four daughters and these troublesome twins who had just been expelled from a fourth college within two years.

Ironically, Scarlett had almost ended the twins' visit earlier when their incessant war talk bored her. She could never endure for long any conversation of which she was not the chief subject. But the promised secret had intrigued her, even though she thought it merely involved Charles Hamilton and Honey Wilkes. Luckily, Scarlett knew how to conceal her feelings behind a sweet and bland face, and although the boys sensed a change in her, they didn't realize the true effect of their secret. She barely heard them explain that this engagement had not been planned for another year but that talk of war had moved it up.

The friendly atmosphere on Tara's porch had cooled and the Tarletons, no longer feeling welcome, took their leave. They were puzzled by Scarlett's sudden change in attitude until their body servant, Jeems, reminded them precisely when her reactions had changed. By then, they should not have let anything about Scarlett O'Hara surprise them. Until the previous year Stuart had courted Ashley's older sister, India, although his fascination for this rather plain girl escaped Brent. Then, during the last summer, they both had noticed Scarlett, a childhood playmate who had since developed into a magnetic young lady. The boys could not understand how she had escaped their attention before, not realizing that Scarlett had merely decided one day to make them notice her. She was constitutionally unable to endure a man's being in love with any other woman and, after seeing Stuart with India that day, had set her devices of charm in motion. As a bonus, she set her cap for Brent as well.

After the twins had left, Scarlett feared Mammy would sense something was wrong so she ran down Tara's driveway to wait for her father. She looked at the winding main road which ran downhill to the Flint River and up the next hill to Twelve Oaks. Mr. O'Hara had visited John Wilkes' plantation to purchase the head woman slave who had recently married Gerald's longtime valet, Pork. Along with Dilcey, who was also a midwife, would come her twelve-year-old daughter, Prissy, whom Scarlett thought to be a sly and stupid creature. As she waited, some of the shock of what she had just heard rushed into the background as she thought of Ashley and the fever returned.

Eventually Gerald O'Hara's horse galloped up the hill and soared, with its master, over the Tara fence. He had been warned against such foolhardy sportsmanship after a broken knee sustained in a riding accident the year before, but, like his oldest daughter, Gerald did as he wished. Mr. O'Hara confirmed the Tarletons' secret and told Scarlett that Melanie and Charles Hamilton were even then house guests at Twelve Oaks. He guessed the reason for Scarlett's concern and tried to placate her with the promise that someday Tara would be hers and the reminder that, to the Irish, land was the only thing in the world that amounted to anything. This did not pacify Scarlett but she was somewhat soothed at home by her mother's gentle touch. She could not help wondering then why this soft-spoken woman had ever married the bellowing Gerald O'Hara in view of the vast differences in their birth, breeding and former lifestyles.

Gerald had come to America quite hastily from Ireland in 1822 with a price on his head for killing an Englishman's rent agent in a quarrel. Two older brothers had previously made the same journey and were then successful merchants in Savannah. Gerald joined his brothers, prospered with them and quickly adapted to Georgia and to poker, which he found the most useful of all Southern customs. Through this game, and an ability to hold his liquor better than his opponents, he had acquired two of his most prized possessions—a valet, Pork, and his plantation, Tara. The latter was a debatable prize with its burned-out house and overgrown fields. The land itself was part of a vast area in middle Georgia ceded by the Indians in 1821. But the white house Gerald O'Hara built there, by slave labor, wore a look of mellowed years even when new and there was an air of stability and permanence about it. He quickly achieved warm friendships with his neighbors—the Wilkeses, the Calverts, the Tarletons and the Fontaines—and richly enjoyed his new life until, at age forty-three, he had decided that he wanted a wife. After traveling to Savannah, he became attracted to a dark-eyed fifteen-year-old girl of French descent and proposed marriage to her.

Ellen Robillard had accepted Gerald O'Hara's proposal and threatened her Presbyterian father with joining a convent to gain his consent. Savannah people speculated on the young girl's motives but only Ellen and her

Mammy knew the real reason. It was in that same year that her cousin, Philippe Robillard, whom she deeply loved, had been killed in a New Orleans barroom brawl. Ellen held her family responsible for having driven Philippe away and agreed to marry the Irishman who was twenty-eight years her senior to escape from the relatives she could not forgive. But the youthful glow had forever left her heart and there was only a gentle shell left for her new husband. A year after their marriage a first child, Katie Scarlett, was born and the following year another daughter, Susan Elinor, who would always be known as Suellen. The last O'Hara child to survive was named Caroline Irene, but called Carreen. Three sons followed but all had died in their infancies.

Ellen and Mammy galvanized the workers at Tara and gave the plantation a dignity, grace and beauty it had never known before. Mrs. O'Hara took charge of the slaves' training from their childhood on, utilizing a curious social system of the time which determined their future either as house servants or in one of the various self-contained professions on the estate. If they showed no aptitude for a trade, they became field hands and, in the opinion of other blacks, had no social standing whatsoever.

Despite Gerald's coarse demeanor, his tender heart was recognized by all who knew him. At Tara only the soft voice of Ellen was obeyed, and there was a silent conspiracy to keep this from him. Ellen, thirty-two years old by 1861 and married seventeen years, was considered a middle-aged woman by standards of the day. Gerald, a head shorter than his wife, had kept an appearance of unworried youthfulness despite his sixty years and curly silver hair. This small man with thickset torso still seemed typically Irish despite his thirty-nine years in America.

Underneath Ellen's quiet, stately grace—inherited from her French mother—she possessed a steely quality which awed the household. She was often absent at all-night sessions of births, deaths or nursing duties with her various neighbors, whether they were comfortable or poor. But nothing ever interfered with the careful training for traditional ladyhood of her three daughters: delicate and dreamy Carreen, fancifully elegant Suellen and the indescribable Scarlett. Although that eldest child was a challenge, Ellen felt she would adapt in time. And the girl, in turn, looked upon her mother as a miracle that lived in their house who awed, charmed and soothed her. The manners imposed upon her by both gentle Ellen and stern Mammy did succeed in subduing some of Scarlett O'Hara's free spirit, at least as far as they could tell.

That evening, during family prayer services, the heartening idea occurred to Scarlett that Ashley had never realized her love for him. She imagined that he thought she really loved one of the Tarleton boys or Cade Calvert and was only marrying his cousin to please the family. As she later lay in bed, Scarlett carefully envisioned the next day's events. After first flirting with all available men, she would maneuver Ashley away from the gathering and let him realize she preferred only him. He would be happily surprised, enough, she hoped, to elope with her even before the evening ball began. Then, afraid of becoming upset by any thought of this plan not working, Scarlett pushed that possibility out of her mind until "tomorrow" and fell asleep.

The morning brought troublesome problems of attire and Mammy's lectures. Scarlett scrutinized her wardrobe with comparisons to Melanie in mind and finally decided on the same green sprigged muslin dress from the previous day as the only one suitable. As she listened to Mammy's admonitions about her behavior and the artificial requisites necessary to catch a husband, she wondered if her past actions, especially with Ashley, had not been too brash after all. Perhaps they had diverted him to the frail Melanie and, if so, it was not too late to change her tactics. She did not realize that her true personality was actually more attractive to men than any traditional pose she might adopt, for in this Southern civilization a lower premium had been placed on feminine naturalness than at any time before.

Tara's overseer, Jonas Wilkerson, was dismissed that morning for fathering a child, who had died, by a poor white girl, Emmie Slattery. Scarlett was relieved that this man's discharge would require Ellen and Mammy to stay behind to settle accounts so there would be no one at the barbecue to reprimand her for the plan of attack on Ashley.

It seemed to Scarlett that the whole County was attending the Twelve Oaks party when she arrived there. She made good her plan by flirting even with Suellen's beau, kindhearted Frank Kennedy, who owned more land than anyone in the County but was a fussy, nervous forty-year-old. Seeing no sign of Ashley or Melanie, Scarlett chattered and laughed with the Tarleton boys until her eyes fell upon a tall, powerfully built stranger. This man with dark eyes and a black mustache, who seemed at least thirty-five, stared at her in a cool, cynically impertinent way. Then, after a courteous greeting from India Wilkes, Scarlett met Charles Hamilton. The boy's shy manner prompted her to tease him and lead him on but she noticed that stranger again, who was named Rhett Butler, watching her entire performance. Cathleen Calvert enlightened Scarlett on a scandal involving Mr. Butler and an unchaperoned girl he had refused to marry. The incident resulted in a duel and afterward he was not received even by his own Charleston family. He was present at this barbecue only because of cotton business being conducted with Frank Kennedy. Scarlett, despite proprieties, secretly felt respect for this Butler man's refusal to marry a girl who was a fool.

Despite Charles Hamilton, the Tarleton twins and four other escorts, the outdoor barbecue itself was no source of pleasure to Miss O'Hara since Ashley had been too occupied with Melanie Hamilton to spend any time with her after a simple first greeting. Melanie, a tiny girl with an underdeveloped body, gave, to Scarlett, the illusion of a child masquerading in her mother's clothes. Although her large timid brown eyes and shy demeanor were not enhanced by any tricks of feminine allure, she projected a touching, sedate dignity that far surpassed her seventeen years. Melanie was as she looked—simple as earth and transparent as spring water.

Scarlett outwardly reveled amidst her admirers in the Twelve Oaks gardens as the other young ladies, including her sisters, glowered at her. Frank Kennedy's attentions to Scarlett infuriated Suellen, while Carreen, whose thirteen-year-old heart was set upon Brent Tarleton, felt close to tears of frustration. But inwardly Scarlett O'Hara was miserable. She noticed that Rhett Butler was again watching her, which brought an uneasy feeling that this man knew what lay behind her forced gaiety. And she thought Mr. Butler not at all a gentleman when, in the midst of a spirited war debate, he reminded the gentlemen guests of the South's shortcomings in the event of war. This fracas, initiated by Gerald, took her beaux momentarily away and, in their absence, shy Charles had found the courage to propose. Scarlett did not take him seriously but was too preoccupied with Ashley to realize that his hopes for this marriage were actually reinforced by her flippant replies.

During the customary afternoon nap period for the ladies Scarlett crept downstairs to the semi-dark library where Ashley found her a few moments later. Her forthright Irish blood defeated her mother's teachings and she blurted out an admission of her love for him. But her well-planned scheme rapidly fell apart as gallant Ashley at first made light of her avowal and then, after she berated Melanie, chastised her. He reminded her of the differences between them, admitted he could never give his entire self to anyone and told her that she would have grown to hate his books and music, which would have come between them if they did marry. Although Ashley, under her questioning, admitted that he did care for Scarlett, he explained to her that love was not enough in marriage and that Melanie was like him, part of his blood, and that she understood him. Confused and enraged, Scarlett struck him across the face, and Ashley quietly departed. To her horror, she then discovered that Rhett Butler, lying on a sofa in the darkened room, had overheard the entire conversation.

When she returned upstairs, Scarlett heard Honey Wilkes insulting her and, worse still, Melanie Hamilton coming to her defense, even against Honey's accusations that Scarlett was in pursuit of Ashley. She hated the Wilkes girl for what she said, including her bragging of a forthcoming engagement to Charles Hamilton. That boy then ran to tell Miss O'Hara the news that Mr. Lincoln had called up troops, signaling the start of war. To spite Ashley, hurt Melanie, get even with Honey and escape from the total mortification she had suffered that day, Scarlett induced Charles to repeat his proposal. She accepted it even while knowing she could never care for him. Within two weeks Scarlett O'Hara was a bride and within two months she had become a widow.

That short interval between engagement and wedding would have been customarily impossible in normal days, but at a time when enthusiastic Southern men knew one battle would end the war and hastened to enlist, traditions were overlooked. The rushed nuptials had been held at Tara on April 30, one day before Ashley's mar-

riage to Melanie. A week after their wedding Charles had left for South Carolina to join the Confederate forces, and seven weeks later there was a telegram informing Scarlett that her husband was dead. The Hamilton boy had died in training of pneumonia, following an attack of measles. On Scarlett's terrified command, tragic Charles had spent his wedding night in an armchair but his few remaining nights of pathetic bliss with a frigid wife did deposit a perpetual reminder with her. Within a year Scarlett gave birth to a son, Wade Hampton Hamilton, named after his father's commanding officer. She had not wanted the child, whom she could not believe was really hers, and motherhood, together with mourning, bored

her even more than the war she refused to acknowledge.

After an unenthusiastic journey to visit relatives in Savannah and Charleston, the Widow Hamilton returned home even more despondent. Her distressed mother, busy doubling the productiveness of Tara to aid the Confederacy, decided to heed the written pleas of Melanie's Aunt Pittypat. With Ashley off at war, Melanie and Miss Pitty longed to see Charles' widow and son. So Ellen dispatched her daughter, grandson and Prissy to Atlanta in May 1862, for a long visit. Scarlett abhorred the idea of living under the same roof with Ashley's wife and this aunt, whom she regarded as the silliest of old ladies, but felt any change might be welcome.

PART TWO
Chapters 8–16, Pages 139–288
(ATLANTA)

Since childhood, Atlanta had always enchanted Scarlet more than any other place. Gerald had told her then that she was exactly the same age as that city and, indeed, it had received its present name in 1845, the year she was born. In 1836 when Georgia authorized the building of a railroad, a town named Terminus had sprung up from the wilderness at the southern end of that line. Later the spot was called Marthasville, then finally Atlanta, and it had leaped to life with its railroads, which eventually connected it—in all directions—with the entire country. Scarlett had not made the twenty-five-mile journey there since the winter before the war began, but she had always sensed this new city was of her own generation, filled with the crudities of youth and impetuously headstrong like herself. Atlanta had become the center of attention in the state, a mixture of old and new, self-willed and vigorous. But Scarlett's arrival was greeted by a new sight: the never-ending loading and unloading of supplies and wounded from the trains. She may have been able to forget the war at Tara, but Atlanta brought perpetual reminders. Scarlett had not known of the city's transformation since the start of the war. Its railroads were the connecting link between the two Confederate armies and were of vital strategic importance. Atlanta was also a manufacturing center, a hospital base and a chief depot for the collecting of food and supplies.

Southerners had once prided themselves on their lack of factories and mechanical skills, but since the Northern blockade of their ports, they had made an effort to become self-sufficient by manufacturing machinery to produce war materials. The throbbing din of Atlanta's newly erected industries, together with a ceaseless roar of trains, set its new pace, which was apparent in the very pulse of this busy, sprawling giant. There were still other compelling changes of atmosphere. Headquarters of various

army departments swarmed with uniformed men, while prostitutes tumbled from bawdy houses in pursuit of the male overflow, and there were other diversions in dozens of new barrooms.

But, for all of this, adaptable Scarlett liked the exciting atmosphere, energy and bustle. Something in it appealed to a crudeness under the fine veneer Ellen and Mammy had struggled to give her. She felt this was where she belonged despite one fly in the ointment—the idea of living with Ashley's wife filled her with a surge of dislike. Yet she learned more about both Melanie and Charles only a short time after moving into their home, almost the last house on the north side of town. The residence had actually been owned by Melanie and Charles—now, after his death, half-owned by Scarlett herself—but, in deference to Pittypat Hamilton's age and position, it was commonly referred to as "Aunt Pitty's."

Sarah Jane Hamilton had been called "Pittypat" by her doting father in recognition of her restless, pattering little feet and, soon afterward, no one called her anything else. But at sixty the pet name had become incongruous with her stout silver-haired appearance. Her tiny feet crammed into too-small slippers made walking any distance impossible and her aimless chatter was delivered breathlessly due to too-tight corseting. Yet these behavioral quirks, together with the swoons she adopted as ladylike pretense, were never taken seriously by anyone.

Scarlett realized that Charles had been subjected to an overly feminine atmosphere and that his devotion to the two unwordly women he lived with easily explained his unsophisticated shyness. He had never received any toughening influence in that gentle home. Melanie had been exposed to nothing but kindness, truth and love, expecting her happiness to reflect in those about her. She saw the best in everyone and was a typical Southern girl, involved in the conspiracy—which lasted from cradle to grave—to make men pleased with themselves. Southern men, in turn, repaid this devotion to women like Melanie with gallant adoration, giving them everything except credit for having intelligence. Although Scarlett Hamilton was also guilty of practicing this same lopsided code, she did it with a studied artistry and skill, always to further her own aims.

Scarlett, Prissy and Wade had been met at the train depot by the Hamiltons' servant, Uncle Peter, a devoted old black man who saved Melanie's father's life in the Mexican-American War. Later he had taken command of her and Charles when their parents died and even adopted the helplessly indecisive Pittypat after she came to live with them. Scarlett found him an even stricter disciplinarian on standards of ladylike conduct than Mammy. Uncle Peter also took it for granted that she would stay with them permanently, finding it inconceivable that Charles' only son might be reared away from his guidance. But Scarlett would make no such commitment before acquainting herself with Atlanta and appraising this close association with her in-laws. Southerners were enthusiastic both as visitors and hosts, and prolonged visits were not at all unusual. Scarlett had come there without any idea of how long she would stay and Melanie and Pittypat immediately campaigned for her to live permanently with them. They flattered her charm and courage, appealed to her patriotism in helping the Atlanta war effort and lured her with the knowledge that half of their house was hers.

Mrs. Hamilton was, in fact, a well-to-do young woman for, in addition to the house, Charles left her farm and town property of which stores and warehouses along the depot had tripled in value since the war began. Scarlett's understanding of these financial interests was aided by Uncle Henry Hamilton, a short irascible bachelor who was Pitty's brother, but virtually estranged from her for years over a minor criticism of her flightiness.

Surrounded by new faces, Scarlett's seventeen-year-old spirits quickly rose to normal and Melanie's attachment to Wade removed an additional source of annoyance. But she unavoidably fell prey to the town's dowagers: imperious Mrs. Merriwether, thin Mrs. Elsing and their co-conspirator Mrs. Whiting. These "pillars of Atlanta" ran their churches, organized charity events, dictated codes of behavior and were authorities on every family's history. They were three finely respectable and closely allied ladies who disliked and distrusted each other heartily. Young Widow Hamilton was drafted by them into "volunteer" hospital work, a duty performed by every Atlanta matron whether young or old. Since the war interested Scarlett not at all—except for a cold terror regarding Ashley's safety—she immediately loathed nursing. Although Melanie did not seem to mind

the delirium, death and smells, her sister-in-law found the hospital an unendurable waste of her charms. Less damaged or convalescent soldiers were in the care of the flirtatious young unmarrieds like Fanny Elsing and Maybelle Merriwether. Wives and widows, on the other hand, drew the bewhiskered, verminous, hideously wounded new arrivals, and Scarlett wished they were all dead.

From this hospital work and through her in-laws, Mrs. Hamilton became well acquainted with the Meade family. Dr. Meade, a tall gaunt man with a pointed gray beard, was as kindly a man as the city possessed. He was, according to his devoted wife, such a necessity to Atlanta's well-being that a petition had been signed begging him not to go to Virginia as an army surgeon. The doctor, considered by his townsfolk as a root of all strength and wisdom, somewhat believed their opinion and displayed a slightly pompous manner. The Meades' older boy, Darcy, was serving in Virginia, while thirteen-year-old Phil ached to join him before the war ended, as everyone was certain it soon would.

The entrapments of mourning kept Scarlett from any social life until she used her wit to suggest that she, along with Melanie and Pittypat, assist at a Confederate benefit bazaar. She was also intrigued by Mrs. Merriwether's account of Captain Butler, the famous blockade runner, whom that abruptly demanding person reasoned should have been bringing in more hospital supplies and less finery for the ladies. But Scarlett's joy at attending the bazaar evaporated when she sensed the guests were filled with emotional commitment to the "Cause"—something which irritated her since it killed men, cost money and made luxuries hard to get. Despite an old admonition from Mammy, she leaned on her elbows and noticed that even the tacky-looking girls were three deep in men. Scarlett's feet patted the floor to the music as they ached to dance. Her entire being longed to be in one of the lovely dresses she saw—instead of just standing like a crow, covered in black to her neck and wrists.

Her heart had sunk when the dancing began and she could not participate. Instead, she must stand in a booth selling useless items to silly old men. Scarlett let her imagination playfully wander at Dr. Meade's mention of a shocking innovation he had planned until she saw a powerful man, dressed like a dandy and vaguely familiar, grinning at her. She threw him a smile but then froze as she realized it was Rhett Butler, and that he was that same blockade runner she had just heard of. Scarlett attempted escape but a nail in the booth caught her skirt, holding her until Rhett reached her side and unfastened it. He toyed with her fan and delivered pleasant greetings to Melanie as he jeeringly forced Scarlett to reveal the tale of her marriage and widowhood. This conversation did not escape the notice of the worthy matrons in the chaperons' corner. A loud burst of applause greeted Dr. Meade's announcement of Captain Butler's presence, and another followed the doctor's sympathetic plea for donations of jewelry for the Cause. Scarlett was too embarrassed to give nothing, although she was secretly thankful her best pieces were at home, and since the significance of her gold wedding ring was as dimmed from memory as Charles' face, she wrenched it from her finger and threw it into the passing basket. Melanie touchingly followed suit and Scarlett was annoyed that she always misconstrued her motives, but knew it was better than letting her suspect the truth.

Mrs. Hamilton disliked Rhett Butler but privately acknowledged his stimulating vitality. He shocked her with the revelation that his blockade-run goods were purchased openly from the vile Yankees in New York, who did not mind selling out the Union to make a profit. Some of her childish illusions might have crumbled if Dr. Meade had not called the attention of all to his new proposal—that to lead a reel with a lady of his choice, a gentleman must bid for her! Before the chaperons recovered from that shock, Rhett Butler had offered $150 in gold to open the first dance with Mrs. Charles Hamilton. Despite Dr. Meade's explanation that a widow could not appear on the floor, the lady accepted. She was Scarlett O'Hara again, she wanted to dance and didn't care if it was with Abe Lincoln himself!

The next day brought a letter from Rhett Butler to the Hamilton home containing Melanie's wedding band, but not Scarlett's—which annoyed her. Rhett had redeemed that gentle lady's ring at ten times its value, which would forever endear him to her, but Scarlett guessed it was less gallantry on his part than a ploy to secure a dinner invitation. Another letter, three days later, was more worrisome since it came from Tara and, along with Ellen's reprovals of her child's conduct, warned that Gerald was traveling to Atlanta to deal with Captain Butler and to escort a wayward daughter back home. Scarlett guessed that Mrs. Merriwether had wasted no time in writing to her parents about the bazaar.

Gerald's fearful arrival was at first softened by tales of the Tarleton twins' bravery in battle. Stuart had renewed his courtship of India Wilkes and Brent was calling at Tara to see Carreen. Scarlett's indignation at the defection of her former beaux almost clouded the issue at hand. But the reckoning came when Gerald acknowledged his daughter was capable of flirting even at the wake of her husband, and then strode off to find Rhett. Late that night Captain Butler brought Mr. O'Hara home quite drunk and without the $500 Ellen had entrusted to him for supplies. Scarlett seized the opportunity to cleverly blackmail her father into letting her remain in Atlanta and into telling Ellen the scandal she had heard was mere gossip. Mrs. Hamilton's relieved imagination whirled with thoughts of future freedom there and opportunities to see men. She was almost grateful to Rhett Butler for the handling of her father.

Although her conscience sometimes stung after certain compulsive actions, like sneaking into Melanie's room and reading Ashley's letters, Scarlett had become adept at postponing unpleasant thoughts with the slogan "I'll think about it tomorrow!" When tomorrow came, the thought was generally forgotten or at least far lessened in impact by the delay. She had feared that Ashley's letters might reveal a deeper love for Melanie than Scarlett could accept. Instead, he wrote of the uselessness of war, his dread for the South's future if it lost and worse, the possibility that—if it won and became a cotton empire—it would be as commercially hardened as the North. These uninteresting ideas bored Scarlett but the letters seemed to her no more than brotherly and she was smugly satisfied that Ashley did not really love his wife.

Still, Scarlett was glad to be done with marriage since Charles had never awakened in her any idea of what passion or tenderness could be, and she regarded the married state only as servitude to a male madness never shared by women. Her feelings for Ashley, however, were different since they were not physical but privately sacred emotions fed on memories and hope.

Although the war's battles went well, the price paid in overflowing wounded and rows of graves was heavy. Southerners no longer bragged that one more victory would end the war. The value of Confederate money dropped in alarming proportion to the soaring prices; many items were impossible to obtain and hospital supplies were frighteningly scarce. But to Scarlett, it was an exciting adventure as former proprieties disappeared and Old Guard citizens prophesied a moral collapse. The exercise of her charms on patients even made hospital work endurable to the merry widow. Life was comparative heaven to her now and she didn't care if the war lasted forever.

Scarlett's life was ideal: it was almost possible to forget Wade, who was cared for so well by others, and it was easier to bear the thought that Ashley belonged to someone else while he was far away. She made a few brief visits home that autumn of 1862, but the demands of the Confederacy kept her parents constantly busy and Tara soon became boring. Thoughts of dancing and beaux lured her back to Atlanta in a short time, as did the frequent visits Rhett Butler made to Aunt Pitty's house.

These unusual times had also brought some respectability to Captain Butler and he was received in many Atlanta homes, despite his unsavory past. He had been expelled from West Point and cast out by his Charleston father at twenty. Then he wandered from the 1849 California gold rush to South America, Cuba and Central America, where he was a gun runner, and had been a professional gambler. This man was mysterious, exciting and glamorous to innocent girls, and a source of delightful gossip for their elders: he was, in fact, becoming the most talked about civilian in Atlanta. Scarlett saw much of Rhett in the months following the bazaar and looked forward to his calls. Although his taunts frequently annoyed her, there was something breathtaking about his physique, manner and eyes which challenged her. She could not even insult him since he admitted everything with laughing dares for her to go further. She felt almost as if she were in love with him, but, since she wasn't, it puzzled her.

A tide began to rise in Atlanta against profiteers and those who held government contracts to provide war supplies. Soldiers at the front lines complained of shoes which wore out in a week, gunpowder that did not ignite or rotten meat and flour. Speculators had bought up goods and were waiting for a predictable rise in prices. Confederate money sank even lower in value, and the wild passion for luxuries among civilians encouraged primary dealings in these nonessentials to the exclusion of necessities. Rhett could not have selected a worse time to be outspoken about his business being for profit only, and sentiment surged strongly against him, concluding with a damaging newspaper editorial by Dr. Meade. Loyal Melanie still defended Rhett and even compared him to Ashley in recognizing the war's futility. Scarlett

reasoned the basic difference between them was that Ashley would be willing to die for the lost Cause and sensible Rhett would not. By 1863, Rhett was excluded from all the houses that had welcomed him in the fall of 1862, except for Aunt Pitty's. Nevertheless, Captain Butler did not forget to bring luxury trifles for Scarlett, even in those critical times.

He had taunted her about her mourning clothes, which expressed a grief she had never felt, and wagered that a new Paris creation would quickly tempt her to change apparel. One morning he arrived with a brightly trimmed hatbox containing a dark green taffeta hat lined with pale jade silk to complement her eyes. When Scarlett mentioned dyeing the bonnet black, Rhett pulled it away and repacked it. He made her promise, before returning it to her, that she would not change it, but Scarlett faced a more vexing problem. Her early training had instilled in her the impropriety of accepting an expensive gift from a man since that might provoke the taking of liberties. Rhett refused to accept cash payment for the hat and she didn't want to give up the first pretty thing she'd gotten in two years, so she almost hoped he would take a liberty —provided it was a small one. He bluntly told her that he was tempting her with gifts for his own purposes,

which did not include marriage, but, for the present, satisfied himself with a slight kiss on her cheek. Scarlett disregarded Rhett's advice to send him packing as a bad influence since she could not fathom his responsibility for her gradual abandonment of traditions. All her selfish little mind could contain was the pretty new bonnet and the satisfying thought that Rhett must be in love with her.

It was only one day later that Scarlett discovered the existence of a relationship between him and the most notorious woman in town. Belle Watling, a prostitute with hair too red to be true, who dressed in overly fashionable clothes, was regarded as scandalous enough for decent women to cross a street rather than cross her path. Belle had hidden herself near the hospital to wait for Melanie, whom she approached with a donation of $50 in gold for the Cause. When Melanie later showed the coins to Scarlett, they were wrapped in a monogrammed man's handkerchief, and the initials "R.K.B." matched those on a similar one Rhett had recently lent her. Scarlett's Irish fury rose but, since she was a lady, there was no confronting him and she promptly burned the evidence.

Meanwhile, Southern hearts were reassured as their forces more than held their own on the battlefronts. The Confederacy had scored an impressive victory at Fredericksburg during the 1862 holiday season, and thousands of Yankees were killed or wounded. In May 1863 the elated populace heard of another Southern victory at Chancellorsville. Union soldiers had also tried to enter Georgia in April to cut off the northwestern railroad to Tennessee and destroy Atlanta's factories but they had been successfully driven back. As July began, Atlanta learned that General Robert E. Lee had marched into Pennsylvania and there was fresh hope in Dixie that a battle there would victoriously end the war. The only discouraging note was that Lee had forbidden looting, which angered Southerners, who were well aware of the devastation Yankees had wrought in the territories they conquered.

On the Fourth of July reports trickled into Atlanta of a battle near the town of Gettysburg and a suspenseful dread swept the city. At the same time the citizens learned that Vicksburg had fallen and the Confederacy was cut in two. Quiet crowds grew larger awaiting news from telegraph or train, and Scarlett, Melanie and Pitty camped outside the newspaper office for first reports. Rhett sympathetically fought the crowds when the casualty lists were distributed to bring Melanie word that Ashley was, at least momentarily, safe. But tragedy had struck scores of Atlanta families and many young men whom Scarlett knew had been killed—Darcy Meade, Raif Calvert, Joe Fontaine, Lafe Munroe and both Stuart and Brent Tarleton, along with their older brother Tom. The next day, Rhett warned Scarlett, might bring even longer lists of casualties. He seemed unusually serious on this sad day and she found herself asking him why a war was being fought over blacks who might have been freed without all this killing. Rhett advised her that slavery was just an excuse and there would always be wars since men basically loved them!

After Gettysburg the Confederate army was tiredly depleted and, while it sought winter quarters in Virginia, Ashley Wilkes was granted a week's furlough for the 1863 holidays. Scarlett even disobeyed her mother's pleas to return home for Christmas rather than miss the opportunity to see him. After warmly greeting Melanie, Pitty and his father and two sisters, who had journeyed from Twelve Oaks, he had gently kissed Scarlett's cheek. She hoped, had the others not been there, it might have been on the lips. Still, she thought of him as hers all that first evening until he opened the bedroom door to let Melanie speed inside and closed it with an abrupt "good night." Ashley was no longer hers—and she was desolate.

That week passed too quickly and Scarlett had not been able to determine if Ashley still loved her. To this end, she had waited until his last morning to present him with a long silk sash made from a shawl Rhett had given her. Alone with her, Ashley extracted a promise—which, to her disappointment, was only to look after Melanie, especially if he should be killed. Although he had told kind lies to the family about General Lee's continued strength, Ashley now admitted to Scarlett that defeat was near, that his men were barefooted in the deep snows of Virginia and that the Yankees were employing foreign mercenaries by the thousands.

Seeing death at his elbow, Scarlett forced a physical embrace that, though she didn't realize it then, made his departure all the sadder for both of them. She had begged him to profess his love, vowing that would be enough to live on for the rest of her life. Instead, his face was the unhappiest she ever saw as his expression mingled love with shame and despair.

The first cold and rainy months of 1864 further crushed the South's army—but not its spirit. Fighting had finally begun in northwest Georgia and there was mention of a ruthless Union general named Sherman. The Confederacy needed fresh troops, but there were never fewer, and supplies were almost nonexistent. The North held the South in a virtual state of siege but Atlanta, heart of the Confederacy, still throbbed at full production beat. The blockade had made paupers of cotton planters and Gerald O'Hara didn't know if he could feed his family and slaves much longer. Venomous feelings toward profiteers were never stronger than those directed at Rhett Butler, who was openly engaged in food speculation.

But all of Scarlett's thoughts were directed to the war's end, even though she had no clear idea of how this could bring Ashley to her. Her staunch Catholic parents would never allow her to marry a divorced man since that would mean giving up the Church. She knew, however, that if there was a choice between her religion and the man she loved, she would have to choose Ashley. Her love for him knew no bounds of religion or society.

Then, in March 1864, with Melanie's announcement of pregnancy, an angered Scarlett suddenly wanted to return home, feeling almost as if her lover had been unfaithful to her. But a telegram informing the household that Ashley was missing changed her plans. Melanie strained her condition with frequent visits to the telegraph office, despite Dr. Meade's warnings that she must remain in bed. To spare her, Rhett Butler used his influence in Washington and found that Ashley was a prisoner in Rock Island, Illinois—the most dreaded prison camp in the North. President Lincoln had stead-fastly refused an exchange of prisoners, feeling that the burden of Union soldiers at Andersonville, Georgia, would weaken the Confederacy. The Southerners had so little for their own forces, much less these prisoners, that hundreds of Yankees had died there. In retaliation Northerners treated their prisoners even worse, and Rock Island became synonymous with pneumonia, smallpox and typhoid. Three-quarters of the Confederate soldiers sent there were doomed. Rhett had also learned that Ashley refused to take an oath of allegiance and enlist for two-year service on the West's Indian frontier in exchange for his release from Rock Island. His family realized then that there would be no way to ascertain his fate until the war was over.

PART THREE
Chapters 17–30, Pages 289–516
(SIEGE)

In May 1864 the Yankees under Sherman again pushed into Northwest Georgia, but Atlanta felt safe that its integral Confederate position would be protected by General Joe Johnston. Aunt Pitty reluctantly decided to kill her last chicken before it died of old age but, fearing it would be selfish to cook him only for the family, had invited guests for dinner. Melanie, five months pregnant, dreaded being seen in her delicate condition but moved her top hoop higher and made the best of it. And, since Rhett was more firmly than ever under Melanie's protection, Pitty was forced to invite him also when he stopped by for a visit—despite the imminent arrival of the Meades. Never one to keep silent, Captain Butler dashed the guests' hopes of victory by comparing Johnston's forty thousand Confederate soldiers to Sherman's forces of one hundred thousand. He also reminded the group of the depletion suffered by the army from "plow furloughs"—men who had temporarily deserted the ranks to tend their farms lest their families starve.

When the Yankees circled behind Johnston and cut the railroad fifteen miles behind him, it forced the Southern general into a retreat to defend a more vulnerable position and allowed Sherman's men to get eighteen miles inside Georgia. Sherman continued to employ that same circling tactic and gained further inroads despite heavy losses. The constant Confederate retreat was necessary to keep the railroad safeguarded, and as the army left these locales so did the frightened Georgian farmers and slaves. Refugees poured into Atlanta, along with the wounded, by the trainloads. Hospitals overflowed and patients were placed, by necessity, in stores, warehouses and private residences. Despite Melanie's pregnancy, even Aunt Pitty's house was crowded with the delirious and gruesomely wounded. What was once a small prob-lem in North Georgia had suddenly become a storm cloud only thirty-six miles away, which blew with it a faint, chilling wind.

General Johnston called desperately and in vain upon Governor Brown to send the Atlanta Home Guard as reinforcements. Suspicions ran high that this group of men, many quite young and strong, were held in Atlanta for reasons of favoritism. Then the Battle of Kennesaw Mountain—only twenty-two miles away—poured even more wounded into the city, requiring the nursing attention of every woman in town. Scarlett, who had danced until dawn at a Home Guard party the night before, cursed the bother of it all since it meant being seen in her raggedest calico frock, which she used only for hospital work. These new wounded were unattractive, smelly, infested, dying men who showed little interest in her.

Unable to fight back nausea at the screams of amputations performed without chloroform, Scarlett sneaked away from the hospital before the noon train brought even more casualties. Meeting Rhett in his carriage, she ordered him to drive where they couldn't be seen, never having felt more indignation against this war she didn't start. As they rode, Rhett's words finally struck home the possibility that the Yankees—now eighty-eight miles into Georgia—would eventually reach Atlanta. Their ride was interrupted when Scarlett noticed Tara's slaves marching with a Confederate captain. The black men greeted her with handshakes as they informed her they had been recruited to dig rifle ditches around Atlanta for protection when the fighting reached there.

The significance of this was not wasted on Scarlett—Gerald had told her of sieges in Ireland resulting in acts of rape and cannibalism, and she had heard Sherman was even worse than Cromwell. But hopeful Rhett advised her to stay for the siege rather than run to Tara since new experiences always enriched the mind! Scarlett accused him of lying to her about Atlanta's danger and he bet her a kiss that the Yankees would reach there in a month. The mention of a kiss quickly changed her fear to glee but she playfully replied that she'd sooner kiss a pig. Rhett countered that there was no accounting for tastes and he had always heard the Irish were partial to pigs.

Atlanta had heard the sound of battle from Kennesaw Mountain for the first time in mid-June, and, as the town wore a preoccupied look, panic lay just beneath the surface. The Home Guard finally marched out, including young boys like sixteen-year-old Phil Meade and old men like Uncle Henry Hamilton, many totally unarmed since there were no rifles or ammunition to issue them. Scarlett was stunned to see John Wilkes, himself almost seventy, riding out among them. Mr. Wilkes told her that only a stiff knee had prevented Gerald from joining this pathetic endeavor. As Ashley's father bade her goodbye, he sent regards to Melanie and mentioned, prophetically, how he would have liked to see his first grandchild.

By July Sherman had still not successfully driven the Confederate troops from Kennesaw Mountain. New hope surged in Atlanta, giving vent to dances and parties of celebration. After twenty-five days of fighting with enormous losses, Sherman again swung his army in a circle and attempted to come between the Southern troops and Atlanta. When he succeeded, Johnston was forced again to retreat and the Yankees then held the railroad north of the battlefront. This allowed a constant replenishment of soldiers for the Union and prevented reinforcements for the Confederates. After several weeks of wild, happy rejoicing, a new wave of terror swept Atlanta as the fighting began only five miles from town. Johnston was removed from command and General Hood took over, giving Atlanta false hope, since it, by then, unfairly blamed its former hero's retreats for the proximity of battle.

General Hood assailed the Yankees one hot July afternoon and grim Atlanta listened to the rumblings of combat. For hours there was no word of the outcome. Since Pitty's house was at the town's north end, the tattered wounded reached there first—sprawling themselves over the lawn. The family ministered help to those prostrate men until evening, when ambulances came for them. Melanie had fainted by then and Pitty's tiny feet had given up supporting her. Scarlett finally realized what Ashley's letters had meant: war was not glory but dirt and misery instead. If this was real, then the world had gone mad.

The defeated army poured into Atlanta by the thousands the following day, exhausted and depleted by seventy-six days of battle and retreat. Some of the wounded had warned Scarlett and the other ladies to evacuate, although they assured them that the city would never fall. But within days the Battle of Atlanta began and, by that time, the town was hemmed in on three sides. Only one railroad to the South was open and this was highly inadequate for Atlanta's desperate needs. Yankee batteries propelled shells into the town, killing people in their homes and destroying streets and buildings. Scarlett and other women sat on rooftops and watched the battle until the falling missiles sent some of them to basements while others packed to leave. That only railroad to Macon, Savannah and points south was Atlanta's sole hope for survival; should Sherman capture it, the town would strangle and fall. Scarlett realized with terror that line ran through Jonesboro, which was only five miles from Tara, and that Sherman would fight fiercely in that area to take it. She wanted to return then to her family, but Dr. Meade forbade a move for fragile, pregnant Melanie, telling Scarlett the clinical reasons why Mrs. Wilkes would have a difficult time giving birth. And Melanie had begged her sister-in-law not to abandon her to the care of Aunt Pitty. Pittypat, meanwhile, donated her horse and carriage to the hospital and fled, with Uncle Peter, on the train to Macon.

In addition to a cold, gripping fear of those bursting shells, Scarlett was filled with apprehension for days as to what she would do when Melanie's child came if Dr. Meade were not available. Prissy calmed that dread one evening when she reminded Scarlett that her mother, Dilcey, was a midwife, and that she also knew how to deliver babies. Days of siege continued, with screeching, ear-splitting shells. Letters from Ellen pleaded with Scarlett to come home, but she remembered her promise to Ashley to look after Melanie. She felt that perhaps Wade and Prissy should go, since her son was terrified to speechlessness and his fears angered Scarlett because they reflected her own. Prissy was, by then, reduced to teeth-chattering idiocy and of little help. But news came that the Yankees had swung to the South and there was fighting near Jonesboro. She knew she must keep them with her after all, which was just as well since she was relying on Prissy's help when Melanie's time came.

Although townspeople tried to adjust to the continued siege, suspense, hunger and wild uncertainty were a constant torment. Scarlett became less frightened because of the brave faces around her, her own natural instincts and the dreamlike quality these events had precipitated in her everyday life. This was a nightmare too terrible to be real. It was inconceivable to her that she could be in this predicament, that her life could have been so altered in so short a time.

Uncle Henry Hamilton, on leave from the front, visited one night in late July to inform Scarlett that John Wilkes was dead and to leave that poor man's effects for Melanie. He related that the Yankees had already captured every route to town except McDonough Road, and that they would soon try to seize the railroad at Jonesboro. He predicted the Confederate army would make a strong stand there to defend it. Henry's words proved true, and at the end of July the Yankees swung around again toward Jonesboro, but were beaten back. Scarlett was frantically anxious for three days until a letter from Gerald assured her that Tara was safe, but that Carreen had contracted typhoid, so she should not return home even if the fighting in that area subsided. She felt that even God had deserted her, the Confederates and the South.

When Rhett visited Scarlett for the first time since the day of their carriage ride, he became angry that Melanie had not left town. As far as Scarlett's safety was concerned, he joked that he would back her against the Yankees any day, and also assured her that she wouldn't be raped if the Union soldiers did enter Atlanta. She hoped that Rhett would declare love for her just so she could get revenge for three years of sarcasm by sweetly letting him down. But when he kissed her hand, something thrillingly electric caressed her body. She knew she loved Ashley, not Rhett, but this experience brought a feeling that made her hands shake and the pit of her stomach grow cold. To her disappointment, Rhett said he did *not* love her but liked her tremendously for the selfish qualities she possessed which were so like his own. Then he played his trump card and asked her to be his mistress. Scarlett's punctured vanity forced a shameless retort that all such a situation could give her would be a passel of brats, a remark she immediately regretted. Rhett's instant delight at her admission embarrassed her even further and she ordered him to leave her sight forever.

Startling quiet descended on Atlanta in late August as the bombardment ceased. The only news from the front was that the troops had marched south to defend the railroad. After thirty days the sound of cannon had given way to a sinister silence, which yielded an even more uncertain strain. When reports arrived, they had a ring of terrifying familiarity: Sherman was once more striking at the Jonesboro railroad. Mail service was broken and for a week, since Scarlett had heard that Carreen was worse, there had been no letter from Tara. Finally, a courier brought her a note from Gerald with the foreboding message that her mother and Suellen had contracted typhoid as well. Scarlett prayed feverishly with an informal promise to be good if God would spare her mother. Atlanta, the town she loved, was no comfort with its dreaded stillness, so reminiscent of a plague-stricken city.

The first day of September was scorchingly hot, even from the morning, with a suffocating immobility broken suddenly by the distant thunder of cannon from the direction of Jonesboro. And on this, of all days, Melanie went into labor. She tranquilly accepted the possibility

of death after Scarlett agreed to take her baby, but refused to allow her to summon Dr. Meade until he was actually needed. Scarlett had resented Melanie before this, blaming her for their imprisonment in Atlanta, but now she felt the girl was a fool for the affection and trust she placed in someone who hated her.

While she herself sat with Melanie, whose quiet face was wrenched with pain, Scarlett sent Prissy first to find Mrs. Meade and later Mrs. Elsing. From each errand, the simple girl returned, at an airy, idle gait, with only reports that a flow of new wounded had taken everyone to the hospital. A last journey to find Dr. Meade proved equally fruitless. Prissy reappeared only to babble that there was fighting at Jonesboro and that Dr. Meade was tending dying men at the depot's car shed, where she had been too frightened to go. Taking her wide straw bonnet as protection from the glaring sun, Scarlett set out down Peachtree Street through crowds of ambulances and wagons. The sight of carriages crowded with furniture and personal effects alarmed her and she stopped a mounted officer who verified that the Confederates were in full retreat and that the Yankees were coming to Atlanta.

Even when she left her house, Scarlett heard the clamor of many voices and it had grown louder as she progressed. Then, in the center of town, she saw the full panic of a city's exodus—mingled with a rush for food from commissary warehouses thrown open by the army for townspeople to salvage what they could. Amid it all were assorted vehicles loaded with wounded and soldiers on horseback rushing and roaring in all directions. Finally, rounding a corner to the depot, she beheld an appalling and bewildering sight.

Hundreds of men—some stiff, some writhing—were stretched in endless rows under the car shed. These wounded, dying and dead men suffered from the pitiless sun as flies swarmed on their bloody bodies. The smell of sweat and excrement in this inferno of pain nauseated Scarlett and she almost couldn't go on. It was, despite her hospital experience, a sight beyond comprehension. She tread carefully to avoid stepping on some poor unfortunate, knowing if she didn't find Dr. Meade soon she would become hysterical. But when she did find him, it was merely to discover that he would not leave hundreds who needed him desperately for one woman and a baby. On her dazed return home Scarlett caught a glimpse of drunken Belle Watling, hanging on a soldier's arm, and other garish prostitutes whose presence gave the panorama a bizarre holiday effect.

Back at the house, matters got even worse when frightened Prissy admitted she knew nothing about midwifery. Although she had never struck a slave in her life, the rage that filled Scarlett at this child's troublesome lie brought a force into her tired arm which slapped that terrified black face. Prissy screamed, more from fear than pain, and Scarlett sent her to round up the necessary items as she trudged upstairs to deliver Melanie's child.

After an endless afternoon of watching the unrelieved sufferings of childbirth, Scarlett was too exhausted even to reprimand Prissy for bragging about her part in the delivery of Melanie's baby boy (this despite her awkwardness, which had almost made it a travesty). She remembered that the Yankees wanted to free the blacks and felt now that they were welcome to them! Soldiers who passed the house told Scarlett they were the last forces retreating in Sherman's wake. She had almost forgotten the Yankees were coming—and under the leadership of a man more dreaded than Satan! The sudden thought of Rhett calmed her, even though she now hated him, and she sent Prissy to his hotel to beg for a rescue.

A faint glow appeared in the sky which grew steadily brighter until leaping flames became visible and Scarlett was certain the Yankees had arrived to burn the town. Deafening explosions rang as torrents of sparks rose and fell. Prissy flew home, half-crazed from terror, to tell Scarlett that the Confederates had set fire to the warehouse district, including seventy freight cars of ammunition, before the Yankees could get it. Prissy had found Captain Butler in a barroom and, although the army had confiscated his horse, he promised to steal another. Ordering Prissy to care for Wade and the baby, Scarlett tried to pack some silver and china but dropped everything she touched.

At last, reliable Rhett—debonair as ever—arrived with an emaciated horse and a rickety open wagon, almost too small to hold all of them. He curiously asked how she planned to escape from a town bottled up by Yankees or to get near Tara, where fighting had raged all day. But her childish determination convinced him to help the effort and he carried the weak Mrs. Wilkes down to the vehicle. At Melanie's request, Scarlett brought Charles' pistol, sword and picture. She looked at her late husband's portrait as she removed it from the wall and realized she hardly remembered him.

Luckily, the last ammunition train had exploded before they reached the warehouse fire. Still, for a tormenting moment, Rhett had to race the wagon through a tunnel of flames, down a narrow street, to cross the railroad tracks. Later, at the outskirts of town, Scarlett noticed an angered bewilderment in Rhett's eyes. But she didn't expect that he planned to leave her and return to help the devastated army. Yet, after an admission that he did really love her and a farewell kiss, he departed in a surge of patriotism to a Cause he had never believed in.

Scarlett continued with her helpless entourage along a rut-filled path, hiding in the woods as unknown soldiers passed on the road so closely she might have touched them. After a short rest until dawn the group renewed its journey along fifteen miles of burnt-out plantations. As she drove on, unprotected from the sun and hating Rhett for abandoning them, Scarlett wondered if Tara would also be gone with the wind which had swept through Georgia.

There was an unearthly quiet about these shell-pitted houses, with their absence of any living thing; only dead soldiers and animals lined the ghostlike countryside. At dusk, only a half-mile from Tara, Scarlett's spirits sank in beholding the tombstone chimneys of the desolate MacIntosh home. Yet she found a cow there, which she took along with them.

Her apprehension in this mad and desolate world was relieved when she found Tara standing grimly silent. Its walls held the tragic news she had dreaded most—her mother had died the day before and was already buried. All of the one hundred blacks had run away except Mammy, Pork and Dilcey, who had recently given birth. These three house servants and a confused Gerald related the events of the preceding days to her. As the enemy approached and the slaves fled, Gerald had met them on the front porch of Tara and told them that the sickness of his wife and daughters prevented their being moved. The Yankees had planned to burn the house but, instead, a sympathetic Union surgeon tended the women, saving Suellen's life. But the invaders had then torn down Tara's fences for firewood, slaughtered the animals, burned the stored cotton and looted the house of furniture, china, food and wine, although Mammy saved the silver by throwing it in the well.

The Battle of Jonesboro had been waged with Tara as a Yankee headquarters, but Mrs. O'Hara's coma fortunately spared her any knowledge of this. The kind Union surgeon had warned Gerald that his wife had undermined herself by strenuous work and nursing and would not recover. Ellen had died calling out Philippe Robillard's name. Scarlett's hopes that Mammy would give her strength ended when that pathetic old woman showed herself so crushed by the death of her mistress that she wished to be in the grave alongside her. It remained for Scarlett O'Hara Hamilton to protect her home and family. Somewhere along that return road to Tara, that nineteen-year-old woman had left her girlhood behind.

The next morning Scarlett sadly realized that Gerald was senile from shock. She walked to Twelve Oaks in a search for food, finding only scorched ruins of the Wilkes house and a few wilted vegetables in their slaves' gardens. After digging up and hastily swallowing a coarse radish, she vomited and fell to the soft earth, where she lay still for a timeless time. Scarlett O'Hara, the sheltered belle of the county, who had been catered to all her life, now lay amidst ruins, too tired to move, and no one in the world knew or cared. She remembered her mother, father, Ashley and a way of living now

gone forever but felt too weak to put those thoughts off until later. When she finally arose, head held high, her mind was settled on forgetting the past and going forward. She swore, before God, to persevere somehow and to never be hungry again. But something of her youth and beauty was gone forever, replaced by an obsessive determination.

For the present, the family was forced to live in total isolation at Tara. Rhett's stolen horse had died the day after Scarlett's return, eliminating any means of communication with the outer world or the still-raging war. Ever-present hunger, increased by unremitting labor, and the whining complaints of her family and servants were Scarlett's new burden. Only Melanie, too sick to move, did not complain, but her gentle hardihood annoyed

Scarlett even more since she could not shout her down like the others. The siege had left deep scars of terror on Wade, whose mother had no time for him, and Melanie was his only source of comfort. But no one dared criticize the bullying new person who walked in Scarlett's body.

Frightened and unsure of herself, Scarlett had found that shouting relieved her overwrought nerves. She impatiently awaited her sisters' recovery to put them to work. None of their mother's fine training was of any value now. All that remained of their past world that was worth working and fighting to keep was the red earth of Tara. And she would keep it even if that meant breaking the back of every person there!

Two weeks later, when Scarlett was alone with the

convalescents, a Yankee deserter wandered across the plantation and rifled the house. Enraged at the thought of losing what little food they had and filled with revenge, Scarlett shot the man in the face with Charles' pistol. Hearing the gunshot, Melanie dragged herself to the scene, holding her brother's sword. She not only condoned this murder but offered to help dispose of the body. In a flash of clarity Scarlett saw unbreakable courage and felt grudging admiration for that gentle person. In addition to a badly needed horse, the soldier's effects yielded a goodly amount of money and stolen jewelry. Afterward, the shell of hardness thickened around Scarlett as she realized that, having committed murder, no unpleasant task was beyond her.

That new horse enabled the family to seek out surviving neighbors. The Fontaines and Tarletons lent them food and the worst of Tara's plight seemed to be over. There was still some cotton in the fields, and although she resented the idea, Scarlett herself joined in the picking. But the blacks had a caste feeling stronger than her own and refused to do field work on the grounds they were house servants. Scarlett accepted no excuses and drove everyone into the cotton rows until Mammy's complaining, Melanie's fainting, Suellen's vehemence and Pork's incompetence left Scarlett, Dilcey and lazy Prissy to do the job alone. Only Carreen obliged willingly, but the young girl was no longer in realistic contact with the world. She had taken Brent Tarleton's death very seriously and, in grief, had turned to a life of constant prayer. Tara had once risen to riches on cotton, as had the whole South, and Scarlett was determined it would rise on it again.

Then, in mid-November, the Yankees returned! Acting quickly, after a warning from Sally Fontaine, all grabbed what they could and hid in the swamp. Melanie rode the precious horse to safety as Scarlett stashed the deserter's wallet in baby Beau's diaper. If she fled to the swamp with the others, she knew the Yankees would burn Tara, which was all they had left. Instead, she summoned courage and went to meet them with Melanie's baby in her arms and Wade clinging to her skirts. They were Sherman's troops, who had begun a path of looting and burning eighty miles wide from Atlanta to the sea. The Yankee soldiers quickly stripped the house, as they ripped open bedding and furniture and stole everything in sight. The sergeant in charge took the deserter's jewelry, which Scarlett had meant to hide, from her hands and seemed satisfied with his plunder. A dispute arose over Charles's sword when Scarlett asked that sergeant to return it for Wade. The man, happy with the jewelry, agreed, but the spiteful private who had found the sword, only to lose it, set fire to Tara's kitchen in revenge. When they left, Scarlett tried to beat out the flames and suddenly was aware of Melanie working beside her. Together the girls extinguished the blaze, saving Tara, and a truer comradeship began as Scarlett realized Melanie was always there when needed.

The Yankees had burned the stored cotton and stolen most of the food, but the O'Haras' neighbors were in a worse plight and there was nothing left to share. The dreadful hunger returned for all. Then Scarlett experienced a haunting dream of being lost in a strange country, encircled in mist, cold and hungry. She sensed spectral hands were reaching out to drag her down but that somewhere ahead there was a haven, which she ran to find but couldn't. The same dream returned again and again whenever she was hungry, which was often.

A Christmas visit from the Confederate commissary troop, headed by Frank Kennedy, informed the family of Atlanta's fate. Scarlett had thought the city burned the first night of September when she left there. But Frank corrected this mistaken notion, reminding her it was only the munitions warehouses that were destroyed that night. When Sherman entered, he forced everyone to leave the town, which he claimed he needed to rest his men and horses. Quite a few citizens forced into the woods during a rainstorm had later died of pneumonia, and many elderly and sick had succumbed merely from the evacuation. Meanwhile, Sherman's troops had disinterred cemeteries and scattered corpses askew in attempts to find valuables. As the Yankees marched out, on November 14, they set the buildings on fire and the town was virtually leveled, although some outskirt homes, like Aunt Pitty's, had survived. House pets had turned savagely wild in the streets and buzzards lined the skies, but pushy, impudent Atlanta wouldn't accept defeat. Already, Frank told them, many of the citizens had moved back—living in tents as they rebuilt. Scarlett realized fully then that she was like Atlanta—that neither Yankees nor a burning could keep her down.

Later, when they were alone, middle-aged Frank movingly asked Scarlett for Suellen's hand, provided he was ever able to reestablish himself, and Scarlett agreed. Then he told her in confidence that the end of the war was in sight.

Although a North Carolina surrender in April 1865 had actually ended the War Between the States, those isolated at Tara never knew until two weeks later when the bedraggled Fontaine boys brought that news on their return home. The "Cause" which had taken the lives of so many Southerners and sadly reduced even more to desolation had fallen forever. But for Scarlett O'Hara Hamilton it was a time of relief from fear, not for tears. Tara had survived, more cotton could be planted and Ashley, if still alive, would be coming home. Yet for weeks afterward they heard nothing of him.

By summer a steady stream of ragged soldiers was arriving at Tara's steps, begging for food and a night's lodging. Despite their long journey by foot, these men were seldom bitter, for they felt they fought a good fight.

They had two things in common, lice and dysentery— but as Mammy steadfastly dosed them with a bitter homemade brew and boiled their clothes, they seemed grateful, perhaps remembering other gentle black hands that nursed them long ago.

Scarlett resented the Southern customs that forced her to feed strangers and sometimes even take them in. It was all so difficult now with dazed Gerald continually searching for Ellen, Melanie always deathly pale and no slaves to help with chores. If Suellen whined she could be slapped into silence, but Carreen was immersed in religion and prayer, mourning the loss of Brent Tarleton, to whom she had become engaged just before he was killed. Town folk might survive under these circumstances but country folk, without blacks to help, would soon become pioneers again, barely able to exist.

Scarlett could not understand the Tarleton family's squandering money on carved marble tombstones for their boys when food was so scarce and expensive. Nor could she fathom why Cathleen Calvert, a pale ghost of the friend Scarlett remembered, was forced to marry her Yankee overseer to give her dying brother a few last days of comfort. But, despite it all, Melanie's philosophy and manners remained the same, almost as if nothing had happened at all. A visit from Uncle Peter showed that Aunt Pittypat had not changed either, since she and her elderly black protector worried more about the appearances of her living alone in Atlanta than the survival of her kinfolk at Tara. But Peter also brought a letter with the rewarding news that Ashley was on his way home.

Although they all knew there were still weeks or months ahead before he could possibly arrive, Tara's hearts beat wildly at the distant sight of each new ragged uniform. But as the weeks dragged on, life settled into its old routine of never-ending work. Scarlett had changed drastically. Even her secret regrets that Melanie had not died in childbirth so that Ashley would be returning to her own arms no longer seemed so dreadful since she wasn't afraid of God anymore. The bargaining process of her religious beliefs had failed her. God had not helped her and she now felt she owed Him nothing.

The never-ending parade of soldiers, all hungry and taking food from the mouths of Tara, continued. Yet the day the family adopted Will Benteen was indeed a fortunate one. A comrade had deposited this one-legged man, who—unconscious and near death with pneumonia —seemed destined for Tara's burial grounds. Even in his delirium, Will's new nurses recognized he was beneath their class, a type of person quite foreign to their upbringing. He survived and, after a long convalescence, proved a quiet and unexcitable comfort, and all, even Mammy, found someone to tell their troubles to. Scarlett even confided her murder of the Yankee deserter to Will and he congratulated her.

Alone in the world, Will showed his gratitude by staying on—mending, trading and working harder than anyone. As he walked about on his ill-fitting wooden peg, Will soon learned everything about everybody at Tara and he gradually became a member of the family. Although he recognized Scarlett as the head of the house, he really cared for Carreen and Scarlett realized this. When Ashley Wilkes did finally return, it was Will Benteen who instinctively held Scarlett back from racing along with Melanie into his outstretched arms.

PART FOUR
Chapters 31–47, Pages 517–846
(RECONSTRUCTION)

In the bleakness of January 1866 the true scourge of Reconstruction came painfully alive as Scarlett discovered that she would lose Tara in a sheriff's sale if she didn't pay an additional $300 in taxes, based on assessments by turncoat Southern Scallawags and invading Northern Carpetbaggers. She now faced eviction of herself and her family into the bleakness of a state virtually under martial law of Yankee soldiers and the cursed Freedman's Bureau. The latter sheltered the emancipated blacks in the name of a protective Republican Party, lest, supposedly, the Confederate Democrats regain strength and reestablish slavery.

Confiding her new problem to Ashley proved of no material help but instead almost provoked a sexual confrontation between them that would have forever violated his code of ethics and honor. She was tempted, momentarily, to run away until Ashley reminded her of Tara's importance. In realization of this, she became infuriated by a visit from their own former overseer, the Yankee Jonas Wilkerson, who was largely responsible for this tax plight since he wanted Tara for himself. Having learned from Ashley and through Aunt Pitty's letters that Rhett Butler had returned to Atlanta and was believed to possess a fortune, Scarlett determined to travel there and seek a loan—even accepting his "mistress" offer if necessary. The family worked together that night to fashion a new outfit for her journey from Ellen's draperies and plucked rooster feathers.

Rhett had been confined in an Atlanta jail and faced the gallows on Yankee charges of murdering a black. He was, at first, touched by the visiting Scarlett's concern and her cheery lies of good times at Tara. But, as calloused working hands betrayed her, he saw through the guise—which provoked her pleas for a loan for which she offered herself as the ultimate collateral. Unfortunately, his money was not readily available, so she had traveled and lowered herself to no avail.

Rain and mud in Atlanta's streets offered no comfort to the dejected lady, but the unexpected offer of a carriage ride from Frank Kennedy proved welcome. Mr. Kennedy, it seemed, had prospered somewhat from opening a store and selling goods left in his charge by the Confederate Army when the war ended. Added to this were his plans to buy a sawmill and acquire even more income from burgeoning lumber-hungry Atlanta for himself and his intended, Suellen. The mention of money was enough in itself to bolster Scarlett's spirits and, with no qualms of conscience whatever at appropriating her sister's beau, the former "belle of the county" cajoled this middle-aged gentlemen into a whirlwind courtship, with marriage following two weeks later.

Scarlett determined to be a good wife, support Frank's business confidence and make a real home for them at Aunt Pitty's with Mammy and little Wade. She wondered feverishly what Ashley would think of her actions and was actively denounced for them in a bitter letter from Suellen. But her most haunting regret was that the price she had paid for saving her home seemed to be a permanent exile from it. The Kennedys' life was sweet and cozy—as long as the lady had her own way. This path included an investigation into the store's business affairs, which uncovered substantial credit given to the "good" people of Atlanta and subsequent pressure on her husband to start collecting these debts. The sawmill savings had gone for Tara's taxes, but that proposition had not lost its profitable appeal to Mrs. Kennedy, and a visit from Rhett Butler, freed through clever blackmail of Union officials, provided new hope. Rhett, who—despite traditions—acknowledged women's endurance, admired the new business lady. He understood why she married Frank and agreed to finance her, but only if she promised not to aid Ashley Wilkes any further. Rhett felt that the ornamental Mr. Wilkes had a wife he did not fully appreciate and found it infuriating to see men supported by women. Scarlett borrowed enough from him to start a mill business but kept the scandalous source a secret from all, even her husband.

The mystified Mr. Kennedy, who couldn't accept without indignation that a woman had a brain, had humored his wife's whims—especially since any protests incited the rages of a wildcat. And Scarlett's new position as a lumber salesperson soon made them unacceptable to Atlanta's "old breed" society. More importantly, further ghastly implications of Reconstruction revealed themselves in some bold attacks on white women by the lowest class blacks—which, if avenged, meant immediate hangings by the Yankees. The Southerners were deprived of voting, dignity, even justice, and they remained in constant danger of property confiscation if considered a danger to the Union. In retaliation, a secret Ku Klux Klan organization sprang up and its hooded members wrought their own brand of reprisal on offending Northerners and blacks.

Sympathetic aid given by the Kennedys to former Tara neighbor Tony Fontaine, who had killed Jonas Wilkerson, placed them on the Yankee's doubtful list. New fear arose then in Scarlett that she could lose all she had acquired, face starvation again and perhaps be given a jail sentence. It had become a time when the singing of "Dixie" was almost equal to treason, newspapers were strictly censored, only Southern blacks had the rights of redress and sometimes even marriage licenses were denied if the applicants refused to take the Yankees' "Iron Clad" loyalty oath.

On the surface, above this misery, the hitherto obscure Atlanta had become a boom town. Its importance had been firmly established by the critical position it held during the war. The prominent railways were, by then, fully reestablished, and, contrary to Southern gentility, Atlanta was a roaring, wide-open city considered by traditionalists to be ill bred and Yankeefied. Fine homes rose for the Carpetbaggers, whose showy elegance contrasted bitterly with the shabbiness of housing and the starvation, consumption and pellagra which were now rampant in the families of the conquered people. In the squalid cabins of the blacks smallpox, typhoid and tuberculosis were frequent houseguests. Some of their abandoned children ran amok in the streets and many of their bewildered elderly begged for help in returning to their once-safe plantation homes. But neither age, disease nor care of the young were a concern to the highly political Freedman's Bureau, which finally tried to return some blacks to their former owners. The Bureau assured them of pay for their future work, without thought as to how the ravished planters could afford such wages. It was in this fevered climate, during the spring of 1866, that Scarlett announced a new pregnancy to her family.

No one loathed the Yankees more than Scarlett Kennedy but the dangers of confiscation kept her silent. She felt forced to court their favor and that of their wives, women who hated and distrusted the blacks in a way Scarlett couldn't comprehend. In realization that her confinement was ever nearing, she pressed affairs at the lumber concern, successfully conducted business on Atlanta's streets and shrewdly bought out another mill owner. Terror of being hungry again drove her, despite her regretted pregnancy, to cast honesty aside, earn more money, repay Rhett's loan, send sufficient funds to Tara and to hoard an amount of cash upon her own person.

When she realized that her conquerors approved of her

but Old Guard society did not, she comforted herself with daydreams of a future security wherein she would be a great lady like her mother. Only Rhett Butler, she thought, understood her motives and the time he spent constantly accompanying her on selling rounds pleasantly puzzled her, since her appearance suffered so from pregnancy. Despite the material rewards of that bustling city she loved and had adopted, Scarlett ached for Tara and to see Ashley again. But the forced loneliness of career success could, she discovered, be eased slightly by a little brandy—sometimes more than a little—and its warm effects lulled her into postponing thoughts of her troubles until "tomorrow," when she would be better able to stand them.

It was a tragic June of 1866 when Scarlett received word from Will Benteen that her father was dead. The sad journey to Tara culminated in hearing a strange story of what poverty had done to her once-proud sister. Suellen, made desolate by her appearance and the restrictions of their financial state, had learned that her father—not a Confederate by birth or army service—might regain the fortune they lost when Sherman's troops destroyed their stored cotton. All Mr. O'Hara had to do was sign the "Iron Clad" oath, swearing he had not sided with the Cause. She had prodded feeble Gerald with brandy to agree and accused him of betraying Ellen's memory by allowing the family to live in poverty. The poor man weakly assented until he learned that "poor white" opportunists were taking this pledge merely for the money. Engulfed in a rage which seemed to restore his old strength, Gerald had raced home on horseback and, while jumping the Tara fence, had been thrown to his death.

Scarlett also learned that her youngest sister, Carreen, would soon enter a convent and that Will planned to marry Suellen. She was grateful to this man, whom she already regarded as a brother and whom she realized was largely responsible for the preservation of Tara. But her most distressing news was that Ashley hoped to relocate to New York with his family. With Melanie's sympathetic help, she coerced the very resistant Mr. Wilkes into coming instead to Atlanta as manager of her second lumber mill. Since Ashley's one sister, Honey, had married and lived in Macon, Melanie made a home for the other, spinsterish India, in their highly modest new home adjacent to the Kennedys'. Their happy Atlanta existence was blighted only by both Dr. Meade's and Dr. Fontaine's warnings that bearing a second child would cost Mrs. Wilkes her life. Scarlett experienced a guilty sense of pleasure in realizing this prevented any real intimacy between Ashley and his wife.

Back in her home town, Melanie unwittingly became the nucleus of the Old South, actively rekindling memories of former days with her kindness, gentility and loyalty. Soon every person of importance who came to Atlanta was the Wilkes' houseguest. Until her advanced pregnancy could be used as an excuse, Scarlett attended Melanie's gatherings but was depressed by talk of war, hard times and what might have been. While these people represented something past, young Mrs. Kennedy wanted to forget it all, even her own acts of wartime heroism, and look to the future.

Ella Lorena Kennedy was born at the very time a new Klan outbreak threatened the safety of every white Southerner in Atlanta. The Yankees threatened mass hangings, and frightened citizens remained homebound. Therefore, even upon recovering from childbirth, Scarlett was forbidden by her husband to venture to the mills alone. Tormented by fears of business loss and realizing that Ashley's management was not a help, her protests induced Melanie to dispatch an embittered old man, Archie, as a protector on the necessary rounds. Archie, who actively hated Yankees, blacks, and women, was strangely silent about his past. Nevertheless, his value as a defender proved so great that Scarlett eventually lent him to other fearful ladies as escort for their errands. Peculiar Archie soon became an Atlanta institution and a bulwark between Southern women and the terrors of Reconstruction.

Scarlett Kennedy had been annoyed by the new baby's interference in her business life and vowed to have no more children. Further irritated by Frank and Ashley, who found time for "political meetings" but not for financial matters, she vowed to get convict labor to increase efficiency and lower operating costs of the two mills. Upon hearing this, Archie revealed himself to be a former convict who would quit if she followed through with this plan. Indomitable Scarlett obtained the prisoners and Archie made good his threat—forcing her then to ride alone.

Rhett Butler returned to Atlanta in December, after an absence of almost six months, and Scarlett felt a queer pang of jealousy about the New Orleans journey he had taken. She feared that someday he might marry a woman from there, but he explained that he had merely been visiting his ward, a young boy. In anger, he then berated her for breaking the promise not to support Ashley, a man he could only pity for not functioning after his world disappeared. He vowed to finance her no further, a disappointment to our lumber lady, who had been planning a future monetary proposition for him.

By March 1867 Georgia was under the strictest federal rule of General Pope for its legislature's refusal to ratify a proposed Constitutional Amendment giving blacks the right to vote. With the Yankee army protecting them, renegade black men got completely out of hand and instances of outrage increased. It was at this time that Scarlett was herself attacked by two derelicts—black and white—near Shantytown. This was a plague spot that even Northerners admitted should have been eliminated but instead had chosen to ignore. Only the intervention of a former Tara slave, Big Sam, whom she had arranged to help return home, prevented the rape attempt from being successful.

That night Frank and Ashley attended another "political meeting," depositing an indignant Scarlett with Melanie and India. The evening induced tension, with mysterious visits first from Rhett and then from Union soldiers. Scarlett slowly began to suspect the horrifying significance of those so-called political gatherings—that they were really the Ku Klux Klan! Her worst dreads became reality when Rhett returned with a wounded Ashley and the news that Frank was dead.

Testimony by Mr. Butler, Belle Watling and her girls that all twelve men suspected by authorities were patrons in Belle's establishment at the time of the Klan raid on Shantytown, persuaded the Yankee Provost Marshal to drop a case against them. But it brought a shame on these Southern families for which their women held Rhett and Scarlett accountable. Melanie, however, planned to personally call on Mrs. Watling and thank her for lying to save Ashley's life. Belle instead drove quickly to their home and, inviting Mrs. Wilkes into the secrecy of her carriage, warned the lady not to jeopardize her reputation by such an association. In a moment of self-revelation the Watling woman disclosed that she too had a young boy, although he lived elsewhere and she had not seen him in years. Melanie expressed a hope they might meet again but Belle realized this could never be.

Stricken by a rarely severe attack of conscience after her husband's funeral and by fear of God's wrath for killing him, bullying him, even marrying him in the first place, Scarlett Kennedy consoled herself with a purloined bottle of brandy. Even attempts to push these torments off until "tomorrow" were of no avail. Frank's only happiness, she feared, had been their daughter and that was not enough to compensate for the way she had so coldly used him. A sympathetic visit from Rhett, so respectful in outward appearance that it verged on the burlesque, soothed her a bit. He assured her that Frank did not have to marry her, nor accept the treatment she gave him. He also intimated the man's life would have been far worse had he married Suellen instead. Rhett calmed some tipsy fears of hell and listened with interest to Scarlett's narration of her recurring dream that had been a plague since the siege of Atlanta—in which she ran through a mist in search of security. Then, joltingly, he proposed marriage as the only course open to catch her between husbands. After some protests, soothed by a few placating kisses, the lady accepted.

Barely a year after the death of her second husband, Mrs. Frank Kennedy became Mrs. Rhett Butler and the newlyweds were then firmly entrenched as Atlanta's most unpopular Southern citizens, having violated every tenet of the unwritten code of behavior. Scarlett weathered the criticisms of many, having been truly hurt only by that of her Mammy. On their New Orleans honeymoon Rhett suggested that she could now tell one and all to go to hell. When she reminded him that he was the principal party she had hoped for such a destination, he promised she could still wish that too anytime it made her happy. It no longer did.

PART FIVE
Chapters 48–63, Pages 847–1037
(RHETT AND SCARLETT)

New Orleans, with its laughing women and reckless men, enchanted Scarlett and taught her that marriage—at least to Rhett Butler—could be fun. The glamour and gaiety she saw masked the Carpetbagging and persecution of honest folk, which was just as rampant underneath as throughout the defeated South. But to Scarlett this honeymoon seemed her life's most pleasurable time since that April before the war and she thrived on it. Never a deep thinker, she found it easy to ignore puzzling conversations about Quantrill's guerillas or Frank and Jesse James, even to forget that the men Rhett introduced her to never talked of a past or future.

Delightful new fashions, without hoopskirts, dazzled Mrs. Butler, and her husband set no limits on purchases. Rhett himself bought some red taffeta to have made into a petticoat for Mammy, whose reaction to their marriage had so hurt his new wife. Scarlett, though, had recovered enough from that insult to gorge herself on meals or even drink too much champagne, singing openly on the streets during one carriage ride home. She realized they were an attractive couple and other women's eyes told her how handsome Rhett really was. This marriage was different. Her husband neither feared nor respected her but, strangely, seemed always to be restraining his emotions. Scarlett imagined this was because he was not really in love with her and she did not trouble herself to understand him. Yet she was often puzzled, upon catching him unaware, to find that he watched her with an alert, eager and waiting look in his eyes.

Although she did not love him, Scarlett acknowledged that Rhett was an exciting person to live with. Her recent past had been serious and bitter but now Rhett made her play and she was again a child, ever on the brink of new discoveries. This mood, unfortunately, was broken with the return of her dream in which she ran through mist searching for an unknown something that was impossible to find. To bolster Scarlett's feeling of security, her husband promised to build her a grand new home in Atlanta.

Rhett's elegant plans were somewhat altered by Scarlett's "execrable taste" but, still, he allowed her every whim. He even offered to help reestablish Tara if Will Benteen's cotton crops couldn't manage that alone. But, although proud of Scarlett's business abilities, he refused to give any monetary support to her store or mills lest this be contributing to the support of Ashley Wilkes.

When the Butlers had returned to Atlanta, the Old Guard women, led by Mrs. Merriwether and Mrs. Elsing, planned to totally ignore their existence—even if their grateful menfolk felt obliged to call and pay respects. These ladies' long disrespect for Scarlett had been fired even further by the innuendoes of India Wilkes, who was tormented by a past jealousy that Stuart Tarleton was once among Scarlett's beaux and by suspicions of a possible hold the lady had on her brother Ashley.

Our Scarlett was untroubled, however, by any lack of cordiality from her former friends since she was surrounded by all sorts of "new people." Aware that the governing of Georgia by its own citizens was impossible, these wealthy but vapid creatures had swarmed there like buzzards to a dying animal. Meanwhile, Mrs. Butler anxiously watched the erection of her new home, which would tower over any on Peachtree Street—indeed larger and finer, she thought, than any other residence in Atlanta. When it was finished, she furnished the house with all the promise her bad taste allowed. Rhett observed that there were as many gilt-framed mirrors as Belle Watling's place had. To little Wade and Ella, the fashionable gloom was overpowering; to Rhett, it was a nightmarish "architectural horror"; but to Scarlett, it was the epitome of beauty and elegance.

Rhett loved to take Scarlett down a peg. When she asked him to suggest a new name for Kennedy's General Store, he offered "Caveat Emptorium," assuring her this name was most in keeping with the merchandise quality. In all innocence, Mrs. Butler had just such a sign painted and would have used it if Ashley had not translated the meaning for her. Scarlett's plans to become Atlanta's foremost hostess were somewhat altered at her first large party when Melanie, Ashley and the few old friends who had attended left when Governor Bullock entered the Butler home. She felt the Old Guard was foolish in not recognizing the Governor and other Republicans since, she thought, their acceptance could help lift Georgia out of its stricken condition. What Scarlett did not realize was that her insincere overtures to these unpopular people had cut her off forever from the old Southern civilization. She had turned, in the eyes of her former neighbors, into a Scallawag, casting her lot with the enemy.

Indifferently, Mrs. Butler busied herself with those new Atlanta acquaintances whose pasts were often morally suspicious. It was a mongrel society whose common bond was money, and it indulged in an orgy of spending such as the city had never seen. Yet this crude and garish era suited Scarlett. With her parental childhood restraints gone and her religious beliefs faded, the lady permitted herself the luxury of doing exactly what she wanted. She actually liked Governor Bullock and the Republicans no more than her old breed friends. The blue uniform still represented the terrors of siege, flight and desperate poverty at Tara, but now she was wealthy and well liked enough to be insulting to these people— and she often was! Rhett was no more popular with older Atlantans than ever, but he was indifferent to their disapproval. All that mattered to him was his young wife, whom he patiently watched with a speculative and waiting gaze. This she still did not understand. Scarlett had made a bargain with Rhett which pleased her and she did not care much if he was satisfied as well.

Unexpectedly, she discovered to her horror that she was going to have another baby and threatened to abort it. Rhett became enraged at this since he had once witnessed a New Orleans girl's death from such a bungled operation. When the baby was born, she was named Eugenie Victoria after two queens. But after Melanie compared the child's eyes to the bonnie blue flag, the girl was known as Bonnie Blue Butler.

Through his gift of the petticoat, but more especially since Bonnie's birth, Mammy finally accepted Rhett as one of her "family," and this new relationship truly pleased the outwardly callous Mr. Butler. Little Wade Hamilton had also grown close to his stepfather. After Bonnie's birth the young man asked "Uncle Rhett" if he were disappointed not to have had a son and was gently told by Rhett that he felt he already had one, who was certainly boy enough for him. Wade tended to boast about the bravery of the father he had never known. Rhett soothed the child's fantasies by assuring him that marrying Scarlett O'Hara had established eternal proof of Charles Hamilton's heroism.

A new servant, Lou, was unable to lace Scarlett back to her former eighteen-and-a-half-inch waistline for a first journey outside after childbirth and Mrs. Butler once more promised herself to have no more children. Then, a visit to the lumber yard provoked an argument with Ashley over convict labor and he accused her of having been brutalized by Rhett. Her childlike mind interpreted this as a wish on Ashley's part that they be physically true to each other, even though married to others. Scarlett informed her husband that evening that she felt three children were enough for one lifetime. Rhett took the news calmly but reminded her that he could divorce her for refusing him his marital rights. However, he added, it would work no hardship on him since the world was full of beds and it seemed a wonder he had not strayed before. After he left her, Scarlett realized how she would

miss the comfort of his arms and suddenly, unhappily, she cried.

After Bonnie's first birthday the Butlers underwent a social change. Aware that eight-year-old Wade had not been included in children's parties given by the Old Guard families, Rhett determined that a similar fate would not befall his daughter. However, he had chosen a particularly bad time to gain respectability. Never before had Republicans and Scallawags—with whom the Butlers were linked—been so hated in face of the corruption of the Carpetbag regime. Nevertheless, Rhett set a campaign into operation which included attending the Episcopal Church and donating funds to it. He cultivated the Old Guard women and contributed to the upkeep of the graves of the "Glorious Dead." Rhett let word spread about his secretly brief Confederate Army service and then took a desk at the bank, working there each and every day. Mr. Butler courted the favor of his sternest foe, Mrs. Merriweather, with bank influence for a mortgage loan and with fatherly concern over Bonnie's trivial childhood problems. When he visited the Watling establishment, it was in the quiet of night—along with the other respectable Atlantan men. And, as often as possible, Rhett proudly walked Bonnie's carriage or rode with her, adding to respect for him as a loving father and to disdain for Scarlett as an uncaring mother.

Scarlett did love her daughter—to the extent she could love anyone—and Bonnie was, in fact, her favorite child. The girl resembled Gerald O'Hara in Irish appearance and sudden temper and Rhett spoiled her to extremes—in spite of Scarlett's and Mammy's attempts to restrain him—until she become fearless of everything—except the dark. This one fear forced her concerned father to take the child from the nursery into his own room to sleep near a lighted lamp. News of this soon carried, allowing Atlanta townspeople the private knowledge of separate Butler bedrooms. Rhett also gave up drinking since the smell on his breath offended Bonnie. He stayed outdoors to ride with her and, as a result, began looking healthier and happier—almost like the younger blockader who had excited wartime Atlanta.

There was a happy bustle of activity at the Wilkes home as preparations were made for a surprise birthday party for Ashley. Melanie asked Scarlett to detain Mr. Wilkes at the lumber yard until five o'clock lest he walk in on the preparations. A sunny April afternoon heralded Mrs. Butler's arrival at her mill, making her aware that this would be the first time she and Ashley would be utterly alone since their romantic confrontation at Tara. Conversation between them drifted to the old days and Scarlett saw that this now-graying man had lost youth and vitality. He seemed as remote from her ideal of him as that Twelve Oaks barbecue was from the present uncertain times. After being moved to tears by unwanted moments of nostalgia, she felt solace as Ashley soothingly took her in his arms. But this tender moment of comforting friendship was awkwardly interrupted by the intrusion of India, Archie and Mrs. Elsing, who misinterpreted what they saw. Terrified at Melanie's and Rhett's possible reactions to the certain ensuing gossip, Scarlett decided to think about it later, when she could stand it, and promptly went home to bed. Awakened by a persistent Rhett, who claimed he could endure a trollop but not a coward for a wife, she was forced by him to face the consequences of Melanie's party guests rather than endanger Bonnie's future.

At the party Melanie Wilkes, as always, ignored the gossip, although it later caused a permanent rift between her and India which even involved the confused Pitty-pat. Rhett had not returned with Scarlett, traveling on from the party, she imagined, to Belle's. At home, still plagued by shame from the day's events and by fear of her husband's wrath, Scarlett decided a few drinks might help bring sleep. But, unexpectedly, she found Rhett quite drunk in the dining room and he argued violently with her over her monotonous unrequited devotion to Ashley. Fear turned into animal courage when he began to manhandle her and she attempted to leave him amidst a cascade of insults. Rhett swung Scarlett from her feet, carrying her in a painfully tight embrace to the quiet of her bedroom. Yet there in the enveloping darkness, she was not afraid and experienced the unknown excitement of surrender. Scarlett O'Hara had finally encountered someone who would be neither bullied nor broken.

In the morning, he was gone but Scarlett felt a warmer appreciation of him. After a two-day absence, she felt alarm for Rhett but, when he returned, bitter words between them prevented her from expressing her new emotions. She refused his request for a divorce, protesting family disgrace, and berated his plans for a trip to Charleston and New Orleans with little Bonnie. Rhett raged at her insinuation that he couldn't properly care for his daughter's welfare and left on the trip with his child and Prissy.

Made desolate by Rhett's absence and driven by her long-dormant Catholic conscience, Scarlett determined to confess her feelings for Ashley to his wife. Melanie would listen to none of it, claiming she knew Scarlett better than anyone. For some unknown reason Scarlett felt incapable now of hurting Melanie with admissions that she once would have been proud to boast of. Scarlett regretted the harm innocently brought to Ashley but, for the first time, Rhett's taunts that Mr. Wilkes lacked manhood seemed more than a remote possibility. Subconsciously, her regard had changed in recent days for the three people most dominant in her life—Melanie, Ashley and Rhett.

The estrangement between Melanie and India divided the Old Guard into separate groups and India's followers made much of Mr. Butler's absence, especially when they heard that Mrs. Butler was pregnant again! Rhett had been gone for three months and his wife had no word from him. She sincerely missed him and Bonnie, too, more than she would have thought possible. Scarlett was aware by then that Wade feared her, and Ella, she acknowledged with annoyance, was a shallow and silly child. But the new pregnancy was not like the others. It was a reminder of her night of rapture and she hoped to have Rhett Butler's son.

Finally Rhett returned, but cross words developed between them on the very day of his arrival. When he sarcastically suggested that Ashley had fathered her expected child, she lunged at him, falling down their staircase, incurring a miscarriage that almost killed her. For days Scarlett remained delirious, imagining herself back in the Atlanta siege. Melanie was at her side except for those moments when she tried to comfort Rhett, who seemed a broken, damned soul awaiting judgment. When she was able to tell him that Scarlett was recovering, Melanie was not prepared to see the man dissolve into tears, fall into her lap and confess all the shameless deeds of his life. To Melanie, who had never seen evil or cruelty, this rambling, drunken confession of a relationship with Belle Watling and past acts of violence was inconceivable. But she fully comprehended then the great extent of Rhett's love for his wife.

After a month of recuperation Scarlett felt the need to return to Tara where she could sort her problems out "tomorrow." In her absence Rhett arranged an anonymous scheme to finance Ashley's purchase of the mill business. But Tara depressed Scarlett since it was merely a farm and no longer a grand plantation. When she returned to Atlanta, Rhett taunted her into agreeing to sell the lumber concern, which she later regretted because it meant losing any future opportunity to see Ashley alone.

Rhett never apologized for the events leading to Scarlett's miscarriage. He treated her with polite disinterest, almost as if there had been nothing between them, and transferred all his former devotion to Bonnie. Scarlett was ashamed of a new jealousy toward her daughter and missed the old days of bickering and retort. She yearned to be foremost in both Rhett's and Bonnie's hearts, but knew they were now forever first with each other.

Mr. Butler had become a humble Democrat and helped persuade the Old Guard to disband the Ku Klux Klan. He discredited many Republicans—their former "new" friends—and was even spending his stored gold to help the Confederates regain power. By October 1871 Governor Bullock had resigned from office and, after an election, Georgia once again belonged to itself and had a Democratic governor. Despite the beliefs of those around her, Scarlett, too, was happy to see the end of Yankee rule but it bothered her to know her husband was highly popular while she remained in disgrace.

Rhett's pampering of Bonnie culminated with buying her a Shetland pony, when she was only four, which the child proudly named "Mr. Butler." Mammy, who was secretly responsible for Bonnie's fear of the dark, then interfered with a criticism which would, inadvertently, lead to tragedy. It was improper for little girls, Mammy cautioned, to ride a-straddle, so Rhett produced a tiny sidesaddle with silver trimming. Over Scarlett's protests he also assented to Bonnie's demands for a totally unsuitable blue velvet riding habit with a long trailing skirt. Then, not satisfied with a jumping bar a few inches from the ground, Bonnie cajoled her father into moving it up to a foot and a half. Riding sidesaddle in that flowing blue garment proved too much for such a young child. She fell going over the hurdle, broke her neck and died.

Rhett collapsed completely into a near-insane state of alcoholic grief and refused to allow his daughter to be buried in the ground where it was dark and fearful. He threatened to murder Scarlett if she tried to force a funeral. She, in turn, tormented him with the guilt of having caused the child's death. Heartbroken Mammy begged Melanie's aid. Realizing how she would feel if Beau died, and despite her fears of his drunkenness, Melanie was once again able to bring Captain Butler back to reality. After she had accepted her child's death, Scarlett sensed something very wrong with her world. She was plagued by eerie fears unlike any she had consciously known before, but more like those of her strange, misty dream. Although contrite over her accusations to Rhett about Bonnie's accident, she never managed to tell him—and he was rarely home. Rhett had become an untidy, helpless drunk relying on servants to put him to bed. Mammy, feeling her work was done, had returned permanently to Tara. Scarlett was lonely and afraid. She now missed the old friends she hadn't cared about for years as she saw herself entombed in that huge mansion with a swarthy, sodden stranger who was disintegrating before her eyes.

She visited Marietta, a nearby town, but was called back by an urgent telegram from Rhett. At the station he told her that Melanie had suffered a miscarriage, was dying and wanted to see her. It was difficult for Melanie even to speak, but she extracted promises from Scarlett to look after Beau, Ashley and Rhett, who Melanie told her, loved her so. Scarlett knew suddenly then how much she had relied on this gentle girl and didn't feel she could go on without her. She was filled with a wild remorse for having cared for Ashley all those years and wished she could bring them back for Melanie's sake. Then, her emotions regarding Ashley also took on new light as she saw him, a bewildered, frightened child, who claimed that Melanie was his only dream that had not yet died in the face of reality. When Melanie died, Scarlett knew she was alone; even her fancied love for Ashley had disappeared at the same time and she knew it had all been a hopeless illusion. All that mattered in her world had gone out of it. These last memories of Melanie and Ashley would hurt all the tomorrows of her life.

She left the grieving Wilkes family and stepped into a thick-chilled, misty night which reminded her of a hundred past nightmares. Scarlett ran quickly until she saw lights, and, unlike her dream, it was a real refuge—the safety of her own home! As if chains had fallen away from her body, the enlightenment came that it was Rhett she wanted, with his strong arms to hold her. It had always been Rhett, she realized then, never Ashley. She had taken him for granted all those years as she had done with Melanie. No longer afraid of the fog, she ran home to tell Rhett that she loved him.

But it was too late. Rhett, affected deeply by Melanie's passing, paid a silent farewell to that lady he respected and then told Scarlett he was leaving her. He suggested she could soon be free to marry Ashley, and her denial that she wanted that and even her profession of love for him seemed not to matter. Although belief showed in his eyes, Rhett expressed little interest. He had waited too long for her, he replied, and then had given his refused love to Bonnie. When the child died, she had taken everything with her. Rhett calmly told Scarlett that, at forty-five, his roaming was over and he would thereafter seek a life of dignity and grace. He hoped that Scarlett, then only twenty-eight, might someday understand what he meant. Since she did not want a divorce, he offered to come visiting often enough to keep gossip down.

Perhaps in this one evening Scarlett had at last attained some degree of emotional maturity and possibly even learned unselfishness—all too late, though, to keep the only man she ever really loved. She forlornly pondered her life and then remembered something that faintly lifted her spirits—she still had Tara! She had returned there once in fear and defeat and had emerged from its sheltering walls strongly armed for victory. A vague comfort filled her as she pictured the white house, autumn leaves and the hush of country twilight. She also wanted to be with Mammy as desperately as when she was a child. Mammy was her last link with the old days and she would be there waiting. Scarlett felt encouraged for, after all, she was still Scarlett O'Hara—daughter of Gerald—and carried the spirit of a people who would not know defeat. She would return to the security of the home she had so valiantly preserved, to the land that was in her blood. And if "tomorrow" there was any possible means, she would find a way to win Rhett back.

1937: The Pulitzer Prize

Throughout 1936 Peggy Marsh had waited for the excitement in her life to wane. In the beginning she had predicted, on the basis of her journalistic experience, that interest in a "local literary celebrity" would subside in three weeks, or two months at the outside. When this did not occur, Peggy could only pray for the day *Gone with the Wind*'s sales would finally diminish and she would be forgotten. As the Christmas 1936 season increased "Scarlett fever" to the manic point, the Marshes assured themselves the New Year would *have* to bring them renewed peace. But *Gone with the Wind* did not take its title's advice in 1937 as it outsold every book of any kind for a second consecutive year—just as *Anthony Adverse* had done, but exceeding Hervey Allen's total sales by the hundreds of thousands. Twelve new printings throughout 1937 would bring the total to forty with almost a million and a half copies circulating in North America alone.

And there were unique problems in 1937 to plague both Margaret and her publisher. February brought an almost humorous annoyance with a plagiarism suit instituted against Macmillan—though not Margaret Mitchell—by Susan Lawrence Davis, a rather elderly lady who had privately published her *Authentic History of the Ku Klux Klan 1865–1877* a dozen years before. The suit was based on such ridiculous charges as that both Miss Davis's book and *Gone with the Wind* had been bound in Confederate gray bindings, and that both had employed terms like "Fort Sumter," "Carpetbagger" and "Scalawag."

Miss Davis's lawyers asked a $5,000 judgment for every infringement, which, if based on Macmillan's thirty-five printings up to that time, would mean a penalty of $175,000. If based, instead, on the number of copies in print—which was possible—it came to a significantly greater amount, which gave Margaret the inspiration to refer to it as her "six billion dollar lawsuit." Although not named in the action herself, Margaret Mitchell became involved and almost hoped it *would* go to court lest anyone think Susan Davis had been "bought off quietly." The case was dismissed without trial by a Washington, D.C., court in July, but Margaret was faced for several years with the unpleasant possibility that the determined Miss Davis might then sue her personally, as it seemed was her right.

In addition to receiving an average of one hundred letters or phone calls each day, Peggy was kept busy refusing to give autographs, write magazine articles, pose for photographs, divulge her age or reveal Scarlett's original name. She also had her hands full denying rumors and published reports that she was getting a divorce from John, preparing to play Melanie in the Selznick film version, squandering thousands of dollars on new fashions, homes and yachts, or worst of all, that she had a wooden leg! The book's success had, it seemed, also inspired a flock of "Margaret Mitchell" impostors who, for either psychological or financial gain, were making impromptu appearances in various cities to autograph copies of the novel, make speeches or pick up men. A rumor that completely bewildered The Macmillan Company was that by sending $1.00 to its New York office, a reader would receive a pamphlet with a final chapter revealing the future of Scarlett and Rhett. The publisher's clerks were kept quite busy returning this money to those inquirers.

Other bedevilments emerged as Margaret saw that

The New York Times *thought* Gone with the Wind's *Pulitzer Prize worthy of front-page attention.*

even some trusted friends had surrendered her letters to them for publication, rudely violating her desire for personal privacy. The journalistic appetite for information about her had seemed to increase with the continued casting controversies in Hollywood. Author Faith Baldwin somehow inveigled a story during a visit to Atlanta and "The Woman Who Wrote *Gone with the Wind*: An Exclusive and Authentic Interview" appeared in the March 1937 issue of *Pictorial Review*. Peggy also allowed her friend Edwin Granberry to write "The Private Life of Margaret Mitchell" for a March edition of *Collier's* and even permitted a page of manuscript from a deleted *Gone with the Wind* chapter to be used as illustrative material. This decision, however, complicated her life further as it brought requests, demands and offers from universities, libraries and even from John Hay Whitney of Selznick International for the complete original. Margaret had previously allowed Macmillan to exhibit two pages from her "final" manuscript at *The New York Times'* National Book Fair. Then, to her irritation, she noted published comments in the media about her liberal pencil corrections—which she very rightly felt were no one's business. Because of all this, Margaret soon thereafter burned all notes, manuscript pages and galley proofs, saving only a small portion of each as proof of authorship if such ever be needed.

She experienced some pleasant surprises in 1937, though, such as receiving the American Booksellers Association's annual Award (later called the National Book Award). Then, on Monday evening May 3, 1937, a telegram was delivered to the Marsh home which read: "TAKE PLEASURE IN ADVISING YOU IN CONFIDENCE [OF] AWARD BY TRUSTEES OF COLUMBIA UNIVERSITY OF PULITZER PRIZE TO GONE WITH THE WIND. ANNOUNCEMENT [IN THE] PRESS TUESDAY MORNING. HEARTY CONGRATULATIONS!—FRANK D. FACKENTHAL, SECRETARY OF COLUMBIA UNIVERSITY." And Atlanta's reporters soon tracked the lady down at her father's house, where she agreed to pose for an "official" Pulitzer Prize photograph. *Gone with the Wind* had thus become the nineteenth novel to be honored in a series established in 1915 through the will of Joseph Pulitzer, publisher of *The New York World*. Prizes were bestowed annually for outstanding achievements in fiction, drama, history, biography, poetry and journalism by Columbia University on recommendation by the advisory board of the Pulitzer School of Journalism. Prizes were not deemed requisite for any year and there were years when no award was given in a specific category. Margaret Mitchell received a $1,000 award for "the most distinguished novel of the last year" and was in the company of playwrights George S. Kaufman and Moss Hart, who won the drama prize for *You Can't Take It with You*.

In early May the actual though not "official" first anniversary of *Gone with the Wind* was marked by sales of

Margaret Mitchell's official Pulitzer Prize photograph.

1,072,037 copies in the United States and 46,813 in Canada. Moreover, 112,686 Book-of-the-Month Club editions had been ordered and 44,691 copies were, by then, sold in Great Britain and British Commonwealth countries. In only a year 1,276,227 *Gone with the Wind*'s had brought Margaret Mitchell over $515,000 in royalties and given The Macmillan Company a profit of almost $117,000. The publisher's first-year accounting, of course, reflected deductions for its outlay in producing the book, as well as nearly $90,000 in advertising expenditures. Macmillan's long-range profit outlook (without those costs) looked even healthier and, in truth, over 138,000 more copies would be sold in the next year alone at that same three-dollar price.

Foreign editions of *Gone with the Wind* began to arrive at Margaret's home that spring but, due to copyright laws, only five of each were allowed into the country. Margaret kept a sample for herself and gave one from each country to her father, to the Atlanta Public Library, to Macmillan in New York and to that publisher's Atlanta branch. Although translations had been legally authorized in 1937 for Germany, Italy, Denmark, Norway, Finland and Sweden, a Dutch publisher boldly "pirated" the book in July. Margaret instituted legal proceedings immediately but learned that the United States had not signed a treaty which would include it in the Berne Convention and thus protect international copyrights for American authors. For several years to come, she would try by letter to influence congressmen in Washington to promote legislation which, though too late for her in this instance, could help others.

Margaret appealed in the same way to her fellow

authors as the case against the Holland book company grew more and more complicated. It seemed that a book would be automatically protected if simultaneously published in a country which was a Berne member, as Canada was. But, with some sleuthing, the Dutch publisher discovered that Macmillan of Canada had merely distributed *Gone with the Wind* copies that had been printed in America, with an alternate imprint—and it used that tack as its line of defense. Margaret's worst fear was that if this practice were allowed to continue, America's image could be distorted in a foreign country through unauthorized erroneous translations of books. This problem was particularly applicable to her own novel with the racial and Civil War reminders it presented.

There were other infringement matters closer than Holland, though, that summer, which might have escaped Peggy Marsh's notice had not *Life* magazine given the event major coverage. The city of Fort Worth, Texas, had engaged showman Billy Rose, at a salary of $100,000, to stage a one-hundred-day spectacular in a mammoth four-thousand-seat theatre café that featured a huge revolving stage. The extravaganza was entitled "Frontier Fiesta" and it highlighted dramatizations of scenes from four recent best sellers: *Lost Horizon, Wake Up and Live, It Can't Happen Here* and *Gone with the Wind*. Mr. Rose soon found himself involved in a lawsuit instituted by one Margaret Mitchell of Atlanta, Georgia, for violating her dramatic rights.

In a more humorous vein was the Hollywood contingent which descended upon Atlanta in late March, consisting of director-to-be George Cukor, assistant casting director John Darrow and Hobe Erwin, who was at that time to design *Gone with the Wind*'s sets. While future reports would refer to this expedition as a "search for Scarlett O'Hara," local men and women—regardless of professional background—were auditioned and interviewed as possible Rhetts, Melanies, Ashleys, Pittypats, Bonnies or Tarleton Twins. *The Atlanta Journal* observed the talent recruiting and assured local readers that there would be no blackface interpretations and that slaves would be portrayed by actual Southern black players. George Cukor admitted, in an interview in that paper, that there was only a bare chance of finding a Scarlett, Rhett or Melanie through these endeavors, but claimed they were sure to immediately recognize potential if they saw it. If they had no luck with these auditions, he rationalized that Hollywood stars would have to be the answer—although he expressed a fear about the dialect problem. George Cukor then praised the book's author as being a great help in taking the California group about the area and old homes than to any part of the talent son." Some observers recorded, however, that Mr. Cukor seemed to be paying far more attention to Georgian landscapes and old homes than to any part of the talent hunt. The "search" continued in other cities afterward—

keeping interest alive, reaping free publicity and, in one case, finding an extremely talented actress, Alicia Rhett. Charleston's Miss Rhett was later brought to Hollywood to test for the parts of Melanie and Carreen, and, although she would eventually play neither, *Gone with the Wind* was very much in her future.

One of the most popular new songs in 1937 America was, not too surprisingly, called "Gone with the Wind," with full credit for inspiration given to Margaret Mitchell's book. The tune—with music by Allie Wrubel and lyrics by Herb Magidson—was recorded simultaneously by Lennie Hayton and also by Dick Robertson on Decca Records, by Guy Lombardo on Victor and by Claude Thornhill on Vocalion. Most interesting was the version by Shep Fields on the Bluebird label, since it employed a song on the reverse side entitled "A Star is Born." The cover on the sheet music for "Gone with the Wind" was actually a replica of the book's own cover design, and that famous pale-yellow dust jacket with its delicate stripes had already become one of the most famous sights in the country.

David O. Selznick had already visualized opening his film version with that notable cover and its title, then progressing with the balance of *Gone with the Wind*'s credits on turning pages. David partially used that device (albeit with a film script) in *A Star is Born*. It was that film also which had given the producer's talent for writing an encore when he decided to retake its final scene. David wrote a new ending in which the heroine introduced herself at a Hollywood premiere by saying "This is Mrs.

A new song, inspired by the already famous book, swept the country in 1937 with sales of recordings and sheet music.

Norman Maine"—thus paying tribute to a man who had killed himself to save her career. This well-received sequence bolstered David's ego and made him all the more critical of Sidney Howard's scenario for *Gone with the Wind*.

Despite his initial pleasure with Mr. Howard's treatment, David could not decide what to keep, what to cut or what parts from the book to reinstate which Sidney had already eliminated. Finally he brought the playwright to Hollywood where they could agonize over it together. And while he had Sidney Howard in his clutches, he used both him and George Cukor for additional work on *The Prisoner of Zenda*, which had already employed the talents of two directors and several writers. When *The Prisoner of Zenda* premiered at the Radio City Music Hall, it introduced, at last, a trademark for Selznick International. The device was simple but majestically impressive: from a carved sign which read "A Selznick International Picture," the camera moved downward to show the facade of the studio's "Mount Vernon" administration headquarters. And composer Alfred Newman, who contributed *The Prisoner of Zenda*'s score, had utilized the sound of bells to signal a most interesting trademark fanfare. Mr. Newman had recently performed a similar chore for Twentieth Century-Fox, composing a trademark fanfare which highlighted drumrolls. Max Steiner would probably have drawn that enviable assignment for Selznick International if he had not just signed an exclusive contract to score the films of Warner Brothers.

Although David's—and M-G-M's—*A Tale of Two Cities* lost its bid for "Best Picture" honors at the Academy Awards, his own *The Garden of Allah* had been nominated for Max Steiner's musical score and had won a very inspiring "first"—a "Special" Academy Award for W. Howard Greene and Harold Rosson's color cinematography. Appreciative David Selznick was more certain than ever that he would film *Gone with the Wind* in Technicolor as well.

Margaret Mitchell had always suspected that the *Gone with the Wind* "talent search" was a little less than one hundred percent sincere. (She would have been even more dubious if she had known David Selznick's plans for *The Adventures of Tom Sawyer*. The producer had told Kay Brown, in regard to the Twain project, that "the greatest publicity story and Horatio Alger story in the history of the picture business would be our finding Tom Sawyer or Huck Finn in an orphan asylum.") Nevertheless, the casting nonsense reached unbelievable publicity heights in 1937, even without inspiration from Mr. Selznick. Margaret asked Kay Brown to let her in on any secret plans, since she hoped to see the cast puzzle solved as eagerly as she looked forward to the day when her book stopped selling. Miss Mitchell's new friendship with Kay Brown also led her to suggest that the Selznick people take Susan Myrick to California in some capacity when filming actually began.

Kay Brown was unable to give Margaret any hints. In fact, under executive orders, she was trying to keep some of the more outrageous casting rumors out of print. All the same, magazines and newspapers insisted on printing whatever struck their fancies. Harold Heffernan had probably started the ball rolling the past December by saying from Hollywood that "authoritative channels indicate clearly there is hardly a doubt" that Gable would play Rhett Butler and that the Scarlett contest was between Miriam Hopkins and Tallulah Bankhead. Then, in February, *The New Yorker* magazine kept the ball in play by publishing a cartoon which caricatured Mr. Gable's Rhett romancing Joan Crawford's Scarlett, with Franchot Tone's Ashley, Janet Gaynor's Melanie and Mae West's Belle Watling thrown in for good measure. Across the continent the *San Francisco News* entered the game with a feature story claiming most movie fans visualized Ronald Colman as Rhett and Miss Hopkins as Scarlett. *Photoplay*'s Cal York learned of "secret negotiations" and reported in the magazine's April issue that the "latest in the business of making *Gone with the Wind* is that Selznick International (which owns the story) and Metro-Goldwyn-Mayer (which has Clark Gable under contract) may join forces for this production. Metro refuses to loan Clark out, and Selznick realizes it can't cast anyone else as Rhett Butler." *Photoplay* even took it upon itself to publish an artist's conception of how Mr. Gable would look as Rhett and, in a subsequent issue, an original drawing of what a "Scarlett" might be like.

Gladys Hall in *Motion Picture* had gotten Ronald Colman to express a few thoughts on the subject of playing the part of Rhett Butler. "Whether I would play it or not, given the chance," Mr. Colman said, "would depend to a great extent on studio agreement as to the concept. . . . There is the Southern accent to be got around. That is important. Robert Montgomery played Rhett on the air, you know, and I have heard several Southerners say that his accent was remarkably right. I should say that, on the whole, the casting of Clark Gable as Rhett might meet with the approval of the greatest number of people. . . . Gary Cooper has been suggested, Basil Rathbone's name has come up and Preston Foster's in private discussions in the all-Hollywood game called 'Casting *Gone with the Wind*'."

The very first issue of *Cinema Arts*, an oversized monthly whose glossy contents cost 1937 readers fifty cents, featured a story by Richard Watts, Jr., called "Director's Dilemma," which proposed that the *Gone with the Wind* casting situation had suddenly become a matter of life or death for millions. The writer narrowed the race for Rhett to either Clark Gable or Fredric March, proposed either Jean Muir or Frances Dee as Melanie, but only Leslie Howard as Ashley. Mr. Watts then sympathized with producer Selznick's unique problem of offending some contingent no matter whom he cast and mentioned that even *Anthony Adverse* had not created a "great cinema-going cult in the fashion of *Gone with the Wind*." There was a reference to Mr. Selznick's thoughts on the value of "new faces" not interfering with readers' illusions and a mention of the recent Southern talent "auditions." Richard Watts then implied that everyone except Martha Raye and Shirley Temple was in the running for the Scarlett role and reminded his readers of support previously given in the press to Tallulah Bankhead, Miriam Hopkins, Irene Dunne, Joan Crawford, Carole Lombard and Jean Harlow. Later historians would single out this edition of the short-lived *Cinema Arts* as containing the first "feature" magazine article devoted entirely to the *Gone with the Wind* casting issue.

David Selznick needed even more sympathy than Richard Watts imagined. Despite the seemingly vast number of candidates, there were reasons—some of them tragic—why certain actors and actresses wouldn't continue in the race. Jean Harlow was stricken with uremia that very June and died only days later—in the midst of filming M-G-M's *Saratoga* with Clark Gable and Hattie McDaniel. There were simultaneous rumors that Miriam Hopkins had become "difficult" to work with and Miss Bankhead had already been discounted. Basil Rathbone, a superb character actor, held no major box-office value as a star and even Joan Crawford began experiencing box-office slippage in 1937. Irene Dunne was considered by many to be "too nice," while there were others who whispered that Ronald Colman was "too old."

Still, David Selznick continued his "filmed auditions" as he hired "candidates" Carole Lombard and Fredric March for his fifth production, *Nothing Sacred*. It was

interesting, too, that Miss Lombard and Mr. March were clients of David's agent brother Myron, as were so many of the other candidates often mentioned—Frances Dee, Katharine Hepburn, Miriam Hopkins, Jean Muir, Margaret Sullavan, Gary Cooper, Thomas Mitchell and Britain's Laurence Olivier. It was generally agreed, also, that *So Red the Rose* had put a permanent damper on ideas of using either Miss Sullavan or her co-star in that film, Randolph Scott.

Nothing Sacred, with a screenplay by Broadway's Ben Hecht, was a successful answer to John Hay Whitney's desire for Selznick International to produce a comedy and, as a Pioneer Picture, it was again a Technicolor production. But it marked the finale of Pioneer as a separate entity since a dispute afterward between David Selznick and Merian C. Cooper concerning a film with director John Ford led to Mr. Cooper's departure from Selznick International. Nevertheless, that did not stop active consideration of Mrs. Cooper, actress Dorothy Jordan, to play Melanie Hamilton. Miss Jordan, once an M-G-M contract player and later an RKO star, had retired after her marriage to Merian Cooper in 1933. As fate would have it, she never was to reactivate her career, despite this temporary temptation. Later in 1937 printed allegations appeared that Fredric March was a member of the Communist Party and his name was removed from further participation in the Rhett Butler contest.

That *Photoplay* report concerning Selznick International had not been without some basis in truth. David had indeed sounded out his father-in-law on the prospects of "borrowing" Clark Gable and discovered that the very least Louis B. Mayer would accept in return was distribution rights but more probably 50 percent of *Gone with the Wind*'s profits as well. A more reasonable offer had come, meanwhile, from the Warner Brothers studio in Burbank. Jack L. Warner proposed the loan of Bette Davis, Errol Flynn and Olivia de Havilland for the Scarlett, Rhett and Melanie roles in return for only 25 percent of the film's profits. For a while David was enthused about the Errol Flynn prospect, listing him—to his staff—third in preference to Clark Gable and Gary Cooper. Miss Davis, on the other hand, was not. After realizing that she might co-star with Mr. Gable, Mr. Cooper or Ronald Colman instead, the inexperienced Mr. Flynn seemed a poor substitute. Bette told her employers of her objection and, meanwhile, David Selznick's enthusiasm cooled. He was afraid that *Gone with the Wind* might become just "another Warner Brothers picture." And since he could make no agreement with any other studio until he had produced *eight* films for United Artists, he decided to go on looking.

No one was more surprised, shortly after, than Bette Davis when Warners bought the 1933 play *Jezebel* as a vehicle for her. She had suggested such a purchase several years before, but the studio had decided against

Photoplay *magazine selected Clark Gable as Rhett Butler in its October 1937 issue and then published a proposed sketch of Scarlett a month later.*

George Cukor's Camille *paired Greta Garbo with venerable character actress Laura Hope Crews.*

it because the Miriam Hopkins production on Broadway had been a quick failure. That drama was set in New Orleans a full eleven years before the Civil War began and climaxed with a yellow fever epidemic. But the selfish heroine's willful actions were thought by many to be so comparable to Scarlett O'Hara's as to make it obvious why the project was activated. David O. Selznick was not at all pleased with these plans, especially since Warners planned a large-budget production under the skilled direction of William Wyler. (Shortly afterward, director Wyler's personal future would be affected by a young starlet, Margaret Tallichet, who was just then under contract to Selznick International and often mentioned as a strong contender for the Scarlett O'Hara role.)

Although there had come a point in late March when David seemed to despair of ever getting Clark Gable, by November the producer's plans for studio affiliation seemed rather evident—his fury at the *Jezebel* resurrection having ended any chance for a Warner Brothers alliance. He instructed his staff to test players who were exclusively M-G-M contractees for various supporting parts. David's prime candidate, at this time, for Belle Watling was Gladys George, who had performed so well in Sam Wood's recent *Madame X* and was preparing to play Madame Du Barry in *Marie Antoinette*. Miss George, however, had health problems which would later remove her from consideration.

Of all the auditions and tests for *Gone with the Wind*, none took quite such *national* "priority" as that of Mrs. Elizabeth McDuffie, who tested in December for the part of Mammy. In addition to her acting aspirations, Mrs. McDuffie happened to be Eleanor Roosevelt's White House maid. Back in Hollywood, David had hopes that Janet Gaynor, the very first

Academy Award winner, might be induced to play Melanie Hamilton. He had placed Miss Gaynor under contract after *A Star Is Born*, but Janet felt that she might risk her star stature by accepting anything less than "first billing," and her salary requirements were higher than he would have liked—considering the price that might be required for a Rhett Butler. Olivia de Havilland had been another early inspiration and her name had made the Warner Brothers offer quite attractive. Even then, Miss de Havilland was appearing with Leslie Howard—a popular choice for Ashley—and Bette Davis in *It's Love I'm After*. Humorously, that Warner comedy gave Leslie Howard dialogue in which he asked Olivia, "Who's Clark Gable?"

M-G-M's Mr. Gable might indeed have wished for some anonymity since, in addition to his unwilling involvement in the casting issue, he suffered dismal critical reception with *Parnell*, a "costume" picture of the type the actor always felt uncomfortable in. Then, as new child singer Judy Garland's recording "Dear Mr. Gable, You Made Me Love You" was blaring from the country's radios and phonographs, Clark's year concluded with his being crowned "King" to Myrna Loy's "Queen" before a "live" and radio audience in Hollywood—the results of a newspaper syndicate's poll of readers.

George Cukor's stock had also risen even further with the January release of his *Camille*, containing probably the finest of Greta Garbo's many luminous screen portrayals. Both he and David Selznick were aware of how great a contribution had been made to the ensemble playing of Miss Garbo and Robert Taylor in that film by veteran character actress Laura Hope Crews. And even though Samuel Goldwyn's publicists stressed that forty-eight famous screen actresses had "tested" for the title role in *Stella Dallas* before the casting of Barbara Stanwyck, the Selznick team took special note of the performance of Barbara O'Neil in her film debut as the "second Mrs. Dallas." Another Goldwyn film, *The Hurricane*, had provided actor Thomas Mitchell with a role many felt worthy of an Academy Award. It also inspired radio's Gracie Allen to predict that *Gone with the Wind* would be *The Hurricane*'s sequel.

But aside from casting, there were myriad other matters to be considered before *Gone with the Wind* could become a completely active project. David had hired noted art director William Cameron Menzies, a client of Myron's, for special work on *Tom Sawyer* and then further engaged him to design and, in fact, serve as architect for *Gone with the Wind*'s entire production, including crucial camera angles and lighting. This valuable man would actually produce a complete script in sketch form, saving Selznick International a small fortune when production was able to begin.

Next, David asked United Artists' sales managers to investigate the possibility of making *Gone with the Wind* into two separate pictures, the second beginning with Scarlett's New Orleans honeymoon with Rhett. A very preliminary budget of $1,500,000 had meanwhile been determined for the entire story as one film, based on Sidney Howard's script—a treatment David was still unable to acept as final. Along with George Cukor, David traveled to New York in early fall to confer with Mr. Howard again—just as Sidney was in the midst of rehearsing his new play *The Ghost of Yankee Doodle*.

Mr. Selznick had employed RKO's Walter Plunkett, who had achieved an excellent reputation for "period" pictures, as *Gone with the Wind*'s costume designer and, in addition, assigned him wardrobe duties for both *Nothing Sacred* and *The Adventures of Tom Sawyer*. The latter production had been in research stages since April of 1936 and would, David hoped, be in the tradition of other great books he had transferred to the screen. Walter Plunkett meanwhile made a research trip to Atlanta to acquaint himself with authentic Civil War clothing and fabrics. Margaret Mitchell proved a willing ally to Walter, accompanying him on local jaunts and advising him how to make contacts. He would later recall that Margaret showed him several homes in the country around Atlanta and said Tara was a composite of them all, not a real location.

What position in all this *Gone with the Wind* madness did actress Katharine Hepburn play? The young Academy Award winner had started her screen career working for both David Selznick and George Cukor in 1932's *A Bill of Divorcement* and had been mentioned often as their "dark horse" Scarlett candidate. In truth, Miss Hepburn was enacting the role of "stand-by" for those gentlemen, although the general public never knew it until thirty-seven years later when she humorously recounted the events on the Dick Cavett Show.

The book was sent to her first by the publisher, Miss Hepburn remembered, and she gave it to someone who was at the head of RKO. They read it and said it was not a sympathetic part for Kate. Then when Selznick bought it, it was going to be directed by her great friend George Cukor, who again thought that it was wrong for her. Then, after they had looked for two years, George thought it was right for her and it was at this point that her career had the most dismal failure and she had gone from offers of $150,000 and a percentage and a piece of everything down to $10,000 for a picture—or no offers at all! In six weeks her career dropped—backfired—just before she did *The Philadelphia Story*.

Katharine then recalled her position of "stand-by.": David Selznick sent for her and he said, "We'd like you to do a test." Katharine said, "Now David, you brought me into the business—you and George—and I'm not going to do a test. You know how I'd play it. And you've gone

out on a limb to find an unknown girl—and you can't tell me you're going to be stupid enough not to find one! So, let us say this, if you get within two days of shooting . . . and the man who's doing the costumes has dressed me many times—Walter Plunkett—he could do the first dress in forty-eight hours . . . you send for me." He said, "I have to start the picture by a certain time." "You send for me," Katharine repeated to David. "You wouldn't have to pay me anything—and I know you well enough to know you *wouldn't* pay me anything."

Katharine Hepburn also remembered cautioning David against making any premature press announcements concerning her possible casting, which could be refuted later if he did find his "unknown." That would break her heart, she told him, and she had to protect herself from incidents which would destroy her. And she didn't want to have it announced . . . and then sort of—whatever happened to Katharine Hepburn?

Meanwhile, crises throughout the world seethed even further in 1937 with increased violence and tension exhibited in Germany, Spain, Italy and in Japan's attacks upon China, while the United States held fast to a policy of "non-intervention." But in England it was a time for rejoicing with the coronation of a new King and Queen, George VI and his wife, Elizabeth. And in that year of celebration actress Vivien Leigh's career took a major surge upward.

Vivien was well aware that segments of the American public were supporting English actors Ronald Colman, Leslie Howard and Basil Rathbone for *Gone with the Wind* roles and therefore saw no reason why she

Katharine Hepburn, a friend of David O. Selznick and George Cukor, was their longtime "Scarlett stand-by."

shouldn't make a try for Scarlett. Fortunately, Miss Leigh's agent, E. G. "Harry" Ham, was the London representative of the Myron Selznick talent agency, so it was not difficult to have her name submitted that February to the New York office of Selznick International shortly before her film, *Fire Over England*, premiered at that city's Music Hall theatre. The Korda production, which teamed Vivien with Laurence Olivier, had provided her with a good supporting role and she hoped this, her best film exposure to date, would make an impression for her in America. Kay Brown relayed Vivien's name to David Selznick in Hollywood but the producer merely replied, "I have no enthusiasm for Vivien Leigh. Maybe I will have, but as yet have never even seen a photograph of her. Will be seeing *Fire Over England* shortly, at which time will, of course, see Leigh."

Vivien Leigh would not remain an unknown quantity to David Selznick for long, however, as she continued to undergo a "star-building" campaign that year, promoted by her employer, Alexander Korda. Mr. Korda and Mr. Selznick, in fact, along with director Frank Capra, would even enter into a tentative 1937 Hollywood partnership in hopes of purchasing United Artists. The proposal stalemated, however, when neither producer would relinquish his desire to be the new president of that distribution company. David had been completely aware of Mr. Korda's shrewd guidance of his stars since he had paid a tidy cash penalty the previous year for breaking a contract with another Alexander Korda discovery, Merle Oberon, to play the lead in *The Garden of Allah*. The casting of a British girl as Scarlett O'Hara seemed a very remote possibility to David Selznick at that particular time.

Despite Mr. Selznick's indifference to her, Vivien Leigh was hardly set back since her schedule that spring and summer was extremely active. In adition to three film roles in Korda productions, she graced the English stage in the short-lived *Because We Must* and, on opening night, presented her co-workers with copies of her favorite new American novel. The filming of *The First and the Last* with Laurence Olivier coincided with an invited appearance in June to Denmark's historic Kronberg Castle at Elsinore, where she played Ophelia to Mr. Olivier's *Hamlet*. It was evident to those around them at the time that these two vital, talented and attractive people had been emotionally drawn together and that their respective mariages would soon end to enable a permanent union to flourish between them.

That summer the Korda enterprise arranged an opportune film assignment for Vivien that would greatly enhance her reputation outside England. The perilous state of the British economy had placed restrictions on both the export of money and the import of foreign motion pictures. One out of every five features distributed in England by a movie company had to be made domestically. To solve this quota problem, and also to utilize its revenues which were frozen in Great Britain, Metro-Goldwyn-Mayer opened its own producing studio there in the summer of 1937. British restrictions also limited the American personnel working on English-made films, so *A Yank at Oxford* was a project to enlist only Robert Taylor, Lionel Barrymore and director Jack Conway from the American headquarters. Luckily, M-G-M contract player Maureen O'Sullivan was from Ireland and, ironically, it was her former schoolmate, Vivien Leigh, who was hired as the second female lead. Later on, it was reported, Louis B. Mayer—on a trip abroad during which he discovered Greer Garson and Hedy Lamarr—raised heavy objections while visiting *A Yank at Oxford*'s set that the "unknown" Miss Leigh commanded such a high salary for her work in the film. Unbeknownst to Mr. Mayer, Americans were just then becoming familiar with the lady's talent, and *The New York Times*, in a review of Korda's *Dark Journey*, called her "England's most charming screen actress." The latter film's director, Victor Saville, would soon be named chief of M-G-M's British studio and then travel to its Hollywood domain, remaining a powerful ally in Miss Leigh's future.

Twenty-nine years after *A Yank at Oxford* was filmed, its star, Robert Taylor, reminisced in an article he wrote for *Variety*: "One of the most beautiful and talented ladies ever to grace a motion picture screen— Vivien Leigh. How well I remember one day between scenes on *A Yank at Oxford* her asking me, in a most interested manner, what an American 'Southern accent' sounded like. . . . I couldn't help wondering if, even then, she wasn't rehearsing. . . ."

Once upon a time . . . there was a very determined young lady from England who had her heart set on playing Scarlett O'Hara.

1938: An English "Rose"

"Don't you let them change any history in my book. I'm very proud of it," were the confidential instructions Margaret Mitchell issued to her friend Wilbur Kurtz as he embarked on a secret journey to California in January 1938. "If they want to let Scarlett marry General Sherman," she pleaded, "that's all right with me. I don't care too much what they do to the story. But don't you let them change my history."

Selznick International had, it seemed, finally taken Miss Mitchell's year-old advice and hired Mr. Kurtz for a three-week assignment to profit from his historical knowledge in regard to the Sidney Howard film script and William Cameron Menzies' proposed designs. Just when so many were beginning to despair that *Gone with the Wind* was a project that would never get off the ground, it was very much in active preproduction stages at the Culver City studio in early 1938. Mr. Howard had tightened his script to 239 pages to please David Selznick, who still agonized over the film's length, and Mr. Menzies had developed more than a hundred watercolor sketches from which the art and budget departments could determine cost estimates. Walter Plunkett had completed extensive costume designs before taking a European vacation, and Hal Kern had been engaged as film editor to offer valuable suggestions for keeping the running time sensible. James Wong Howe was tentatively promised photography duties, and a young Southern dialogue director, Will Price, trained acting candidates for their auditions. Selznick's research department employees were indexing dialogue, backgrounds and properties needed directly from the novel and, upon his arrival, Mr. Kurtz was asked to review the script, sketches and proposed props for anachronisms. Wilbur also drew his own blueprints for difficult assemblages and made lists of antique trivia which he might find back in Georgia. When he departed, Wilbur Kurtz was assured that he would be recalled when actual filming began. Meanwhile, rather than remain idle, George Cukor had accepted an assignment at Columbia Pictures to direct Katharine Hepburn in *Holiday*.

Auditions were going full force on the Selznick lot as all Hollywood studios sent their newer contract players there in hopes of reaping a portion of the *Gone with the Wind* bonanza. RKO volunteered Joan Fontaine, who was Olivia de Havilland's younger sister, and redheaded starlet Lucille Ball. Miss Fontaine made a good enough impression to be remembered importantly by both George Cukor and David Selznick in the future. And Miss Ball began rehearsing her lines alone as she knelt by a coffee table—not realizing until her audition was

over that she had never risen from that position. Meanwhile, Paulette Goddard, so striking in Chaplin's *Modern Times*, was signed to a rare personal contract by Mr. Selznick and immediately prepared to test for the role of Scarlett.

Actual screen tests were photographed silently with black and white, not color, film for economy's sake and, whenever possible, a former performance would be viewed instead—to judge if a screen test were even feasible. Far fewer filmed tests were made than columnists and Russell Birdwell's staff would have had the public believe, since most candidates never got beyond reading lines for an audition. Only if a filmed candidate looked particularly promising would that player be requested to film another test, the second time most likely with sound equipment. Published reports on February 3 that Paulette Goddard had been cast as Scarlett were not taken too seriously by anyone familiar

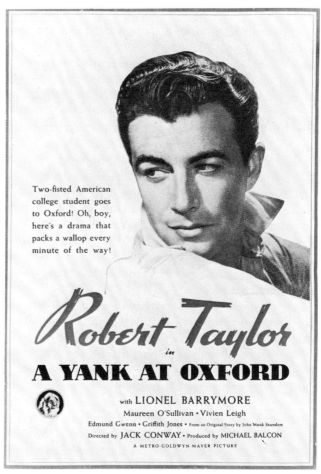

Two-fisted American college student goes to Oxford! Oh, boy, here's a drama that packs a wallop every minute of the way!

Robert Taylor
in
A YANK AT OXFORD

with LIONEL BARRYMORE
Maureen O'Sullivan · Vivien Leigh
Edmund Gwenn · Griffith Jones · From an Original Story by John Monk Saunders
Directed by JACK CONWAY · Produced by MICHAEL BALCON
A METRO-GOLDWYN-MAYER PICTURE

Vivien Leigh's performance in A Yank at Oxford *was far more noticeable than her official M-G-M billing.*

with the goings on, but she was one of the few at the time to receive two successive screen tests in varying makeup, her second being completed on February 11.

Only five days later David Selznick saw an M-G-M screening of *A Yank at Oxford* and realized exactly why Alexander Korda was so intent on making Vivien Leigh a star. Her striking performance as a coquettish, unfaithful wife and her natural and overpowering beauty sowed a seed in David's mind that was to become the most closely guarded secret of his filmmaking career. It wouldn't be, actually, until after his death twenty-seven years later that his personal effects would uncover a masterful public deception. These effects yielded a privately owned print of *A Yank at Oxford*, rental receipts for all of Miss Leigh's British films and various photographs of her—all date-stamped between February and August of 1938. His confidential correspondence of that time included a thank-you to M-G-M for the print of Miss Leigh's film and discussions with Myron Selznick asking that his client, Laurence Olivier, postpone divorce proceedings until after *Gone with the Wind* began.

Not too coincidentally, considering her agent's link with Myron Selznick, there was a suggestion then at David's studio proposing Vivien for a part in *The Gay Banditti*, scheduled to start quite soon. Since the story involved an English family, it seemed sensible for London's Harry Ham to suggest his client. Miss Leigh, of course, desperately wanted the opportunity to work for the American producer. David decided against using Vivien then, feeling such exposure could detract from her relatively "unknown" stature in America. But his most guarded correspondence later showed that from February on Vivien Leigh had the inside track to play Scarlett O'Hara. Mr. Selznick began negotiations with Alexander Korda to secure her services for a commitment later that year and found the overseas movie man was not immediately receptive to the idea. However, Vivien was informed of the Selznick interest, sworn to secrecy and told that a screen test was not presently necessary since David Selznick could view her previous films instead.

For the moment David was confronted with an even more pressing problem—a Rhett Butler! Negotiations with M-G-M for Clark Gable were still completely viable, but dealing with Louis B. Mayer, he knew, would command a heavy price—and more of a loss to United Artists than to anyone else. He made a final appeal to Samuel Goldwyn, as a principal in United Artists, for the loan of Gary Cooper, but when Mr. Goldwyn remained noncommittal, David was forced to visit his father-in-law, who was waiting with open arms.

Gone with the Wind finally did fall off America's best-seller lists in March 1938 and Margaret Mitchell thanked God! Now it was time for other fine books like *The Yearling* by Southerner Marjorie Kinnan Rawlings, *Rebecca* by Daphne du Maurier, *The Rains Came* by Louis Bromfield, *Northwest Passage* by Kenneth Roberts or *The Citadel* by A. J. Cronin to capture their rightful place in the year's sales spotlight. And it was a surprise to no one that all those novels were immeately purchased by movie studios. It seemed Peggy and John Marsh could finally get their wish for peace as the volume of incoming mail and visiting tourists slowed down and reporters no longer lay in wait to catch their every move. Now, Margaret felt, it was possible to watch the foreign progress of her novel comfortably, and to possibly appreciate the whole phenomenon. Macmillan informed her, after the book's forty-first printing in February, that the company had no immediate plans for future orders. By May Margaret had earned an additional $90,000 in royalties and was more than satisfied to let it remain at that.

She looked forward to receiving samples of the editions published that year in Czechoslovakia, Hungary and Latvia, and there was even time to study the mountains of clippings and memorabilia her book had inspired. There had been countless cartoons and merchandising ads utilizing either her title or characters. Designer Hattie Carnegie of New York, for example, advertised "Scarlett might have worn this glamorous gown," while *Women's Wear Daily* suggested that retailers use "Scarlett green" as a promotional gimmick. There were the popular "Scarlett O'Hara bonnets"—considered stylish but which Margaret hated—and an interior decorator in New York requested permission to sell *Gone with the Wind* wallpaper. New York's Bonwit Teller's had employed layout copy which read, "Southern Belle sensation—latest development in our series of highly romantic Civil War fashions dedicated, with a bow, to *Gone with the Wind*." And an eye specialist from that city had told potential customers that it was "A truly remarkable book—but impossible to fully appreciate and enjoy if your eyes are not in perfect condition." There were bookends, perfume decanters and statuettes modeled after Scarlett and Rhett along with a "Scarlett O'Hara Morning Glory" which had won a gold medal from the All American Seed Selection Society.

Wilbur Kurtz's Western journey provided some humorous side effects as news that an Atlantan had traveled to Hollywood inspired a new batch of national rumors which insisted that the person was Margaret Mitchell herself, that she was engaged in the filmmaking and would write a sequel while there, and that she was really the one who would play Scarlett. Somewhat less amusing to Miss Mitchell were current references to her as "the Atlanta midget." But even though the Dutch "piracy" case dragged on and seemed to go nowhere, Margaret's business pride was satisfied when the Billy

Rose affair was settled, with that showman sending her $3,000 and an apology. She had even thought of a solution to the continual questioners or debaters she encountered on the casting issue. Placing her tongue firmly in her cheek, she innocently suggested that Selznick International would be delighted to hear these people's views.

The Selznick studio had long been prepared for this type of mail, however, and answered it with a very sincere form letter which actually revealed nothing at all:

SELZNICK INTERNATIONAL PICTURES, INC.
9336 WASHINGTON BOULEVARD   CULVER CITY, CALIFORNIA

Dear ———

Thank you for your letter on GONE WITH THE WIND. We are grateful for such expressions from the public as yours, and it is our earnest desire to be guided as much as possible by the public's wishes.

When you eventually see the picture on the screen, please keep in mind these two facts: First, that with such a wide difference of opinion among enthusiasts of the book, we cannot hope to make everyone happy with the final choice; and, second, that most stars are under exclusive contract to different studios. To show the reverence with which we treat important original material and the accuracy with which we attempt to cast, we refer you to our productions of LITTLE LORD FAUNTLEROY, THE PRISONER OF ZENDA, THE ADVENTURES OF TOM SAWYER, ETC.

Please be assured that your suggestions will have the most careful consideration and that your interest is greatly appreciated.

Your very truly,

(signed)
Charles Richards,
Casting Director

At the tenth annual Academy Awards ceremonies that March, David Selznick's *A Star Is Born* had been honored with an almost unprecedented seven nominations for production, actress, actor, director, assistant director and two writing categories. And *A Star Is Born* brought Selznick International its second consecutive Award for Technicolor photography, a special honor "recommended by a committee of leading cinematographers after viewing all the color pictures made during the year." It was an even more personal tribute to David's writing talents when the film won a statuette for "Best Original Story." After accepting the golden token—by then nicknamed "Oscar"—William Wellman turned to David and said, "You ought to get this—you wrote more of it than I did." A very special Academy Award had been inaugurated that year in memory of

Irving Thalberg—and bearing his name—to honor producers for a consistent level of quality. The first enviable recipient was Darryl F. Zanuck.

David also noted with interest that Awards evening how Victor Fleming's direction of M-G-M's *Captains Courageous* had helped Spencer Tracy to win the "Best Actor" trophy and guided the film itself to a "Best Picture" nomination. Mr. Fleming, long known as a dependable Hollywood craftsman, was suddenly gaining a reputation for work on "quality" films. His *Test Pilot*, which featured Mr. Tracy, "King" Clark Gable and "Queen" Myrna Loy, was already rumored to be a big success and the director had even been able, in that film, to induce the manly Mr. Gable to shed tears—not once, but in three separate scenes. Additionally, M-G-M had recently called Victor in as a replacement to helm some difficult scenes in their expensive musical, *The Great Waltz*.

As far as his own studio product was concerned, the anxiously awaited release of *The Adventures of Tom Sawyer* brought David a bit of a jolt. In the midst of continued *Gone with the Wind* casting controversies, *The New York Times* opined that *Tom Sawyer* "suggests that most of the temporal budget in this case was

Warner's Jezebel *brought Bette Davis a second Academy Award but eliminated her from "the search for Scarlett."*

spent on the comparative luxury of talent hunting." To add further insult, the reviewer questioned, "Is it Mark Twain we have been led to anticipate or Mack Sennett?"

When Warners' *Jezebel* pursued *Tom Sawyer* into the Radio City Music Hall a few weeks later, that same paper felt it necessary to mention in its review "a Southern cycle is in the offing, where it has been since Mr. Selznick started looking for Scarlett." Any such comparisons to that picture infuriated David since, although he admired the film's quality, he felt it had only been produced to commercialize on his own upcoming epic. Although Margaret Mitchell admitted she liked *Jezebel* and insisted no one had a copyright on the "Old South," David was incensed by Warner advertising and publicity, which carried repeated echoes of *Gone with the Wind*.

He was even less enchanted when a *Liberty* magazine story entitled "Jezebel's Revenge" insinuated that Bette Davis had been ruled out as Scarlett only because George Cukor had fired her from a Broadway play nine years before. In what appeared to be a "last-ditch" journalistic appeal to give Bette that part, the magazine's writer insulted both David and George by saying, "What does it [*Jezebel*] do to producer Selznick's dreams re *Gone with the Wind*? Will it be put on the shelf for another two years? Does the man who is to direct the most highly prized motion picture plum in recent years find himself holding the bag with *the Wind* gone out of it . . . ?" In truth, the release of *Jezebel* seemed forever to end any possibility that Bette Davis might play Scarlett O'Hara.

Placing *The Gay Banditti* into production with its new title, *The Young in Heart*, had served a triple purpose for David O. Selznick and his studio. It provided a seventh—and next to last—obligatory picture for United Artists, kept overhead down with its modest budget and black-and-white photography and "auditioned" a whole cast of players David was considering for various *Gone with the Wind* roles—Janet Gaynor, Douglas Fairbanks, Jr., Paulette Goddard, Billie Burke and newcomer Richard Carlson. With only one more celluloid effort owed to his present distributor, David hoped his father-in-law might demand *only* distribution rights in return for Clark Gable. The shrewd Mr. Mayer, however, had

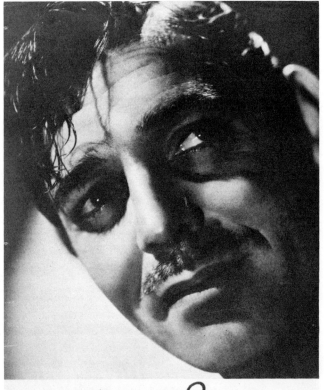

The great Rhett Butler-Scarlett O'Hara controversy appears to be over at last, with Clark Gable (above), and Norma Shearer (at right, as "Marie Antoinette"), announced for those much-coveted roles in "Gone With the Wind"!

In September 1938 Screen Guide *Magazine told its readers that Norma Shearer and Clark Gable had won the leads in* Gone with the Wind.

complete faith in his son-in-law's abilities and at first offered to buy the *Gone with the Wind* property outright, including David's own services as producer. When John Hay Whitney refused that offer, Louis B. Mayer countered with an even more demanding one—Gable plus half of the film's budget of $2,500,000 would be donated in exchange for 50 percent of the profits going to M-G-M with distribution to be credited to Loew's, Inc., the parent company. Loew's would also receive remuneration in the form of 15 percent of the film's total gross. Tired of delays and annoyed by derisive Hollywoodites who swore the film would never be made, David accepted.

Feeling it was his duty to inform the author immediately, Mr. Selznick sent word to Atlanta that *Gone with the Wind* would be in production "positively between now and December." The M-G-M agreement was to remain confidential until Selznick International was able to put its eighth film into production, with which it would fulfill the obligations of that 1935 contract. At any time thereafter *Gone with the Wind* would be free to start. However, M-G-M needed immediate publicity for a very risky venture which it was about to reveal to the public.

Only days before the world premiere of Norma Shearer's return to the screen in *Marie Antoinette*, M-G-M studio publicists released a news break that Miss Shearer and Clark Gable had been selected by David O. Selznick to play the leads in Margaret Mitchell's epic. It was not too sensible, in retrospect, for those publicity folk to have circulated photographs of Miss Shearer from her new film—elegantly gowned and wigged—to advertise her as the Scarlett O'Hara who had been reduced to wretched poverty by the Civil War. A completely new controversy broke out in the press over this "final" casting, with Louella Parsons dutifully reporting to her readers that Norma planned to resolve the difference in images by asking David Selznick to rewrite the entire second portion of the *Gone with the Wind* script to make Scarlett O'Hara more sympathetic. This bulletin was about as accurate as a similar Parsons report of the time which had Sigmund Freud traveling to Hollywood to act as technical advisor for Warner Brothers' *Dark Victory*.

Unfortunately for Margaret Mitchell, the news release broke just as she was innocently visiting New York City and that town's reporters plagued her with questions about the proposed script changes for which the startled author had absolutely no reply. While in New York, Margaret finally managed something she had hoped to do as soon as the "fever" showed signs of subsiding—something that would be remembered at The Macmillan Company until each of its present employees had retired and that would remain a publishing legend. She visited the 60 Fifth Avenue offices where her novel

had been published and personally shook hands with and thanked every person on all six floors for helping make her book a success.

The "Shearer controversy" did not upset Margaret at all since she had never cared who played Scarlett or Rhett, feeling any competent performers would do nicely. But she was truly alarmed at another rumor concerning George Cukor, a man she regarded as brilliant and whom she had liked and respected on his visit to Atlanta. With her book in Mr. Cukor's hands, Margaret had always felt secure since she expressed complete faith in his judgment. This rumor, unfortunately, did have some basis in truth. David Selznick had become unhappy that George Cukor was not more receptive to accepting other Selznick assignments while awaiting the start of *Gone with the Wind*, even though he had remained on salary since early 1937 at $4,000 a week. Mr. Selznick even flirted with the idea of replacing George with Victor Fleming, who had shown such a fine track record that past spring.

Norma Shearer, meanwhile, had actually been indifferent about whether she played Scarlett O'Hara or not. Norma portrayed a teenager in *Romeo and Juliet* successfully enough two years before to win an Academy Award nomination, but agreed to this new casting ploy more or less as a favor to her friend David Selznick—if he could find no "newcomer"—and because of her vested interest in Metro-Goldwyn-Mayer. The "announcement" had been made primarily as publicity to help offset the financial risk of Miss Shearer's return venture, which had cost

Margaret Mitchell's book was sent on a trip to the future with the time capsule buried in New York in 1938.

Actress Susan Hayward was fated to be a "reel-life" Scarlett O'Hara throughout her illustrious screen career.

M-G-M $1,800,000 and employed a dangerously long running time. It could also do no harm as advance publicity for *Idiot's Delight*, Robert E. Sherwood's Pulitzer Prize play, which M-G-M was about to begin with Norma Shearer and Clark Gable in the leading roles. Only a month later it was revealed that "public protests" had forced Norma Shearer to permanently withdraw her offer to play Scarlett. "The one I'd like to play is Rhett," the lady humorously quipped to reporters.

Made for Each Other, starring Carole Lombard and M-G-M's James Stewart, began production in late August, and with the start of his studio's eighth film David Selznick was free to publicly announce that Clark Gable would play Rhett Butler. Contract-signing pictures of the actor with both Mr. Selznick and Louis B. Mayer were released to the press on August 25, assuring Americans that Margaret Mitchell's story was on its way to the silver screen.

As the innocent pawn in these dragged-out proceedings, Clark Gable had rarely been consulted as to his personal feelings in the matter. In truth, he looked upon the *Gone with the Wind* phenomenon with about as much enthusiasm as Margaret Mitchell did—and with as much trepidation. The actor later told writer Pete Martin: "It struck me that the public's casting was being guided by an elaborate publicity campaign. . . . People didn't just read it [*GWTW*], they lived it. They formed passionate convictions about its characters. . . . One thing was

certain: they had a preconceived idea of the kind of Rhett Butler they were going to see. Suppose I came up empty? . . . It was a challenge. I enjoyed it from that point of view." Much speculation would later be offered that Clark needed *Gone with the Wind*'s bonus money to settle divorce proceedings, which would free him to marry Carole Lombard. Actually, as an M-G-M contract player —and a highly professional one—he was in no position to refuse any role assigned to him.

While David Selznick promised United Artists' management that he would certainly return to their fold with his future films, he simultaneously assured his studio staff that *Gone with the Wind* would remain their own production. With financing settled, David authorized model set construction and costume manufacture to begin, with all costs to be accrued against the official production charge number of *Gone with the Wind*—"S.I.P. #108!" Filming was slated to begin "somewhere between November 15 and January 15," depending on Clark Gable's completion of *Idiot's Delight* and the fulfillment of other casting requirements. George Cukor, in the meantime, accepted an outside assignment at Paramount Pictures to direct Claudette Colbert in *Zaza*.

At a time when full-scale war in Europe seemed inevitable and Hitler's persecution of German Jews drew condemnation throughout the free world, Margaret Mitchell was grateful to be off the front pages. Yet she was singularly touched to have her work included in a message sent to posterity from a civilization facing one of its greatest crises. On Friday, September 23, 1938, a "5,000-Year Time Capsule," quoted as "containing a condensed record of present day civilization for inhabitants of the earth in the year 6939," was deposited in an Eternal Well in Flushing Meadows, New York, on the grounds of the soon-to-open 1939 World's Fair. Holding more than one hundred items to represent a cross-section of life in 1938, the capsule would eventually yield a woman's hat, a Mickey Mouse plastic cup, an alarm clock, coins, fabrics and a fifteen-minute newsreel with scenes of President Roosevelt, athlete Jesse Owens and a preview of that upcoming World's Fair. Additionally, microfilm enclosures in the capsule incorporated more than 10,000,000 words and 1,000 pictures, which highlighted prayers, magazines, dictionaries and two complete novels—*Arrowsmith* by Sinclair Lewis and *Gone with the Wind* by Margaret Mitchell.

But Margaret's long-awaited peace proved short-lived as the fall season brought her renewed press attention, controversies and business dealings. After trying for two and a half years to keep a low profile, she now saw herself nominated by *Scribner's* magazine as one of "The Most Overrated People in America" for a contest designed to amuse its readers. (At least she was in the impressive company of Tallulah Bankhead, Jack Benny and Eleanor Roosevelt!) Then, when Clare Boothe's *Kiss the*

Boys Goodbye opened on Broadway in September, it unveiled a quite obvious parody in depicting an Alabama girl who aspired to win the movie role of "Velvet O'Toole."

Despite the publicity, it was a truly appreciated gesture in late October when the Southeastern Library Association voted Margaret the Carl Bohnenberger Memorial Medal for "the most outstanding contribution to Southern Literature" in the previous two years. But she did not appreciate, a few days later, the announcement in a New York newspaper that her innocent remark of how well Katharine Hepburn looked in *Little Women*'s hoopskirts was actually an endorsement for that actress to play Scarlett O'Hara. Then, on November 1, Macmillan published a "limited cheap edition" of *Gone with the Wind*—priced at $1.49—and a new deluge of publicity arose as buyers, rejuvenated by the movie publicity, flocked in droves to purchase the entire stock of 338,000 printed copies.

The historical-novel rage was again providential for The Macmillan Company when it published Rachel Field's *All This and Heaven Too* at the same time. Miss Field's excellently reviewed book became an instant best seller and Warner Brothers purchased movie rights soon afterward with plans of imitating *Gone with the Wind* through a massive publicity buildup. As far as her own book's imminent movie start was concerned, Margaret was encouraged when Wilbur Kurtz was asked to return to California by December and her friend Susan Myrick was likewise retained by Selznick International to give the cast instructions in Southern manners and diction. However, Margaret now encountered a nemesis far greater than any she had endured before—Metro-Goldwyn-Mayer's Publicity Department! With no basis whatsoever in fact, this new crew planted press items quoting Margaret in every way imaginable concerning the picture, which, for a while, stunned the lady author into total silence. Despite her rigid determination to keep her life private and let her novel speak for itself, Margaret kept forgetting that she had become a "star" in an era when the public expected and demanded intimate knowledge of its idols—at whatever cost to them.

The Selznick casting dilemma continued! Still very impressed with Olivia de Havilland as a Melanie, David noted that the Warner family thought well enough of the actress to feature her in two of their only four Technicolor features that year—a rarity for any performer at the time. Miss de Haviland photographed beautifully in that process, which was not necessarily kind to those it came in contact with. But the Burbank brothers remained steadfast in refusing to lend Olivia's services to another studio. Instead, they dangled almost their entire list of younger contractees before the Selznick eyes, hopeful of a career boost for any of them. Warners' Humphrey Bogart, Ann Sheridan, Priscilla Lane, Jane Bryan, Jeffrey

Lynn and Geraldine Fitzgerald were freely offered as was young Susan Hayward, whom the Warner regime had decided to dismiss after minor appearances in six of their films.

Miss Hayward's story was quite unique. Not unlike Margaret Mitchell, she would always remain silent about her early life and career, although later legends attributed her discovery to Irene Mayer Selznick and George Cukor. Mrs. Selznick and Mr. Cukor, it was said, noticed the girl—whose name was then Edythe Marrener—while on a talent-scouting trip to New York, where Edythe was a model. They arranged for her to travel to Hollywood to compete for the Scarlett O'Hara role, and upon her arrival, the girl secured a contract and a new name from Warner Brothers. In the fall of 1938 she *did* receive the opportunity to film a test for *Gone with the Wind* and David Selznick then kept her on his payroll for a while to do stand-in work and to test with other candidates. But in mid-November, David gave the girl a fatherly talk, telling her to "go home" and study acting further.

Susan decided against Mr. Selznick's advice and, within months, was employed at Paramount, where she would soon make a noticeable impression in *Beau Geste*. For more than three decades afterward Susan Hayward continued to perfect her remarkably individual acting technique, winning four Academy Award nominations plus the Award itself along the way. Strangely, the redheaded Susan—more than any other actress fated to enjoy screen success—typified the Scarlett O'Hara tem-

Ann Rutherford, Lana Turner and Paulette Goddard "auditioned" for David Selznick in M-G-M's Dramatic School, *but only Ann was chosen.*

perament and image in her various performances: fighting, tempestuous, often vixenish but always sympathetic. Miss Hayward also continued, throughout her career, to keep a veil of reticence around her private life, frustrating journalists as much as Margaret Mitchell did. Ironically, it would be in Georgia—birthplace of the heroine she would so like to have portrayed—where Susan Hayward later found her most rewarding personal happiness. And it was in that Southern state where she was eventually laid to rest.

As the Warner clan delivered packages of their recent films for David Selznick to study, he observed Barbara O'Neil and Thomas Mitchell playing husband and wife in *Love, Honor and Behave*, saw the reliability of character actor Harry Davenport in numerous Warner roles, and noted the contributions by Laura Hope Crews, Isabel Jewell, Ward Bond, Jane Darwell, Victor Jory and black performers Hattie McDaniel and Eddie Anderson.

Although Technicolor had created new 1938 audience excitement in Walt Disney's *Snow White and the Seven Dwarfs*, M-G-M was unconvinced as to its future and questioned David about the advisability of adopting the technique for *Gone with the Wind*. The studio was already experiencing some financial disappointment with *Marie Antoinette*, a black-and-white picture, and cautioned its new partner against overspending and overlength. The Norma Shearer film, at two hours and forty minutes, limited per-day performances and thus constricted profit. Most of all, M-G-M felt, Technicolor added expense to a production without guaranteeing any added returns. At the time the Mayer enterprise had cautiously used the new color on only two of its features, one of which, *The Wizard of Oz* (just then filming), was designed to be partially in black and white.

The filming of that expensive M-G-M fantasy destroyed David's hopes of securing Victor Fleming as *Gone with the Wind*'s director, and it also ended his former thoughts of casting Judy Garland as Carreen O'Hara. That talented teenager was obviously far too important by then to be considered for such a small role. M-G-M's Lionel Barrymore was also eliminated from portraying Dr. Meade since crippling arthritis had just confined him to a wheelchair. But David was offered liberal use of many other M-G-M contract players for varied roles: Lew Ayres, Melvyn Douglas, Lewis Stone, Robert Young, Julie Haydon, Billie Burke and two of Judy Garland's recent co-stars in *Love Finds Andy Hardy*—Ann Rutherford and Lana Turner.

Miss Turner had actually begun her Hollywood climb at Selznick International with extra work in *A Star Is Born*. From there she traveled to Warner Brothers and created a sensation as a Southern girl in 1937's *They Won't Forget*. Redheaded Lana exuded an innocently provocative sex appeal that might have fit Scarlett, but her Selznick screen test, with Melvyn Douglas as Ashley, showed the demanding role was still beyond her experience. Within two years however, Miss Turner had changed her hair color to blonde and began skyrocketing toward a luminous screen career which lasted for decades and made her name a household word synonymous with the ultimate in feminine allure.

As an additional favor to David, M-G-M had cast two Selznick International contract players, Paulette Goddard and Alan Marshall, in *Dramatic School* along with Miss Turner and Miss Rutherford as a sort of group "audition." Afterward, Alan Marshall's name was dropped from the contest but David remained impressed with Ann Rutherford and a young man who made his debut in that film, Rand Brooks. All this time Paramount Pictures had been trying to interest the Selznick people in their young players but the only two to receive more than cursory consideration were leading man Ray Milland and their new Southern discovery, Evelyn Keyes. Selznick International itself had continued tests and training of three young girls recruited on the studio's Southern scouting trips: Alicia Rhett, Marcella Martin and Bebe Anderson. Margaret Mitchell was especially interested in Miss Rhett's progress since she had heard reports of her talent and was intrigued, of course, by her last name—which, coincidentally, was her natural one.

When Janet Gaynor delivered an absolute refusal to the price and billing David had offered her to play Melanie, the producer turned once again to his friend Dorothy Jordan. Meanwhile, Olivia de Havilland realized the esteem felt for her at Warner Brothers was actually resulting in a punishment—by prohibiting her from a role she wanted and was wanted for. Olivia sought the sympathetic help of Mrs. Jack Warner and, as a result, the path finally seemed to clear, although there would still be weeks of tension ahead before final permission might be granted.

Confidential correspondence between David Selznick and Leslie Howard at this time would later make for humorous reading, although neither gentleman was even slightly amused by the situation then. Mr. Selznick, despite former doubts, realized the public—especially in the South—wanted Leslie Howard to play Ashley. David was willing to make any sort of handsome offer to induce the British actor to accept the part. Leslie, on the other hand, was just then enjoying his finest screen success in *Pygmalion* and didn't want a comparatively minor role for which he felt too old and quite ill-suited. David continued to press the issue, and Leslie, eager to please him, offered to do *anything* else but *Gone with the Wind*, suggesting his talents in a variety of capacities. David wracked his brain and came up with a counterproposition: executive duties and the acting lead in *Intermezzo*, a project he was preparing for a new Swedish actress, Ingrid Bergman, whom Kay Brown had discovered. But the *Intermezzo* proposal would be only *in addition to* Leslie Howard's participation in *Gone with the Wind*, not instead of it.

Hollywood's popular blonde ingenue, Joan Bennett, had made a fine impression a few years earlier in George Cukor's *Little Women*. In 1938 she donned a black wig for United Artists' *Trade Winds*, and resulting comparisons to M-G-M's Austrian sensation, Hedy Lamarr, were so noteworthy that Joan decided to remain a brunette. With her new appearance she also felt worthy of consideration for a Scarlett O'Hara screen test. David Selznick agreed—Joan was a friend, after all—but couldn't help noticing the even more striking resemblance the "new" Joan had to Vivien Leigh! Especially since there had been some stumbling blocks along the way in finalizing agreements for Miss Leigh's services.

David had been aware through the past summer months that Vivien Leigh would be ending her marriage and that there was a child involved, as was true in Laurence Olivier's case. He feared adverse public reaction if these dual divorces broke in the midst of *Gone with the Wind*'s production. Through the secret negotiations of Myron Selznick and Harry Ham, the producer received assurance that both performers were willing to wait a "decent" length of time before ending their marriages if Vivien were to be cast as Scarlett. However, there was a more troublesome block. Alexander Korda, who held Vivien's contract, did not want her to accept the *Gone with the Wind* assignment. Mr. Korda had gone to considerable trouble in the last three years to establish Vivien as an "impetuous, but sweet English 'rose' " and felt exposure as Scarlett O'Hara could destroy that image completely. Meanwhile, the uncertain David Selznick was forced to consider more established American actresses such as George Cukor's friend Katharine Hepburn, his own longtime friend Jean Arthur, new entry Joan Bennett and Loretta Young, suddenly "at liberty" after several contractual years at Twentieth Century-Fox.

Even if the Vivien Leigh dealings eventually did go through, David had decided not to announce that casting until the film had actually begun. The surrounding excitement, he felt, would overshadow any possible objections to an English actress playing America's foremost literary character. He even kept the news absolutely secret from Louis B. Mayer, which also meant keeping it from his wife (after all, Irene was Mr. Mayer's daughter!). The overpowering Louis B. would most certainly have insisted upon using an established M-G-M star instead, such as Joan Crawford, Myrna Loy, Margaret Sullavan or Rosalind Russell, and David had seen from the Norma Shearer "trial balloon" how the public had reacted to actresses with preconceived images.

Meanwhile, in England, Vivien Leigh hoped for the best as she reread the Mitchell book to the point of memorization. She turned down an offer from director

Joan Bennett donned a black wig for Trade Winds *and became a late entry in the "Scarlett O'Hara contest."*

William Wyler to play a secondary role with Laurence Olivier in Samuel Goldwyn's *Wuthering Heights*, hoping to be in Hollywood at the same time Laurence was with her own project. But that undertaking was then still far from readiness as David Selznick tried to dispel his long-standing vexation—the script!

The production costs, of which M-G-M had agreed to pay half—or $1,250,000—had been estimated on Sidney Howard's adaptation. Yet David had never been fuly satisfied with it. Mr. Howard had eliminated a great deal from the novel—which was recognized as a necessity—but had imaginatively created original sequences that disturbed David's sense of loyalty to the *Gone with the Wind* ideal. The first-person existence of Belle Watling, for example, barely existed in the book. She was seen in passing or talked about, but materialized with dialogue only in a carriage sequence with Melanie. Yet Sidney Howard had built up her part considerably and this detracted from Scarlett's being the center of all action and events. David was to remain so uncertain as to Belle's final outcome that hers would remain the last role cast for the film.

Finally, David took a Bermuda vacation in November, where, away from distractions, he could concentrate completely on the script problems. Since Sidney

Howard had refused to work any further on the adaptation, David temporarily daydreamed that Margaret Mitchell might join him in Bermuda to help with the revisions. Wishful thinking! From Bermuda, Mr. Selznick traveled to New York City, where it had been arranged for scriptwriter Oliver H. P. Garrett to join him, along with Wilbur Kurtz, for the train ride back to California. Although there was heavy script work on that trip, David did volunteer a press conference in Chicago during which he admitted to having three or four Hollywood-type actresses in mind for Scarlett O'Hara but that Bette Davis was definitely *not* one of them.

Upon his return to California, David would require "dialogue" help, for he hoped to have not one "original" word in the script, a task which would require transposing Mitchell dialogue from one scene to another. The problems were vast. To reinstate Margaret Mitchell sequences would add to the costs he had already agreed upon with M-G-M. To delete Sidney Howard interpolations might damage the structure which the playwright had carefully built. It was evident to those around him that David's ideas were almost impossible to convey to any other writer. It seemed, to get the picture he wanted, David Selznick would have to write the script himself.

If there were those who felt scriptwriting was beyond David, they obviously did not realize his contributions to *A Star Is Born*. Nor had they ever received one of his famous memorandums. Actually, unlike Margaret Mitchell, David had a healthy respect for his own words and dictated or wrote endless "memos" covering all aspects of every production at his studio. His knowledge, ideas and "storytelling" technique culled from these "memos" would later make marvelous reading in situations removed from the pressures of work their recipients were then undergoing. Some of his inspirations were a bit grandiose, however, as he "memoed" almost every thought in his head and aspired to such lofty heights as casting Tallulah Bankhead in the Belle Watling part and even Lillian Gish or Cornelia Otis Skinner in the small role of Ellen O'Hara.

As a production start on *Gone with the Wind* came closer, David's memos drew attention to another aspect which was, to say the least, quite necessary—a cameraman. James Wong Howe had dropped out of the proceedings long before but David had his choice from many expert M-G-M cinematographers. Still, he opted for someone whose skill might be unique. At the same time, he demanded total cooperation from the Technicolor company since he planned to experiment with semi-lit interior photography, something that had not been done before with the Technicolor process. Against M-G-M's wishes, David was determined to employ color photography just as, where M-G-M had warned him

on length, he publicly announced that *Gone with the Wind* might very well be the longest movie ever made! Then, in a varying mood, he decided to cut the script to bring estimated costs down to $2,000,000. Such contradictory decisions showed a mind obsessed with an overwhelming project and David was not immune to periods of depression over the entire scheme. In a black moment the producer despaired and feared that he would let the book's author down, bemoaning, "Miss Mitchell has such a childlike faith that I'm going to make a good picture!"

Some of David's memos invoked a flair for the theatrical. "Still hoping against hope for that new girl," he would write, while knowing full well that such a lady was just then busily rereading *Gone with the Wind* in England for the umpteenth time. At varying times he would either assure his staff that there were "a few good Scarletts in reserve" or individually discourage the use of any one of them. And finally, when it seemed that Vivien Leigh might be coming to America, David invented an excuse to his staff for having bypassed an "unknown" who had previously been suggested to him. He issued a self-blameless bulletin: "I have long felt that there is a very good chance that we have passed up Scarlett with our cavalier attitude about a number of the girls that have applied, through not taking sufficient pains to see personally more of these applicants." The Selznick International staff, still reeling from two years of auditions, was more than a little dumbfounded by that priceless announcement.

Thousands of miles lay between the domains of David O. Selznick and Alexander Korda, but they continued to share a mutual knowledge of, and respect for, each other's filmmaking talents. Mr. Korda was a principal in United Artists but had recently encountered financial difficulties. By late 1938, in fact, Alex was faced with an unusual problem. After a 1937 dispute with his United Artists partners, he had won the right to produce films for other American companies. But, after signing a 1938 contract with Columbia Pictures, his immediate financial situation posed an inability to fulfill that pact. Then, he was inspired to resurrect one of his formerly "shelved" productions, *The First and the Last*, with Laurence Olivier and Vivien Leigh. Mr. Olivier had already established himself in Hollywood and was just about to play opposite the future Mrs. Korda, Merle Oberon, in *Wuthering Heights*. It would likewise do no harm for the film's box-office appeal to Columbia if Miss Leigh were also better known to Americans. Mr. Korda knew all too well of Vivien's desire to play Scarlett O'Hara and had thought the issue a closed one. Now, however, there was business to be considered—always a more pressing matter than art!

Alexander Korda therefore, by necessity, as holder of

her contract, became a party to the "secret" journey Vivien Leigh made in November 1938 to New York, where David O. Selznick was staying after his return from Bermuda. Alex assured both actress and producer that he would travel to Hollywood himself in January of 1939 to settle contract matters if Vivien's auditions appealed to the Selznick company. As a bonus, he recommended to David Selznick an American cinematographer, Lee Garmes, who had recently been working in England. Mr. Korda would indeed think well enough of Mr. Garmes to employ him in the near future as "associate producer" and photographer for one of his own productions. Additionally, Mr. Garmes had worked at great length, two years before, with William Cameron Menzies on Korda's abortive *Conquest of the Air.*

But in return for surrendering Miss Leigh's services for *Gone with the Wind* and a future share in her contract, which he knew David Selznick would require, Alexander Korda wanted something urgently. He was about to begin a cherished project, *The Thief of Bagdad,* which required unique imaginative creativity that only one man he knew possessed—the brilliant art director William Cameron Menzies. For Mr. Menzies, who had directed and helped design Korda's remarkable *Things to Come* in 1936, it would be a difficult assignment since he had contractually agreed to remain with Selznick International throughout the filming of Margaret Mitchell's book. Alexander Korda's fantasy, which would become his own *Gone with the Wind,* was to begin London filming in March of 1939, requiring William Cameron Menzies to simultaneously plan designs for two huge projects—an ocean apart. (Actually, his production designs for Selznick were, by late 1938, virtually complete.) For Alexander Korda, however, it was a bittersweet trade since Vivien Leigh was his original choice to play the Princess in *The Thief of Bagdad.* Now, Mr. Korda had to find his own "unknown."

The official story was well rehearsed. Miss Leigh was to say she had sailed to America in possible hopes of replacing Merle Oberon in *Wuthering Heights,* an absurd idea since Miss Oberon was a Goldwyn contractee and it was Laurence Olivier who might have been replaced if that project went badly. Vivien was also to maintain that she had caught a connecting flight to California with no time whatever spent in New York, where she might have seen Selznick people. Then she was to "lay low" in Hollywood until a properly staged "entrance" could be arranged. That, it was decided, would come on Saturday night, December 10, when Myron Selznick would "introduce" her to his brother during the spectacular filming of fire sequences to be utilized in *Gone with the Wind.*

Very few Selznick studio personnel were even aware of Miss Leigh's presence in Hollywood until that night and there were few slip-ups in secrecy. Myron almost "botched" his role in the drama by appearing after the fire was extinguished and being a bit drunk. Vivien Leigh and Laurence Olivier had arrived just before the fire was to be ignited, but had to wait for Myron to "introduce" them to his brother. As they strolled around the lot awaiting their cues, Wilbur Kurtz couldn't help noticing the strikingly beautiful young lady. When he asked David's secretary, Marcella Rabwin, who the girl was, Miss Rabwin cupped a hand to her lips and whispered, "Vivien Leigh—Mr. Selznick is seriously considering her." Wilbur also noticed that when David left, after the fire and Myron's very late arrival, the producer was holding Miss Leigh by the arm.

All Selznick correspondence up to that time had referred to Vivien Leigh in a secretive and disguised manner. But on the Monday morning after the fire shots, unable to hold back his delight at the "introduction," David wired his wife in New York—referring to Vivien Leigh as "the dark horse" for Scarlett. (This, supposedly, even before she had been given a reading or screen test.) Although David admitted in that wire to Irene that Myron had arrived *after* the set burning was completed, all official Selznick stories would later refer to the flames "lighting up her face," which convinced him she *might* be right to test for Scarlett. Yet Myron Selznick, it was said, introduced them.

Strangely, in a cynical America where the debunking of Hollywood Cinderella stories was almost a journalistic prerequisite, few writers then or in the future would pick up the delightfully obvious hoax that had been perpetrated on them. Only Bosley Crowther in *The Lion's Share,* a history of M-G-M, would later note: "her [Miss Leigh's] trip to America to see her good friend, Laurence Olivier, who was busy in Samuel Goldwyn's *Wuthering Heights,* was suspiciously timed. It turned out that Myron had already made arrangements for her to be tested, through Selznick's right-hand man, Danny O'Shea." But until his last day on earth David O. Selznick maintained that the "introduction" story was true. After all, the press would not have taken too kindly to the revelation that "the search for Scarlett" was really more like window shopping—not to mention the possible ire of those disappointed ladies who thought all along that they had a chance.

No matter. What was truly important was what had happened on that Saturday night—production on *Gone with the Wind* had started! The great wall from the native village of *King Kong,* disguised to resemble the environs of the Atlanta depot, had been laced with pipes—controlled from a central station—through which were fed one thousand gallons of fuel per minute. Upon igniting, flames lashed two hundred feet into the air and, within minutes, the wall crumbled into ashes.

And then David O. Selznick had "met" his Scarlett O'Hara.

Vivien Leigh—subject of David O. Selznick's best-kept secret.

THE MOVIE
The Fever Spreads

"I wrote a book about old Atlanta without ever having seen it except in my mind. Now I will see the old streets of the little Atlanta I wrote about and the old houses which have been gone for seventy-five years, and the people. It will be a strange and unbelievable experience."

—Margaret Mitchell
December, 1939

1939: Lights! Camera! Confusion!

Nineteen hundred and thirty-nine . . . Ninotchka laughed, Mr. Smith took a trip and Dorothy soared over the rainbow . . . John Ford rode a stagecoach to glory, Bette Davis was victorious and Emily Bronte's vision materialized . . . the rains came and so did Ingrid Bergman, William Holden and even Greer Garson, who said goodbye to Mr. Chips . . . Irene Dunne and Charles Boyer had a love affair worth remembering while Beau Geste's new sweetheart was Susan Hayward . . . it was a world of idiot's delight, mice and men, babes in arms, the women and Shirley Temple in Technicolor . . . there were drums along the Mohawk and more of Fred with Ginger while Gulliver, Juarez, Destry, Gunga Din and Jesse James were in the company of Elizabeth and Essex . . . throughout the real world tremors of destruction prevailed and the need for escape had never been so great as Americans realized their safe civilization could soon end . . . it may have been the last completely romantic time for Hollywood films—to be cherished for decades thereafter . . . it was the year of GONE WITH THE WIND.

David O. Selznick's film version of Margaret Mitchell's novel was only one of 469 feature motion pictures released by Hollywood's major studios in 1939—which was a year, later film historians would note, never to be paralleled for its abundance of quality product. Although the vast differences between the picture and the book were to irritate many readers upon their first encounter with the film, repeat viewings over the next few years eventually soothed most of those who had been disappointed. In fact, through the illusion of celluloid, the movie version would become so identified in the minds of the masses that Margaret Mitchell's novel eventually took a back seat to its preeminence. Those four words in its title were forever after to conjure visions of Clark Gable and Vivien Leigh and would cloud any preconceived character impressions original readers might have had.

And then, to the eternal confusion of future writers, typographers, proofreaders and the public in general, Mr. Selznick and his forces took the liberty of capitalizing the first "w" in Miss Mitchell's title—making it *Gone With the Wind*—in all publicity stories and in the souvenir program (on the screen, the title appeared in block capital letters so no difference was discernible). And that movie "adaptation" of the title became so generally accepted that even the book's original publisher would become confused in later years when referring to it.

But back in 1939, Mr. Selznick's long-awaited project began in a disjointed and frustrating manner. Even the "discovery" of Vivien Leigh in December 1938 had not immediately solved the Scarlett O'Hara problem. Both Susan Myrick and dialogue coach Will Price spent a great deal of time with Vivien helping her exchange her British accent and mannerisms for those of an American Southern belle—yet careful not to overdo them to the point of caricature. Once again, Miss Leigh's determination showed through.

Vivien had begun filming a series of tests in the days immediately following the highly publicized fire episode and they seemed, from the first, remarkably promising. But similar tests were given to the three other remaining candidates (Paulette Goddard, Joan Bennett and Jean Arthur) at the same time. On December 20, 1938, for example, George Cukor had directed Paulette Goddard in a filming (with sound) of "Scarlett and Ashley in the Twelve Oaks Library" with Charles Quigley portraying the poetic Mr. Wilkes. At two o'clock that same afternoon, Vivien Leigh performed the same sequence (also with Mr. Quigley) and—as she later recalled—"the day that I tested for it, I remember the costumes being taken hot off somebody else's body and put on mine. It was quite unpleasant."

David spliced the tests of the four finalists together in various interrelated orders to judge their effectiveness but no matter how they were arranged, Vivien's rendition stood out. Her tests would be remembered by eyewitnesses as being, in fact, even more effective than her finished performance in those particular scenes. By late December Miss Leigh was being tested in Technicolor (along with Leslie Howard) and word was spreading through Selznick International that the part was hers. Simultaneously, the reluctant Leslie Howard and the eager Olivia de Havilland became certain of their assignments. And Clark Gable, who had little say in the matter, prepared for his role by reading the best-selling novel.

Meanwhile, Wilbur Kurtz had been viewing "rushes" of the fire scenes and realized the footage was monotonously overlong. David Selznick had envisioned a spectacular sequence to be projected on a triple-panel screen for its engagements in New York and at Hollywood's Carthay Circle Theatre. He hoped to advertise this as "the burning of Atlanta" despite Wilbur's continued reminders that Atlanta had *not* been burned on the night Rhett and Scarlett escaped and that the city had survived, in fact, for two and a half months afterward. The disappointed producer finally bowed to historical accuracy after viewing the repetitive footage himself and the fire eventually reverted to its normal story perspective of the depot area only. Nevertheless, its brief finished form was destined to become a memorable highlight in the completed picture. And despite the efforts of Wilbur Kurtz and even David Selznick himself (in later publicity instructions), it was destined to be forever erroneously termed as "the burning of Atlanta!"

Despite some early press leaks (notably one to columnist Ed Sullivan which seemed intentional), Mr. Selznick held back the official announcement of Vivien Leigh's casting until January 13, 1939. This allowed the producer the gentlemanly privilege of excusing himself to the other three contenders through an unlucky act of fate—since the thirteenth fell on a Friday! The disappointed ladies received orchids and personal notes that day shortly before the news was made public.

David allowed the "first" announcement honor to be granted to Margaret Mitchell, whose former newspaper colleagues rather expected that "scoop." Western Union wires with news of the Leigh-Howard-de Havilland casting were sent to the Marshes in Atlanta along with a studio-authorized biography of Miss Leigh. (David had saved contract signing of his Melanie and Ashley for that same day to make it a real "event.") Peggy Marsh then hand-delivered the wire stories to *The Atlanta Constitution* just in time to make the first page of its next morning's edition.

The three performers simultaneously sent telegrams to the author that evening with the ladies acknowledging the importance of the assignments to their careers and expressing hopes that they would not disappoint her. Leslie Howard, however, did not veer from his policy of entrapment as he wired ". . . I feel it a great honor to have been selected to enact one of the roles of your book, the title of which escapes me at the moment."

Script problems were a continuing plague to the *Gone With the Wind* film project, which amused Margaret Mitchell, who had never thought of her book as movie material. At one point, when David was desperately enlisting the aid of Ben Hecht (whose eventual contributions were minimal), the author wrote to Susan Myrick: "Now they have run into exactly the problems I foresaw, and may God have mercy on their souls." Although neither the public, the press nor even the Selznick staff was aware of it, Miss Mitchell was better informed of the film's progress (by her friends Wilbur Kurtz and Susan Myrick) than anyone outside Hollywood that year. And through those two technical advisors, Margaret was even able to send hints or criticisms on various problems she learned of from their letters or from the "still" photographs sent to her. But officially, she kept rigidly to her non-involvement policy.

Although she had been aware of the various rewriters and polishers brought in by David Selznick to revise the script, Margaret was most impressed to hear that F. Scott Fitzgerald was working on the screen treatment of "her book" in early 1939. But she would have been truly dazed to learn (from that illustrious writer's own de-

Friday the thirteenth: A lucky day for David Selznick, Leslie Howard, Vivien Leigh and Olivia de Havilland.

scriptions) that he was ordered to continually consult her novel and employ only "Mitchell dialogue" in various scenes. But no one was ever able to point out with certainty afterward exactly what, if any, Mr. Fitzgerald's contributions to the finished project actually were. David Selznick later disclaimed all writing contributions to the film other than his own, Sidney Howard's, structural innovations made by Jo Swerling and a few lines of dialogue from Ben Hecht and John Van Druten.

Gone With the Wind's various scripts would later become extremely valuable collector's items, especially the original Sidney Howard version. The Oliver H. P. Garrett rewrite was the first actual "shooting script," but during the film's production new pages were constantly added—sometimes on a daily basis. These new additions were printed on varying colors of paper and the resulting "rainbow scripts" were collected by the producer from cast and crew members upon the film's completion. In return he eventually gave them leather-bound copies of a script derived from the complete and edited film, which showed none of the rewrites or deletions. None of the "rainbow" versions were known to have survived destruction by the shrewd Mr. Selznick.

"Movieola scripts" were also prepared by the studio. These recorded the dialogue and action in a frame-counted foot-by-foot breakdown of the thirteen reels (eleven of which were double reels with "A" and "B" sections). But shortly after all those post-production scripts were prepared, David Selznick decided on more changes. He added a two-and-a-half-minute overture to precede the film, as well as four minutes of intermission music, a minute-and-a-half overture for Part Two, and four minutes of exit music. Now faced with overlength, David once again went through the 19,880 feet of film reflected in the "movieola script" and pared lines of dialogue and entrances and exits wherever possible. As a result, no script in existence would ever be totally representative of the finished film. And the release version of *Gone With the Wind*—including its overtures—ran three hours and forty-seven minutes.

Even after his film was "frozen" and sent to the Technicolor laboratories for multiple print manufacture, David continued to supervise other affairs related to it. One was the twenty-page souvenir program which was printed on soft parchment paper (so page rattling would not distract audiences) and was to be sold in theatres for twenty-five cents a copy. While preparing the program David corrected some errors that had been made in the film's titles (the spelling of Barbara O'Neil's name, the character played by George Reeves) and also generously gave credit to thirty-five individuals whose contributions were not listed on the screen at all.

Within only a few weeks of the film's actual start, George Cukor had been discharged from his duties as director. Later history would prefer to believe that change was made at the insistence of Clark Gable, whom inventive gossips saw as jealous of Mr. Cukor's attention to the female leads. Since *GWTW*'s first half quite obviously revolved around Scarlett and Melanie—with Rhett drifting through only occasionally—this theory could hardly be valid. Three decades later Mr. Cukor expressed his feelings about the Clark Gable rumor to author Gavin Lambert: "It may or may not be true. I honestly don't know. Perhaps Gable mistakenly thought that because I was supposed to be a 'woman's director' I would throw the story to Vivien. . . . as I say, I don't know for sure. Gable was always very polite with me."

Since Mr. Gable remained permanently silent on the issue, a more sensible version of the change was reflected in a letter of explanation written by Susan Myrick—a first-hand witness—to Margaret Mitchell in early February. "George finally told me all about it," Miss Myrick wrote. "He hated it very much he said but he could not do otherwise. In effect he said he is an honest craftsman and he cannot do a job unless he knows it is a good job and he feels the present job is not right. For days, he told me, he has looked at the rushes and felt he was failing. . . . the thing did not click as it should. Gradually he became convinced that the script was the trouble. . . . So George just told David he would not work any longer if the script was not better and he wanted the Howard script back. . . . he would not let his name go out over a lousy picture. . . . And bull-headed David said 'OK get out!'"

M-G-M contract director Victor Fleming was taken away from *The Wizard of Oz* during its last weeks of shooting and sent in as a *GWTW* replacement Another

veteran director, King Vidor, remembered it this way: "David Selznick, who had also talked to me about taking over *Gone With the Wind* after Cukor was leaving the film, asked me if I would be willing to take over the remaining part of *The Wizard of Oz* if Fleming would come and undertake *Gone With the Wind*. Strange as it may seem, to me the script of *GWTW* needed so much work that I was glad to do *The Wizard of Oz*. I spent one day with Fleming . . . and I took over the film. I do remember that I shot the scene with the very popular song 'Over the Rainbow.' Mr. Vidor also explained, "I didn't ask for any screen credit for taking over the last three weeks of production." Mr. Vidor's recollections also exonerated Clark Gable in *GWTW*'s directorial switch, since he was asked even before Clark's friend, Victor Fleming, was sought. And, ironically for Victor, even though he received sole directorial credit for two American film classics released in the same year, he was not the sole director of either one.

Victor had his hands full on *The Wizard of Oz*, and one of his last duties was the management of a troublesome group of midgets employed to play the "munchkins" in the Frank Baum fantasy. Their misbehavior, however, did *not* involve incorporating off-color lyrics into their songs as some later historians would claim. This would have been impossible since, in the words of King Vidor, "singing scenes done in major motion pictures are photographed to prerecorded sound tracks" (in the case of "munchkins," their song sequence was technically augmented as well). Nevertheless, the Technicolor musical had been in production since mid-1938 and had become something of a nightmare to its principal cast and crew members.

The idea of using the reliable Mr. Fleming on *Gone With the Wind* was a good one, except that leaving one exhaustive project to undertake another—with no rest in between—led to the director's collapse a month and a half later. A subsequent two-week furlough for Victor then required still another director to step in. Although David Selznick had seemingly ignored George Cukor's dire warnings on the script issue, the producer did shut down production for two weeks after George's departure to rectify the problem. Nevertheless, when filming resumed at the beginning of March under Victor Fleming's guidance, it was still based on an ever-changing script. Even Sidney Howard once again lent his talents in April, ironically coinciding with Mr. Fleming's temporary defection from the project. Another M-G-M director, Sam Wood, was dispatched to fill the gap until Victor's return and found himself staying on until the project was finished and his Metro contract had expired.

Sam Wood, whose directorial career had not been particularly distinguished beforehand, received an unexpected bonus from his *GWTW* employment. He began a working relationship with William Cameron Menzies which was to extend to other successful ventures (*Our Town, Kings Row, For Whom the Bell Tolls*) and he would thereafter establish himself as one of Hollywood's foremost directors for the final decade of his life. But, ironically, Sam's first post-*GWTW* assignment added a humorous footnote to the directorial merry-go-round which had surrounded Selznick International that year. Shortly after he and Olivia de Havilland had departed for the Samuel Goldwyn Studios to work on *Raffles*, Sam fell ill, and that project was assumed by William Wyler—himself recently replaced on Mr. Selznick's *Intermezzo*.

Meanwhile, George Cukor had returned to M-G-M to find "Scarlett runner-up" Paulette Goddard waiting for him on the set of *The Women* along with an assortment of other one-time *GWTW* candidates—Norma Shearer, Joan Crawford, Rosalind Russell and Joan Fontaine! (George replaced Ernst Lubitsch on *The Women* and Mr. Lubitsch was moved to *Ninotchka*, a project far more in keeping with his special talents.) For George Cukor, the abortive *GWTW* interlude cast no shadow on his career, and his greatest successes were still to come.

On June 12, 1939 Margaret Mitchell was awarded an honorary degree of Master of Arts from Smith College and the author made one of her rare journeys when she traveled to Massachusetts to receive that honor in person (although she declined the opportunity to make a speech). Otherwise, though, the "movie situation" made 1939 a difficult year for Peggy and John Marsh, since it renewed the vast public interest in her that had formerly seemed to subside. She found herself once again refusing David Selznick's pleas for help on the *GWTW* script while also learning that a "Tara" replica was planned to house Georgian exhibits at the New York World's Fair (a proposal she later vetoed). Peggy also found her relationship with Hollywood temporarily strained when M-G-M asked her to appear in a filmed promotional "trailer" to advertise the picture. Metro publicists had also felt free to invent Mitchell endorsements for the various cast members, especially outright raves about Vivien Leigh. Margaret was almost ready to take legal measures when David Selznick stepped in to act as peacemaker, as he cautioned M-G-M against using her name or contacting her for any purpose.

That World's Fair might have had Scarlett O'Hara in mind, since its theme was the "world of tomorrow." It was the largest international exposition in history—commemorating the One Hundred and Fiftieth Anniversary of George Washington's Inauguration—and was officially dedicated by President Roosevelt on April 30, 1939. The Fair attracted millions of visitors (including the King and Queen of England) who were reminded of *Gone with the Wind* when they read the contents of the time capsule buried there.

Television was also displayed at the World's Fair, although an impending world conflict would delay commercial manufacture of that novelty for several more years. But television would nevertheless have its first rendezvous with *Gone With the Wind* later that year at New York's Capitol Theatre. Another *GWTW* "first" involved Macmillan's announced plans to publish the novel in a *paperbound* movie edition. This was the very year, incidentally, when Pocket Books began the innovation of marketing such "paperbacks" to American readers. Although the company published only thirty-four titles in its first year (with average print orders of 10,000 copies each), the idea caught on and inspired a host of competitors, the first of which was Avon. Both Pocket Books and Avon had future dates with *Gone with the Wind*.

Tragedy struck those closely linked to *GWTW* for the first time in August of that year when Sidney Howard was killed in a tractor accident on his Massachusetts farm. And a pall of far greater significance was thrown over the entire world on September 1 when Nazi forces invaded Poland, causing outraged England and France to declare war on Germany two days later.

Ironically, *Gone with the Wind* had just made its first appearance in France (as *Autant en Emporte le Vent*) in February and Margaret Mitchell also received confirmation of Poland's publication of Volume II shortly before the tragic devastation of that country. (Volume I had appeared in Poland in the fall of 1938.) There was also news for Margaret from the chaotic Orient that the novel had been "pirated" by China and—worse still—

Before the "Evening Prayer" scene was photographed, this test chart was used to compare the tones of Vivien Leigh's makeup and costume to the Technicolor hues desired.

William Cameron Menzies and Vivien Leigh on the set of Gone With the Wind.

that under a permissive United States treaty it had been published in Japan without her knowledge, consent or financial remuneration. The Japanese three-volume edition of *Gone with the Wind* sold an immediate 150,000 copies, and its author received polite letters—but no money—from its publisher. However, a relationship bordering on fanaticism began at the time between Japan and Margaret's story that would continue for decades.

Journalistic interest in the film version of *Gone With the Wind* never subsided throughout the year. *The Family Circle* magazine captured the honor of first "cover story" with a color photograph of Vivien Leigh in her green-sprigged muslin dress adorning its June 30, 1939 edition. *Look* magazine was not far behind as it showed Vivien in her provocative burgundy velvet costume on the cover of its July 18 issue. Later in the year, as interest heightened, Vivien and her "drapery dress" won the enviable honor of a *Time* cover dated Christmas Day 1939. *Photoplay, Movies, Silver Screen* and *Hollywood* likewise decided on Miss Leigh and/or Clark Gable for the first issues of their magazines to go on sale at the start of 1940.

Although the popular *Life* magazine did not elect a *GWTW* cover, it devoted space in two successive year-end issues to the phenomenon. *Life*'s December 18 edition, published just as the world premiere was taking place, included a feature story entitled "Hollywood's Selznick" which recapped the background of the book's success and the film's casting problems. The article also offered its own account of the filming which, though interesting, included some distortions. Then in *Life*'s December 25 issue the very first news story of the week was a pictorial essay entitled "Atlanta Premiere Stirs South to Tears and Cheers." From a photograph of Margaret Mitchell meeting Clark Gable, to some candids of the stars at the pre-opening ball, through other shots of the festive Atlanta event itself, *Life* brought the Southern celebration into the homes of millions of anticipatory Americans.

For Clark Gable, who married Carole Lombard during the filming, *Gone With the Wind* was a far more pleasant —if challenging—experience than he foresaw. And he was later quoted as having found it financially rewarding as well: "Selznick had offered me a flat rate for the picture. M-G-M played very fair with me and let me make my own deal. I put it on a week-to-week basis. Six months at that rate was mighty sweet sugar." But he also remembered: "Actually, in production, however, I discovered that Rhett was even harder to play than I had anticipated. With so much of Scarlett preceding his entrance. . . . What I was fighting for was to hold my own in the first half of the picture. . . . I, for one, was a stranger in a strange studio. Somehow, I'd never met Olivia de Havilland or Leslie Howard before. . . . It took all the stamina I've got, which is enough, but I can't imagine what it must have taken out of Vivien, who worked twice as much as I did."

Clark's assumption was correct. Of the one hundred and forty days officially recorded on the Selznick shooting schedules, Vivien Leigh worked for one hundred and twenty-five of them while Mr. Gable worked seventy-one days, Olivia de Havilland fifty-nine and Leslie Howard thirty-two. M-G-M publicists would be quick to acclaim Vivien's feat as "the longest period for any actress in a single picture." On many occasions, her presence was needed until midnight or later through five grueling months of six-day work weeks. Some of Vivien's biographers would cite this experience as an initial contribution to her later health problems (which ranged from tuberculosis to mental depression). Others noted that the majority of candid photographs taken of her on the *Gone With the Wind* set caught her with cigarette in hand—hardly helpful for a tubercular person.

David Selznick himself faced the most pressing mental and emotional (if not physical) endurance test wrought by the *Gone With the Wind* filming. Against his previous resolutions David also had two other films— *Intermezzo* and *Rebecca*—simultaneously in some stage of preparation, active production or release throughout *GWTW*'s entire eleven-month schedule. And as director problems cropped up on *GWTW*, so did they extend to *Intermezzo* when he replaced William Wyler with Gregory Ratoff just as its filming began.

Since he felt *Rebecca* was the most popular literary property since Margaret Mitchell's novel, David authorized another "search" for a female star—wisely limiting it to established players this time. For that film he imported British director Alfred Hitchcock and cast Laurence Olivier in the leading male role. Naturally, then, Vivien Leigh wanted the other part but, ironically, Olivia de Havilland was the producer's own first choice. Miss de Havilland declined in favor of her sister, Joan Fontaine, who was also George Cukor's recommended choice. That gesture of George's—giving his opinion—

was particularly kind since it followed by only a few months his discharge from duties on *Gone With the Wind*. But Mr. Cukor held no grudges and, in fact, his congratulatory telegram would be among the first David Selznick received when the film finally premiered.

David Selznick strenuously objected to the public release of any *GWTW* scene "stills" prior to the motion picture's debut, for fear of overexposure. The story was already so well known, he felt, that all the public needed was familiarity with the cast and scenes to deem the entire project "old hat" or something they had seen already. The producer even expressed, at one point, the desire to destroy all the "stills" after some managed to "escape" and had been published in magazines and newspapers. (Later historians would conclude that he did destroy at least *some* of them.) Accordingly, he also forbade Macmillan to publish an illustrated "photoplay" edition until two months after the film opened.

However, when finally convinced by M-G-M publicists that simultaneous publication of that movie edition when the picture opened could only help the film's financial future, David relented just before the scheduled debuts. On December 12, 1939, The Macmillan Company announced: "Macmillan is publishing a motion picture edition of *Gone with the Wind*, priced at 69¢. This edition is paper bound, includes the complete text, unaltered from the original, and fourteen full-color page illustrations from the motion picture. Through the cooperation of Selznick International Pictures, Inc. and Loew's Inc., arrangements have been made to release the book by cities before February 15 (the publication date under the original contract). This motion picture edition may now be released in the cities in which the picture opens, simultaneous with the opening." (Macmillan also reminded everyone: "Margaret Mitchell's book was first published in June 1936 and 2,153,000 copies have been printed to date in this country alone. The book has been translated in full into sixteen foreign languages.")

Initial sales reaction to that illustrated movie edition was spectacular, as the moviegoing public purchased over 600,000 copies within the first two months after its appearance. Macmillan would place extensive reprint orders in both January and February of 1940 but, despite the book's low price, public apathy set in soon afterward and the publisher realized it had overestimated the potential and was soon faced with a non-moving surplus of 350,000 copies of the million it had printed.

Macmillan proceeded more cautiously in reissuing its standard version of the novel on December 7, 1939 with —for the first time—a three-color dust jacket (a splash of red made the difference). Almost all of the 14,000 copies printed of these (to retail at $2 each) were ordered by stores and sold within the months following the film's massively publicized debut. Not as successful, however, was a thousand-copy order of a two-volume

edition printed by Macmillan that November for the Davison-Paxon Company to be sold only through its Atlanta retail store operation (in conjunction with the premiere). Despite heavy advertising in that area, the handsome slipcased set was ignored even by many *GWTW* followers in the festive premiere atmosphere since its retail price of $7.50 was inordinately steep and it had to compete with both the reissued hardcover and the inexpensive movie edition. As with many such financially disappointing products, the Davison-Paxon set would become an extremely rare and valuable collector's item within only a few years.

In addition to sacrificing half of *GWTW*'s profits to M-G-M, David Selznick was also obligated to return favors to Jack L. Warner in return for the services of Olivia de Havilland and composer Max Steiner. He surrendered to Warner Brothers the future services of newcomers George Reeves and Mary Anderson, as well as those of Barbara O'Neil and Hattie McDaniel, whose exposure in *GWTW* had greatly enhanced their commercial value. However, through this arrangement he was able to secure Warner's Ernest Haller as replacement cinematographer immediately after discharging Lee Garmes. Mr. Garmes was temporarily blamed for technical problems inherent in the Technicolor process, although David later realized the haste and unfairness of this action.

In mid-production, costs on *Gone With the Wind* had almost predictably exceeded the estimated $2,500,000 and David arranged for the loan of an additional $1,000,000 from the Bank of America in Los Angeles to finish the picture. Upon its completion, Selznick International and M-G-M declared that *GWTW*'s "negative cost" was computed at $3,957,000, but with advertising and prints the final tally was in the neighborhood of $5,500,000. (M-G-M publicized various cost breakdowns —ranging from $466,688 for cast salaries to $10,000 for costume cleaning—but at no time was a total itemized budget made known.)

David Selznick realized he had risked his professional reputation and his studio's financial future on this one project and that every caustic wit in the country was awaiting with relish its possible failure. He decided to take a period of retrenchment, and upon completion of Selznick International's eleventh film, *Rebecca*, closed his studio indefinitely. It was never to reopen.

The *GWTW* suspense continued unabated throughout 1939 until the night of December 15, when two and a half years of maddening speculation finally ended at Loew's Grand Theatre in Atlanta. The house lights dimmed and curtains parted as the bells of Selznick International's trademark rang throughout the auditorium. Vivien Leigh's heart beat faster, Margaret Mitchell held onto her seat and David Selznick held his breath—the hour of truth had arrived!

Three Important Directors

Victor Fleming

[FEBRUARY 23, 1883–JANUARY 6, 1949]

No director of his time knew more about the motion-picture camera than Victor Fleming, who was born in Pasadena, California, almost next door to the movie industry. He was only twenty-seven when he began a film career in 1910, and within a few years was considered a top-flight cinematographer because of his natural aptitude for mechanics at a time when the cameraman had to repair his own equipment or design any new apparatus needed. One of Victor's most valuable early champions (and closest friends) was Douglas Fairbanks, Sr., who was an initial exponent of lively action films. In Mr. Fleming's own words: "I learned much from Doug. We spent hours discussing the subject of camera technique, agreeing that the camera can never fully tell a story standing still. Later, during the first World War, I filmed instruction pictures in gunnery for the army and I learned something more about the value of action pictures."

As a result, after becoming a director on Mr. Fairbanks' *When Clouds Roll By* in 1919, Victor was much in demand at Paramount Pictures during the decade of the Twenties. His *The Way of All Flesh* was nominated as "Best Picture" while its star, Emil Jannings, became a winner in the very first Academy Award presentations on May 16, 1929. And because he knew his cameras and was dedicated to action, Victor was one of a few Hollywood directors not confused by the introduction of "talking" pictures. When assigned to Paramount's *The Virginian* with Gary Cooper in 1929, he decided to make

dialogue secondary to movement, a rarity in those early days of sound. "By rigging the microphone to travel along with the camera," Victor said, "we got the sound and action in a natural way. . . . It was the first attempt, I have since been told, to use a traveling microphone." When Victor joined M-G-M in 1932, that studio recognized his attributes and assigned him films like *Treasure Island, Captains Courageous* and *Test Pilot*, all destined for immense screen popularity with the latter two receiving "Best Picture" Academy Award nominations. Victor had worked with Clark Gable twice (in 1932's *Red Dust* and 1938's *Test Pilot*) before taking the reins on *Gone With the Wind*, and worked with him once again (in 1946's *Adventure*), but was hardly the great influence on Mr. Gable's career that later historians would have portrayed. It was not too surprising that after his peak year of 1939 Mr. Fleming chose to work on only a few occasions. And his later works—fascinating, if uneven, films—were destined for the same lack of recognition that the director's career would later inspire. Ironically two of his five post-*GWTW* films, *Dr. Jekyll and Mr. Hyde* (with Spencer Tracy, Ingrid Bergman and Lana Turner) and *A Guy Named Joe* (with Mr. Tracy and Irene Dunne), were successful enough for M-G-M to reissue them a decade later. And *Adventure*, an unusual and thoughtful film, did not deserve the limbo it was sent to. Nor did the ponderous *Joan of Arc*, in which Ingrid Bergman gave a magnificent performance.

But totally uninformed future writers dismissed any talents Victor Fleming possessed and dedicated specious and unfounded critiques which discredited almost all his contributions—even *Gone With the Wind*. These came, of course, at a time when there was no one left to defend Victor's reputation. A careful reevaluation of his film career, with prior knowledge of his marvelous penchant for camerawork, could really leave little doubt as to the directorial authorship of *GWTW*, from the excitement of its Atlanta exodus, to the fluid camerawork in the wounded soldier/depot sequence, through the totally professional performances of its ensemble. Nevertheless,

Victor Fleming fiddled on the GWTW *set (while the Atlanta depot burned?).*

Victor Fleming was fated to be forgotten by history despite the fact that by the end of 1939, the year for which he was granted his well-earned Academy Award, the director had guided two of the most enduring classics of the American screen—*Gone With the Wind* and *The Wizard of Oz.*

George Cukor

Often mistakenly referred to by the limiting term "women's director," George Cukor's talented guidance was responsible for Oscar-winning performances by James Stewart, Ronald Colman and Rex Harrison. And he gave equally invaluable assistance to Fredric March, Charles Boyer, James Mason and Anthony Quinn in gaining Academy Award nominations.

George was born in New York City on July 7, 1899, attended public schools there and enlisted in the Students Army Training Corps during World War I. At war's end, he secured a position as stage manager in Chicago and eventually worked his way into similar positions in the New York theatre. By 1920 George had been given the opportunity to direct at a Rochester, New York, summer stock company (to which he would regularly return over the next eight years), and this led to his first Broadway directorial assignment, *Antonia*, in the fall of 1925. This was followed by a theatrical adaptation of *The Great Gatsby* in early 1926. George's legitimate stage career continued through early 1929 (during which time he worked with Leslie Howard in *Her Cardboard Lover*). Afterward, he was lured to Hollywood, then in the midst of its "talking screen" revolution. It was George's ex-pertise in handling dialogue that had attracted the filmmakers. After two years of co-directing at Paramount, he made his solo debut by directing Tallulah Bankhead in 1931's *Tarnished Angels*. Success with Paramount's *One Hour With You* led to an RKO contract and a friendly working relationship with David O. Selznick beginning with *What Price Hollywood?* in 1932. Their *A Bill of Divorcement*, which introduced Katharine Hepburn to the screen, started a lifelong friendship between actress and director which involved seven other mutual films over the next twenty years, including several with Spencer Tracy. It was during George's subsequent twenty-five-year relationship with M-G-M that his career reached its zenith with Selznick's *Dinner at Eight* and *David Copperfield*, as well as films like *Romeo and Juliet, Camille, The Women, The Philadelphia Story, Gaslight* and *Adam's Rib.* Other memorable Cukor creations included *Holiday, A Double Life* and the 1954 musical remake of *A Star Is Born.* Along the way, there was also service in World War II and George lent his talents to a number of military training films. Although George helped Ingrid Bergman and Judy Holliday win Oscars, he remained a "loser" himself for many years despite four Academy Award nominations. Then, in April 1965, he finally received his industry's highest honor for directing the Academy Award-winning "Best Picture of 1964," *My Fair Lady.*

Sam Wood

[JULY 10, 1883–SEPTEMBER 22, 1949]

The early student leanings of Philadelphia's Samuel Grosvernor Wood were not toward the arts but totally in the direction of athletics. Adventurous Sam embarked with a friend on a hitchhiking journey across the country in 1901, arriving in Los Angeles a year later. He then drifted successfully into the real estate business until, five years later, a film company hired one of his properties as a location. Sam was fascinated by what he saw and soon entered the motion picture industry as an actor under the name Chad Applegate. He married Clara Louise Rousch in 1908 and it was his new wife who urged him to consider films as a permanent career. By 1910, Mr. Wood was a production assistant in the fledgling California industry, and in 1914 he became an assistant director working with Cecil B. DeMille. Several hundred pictures later, in 1919, Sam was elevated to full director status on Paramount's *Double Speed*, starring the popular Wallace Reid, an actor he would work with on four other films. Sam Wood's prolific relationship with Paramount Pictures lasted until 1926, during which time he directed Gloria Swanson in ten films, including one with Rudolph Valentino. From there it was on to M-G-M where Sam successfully made the transition to director of sound films and remained until 1939. His *Gone With the Wind* chores were the last under his M-G-M contract and he afterward began a free-lance career which brought his greatest artistic recognition. Although *A Night at the Opera* and *Goodbye, Mr. Chips* were classic Wood/M-G-M productions, Sam's post-*GWTW* era witnessed far greater contributions by him to cinematic art such as *Kitty Foyle, Kings Row, For Whom the Bell Tolls* and *Saratoga Trunk.* Although he was nominated three times for an Academy Award, that final honor always managed to escape him. Nevertheless, Sam Wood brought his early interest in sports to the two finest Hollywood films ever made on baseball, *The Pride of the Yankees* and *The Stratton Story*, the latter being released only four months before his death.

The Players

AT TARA
The O'Hara Plantation in Georgia

Gerald O'Hara	**Thomas Mitchell**
Ellen, his wife	**Barbara O'Neil***

THEIR DAUGHTERS:

Scarlett	**Vivien Leigh**
Suellen	**Evelyn Keyes**
Carreen	**Ann Rutherford**

SCARLETT'S BEAUX:

Stuart Tarleton	**George Reeves**
Brent Tarleton	**Fred Crane**
Jeems, their groom	**Ben Carter†**

THE HOUSE SERVANTS:

Mammy	**Hattie McDaniel**
Pork	**Oscar Polk**
Prissy	**Butterfly McQueen**

IN THE FIELDS:

Jonas Wilkerson, the overseer	**Victor Jory**
Big Sam, the foreman	**Everett Brown**
Elijah	**Zack Williams‡**

AT TWELVE OAKS
The nearby Wilkes Plantation

John Wilkes	**Howard Hickman**
India, his daughter	**Alicia Rhett**
Ashley, his son	**Leslie Howard**
Melanie Hamilton, their cousin	**Olivia de Havilland**
Charles Hamilton, her brother	**Rand Brooks**
Frank Kennedy	**Carroll Nye**
Cathleen Calvert	**Marcella Martin**
A Guest	**Marjorie Reynolds‡**

AND A VISITOR FROM CHARLESTON

Rhett Butler	**Clark Gable**

* Her name was misspelled on the film's credits (as Barbara O'Neill).
† Performance deleted before the film's release.
‡ Received no billing in the film.
§ Received featured billing in the film.

IN ATLANTA

Aunt "Pittypat" Hamilton	**Laura Hope Crews**
Uncle Peter, her coachman	**Eddie Anderson**
Doctor Meade	**Harry Davenport**
Mrs. Meade	**Leona Roberts**
Phil Meade	**Jackie Moran§**
Mrs. Merriwether	**Jane Darwell**
Maybelle Merriwether	**Mary Anderson§**
Mrs. Elsing	**Mary Young†**
Fanny Elsing	**Terry Shero‡**
Rene Picard	**Albert Morin‡**
One-armed Soldier	**Harry Davenport, Jr.‡**
Old Levi	**William McClain‡**
Mrs. Tarleton	**Margaret Seddon†**
AND	
Belle Watling	**Ona Munson**

AT THE HOSPITAL

Reminiscent Soldier	**Cliff Edwards§**
The Sergeant	**Ed Chandler‡**
A wounded Soldier in pain	**George Hackathorne‡**
A convalescent Soldier	**Roscoe Ates‡**
A dying Soldier	**John Arledge‡**
An amputation case	**Eric Linden§**

DURING EVACUATION AND SIEGE

A commanding Officer	**Tom Tyler‡**
A mounted Officer	**William Bakewell§**
The bartender	**Lee Phelps‡**
A collapsing Soldier	**Junior Coghlan‡**

AT TARA AFTER SHERMAN

A Yankee deserter	**Paul Hurst§**
The Carpetbagger's friend	**Ernest Whitman‡**
A returning veteran	**William Stelling‡**
A hungry Soldier	**Louis Jean Heydt§**
Emmy Slattery	**Isabel Jewell§**

DURING RECONSTRUCTION

The Yankee Major	**Robert Elliott§**
His poker-playing Captains	**George Meeker‡**
	Wallis Clark‡
The Corporal	**Irving Bacon§**
A Carpetbagger orator	**Adrian Morris‡**
Johnny Gallegher	**J. M. Kerrigan§**
A Yankee businessman	**Olin Howland§**
A renegade	**Yakima Canutt§**
His companion	**Blue Washington‡**
Tom, a Yankee Captain	**Ward Bond§**
Bonnie Blue Butler (aged 2)	**Phyllis Callow‡**
Bonnie Blue Butler (aged 4)	**Cammie King§**
Beau Wilkes	**Mickey Kuhn§**
Bonnie's nurse in London	**Lillian Kemble-Cooper§**

94

Lillian Kemble-Cooper

Jackie Moran

Robert Elliott

J. M. Kerrigan

Junior Coghlan

Irving Bacon

Notes on the Cast

"Superman," "Jiminy Cricket," "Rochester," "Polly Benedict" and "Beulah"—such were the occasional professional identities of several fascinating members of *GWTW*'s cast. Aside from the twenty-four performers whose lives and careers were briefly detailed for the following pages, the film's players included many lesser-known but highly dependable and familiar character actors, and even two former child stars (Jackie Moran and Junior Coghlan)—some pictured here, others in the costume or filming sections. And there were two others whose individual stories were particularly intriguing. Yakima Canutt (*at the right*), who doubled for Clark Gable in the fire sequence and played a Shantytown marauder, had been a reliable movie "stuntman" long beforehand. His contributions to films became so noteworthy that he was granted the title of assistant or second-unit director in later years. And, in April 1967, Mr. Canutt was given a special Academy Award for "pioneering film stunt work."

Alicia Rhett (*at right*) was a young lady from Charleston, South Carolina, who was brought to Hollywood as part of the "talent search." Although she made a striking impression as India Wilkes, she never again returned to the film world, preferring instead to employ her considerable artistic talents in commercial and aesthetic endeavors. She later recalled her famous Selznick venture as "a delightful memory. I enjoyed it."

Yakima Canutt

Alicia Rhett

Clark Gable (Rhett Butler)

[FEBRUARY 1, 1901–NOVEMBER 16, 1960]

Christened "the King" in a thirties newspaper popularity poll, that title adhered to Clark Gable as naturally as a friendly nickname and remained with him for the balance of his life and career. Clark was born to a Cadiz, Ohio, oil driller and his frail wife who were both of German descent ("Gable" was a name once anglicized from "Goebel"), but that ancestry was kept quite secret by Hollywood publicists in the days when Nazism threatened the world. The boy who was known as Billy in his youth—his father's name was William—lost his mother when only nine months old but was raised by an affectionate stepmother who guided him in the direction of the arts. Clark left his home town's Edinburgh High School after two years and moved to Akron to make his own living, and soon fell under the hypnotic illusion of that Ohio city's local legitimate theatre.

During the next few years Clark Gable traveled and worked a variety of jobs (whenever possible seeking employment with theatrical stock companies) and by 1924 arrived in Hollywood. Although he found extra work in films like M-G-M's *The Merry Widow*, Clark still preferred theatre assignments. It was, in fact, a Los Angeles stage production of *The Last Mile* that finally attracted the active attention of filmmakers after it opened in June 1930. His first featured film role, in *The Painted Desert*, was seen by audiences in early 1931 and this was the same year he began a twenty-four-year relationship with Metro-Goldwyn-Mayer. That Culver City star-making enterprise guided the newcomer's progress carefully by casting him opposite three of the screen's most popular actresses in his first year: Joan Crawford in three films, notably *Possessed*; Greta Garbo in *Susan Lenox, Her Fall and Rise*; and Norma Shearer in *A Free Soul*. The last film caused a sensation among America's women with a magnetically unsympathetic performance by Clark which would prove to be totally unlike his future screen image. M-G-M's new actor achieved full stardom by 1932, joining the ranks of other noted Metro players who were known the world over by their last name alone. And there were more leading ladies: Jean Harlow, Marion Davies, Myrna Loy and Helen Hayes at M-G-M and Carole Lombard, Loretta Young and Claudette Colbert on outside assignments. Both Clark and Claudette found their "loan-out" to Columbia Pictures mutually fortunate since they both won Academy Awards for the similarly honored 1934 film *It Happened One Night*. Mr. Gable would be nominated for that honor two more times—for 1935's *Mutiny on the Bounty* and 1939's *Gone With the Wind*—but would never win again. Although only a handful of his pictures would be remembered as examples of screen art, through-

out the thirties he appeared in many crowd-pleasing films such as *Manhattan Melodrama*, *Call of the Wild*, *China Seas*, *San Francisco*, *Saratoga*, *Test Pilot* and *Idiot's Delight*. And by the start of the forties, Clark found his own screen presence was being used to assist young actresses on the rise such as Lana Turner and Hedy Lamarr.

Clark Gable was married several times, with his most publicized union being to the vivacious Carole Lombard. Their wedding, which occurred during the filming of *Gone With the Wind*, culminated a three-year romance and was regarded as the perfect match between two talented and respected individuals. After Miss Lombard's tragic death in an early-1942 plane crash, Clark enlisted in the armed forces and was off theatre screens for the duration of World War II. When he returned, M-G-M began pairing him with an altogether new parade of notable actresses—Greer Garson, Deborah Kerr, Anne Baxter, Alexis Smith, Barbara Stanwyck, Ava Gardner, Grace Kelly and Gene Tierney. Many of these later M-G-M films were considered by critics to be under par for the star's well-earned stature. Nevertheless, his enormous popularity and screen image remained unchanged. Clark, with his natural and approachable qualities, inspired equal admiration from men and women. Unfortunately, it was those same factors which belied the genuine acting talent that he did possess and prevented him from recognition for it in his lifetime.

In 1954, after making fifty films for M-G-M (and eight for other studios in that period), Clark began a career as a freelancer that spanned another six years and nine films. Even then, various studios enticed him to accept assignments with one final and significantly famous cavalcade of younger co-stars—Susan Hayward, Jane Russell, Eleanor Parker, Yvonne DeCarlo, Doris Day, Sophia Loren and, last of all, Marilyn Monroe. "Gable and his ladies" in films painted a fairly complete portrait of Hollywood in the Thirties, Forties and Fifties. "The King" continued working virtually until his death—and there was never a successor to his throne.

Vivien Leigh (Scarlett O'Hara)

[NOVEMBER 5, 1913–JULY 8, 1967]

Although Vivien Leigh's Christian name would often be misspelled by journalists, it was never too cardinal an error since the lovely actress had actually been christened Vivian Hartley shortly after her birth in Darjeeling, India, in 1913. Like Scarlett O'Hara, Vivian had a partial Irish, French and Roman Catholic heritage. She was educated, as a child, in convents in England after her family returned her there in 1920.

The young Miss Hartley showed enthusiasm for performing as early as her seventh year and soon thereafter decided to become an actress. Quite in accordance with this, she enrolled in the Academy of Dramatic Art directly upon completion of her formal schooling in London and Paris. An early marriage to English barrister Herbert Leigh Holman in 1932 and motherhood late the following year interrupted these studies. Yet within another year Mrs. Holman had successfully entered the British film industry, making her debut with a minor role in a comedy about a girls' school entitled *Things Are Looking Up*. And with this new career came an even more significant change: Mrs. Holman changed the spelling of her name to Vivien and adopted her husband's middle name, Leigh, as her professional one.

The London film colony was not too devastated by young Vivien Leigh in 1935, although she did secure parts in three more films. However, after obtaining an important stage role in *The Mask of Virtue* and receiving highly favorable reviews, she attracted the attention of famed producer Alexander Korda, who placed the twenty-two-year-old actress under contract to London Films and cast her as a lady-in-waiting in *Fire Over England*, a historical drama of Queen Elizabeth I. Miss Leigh came to know another cast member, Laurence Olivier, at this time and one of the more famous love stories of this century had its beginning. Three more films for Mr. Korda followed: *Dark Journey* with Conrad Veidt, *Storm in a Teacup* with Rex Harrison and *The First and the Last* with Mr. Olivier. The last of these was completed in 1937 but, for one reason or another, was not granted a general release.

But Vivien could not be too concerned with that small disappointment since her Korda contract allowed outside stage work, her friendship with Laurence Olivier had become romantic reality and Metro-Goldwyn-Mayer was seeking her services. That mammoth American enterprise had set up studio facilities in Denham, England, and the first film there was *A Yank at Oxford*, starring Hollywood's Robert Taylor. Although cast in a supporting role, Miss Leigh made the most of her vixenish assignment as an unfaithful wife, realizing that this film would receive more worldwide exposure than any of her previous movies had. And there was another, more hidden reason. A book had been published in England in late 1936—following its phenomenal acceptance in the United States—about a young woman's struggle throughout the American Civil War. A motion picture version would soon be made and the leading role was one that many determined actresses were praying for. There have been few thespians in history, however, more determined than Vivien Leigh.

A Yank at Oxford, released in early 1938, received the attention and reviews Vivien had hoped for and did, by no means, go unnoticed by producer David O. Selznick. Another Korda loan of her services to Charles Laughton's Mayflower Productions (with release by America's Paramount Pictures) for *St. Martin's Lane* gave Miss Leigh further opportunity to show her talents in a selfish, unsympathetic role. When the announcement was made in early 1939 that England's Vivien Leigh would portray Scarlett O'Hara in *Gone With the Wind*, this Laughton film (retitled *The Sidewalks of London* in America) was the most referred to in identifying the foreign actress to her new country of admirers.

Gone With the Wind would bring Vivien Leigh an Academy Award and, within the next years, roles in two distinguished films: *Waterloo Bridge*, again with Robert Taylor, and *That Hamilton Woman*, once more with Laurence Olivier, who was by then her husband. Their 1937 film even found release at this time under the new title of *21 Days Together*. Mr. Olivier was knighted in 1947, and for the next decade—until their marriage ended—Vivien Leigh would be known in her homeland as Lady Olivier.

There would be only six more films in the years left to Miss Leigh but one of them, *A Streetcar Named Desire*, in which she once again played an American Southerner, would bring her into the select circle of performers twice honored by Hollywood's Academy. However, there was a vast amount of stage work, including much with Sir Laurence, and a Broadway "Tony" Award. There was illness too, both physical and emotional, dimming perhaps the body's ability but never the spirit. In her later years Vivien Leigh publicly expressed some doubts about her most famous assignment, fearing that perhaps Scarlett O'Hara had become an identity too great to escape from. Privately, however, there were never any real regrets.

Leslie Howard (Ashley Wilkes)

[APRIL 3, 1893–JUNE 1, 1943]

Leslie Howard Stainer had not initially planned an acting career, starting adult life instead in his native London's banking world. And what he had really desired was to become a writer. But then World War I changed the course of his future. Shortly after marrying Ruth Martin in 1916, Leslie enlisted for a tour of duty in France. After a year at the front lines, young Mr. Stainer was returned home—a victim of shellshock. Upon his recovery, Leslie decided to try for a position in the London theatre, since so many actors were still serving in the military. He secured assignments in touring versions of *Peg O' My Heart* and *Charley's Aunt* and, for this new career, dropped the family surname—becoming "Leslie Howard."

After returning to London, Leslie continued to find employment in an assortment of small acting roles, then traveled to America in late 1920 for Broadway's *Just Suppose*. Resulting success on the American stage induced Leslie, his wife and their son Ronald, born in 1918, to become residents of the United States. His more famous theatrical vehicles at that time included *Outward Bound* with Alfred Lunt, *The Green Hat* with Katharine Cornell and *Her Cardboard Lover* with Jeanne Eagels. And it was during this period that the Howards welcomed their second child, daughter Leslie Ruth.

Mr. Howard returned to England for a version of *Her Cardboard Lover* with Tallulah Bankhead and remained there for productions of *Berkeley Square* and *Candlelight* (with Gertrude Lawrence). *Berkeley Square* would, shortly afterward, become an immense success for him in America as well and, after its initial run, he traveled to Hollywood for a film debut in the 1930 Warner Brothers version of *Outward Bound*. Leslie then contracted with Metro-Goldwyn-Mayer for three 1931 films beginning with *Never the Twain Shall Meet*. After co-starring with Marion Davies in *Five and Ten*, he was cast in *A Free Soul* with Norma Shearer, newcomer Clark Gable and Lionel Barrymore (in his Academy Award-winning role).

After another success on Broadway in *The Animal Kingdom*, Leslie repeated his part for David O. Selznick in the RKO film treatment. During that year (1932) he essayed another M-G-M film with Norma Shearer, *Smilin' Through*, and then romanced Mary Pickford in her last film, *Secrets*, released in 1933. For recreating his stage role in the Fox Films version of *Berkeley Square*, the mystical love story of a man who regressed through time, Leslie Howard received his first Academy Award nomination as "Best Actor of 1932–1933," losing to Charles Laughton. Among the most notable moments of Leslie's film career was the 1934 RKO film version of Maugham's *Of Human Bondage*, directed by John Cromwell and featuring the brilliant young Bette Davis.

"Scarlet" first entered the actor's life in Alexander Korda's *The Scarlet Pimpernel*, filmed in 1934, and the following year he was back on Broadway in *The Petrified Forest* with newcomer Humphrey Bogart. The Warner Brothers were able to induce Leslie to repeat his performance in a film version, opposite Bette Davis, only by obeying his mandate that Mr. Bogart be allowed to recreate his role as well. The future "Bogart legend"—greater after that actor's death than during his lifetime—would owe its beginnings to this particular comradeship.

It was in 1935 also that Leslie Howard agreed to play "Romeo" to Norma Shearer's "Juliet" in Irving Thalberg's expensive M-G-M production of the Shakespearean classic to be directed by George Cukor. *Romeo and Juliet* was later acknowledged to be among the better pictures of 1936. Another fling with Bette Davis in 1937's *It's Love I'm After* introduced Leslie to young Warner actress Olivia de Havilland, after which he contracted with Gabriel Pascal for the screen version of George Bernard Shaw's *Pygmalion* to be filmed in England. There was much critical acclaim for the M-G-M release and a second Academy Award nomination for Leslie, as "Professor Henry Higgins." He against lost that contest—to Spencer Tracy—and was thereby fated to be the only one of *Gone With the Wind*'s six major players never to receive an Oscar trophy.

Leslie had not read *Gone with the Wind* and did not want to play Ashley Wilkes, but clever Selznick bribery lured him into the fold. After one other Selznick film, *Intermezzo*, he patriotically returned to his native England just as that country entered the Second World War. The performer devoted the next four years to aiding the war effort through films and radio broadcasts. In the late spring of 1943, as he returned from a lecture tour in Portugal, Leslie Howard's plane was shot down by the Germans over the waters of the Bay of Biscay.

Olivia de Havilland (Melanie Hamilton Wilkes)

Mr. Walter de Havilland of England held an important legal position in Tokyo when on July 1, 1916, his wife Lillian gave birth to their first child, Olivia. Even though a second daughter, Joan, was born soon thereafter, the marriage was not fated to last and Mrs. de Havilland, with her children, left Japan for America a few years later and settled in Saratoga, California. Lillian remarried in 1925 and young Joan would later adopt the surname of her stepfather, George Fontaine.

By 1934 Olivia's immediate goal was college and eventually a teaching career but while portraying "Puck" in a local production of *A Midsummer Night's Dream*, she won the attention of a talent scout for Max Reinhardt, who was preparing a presentation of the same work at the Hollywood Bowl. Signed only as second understudy, Miss de Havilland herself played the role of "Hermia" on Mr. Reinhardt's opening night—in true Hollywood Cinderella fashion. Olivia was persuaded to change her future plans in order to repeat this part in a film version of the Shakespeare classic and was further tempted by a long-term contract at Warner Brothers Studios.

The transition to film was quite successful for her and she was soon playing opposite young newcomer Errol Flynn in the swashbuckling Sabatini adventure, *Captain Blood*. Movie audiences in 1935 had been introduced to actress de Havilland at the same time the best-selling novel *Anthony Adverse* was capturing the imagination of thousands. When Olivia was cast in the 1936 motion picture version, she thought her future as an actress a charmed one. However she didn't realize that the Brothers Warner, almost more than other filmmakers, produced a great succession of strictly commercial pictures and the terms of her contract meant she had to endure the likes of *Alibi Ike*, *The Irish in Us* and *Hard to Get*. There were, however, the benefits of working with directors like Michael Curtiz, Mervyn LeRoy and Raoul Walsh and with performers like Bette Davis and Leslie Howard in *It's Love I'm After*.

When David O. Selznick first suggested borrowing Miss de Havilland for *Gone With the Wind*, her employer was not immediately agreeable. But she combined a determination to improve her career with the sympathy of Jack Warner's wife and the role eventually became hers. Mr. Warner had feared that if Olivia tasted this freedom she might not be satisfied with routine assignments in the future. The acclaim surrounding Selznick's production, a subsequent Academy Award nomination, further loanouts to Samuel Goldwyn for *Raffles* and to Paramount for *Hold Back the Dawn* (bringing a second nomination) all proved Mr. Warner's prediction quite valid. Olivia had lost on both Oscar tries (first to co-star Hattie McDaniel, then to her own sister in *Suspicion*)

and feared that her home studio might never provide a role that could earn her that desirable prize. Interesting assignments in *Strawberry Blonde* with James Cagney, *The Male Animal* with Henry Fonda and *In This Our Life* with Bette Davis were temporary pacifiers. But by 1943 Miss de Havilland decided not to renew the working relationship.

In spite of fulfilling twenty-four assignments and four loan-outs, there had been other roles which Olivia refused to play, feeling them unsuitable, and in return she was placed on suspension without salary. Therefore, when her contract expired, she was informed that the studio expected her to remain and work out this suspension time. Invoking an existing California law, Miss de Havilland preferred to fight this unreasonable request in the courts. After two costly years of unemployment the case was decided in her favor and a new, far more enriching career phase began.

Under Mitchell Leisen's direction in Paramount's *To Each His Own*, Olivia poignantly recounted the story of an unwed mother and received that long-awaited Academy Award as "Best Actress of 1946." The following year Darryl F. Zanuck filmed Mary Jane Ward's best-selling *The Snake Pit* with the new Oscar winner in its leading role and this film's 1948 release brought her the New York Film Critics' Award as well as a fourth Academy nomination. Another New York Critics' laurel and a second Academy Award were the rewards for working in William Wyler's 1949 production *The Heiress*, based on Henry James's *Washington Square*.

Marriage to author Marcus Goodrich in 1946 had coincided with Olivia's return to the screen and the birth of their son, Benjamin, occurred during the same month, October 1949, that *The Heiress* premiered at New York's Radio City Music Hall. In 1951 Miss de Havilland turned to the stage and afterward interspersed film roles with theatre and television appearances. Among her more interesting later pictures were *My Cousin Rachel* with Richard Burton, *Not As a Stranger* with Robert Mitchum and Frank Sinatra, *The Proud Rebel* with Alan Ladd and *Hush . . . Hush . . . Sweet Charlotte*, in which she played for the fourth time with Bette Davis. On the stage she was seen in *Candida*, *Romeo and Juliet* and in *A Gift of Time* with Henry Fonda.

A second marriage to Parisian editor Pierre Galante in 1955 was the occasion for a move to France, which then became her home, and the Galantes welcomed a daughter, Giselle, in 1957. Loyal to America and the Hollywood which brought her international fame, Olivia de Havilland later participated in several Academy Award presentations and traveled to Atlanta in 1961 and 1967 for new "premieres" of *Gone With the Wind*.

Hattie McDaniel (Mammy)

[JUNE 10, 1895–OCTOBER 26, 1952]

"I just had a picture of what Mammy must have been," Hattie McDaniel later said. "I had it deep in my heart." Although that great black actress's performance in *Gone With the Wind* would later be a focal point in disputes concerning the picture's "racist" attitude, to Hattie it was a sought-after opportunity for which she was forever grateful. Miss McDaniel was born in Wichita, Kansas, the thirteenth child of a Baptist minister, but moved to Denver, Colorado, with her family while still an infant. After an elementary education and two years of study at East Denver High School, Hattie debuted as an entertainer by singing with Professor George Morrison's Orchestra over the airwaves.

A year later, when she was eighteen, Hattie won a gold medal from the Women's Christian Temperance Union for a recitation she gave and then toured Southern vaudeville houses in a one-woman act with script, music and lyrics written by herself. By 1924, she was a headliner on the famous Pantages circuit and Miss McDaniel so impressed her audiences that she was often called "the colored Sophie Tucker" or "the female Bert Williams." But there were in-between periods when, like all show business veterans, Hattie was "at liberty." There were days, she would later tell, when she hired out as a domestic or even as a night club's rest room maid. It was during just such a latter-type stint that she substituted for another performer and became the Cinderella of her

day—starring in that club's show for two subsequent years.

It was 1931 when Hattie McDaniel arrived in Hollywood, bent on film employment and she made the rounds of movie companies and occasionally found some extra or bit work. To exist in lean times then Hattie took in washing or even worked as a cook. That was all ended by 1935, however, when recognition came to stay. Hattie was even able, at times, to demonstrate her ingratiating musical talents in films like *Showboat* and *Saratoga* (singing with *GWTW*'s Clark Gable and Cliff Edwards). But her career was unfortunately limited by the racial discrimination of her time and she did not hesitate to take extremely small roles even after making marked impressions in *The Little Colonel*, *China Seas* and *Alice Adams*. For example, in 1938 (only one year before *GWTW*) the actress played a one-scene bit with Ginger Rogers in *Vivacious Lady* with absolutely no screen billing—but to hilarious results.

Although she was married several times, Hattie McDaniel—"mother" to all through her screen image—had no children of her own. Instead, she led a totally fulfilled life in her later years and enjoyed the comforts her successful career provided. When criticized, even in her lifetime, for continually accepting roles as domestics, Hattie reflected on the days when she had actually done such work and offered the vast difference in salaries as a defense to other members of her race.

Among Hattie's many, many later film performances Disney's *Song of the South*, Warners' *In This Our Life* (again with Olivia de Havilland) and particularly Selznick's *Since You Went Away* remained affectionately remembered long afterward. Hattie also devoted much time to the radio medium, on which she had gotten her start, and had just begun to interpret her famous "Beulah" character on television when stricken with terminal cancer.

"As for *Gone With the Wind*," Hattie once remembered, "I just gave myself that part. I got the book, read it, lived it. When I was finally tested for the role, I just opened my heart and let the words flow." Hattie McDaniel was the first black performer to win Hollywood's valued Academy Award, and for the better part of four decades afterward remained the only black woman to have done so.

Thomas Mitchell
(Gerald O'Hara)

[JULY 11, 1892–DECEMBER 17, 1962]

One of Hollywood's most versatile character actors, and one of the few performers ever to win the top prizes of stage, screen and television had originally followed his father into a journalism career. Like the lady from Atlanta whose last name he shared, Thomas Mitchell entered professional life as a reporter on his hometown Elizabeth, New Jersey, newspaper. Tom's ambitions soon reached beyond the newspaper life and, in spare time away from duties on the *Elizabeth Daily Journal*, he began writing theatrical skits and making plans to become an actor.

By 1920 he was appearing on the Broadway stage and for the next fifteen years alternated as an actor (*Clear All Wires*), playwright (*Glory Hallelujah*), director (*Forsaking All Others*) and as a uniquely gifted "play doctor." With *Little Accident* in 1928 and *Cloudy With Showers* in 1931, Thomas served in the triple capacities of actor, director and co-author. Eventually lured into films by a Columbia Pictures contract, Tom's first year in Hollywood (which coincided with the publication of *Gone with the Wind*) granted him a quick succession of important acting roles.

His former Broadway co-workers could follow Tom's progress at New York City's Radio City Music Hall when the Pulitzer-Prized *Craig's Wife* opened and was followed by *Adventure in Manhattan*, *Theodora Goes Wild* and *When You're in Love*. In 1937 Mr. Mitchell appeared in Frank Capra's immortal *Lost Horizon* with Ronald Colman and Isabel Jewell, and then in John Ford's *The Hurricane*, for which he received an Academy Award nomination as "Best Supporting Actor."

By early 1939, having already completed Mr. Ford's *Stagecoach*, Tom's reputation was such to make him a popular choice for the father role in *Gone With the Wind* and for an important role in *Mr. Smith Goes to Washington*. It was no great surprise, therefore, when he was voted "Best Supporting Actor" of that year. Although the Oscar was nominally granted for his superb performance as "Doc Boone" in *Stagecoach*, it would often be conceded that Mr. Mitchell's work for the entire year had actually been recognized.

Shortly after this triumph Thomas was seen in the film version of Thornton Wilder's Pulitzer Prize-winning *Our Town*, directed by Sam Wood. Later in 1940 he followed with another brilliant performance in John Ford's trans-lation of four Eugene O'Neill short plays entitled *The Long Voyage Home*. Other notable films that showcased the Mitchell talent in the next few years included *This Above All*, *Tales of Manhattan*, *The Immortal Sergeant*, *The Sullivans*, *Wilson*, *The Keys of the Kingdom*, and Howard Hughes' once-notorious *The Outlaw*. A touch of the past came in 1944 when Nunnally Johnson adapted and produced the sixteen-year-old Thomas Mitchell–Floyd Dell *Little Accident* for the screen as a vehicle for Gary Cooper. Sam Wood directed the film and it was released under the title *Casanova Brown*.

In 1946 Tom was reunited with Clark Gable and Victor Fleming in *Adventure* and with Olivia de Havilland in *The Dark Mirror*. But his first love was still the stage and when, in 1950, he replaced Lee J. Cobb in Arthur Miller's Pulitzer Prize-winning *Death of a Salesman*, he found a role that actors wait a lifetime for.

These were also the early days of "live" television, and to Tom Mitchell this new medium was as interesting a challenge as the theatre. He adapted himself to it immediately and won an "Emmy" Award for "Best Television Actor" of 1952.

After a return to films for Fred Zinnemann's *High Noon* with Gary Cooper, it was back to Broadway for *Hazel Flagg*, a 1953 musical version of David O. Selznick's classic film *Nothing Sacred*. And for his performance as "Doc Downer," collaborator in a radium-poisoning hoax, Mr. Mitchell received the Antoinette Perry Award as "Best Actor of the Year in a Musical."

Over the next eight years Thomas alternated between films and numerous dramatic appearances on television, including two series, *Mayor of the Town* and *Glencannon*. Frank Capra's *Pocketful of Miracles* in 1961 was to be the last of Tom's sixty film performances but he continued active television work until only weeks before he died of cancer in December 1962.

ONA MUNSON (Belle Watling)

[JUNE 16, 1903–FEBRUARY 11, 1955]

Ona Wolcott (a name she would later change) was born in Portland, Oregon, but after her education there joined the itinerant world of vaudeville in 1922. By 1925 Ona was playing the title role in a touring company of *No, No, Nanette* and, a year later, assumed that important ingénue role in the Broadway production. That opportunity led to more leading parts on the New York stage, including 1927's *Manhattan Mary* and 1928's *Hold Everything* and from there it was on to Hollywood. In 1931 Ona was seen in four films, including First National's *Five Star Final*, starring Edward G. Robinson, a picture nominated for that year's Academy Award. Ona was in demand on Broadway in the Thirties in plays like *Hold Your Horses* and *Petticoat Fever* but she also gained a following in musical and dramatic roles on the airwaves. In fact, when her casting for *GWTW* was announced, publicity releases called attention to the fact that she had played "Lorelei" (opposite Edward G. Robinson again) in radio's popular *Big Town* series. Ona completed the role of Belle Watling in little over a month but the actress—who began as a singer and dancer—felt the Selznick film had forever typecast her in producers' minds. Her later screen career was limited to similar supporting roles in important films or leads in westerns. In the early Fifties she underwent major surgery and suffered increasingly from depression afterward. Then in 1955 Ona was found dead near an empty box of barbiturates and a note to her husband, which read, "This is the only way I know to be free again."

BARBARA O'NEIL (Ellen O'Hara)

The talented actress who was equally believable as the warmly sympathetic second wife in *Stella Dallas* (her film debut) and the vicious shrew in *All This, and Heaven Too* (an Academy Award nomination) owed her acting strength to disciplined years in the theatre. Barbara was born in St. Louis, Missouri, on July 10, 1909, the daughter of a wealthy and social family. By 1930 she was on Broadway in *Saint's Parade* and immediately after joined the University Players Repertory Theatre of Falmouth, Massachusetts. There she met actor (and future director) Joshua Logan, to whom she would later be briefly married. With Mr. Logan, James Stewart and Mildred Natwick, Barbara went back to Broadway for 1932's *Carry Nation*, followed by six other plays in the next half-decade. Hollywood summoned in 1937 and two years later she was cast in *Gone With the Wind*. After ten films Barbara returned to New York where she appeared in four major plays during the war years, notably *The Searching Wind*. Later on she alternated stage appearances such as *Affairs of State* and *Portrait of a Lady* with choice character roles in films like *I Remember Mama*, *Whirlpool*, and *Angel Face*. After a small but powerful role in Fred Zinnemann's magnificent *The Nun's Story* with Audrey Hepburn, Barbara became artist-in-residence at the University of Denver between 1958 and 1960. Then there was one more Broadway return in 1960 for *Little Moon of Alban* before Barbara O'Neil decided to retire to the restful life of her family's Connecticut home.

EVELYN KEYES (Suellen O'Hara)

Although born in Port Arthur, Texas, on November 20, 1919, Evelyn Louise Keyes was raised and educated in Atlanta, Georgia, and always regarded Margaret Mitchell's city as her home town. Traveling to Hollywood while still in her teens, Evelyn was successful in obtaining a contract with Cecil B. DeMille and made her film debut in that producer's *The Buccaneer* and followed up with a role in his *Union Pacific*. After her performance in *Gone With the Wind*, she began an eight-year association with Columbia Pictures, becoming one of the screen's more popular leading ladies in *Here Comes Mr. Jordan, Ladies in Retirement, A Thousand and One Nights* and, most notably, *The Jolson Story*. After leaving Columbia to freelance, Evelyn continued her career in such important features as *Enchantment, Mrs. Mike, The Prowler, The Seven Year Itch* and played a cameo role in Michael Todd's *Around the World in 80 Days*. Miss Keyes was married to directors Charles Vidor and John Huston and later to musician Artie Shaw. In recent years she dabbled in stage work, starring with Don Ameche in a nationwide tour of *No, No, Nanette*, and also decided to try her hand at serious writing. In 1971 her first novel, *I Am a Billboard*, was published and it described—from firsthand experience—a Southern girl's struggle to become a Hollywood star. Then, in late 1976, Evelyn Keyes completed work on her autobiography, which she appropriately titled *Scarlett O'Hara's Younger Sister*.

ANN RUTHERFORD (Carreen O'Hara)

With an operatic tenor for a father and a film actress for a mother, pert Ann Rutherford was certainly destined for a performer's life. And that varied career eventually brought her to Hollywood's most famous studio and a role in its best-remembered movie. Ann was born on November 2, 1917, in Toronto, Canada, moved to California at age eleven and started it all with assignments in the radio medium. Within a few years there were minor roles in films (such as those opposite a young John Wayne) and then an M-G-M contract in 1937. Twelve "Andy Hardy" pictures followed over the next five years in which, as "Polly Benedict," Ann was the buffer between Mickey Rooney and Judy Garland (or a dozen other lovely ladies). But there were many other M-G-M roles, including prestige pictures like *Of Human Hearts, A Christmas Carol* and *Pride and Prejudice*. After leaving Metro, Ann freelanced for a while (*The Secret Life of Walter Mitty, The Adventures of Don Juan*) until, in the Fifties, she decided to try private life as Mrs. William Dozier—and became stepmother to Olivia de Havilland's niece! One of her happiest career memories was Glenn Miller playing the standard song "At Last" as her theme in Fox's *Orchestra Wives*. But there were a few later lures back to the world of entertainment and, of course, occasional doings in Atlanta. Through the years Ann traveled to the South for three separate "premieres" of *Gone With the Wind* and often contributed some delightful "inside" anecdotes about the film's production.

LAURA HOPE CREWS
(Pittypat Hamilton)

[DECEMBER 12, 1879–NOVEMBER 13, 1942]

Born into a theatrical tradition, Laura Hope Crews's mother had been an actress and transferred those ambitions to the youngest of her four children. Laura debuted on stage in her native San Francisco at age four and remained a child actress until retiring in favor of a formal education. After high school graduation she joined the Alcazar Stock Company, arrived in New York City in 1900 and enjoyed her first Broadway success in *Merely Mary Ann* in 1904. Then she fortunately came under the directorial guidance of Henry Miller, who shaped a highly successful stage career for her. Throughout the 1920's Miss Crews charmed Broadway audiences in *Mr. Pim Passes By*, *Merry Wives of Gotham* and *Pomeroy's Past*. With Noel Coward's *Hay Fever* in 1925, Laura also acted as director and guided an actor with whom she would eventually play in *Gone With the Wind*, Harry Davenport. Her striking performance in Sidney Howard's *The Silver Cord* in 1926 brought even more recognition and, three years later, she accepted an offer to travel west and instruct screen players like Carole Lombard who were preparing to enter the devastating world of "talkies." Soon there were acting offers as well and, after Laura made her film debut in 1929's *Charming Sinners*, she essayed over thirty character parts throughout the 1930s. Among her memorable film performances were the recreation of her stage role in *The Silver Cord* and the delightfully wicked Prudence in George Cukor's *Camille*. Miss Crews never married, devoting her life instead to the demanding career of a dedicated actress.

HARRY DAVENPORT (Dr. Meade)
[JANUARY 19, 1866–AUGUST 9, 1949]

In an article devoted to the longest show business careers in America's history, *Variety* once noted that Harry Davenport had debuted on stage in 1871 (at age five) and remained a performer until his death—giving him a seventy-eight-year professional career! After Harry's birth in New York City as the son of noted Shakespearean actor E. L. Davenport, family tradition almost dictated the pursuit of a theatrical life. In the latter part of the nineteenth century and the early years of the twentieth, the younger Mr. Davenport's stage career brought him into contact with the most notable performers of the era and one of them, Phyllis Rankin, became his wife. Harry entered the new world of motion pictures in 1912 as actor and sometime director with the Vitagraph Company in New York. He alternated stage and film assignments until the mid-1930s when he settled into the California life and an enduring career as a sought-after character actor in scores of films for all the major studios. Aside from *Gone With the Wind*, Harry's warm performances as "Grandpa" in *Meet Me in St. Louis* and that of the elderly hermit in *The Enchanted Forest* remained just as memorable for future generations. Harry Davenport renewed his *GWTW* working relationships with Barbara O'Neil in *All This, and Heaven Too*, with Olivia de Havilland in both *Princess O'Rourke* and *Government Girl* and with Clark Gable, Thomas Mitchell and Victor Fleming in *Adventure*.

BUTTERFLY McQUEEN (Prissy)

An ambitious actress in an era when roles for blacks were limited, Butterfly McQueen was additionally hampered by an unmistakable speaking voice and too-complete identification with the role she played in *Gone With the Wind*. Born in Tampa, Florida, on January 8, 1911, young Thelma McQueen moved to New York City and joined a theatrical Harlem youth group in 1935. After dancing the "Butterfly Ballet" in *A Midsummer Night's Dream*, Thelma adopted a new, distinctive professional name. In 1937 she made her Broadway debut in George Abbott's *Brown Sugar* and the following year found added success in his *What a Life!* Next came the movies and the role of Prissy—but Butterfly's Hollywood future was to be limited, highlighted only by *Cabin in the Sky* with Eddie Anderson and Joan Crawford's Oscar-winning *Mildred Pierce* (in which, despite a sizable role, Butterfly received no billing). David Selznick tried using her as a good-luck charm again in his ponderous *GWTW* follow-up, *Duel in the Sun*, but after that her film career literally halted. Nevertheless, the determined little lady furthered her education, eventually receiving a bachelor's degree in political science, and also devoted her time to charitable and civic work in Harlem. In 1975 she was one of twenty artists honored by the Black Filmmakers Hall of Fame. Butterfly McQueen did not like portraying shallow Prissy, but her artistry created a character of far more dimension than even Margaret Mitchell had visualized.

CARROLL NYE (Frank Kennedy)

[OCTOBER 4, 1901–MARCH 17, 1974]

Like Clark Gable, Carroll Nye was born in Ohio (Canton, to be exact), migrated to California, became active in stage work and finally broke into motion pictures. After a silent-screen debut in *Classified* (based on Edna Ferber's short story) and several subsequent assignments, Mr. Nye gained the romantic lead in Lon Chaney's *While the City Sleeps* in 1928 and seemed headed for stardom. But that plateau eluded him for the next decade until he won the part of Scarlett O'Hara's second husband and seemed on the verge of a second chance. The spotlight turned away from him again and Carroll left acting behind to enter the newspaper world, becoming radio editor for *The Los Angeles Times* soon after. Over the years Carroll Nye's diverse careers included radio broadcasting, public relations and a position with ABC Television. His brother, Ben Nye, was associate makeup director for *Gone With the Wind* and later head of the makeup department at Twentieth Century-Fox Studios. It was through his brother's technical expertise, the actor later gratefully admitted, that he secured the part of "aging" Frank Kennedy.

JANE DARWELL (Dolly Merriwether)

[OCTOBER 15, 1879–AUGUST 13, 1967]

The fifth member of *Gone With the Wind*'s cast to win an Academy Award, Jane Darwell once said she originally wanted to be a circus fat lady. But Patti Woodward (born in Palmyra, Missouri, the daughter of a railroad president) was discouraged by her father from pursuing that unusual occupation. Instead, she studied music and dramatics and made her stage debut in Chicago in 1906. As Jane Darwell, the actress began a fifty-year screen career in 1914 in Cecil B. DeMille's *Rose of the Rancho*, played in many silent films and successfully overcame the "sound barrier" in 1930. Jane's skill was such that she could essay unsympathetic roles in *The Ox-Bow Incident* or *Caged* as easily as the heartrending part of Ma Joad in John Ford's *The Grapes of Wrath*, which won her that Oscar. Miss Darwell also appeared in six of Shirley Temple's successful movies, and in five additional John Ford films, as well as 150 other pictures. Her final, and very touching, appearance was in the 1964 Walt Disney classic *Mary Poppins*. As with Hattie McDaniel, Jane Darwell's image was the eternal mother (or grandmother), and like Hattie, she died childless.

Butterfly McQueen

Carroll Nye

Jane Darwell

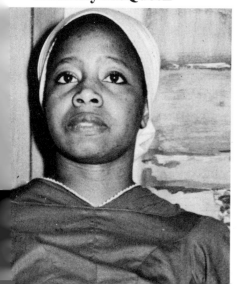

Rand Brooks **Isabel Jewell** **Victor Jory**

RAND BROOKS (Charles Hamilton)

Scarlett O'Hara's first husband, Marilyn Monroe's first leading man and "Hopalong Cassidy's sidekick" were some of the distinctions Arlington Rand Brooks, Jr., earned during his movie career. Born in Los Angeles on September 21, 1918, Rand had planned a teaching career but turned to acting, obtained an M-G-M contract and debuted in that studio's *Dramatic School* in 1938. After a few years of toil in such films as *The Old Maid*, *Babes in Arms*, *Cheers for Miss Bishop* and *Lady in the Dark*, Mr. Brooks served in the armed forces during World War II. Afterward he adopted the identity of "Lucky Jenkins" in 1946 for a series of western films with actor William Boyd. Then in 1948 Rand was a very young Marilyn Monroe's heart interest in *Ladies of the Chorus* and also played in Victor Fleming's very last production, *Joan of Arc*. When the "Hopalong Cassidy" films were nationally televised soon after, he achieved even greater recognition because of the phenomenal popularity they enjoyed with America's youngsters. Rand Brooks married the only child of immortal comedian Stan Laurel and later deserted acting in favor of the pleasant life of ranching.

ISABEL JEWELL (Emmy Slattery)

[JULY 19, 1909–APRIL 5, 1972]

Two of Isabel Jewell's most remembered screen roles were limited in running time but very effective in impact. Although the character Emmy was discussed from the very start of *Gone With the Wind*, Isabel was actually in but a single sequence and had only one line of dialogue. And in David Selznick's *A Tale of Two Cities* her appearance in the finale was another small, although highly touching, "bit" as she accompanied Sydney Carton (Ronald Colman) on a journey to eternity. "Small" seemed the keyword for Miss Jewell who, like Margaret

Mitchell, was under five feet tall—a fact she often felt hampered her career. The actress was born in Shoshoni, Wyoming, daughter of a medical doctor/researcher, and she studied dramatics in junior college. She trained with a Lincoln, Nebraska, stock company for eighty-seven weeks and, after attaining lead status, gained further stage experience in New York, Chicago and Los Angeles before entering films in 1932. The other "gems" in Isabel Jewell's long career of supporting roles were Frank Capra's *Lost Horizon* (with Thomas Mitchell) and Warners' *Marked Woman*, for which she earned fine reviews and third billing to Bette Davis and Humphrey Bogart.

VICTOR JORY (Jonas Wilkerson)

Not too long after his birth in Dawson City, Alaska, on November 23, 1902, Victor Jory decided to follow an athletic career. After prizefighting briefly and then becoming champion wrestler of the National Guard, Victor decided he was more partial to the acting skills he had acquired while attending the University of California. He began a new career on the stage and continued to accept theatrical assignments (and even to write plays) whenever possible after his 1932 film debut. But he found himself much in demand among movie producers since he could ideally project the image of an arch-villain such as "Injun Joe" in *The Adventures of Tom Sawyer* or Jonas in *GWTW* (replacing Robert Gleckler, who died during production). Like two of his *GWTW* co-stars, Mr. Jory also appeared in several "Hopalong Cassidy" films, but the most famous other titles on his long list of movie credits were *A Midsummer Night's Dream*, *The Miracle Worker* and *The Fugitive Kind*. Victor Jory traveled to Atlanta for the 1967 "premiere" of *Gone With the Wind* and utilized his resonant speaking voice to record the narration for that city's famed Cyclorama.

EDDIE ANDERSON (Uncle Peter)

[SEPTEMBER 18, 1905–FEBRUARY 28, 1977]

As a twelve-year-old working boy Eddie Anderson strained his vocal cords hawking newspapers in his native Oakland, California, but the gravel-voiced result would provide him with a lifelong trademark. Since Eddie's father was a minstrel performer and his mother a circus tightrope walker, it was natural for him to enter show business at the age of fourteen, appearing in an all-black revue. After touring in vaudeville, first with his older brother and later as a solo song-and-dance man, the entertainer reached Hollywood where he found another career as a movie character actor. But national fame began for Eddie Anderson on Easter Sunday 1937, when he created a character on the extremely popular *Jack Benny Show* that drew such favorable response from radio listeners it became a staple. As "Rochester," Mr. Benny's brash valet, he transcended the program's transfer to television in the early 1950s, remained with it for the next decade and, after its demise, returned for various Jack Benny "specials." Among Eddie Anderson's more notable film credits were *The Green Pastures*, *Jezebel*, *You Can't Take It With You*, *Kiss the Boys Goodbye* and, most importantly, M-G-M's *Cabin in the Sky* in which he starred.

WARD BOND (Tom, a Yankee Captain)

[APRIL 9, 1903–NOVEMBER 5, 1960]

One of the screen's most durable character actors, Ward Bond of Denver, Colorado, originally thought of a medical career but was studying engineering at the University of Southern California when Director John Ford recruited him and his friend John Wayne for roles in 1929's *Salute*. Although he received his degree, Ward turned to acting permanently and his list of over one hundred credits represented three decades of film history.

In addition to parts in such memorable pictures as *The Maltese Falcon, Sergeant York, The Sullivans* and *It's a Wonderful Life*, Ward appeared in a total of seventeen films with John Wayne, in sixteen other John Ford productions, with Clark Gable in one other film (*It Happened One Night*), in Victor Fleming's *A Guy Named Joe* and *Joan of Arc*, and in Selznick's *Made for Each Other*. From 1957 until his sudden death, Ward was starring in the television series *Wagon Train*, which gave him the greatest solo recognition of his career.

GEORGE REEVES (Stuart Tarleton)*

[APRIL 28, 1913–JUNE 16, 1959]

Although George Bessolo was born in Ashland, Kentucky, he moved to Southern California during his elementary school days and acted in local theatre groups there during his teen years. Then, after enrolling in Pasadena Junior College in 1932, he excelled in extracurricular boxing activities. Next came apprenticeship at the Pasadena Playhouse, and it was there that Max Arnow, Selznick International casting director, signed him for a small but prestigious part in *GWTW*. As a means of returning favors to Jack Warner, David Selznick traded George to the Warner Brothers studio where he was renamed George Reeves. The young actor's career was doing extremely well, with assignments opposite Merle Oberon in *Lydia* and Claudette Colbert in *So Proudly We Hail*, until it was interrupted by World War II, in which he served as an entertainer. (He appeared at that time in George Cukor's *Winged Victory*.) The postwar years proved difficult for George in reestablishing his career until he found phenomenal success as the lead in the "Superman" television series. But, like Ona Munson, he later despondently felt his career was ruined by too-close identification with one role and, in 1959, George Reeves died of a self-inflicted gunshot wound.

* NOTE: Mr. Reeves was wrongly credited on screen as Brent Tarleton.

Eddie Anderson

Ward Bond

George Reeves

MARY ANDERSON
(Maybelle Merriwether)

Her name was Bebe Anderson when she raised the Confederate flag for official ceremonies signaling the start of *Gone With the Wind* and Mary Anderson when the film was released. Although the young Southern lady (who was born in Birmingham, Alabama, on April 3, 1921) was almost totally eliminated from David Selznick's finished picture, the publicity Mary received actually promoted her screen career. After subsequent roles in *All This, and Heaven Too* and *Cheers for Miss Bishop* (with Rand Brooks), Mary scored a major success on Broadway in *Guest in the House* and won a contract with Twentieth Century-Fox. At that studio she was cast in important roles in *Lifeboat*, *The Song of Bernadette* and *Wilson*, and later traveled to Paramount where she was reunited with her *GWTW* co-star Olivia de Havilland. Mary's pivotal role in *To Each His Own*, for which Miss de Havilland won her first Oscar, would later be remembered as the highpoint of her screen career. Mary wed Fox's Academy Award-winning cinematographer Leon Shamroy in 1953 and, in the next decade, once again crossed paths with a famed bestseller when she accepted a role in the television series *Peyton Place*.

CLIFF EDWARDS
(A Reminiscent Soldier)

[JUNE 14, 1895–JULY 17, 1971]

Although heard but not seen in *Gone With the Wind* (in the Atlanta church/hospital's "shadow scene"), Cliff Edwards had already established himself by then as a world-famous entertainer. A native of Hannibal, Missouri, his singing and playing won him the title of "Ukelele Ike" as a vaudeville headliner and as a featured player in a score of M-G-M's early sound films. Cliff's recordings sold in the millions, especially "Ja Da" and the classic "Singin' in the Rain," which he—along with most of M-G-M's star stable—introduced in *The Hollywood Revue of 1929*. Among his more notable other films were Sam Wood's *So This Is College*, *Saratoga* (in which he sang with Clark Gable and Hattie McDaniel), *Maisie* and *His Girl Friday*. But Cliff Edwards's greatest claim to film immortality was another instance when he was heard but not seen—as the voice of Jiminy Cricket in Walt Disney's *Pinocchio*, in which he introduced the 1940 Academy Award-winning song "When You Wish Upon a Star."

MARJORIE REYNOLDS
(A Guest at Twelve Oaks)

Unlike Cliff Edwards, Marjorie Reynolds was seen but not heard in *Gone With the Wind* (her one line of dialogue on the Twelve Oaks staircase with Melanie and India was delivered off-camera). Marjorie Goodspeed and her family left their native Buhl, Idaho, where she was born on August 12, 1921, to relocate in California. After high school and a novice period of minor film roles, Marjorie secured a Paramount contract, a new name and, by 1942, was leading lady to Bing Crosby and Fred Astaire in *Holiday Inn*. Miss Reynolds remained in films —including *Star Spangled Rhythm*, *Dixie*, *Duffy's Tavern*, *Ministry of Fear* (with Ray Milland), *That Midnight Kiss* (with Mario Lanza) and *Home Town Story* (with Marilyn Monroe)—until television provided her with a completely new career opportunity. As "Peg Riley" opposite William Bendix in the second version of *The Life of Riley*, Marjorie Reynolds gained even more lasting recognition than in her films. The highly popular series, which began in 1953 and continued for more than five years, would remain in syndication on local stations for over a decade afterward.

Mary Anderson

Cliff Edwards

Marjorie Reynolds

Walter Plunkett's masterful designs for *Gone With the Wind*'s costumes magnificently captured the essence of Margaret Mitchell's novel from Old South innocence through wartime rags to Scarlett and Rhett's Reconstruction grandeur. In some cases, such as the drapery dress or Bonnie's riding habit, Mr. Plunkett faithfully captured important details of Miss Mitchell's narrative. In others, such as Scarlett's burgundy velvet gown, he brought his own creativity into play. The collective results enhanced the memorable film with historical authenticity. The rare costume tests on these pages were never meant to be seen by the public. Their purpose was merely to determine how the cast's apparel photographed or to match sequences interrupted before completion. But through them a permanent record of Walter Plunkett's achievement was preserved for evaluation and appreciation.

Initial filming began with Scarlett, as in the book, wearing a green sprig muslin dress (*above right*). Vivien Leigh here held a slate significantly marked: "Change #1, Sequence #1." But her work with the Tarleton boys (Fred Crane and George Reeves, *above*) and Thomas Mitchell (*below right*) as Gerald was in vain as all these scenes would be discarded later when she changed dresses and Mr. Mitchell lost his curly hairdo. Even a "Quittin' Bell" scene with black children (*below*) was later redone.

The Costumes

Barbara O'Neil (*above*) was a model of elegance as she and Susan Myrick awaited cues for Tara's "evening prayers." Vivien Leigh prepared to pray ("Scarlett Costume #1-A," *above right*), totally unaware then that this white dress would also be used in the film's opening scenes, which were refilmed more than half a year later. Although viewers were generally unaware of it, even Mammy's costumes underwent subtle changes in neckerchiefs and headrags. Hattie McDaniel (*below left*) was ready to lace up Scarlett and (*below right*) about to warn her not to wait for Ashley in Atlanta "just like a spider!" Miss O'Hara's pantalets and hoop-skirted petticoat (*below center*) had to be removed for the young ladies' nap interval shortly after arrival at the Twelve Oaks barbecue.

The film's four stars modeled their barbecue costumes here for the first time. It appeared that Mr. Gable (*above*) was not in on the fun Vivien and Miss Myrick shared behind him. Miss Leigh's green muslin dress from the original opening sequence was now accessorized with bonnet and parasol to become "Scarlett Costume #2-A." There may well have been some chauvinism in 1939 Hollywood since, it seemed, the two male stars never had to hold their own slates in these photographic tests.

Evelyn Keyes (*above left*) and Ann Rutherford (*above right*) were destined to attain more screen prominence than the other members of *GWTW*'s subordinate cast. Evelyn seemed dazzled by the opulence of Suellen's barbecue gown, while Ann was obviously "pleased as punch" with Carreen's attractive ensemble. Prudent Ann felt compelled to caution Producer Selznick that her expensive shoes and underthings would never be seen by the audience. Mr. Selznick countered that as long as she remained aware of them and this helped influence her characterization, it was money well spent. The Twelve Oaks festivities also provided the one film occasion for all the gentlemen in Scarlett O'Hara's life to be gathered around her. In addition to Ashley and Rhett, the guests included (*below from left*) her father Gerald (Thomas Mitchell), Charles Hamilton (Rand Brooks), Frank Kennedy (Carroll Nye), and the host John Wilkes (Howard Hickman), a man she hoped would someday be her father-in-law.

The first gown executed for Alicia Rhett to wear at the Twelve Oaks party (*above left*) was an effort audiences would not see. Miss Rhett was herself quite attractive and a change of costume (*right, above*) successfully subdued her charms and emphasized the spinsterish qualities synonymous with India Wilkes. Star-to-be Marjorie Reynolds (*below left*) may have been nervous even with her small contribution as a barbecue guest, not realizing that within a few years she would herself be a leading lady. Marcella Martin (*right, below*) was one of a select few belles from the South to win a part in the film (as Cathleen Calvert). A Hollywood career was not, however, to be in Miss Martin's future and, in fact, her entire part would be redubbed by another voice that sounded "more Southern."

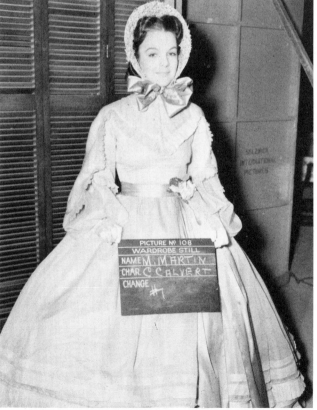

Scarlett's nuptials to Charles Hamilton presented her with the film's only opportunity to wear a wedding gown, despite two later marriages. Miss Leigh's slate for this costume change (*left*) was unnumbered, which provided some temporary confusion. There was new finery too in this brief sequence for Ashley and Melanie (*above*), but Leslie Howard wrote to his family after seeing himself in this uniform, "I . . . looked like a fairy doorman at the Beverly Wilshire—a fine thing at my age."

If Barbara O'Neil (*left, below*) was ever unhappy that her name was misspelled in the movie's credits, she had only herself to blame: the spelling on this costume slate she held made the same error (O'Neill). She was dressed here to comfort her newly widowed daughter, who hadn't been able to resist donning a fancy hat (*below*) instead of the customarily dreary black bonnet. The numeral on Miss Leigh's slate (#3) should have been advanced by one but the mistake was rectified soon thereafter.

Atlanta's "monster bazaar" provided Clark Gable (*above left*) with a truly impressive entrance. The orchestra of black men (*above right*) was barely visible in the film but it helped create a background illusion for the delightful moment when Scarlett (*right*) scandalized the Old Guard by dancing with Rhett. At the bazaar audiences also met several of the book's most famous characters (*below from left*): Aunt Pittypat (Laura Hope Crews), Dr. Meade (Harry Davenport) and Maybelle Merriwether (Bebe Anderson). Miss Anderson would change her first name to Mary just before the movie was released and enjoy a nice little acting career in films.

Scarlett ("Costume #6," *left*) received a gift from her new admirer, Rhett Butler (*above*). The costumes pictured here were, again, for a scene directed by George Cukor which would afterward be totally remade. In the revised "Paris Hat" sequence Mr. Gable traded in his cravat for a bow tie and Miss Leigh added front curls to her hairdo. (Even the hat itself underwent change.)

Scarlett (*below left*, "#7") was still in mourning for Charles Hamilton while she awaited the Gettysburg casualty lists. Clark Gable (*below center*) took the seriousness of it in his stride, while Eddie "Rochester" Anderson (as Uncle Peter, *below right*) was probably rehearsing his script for that Sunday's Jack Benny radio program.

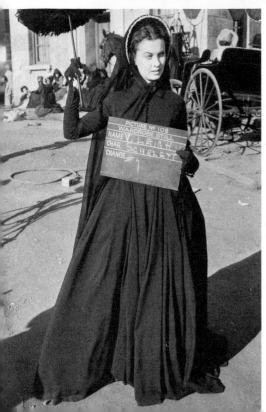

Ashley Wilkes was granted a furlough for the 1863 holiday season and returned to *both* of the women who loved him. Leslie Howard (*above*) seemed little affected by the Civil War tragedy as he prepared for arrival at the Atlanta depot. Vivien Leigh displayed her eighth change of wardrobe and the new Paris hat when she met Ashley's train (*right*). But she was far more radiant without coat and hat (*below left*) for Christmas dinner with Aunt Pittypat (*below center*). The next morning Scarlett had a gift for Ashley and another new dress for herself ("Costume #9," *below right*).

Wartime Atlanta was not exactly a fashion show for Melanie (*above left*) or Scarlett (*above center*) as they nursed wounded soldiers. (*Ordeal* by Nevil Shute was a project planned for filming by Selznick International that was canceled because of the spread of war.) This marked viewers' first encounter with the calico dress worn by Miss Leigh, but it would not be the last! ("Costume #11").

Upon leaving her nursing duties, Melanie (*above right*)

met Belle Watling (*below left*), who had evidently found Scarlett's lost secret of fancy wardrobe. Vivien's alternate hospital uniform (officially catalogued as "#10," *below center*) was used in the frightening panorama of Atlanta's exodus, after which she was driven home by Rhett Butler (*below right*). Upon reflection, moviegoers would often incorrectly remember Vivien playing these last scenes in her calico—but it was plainly a quite different design.

Poor Scarlett had to look up Dr. Meade in that same old calico frock (*left*), and even Prissy's duds (*above*) were not worth borrowing. Big Sam (Everett Brown, *below left*) didn't seem to mind but she certainly hoped Rhett Butler (*below center*) and Belle Watling (*below right*) wouldn't see her.

Walter Plunkett would cause later havoc with *GWTW* historians when he said in an interview that there were twenty-seven different copies of Scarlett's calico dress employed in the film. Future writers took Mr. Plunkett at his exact word and even went so far as to challenge moviegoers to "count them" when they viewed it. Walter, as designer, certainly would have known how many individual calicos had been manufactured for stand-ins, doubles or as replacements in the event any damage occurred to an original. But as far as the number of designs actually evident on Vivien Leigh in the completed film, it was much more like *five*, with various shawls, aprons or bonnets used to accessorize them. None of the shooting schedules for those scenes involving the dress were so prolonged as to require multiple copies for Miss Leigh herself. So, herewith the calico dresses—count them!

The costume *first* materialized over hoopskirts and with an apron for Vivien's "Shadow" scene with Olivia de Havilland and Cliff Edwards at Atlanta's church/hospital. Immediately thereafter (*above left*) Miss Leigh removed the apron but added a bonnet and shawl as she encountered Belle Watling outside that building. This sequence represented incidents in the winter of 1863 and was catalogued by the filmmakers as "Costume #10A" or #11." The following September, with the city under siege, hoopskirts proved impractical and she discarded hers (*above center*) to help deliver Melanie's baby. A sunbonnet was an added help (*above right*) in the search for Dr. Meade. This year-old calico variation was described by the wardrobe department as "Scarlett Costume

#11—Aged 1." This alteration encored that night when Rhett came to the rescue. (As they drove through the burning depot, a black hat "magically" appeared on her head, without prior explanation. In the book Scarlett had intentionally taken Melanie's black mourning bonnet but this detail was lost in the film's final editing.) It was also that same copy worn upon return to Tara the following day and used for Scarlett's famous starvation oath. Several months later the *third* calico debuted (*below*) for "cotton picking" ("Scarlett Costume # 12").

After the third calico was reprised by Vivien for the "Yankee Soldier" sequence (*above left*) she seemed rather amused by the *fourth* calico modification (*above, second from left*) worn with an apron in September 1865 when she gave Frank Kennedy permission to marry Suellen and when Ashley returned to Tara ("Scarlett Costume #13"). But two months afterward she was more somber in the *fifth copy* ("#14," *second from right*), which was far more tattered for the paddock interlude with Ashley and a Jonas Wilkerson visit which resulted in Gerald's death. This fifth version was again employed (*above right*) when Scarlett gave Gerald's watch to Pork and then tore down draperies to adorn herself for an Atlanta visit to Rhett (labeled "Scarlett #15"). If Miss Leigh looked rather apprehensive here, it may have been her realization that the recurring calico—worn longer than any other costume in the picture—had appeared for the very last time. She now eagerly prepared for the premiere of *Gone With the Wind*'s most immortal garment. (Walter Plunkett's original sketch for that drapery dress reproduced at the *right*.)

125

While waiting for that new dress to replace her calico rags, Scarlett could take heart that her friends and family were no better off. Rhett (*above left*) went off to war more than somewhat bedraggled after the escape from Atlanta. Mammy (*above right*), along with Gerald, Suellen and Carreen (*below from left*), were all in tatters, while Frank Kennedy (*below far right*) was even reduced to wearing a blanket.

Ashley (*above left*) and Pork (*above right*) tried to make the best of the new hard times at Tara. But then that nasty Jonas Wilkerson (*below left*) visited with Emmy Slattery (*below center*) in all their finery—just to make everyone "pea green with envy!" Melanie (*right*) was in the best spirits of all, however, as she celebrated the end of the war.

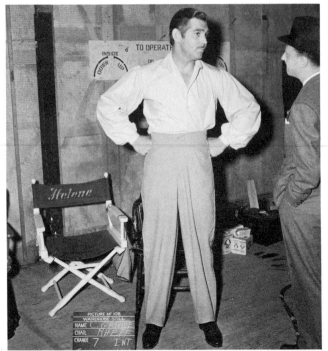

The drapery dress (*right*)—symbol of Scarlett O'Hara's determination to survive! Rhett Butler (*above left*), dressed for the Yankee jail scene, was not impressed enough by it to find her any tax money. But Frank Kennedy (*above right*) was swept off his feet and married her. Belle Watling (*below*) didn't care about it at all when they met at the jail, since she could afford to *buy* her clothes! Mr. Plunkett's green velvet masterpiece officially became "Scarlett Costume #16."

The new Mrs. Frank Kennedy was the lady in red when she returned to Tara ("#17," *above left*) to ask Ashley (*above center*) to help manage the new lumber mill. Her fancy apparel as a business woman (#18, *above right*) may have seemed out of place for the difficult Reconstruction era compared to Melanie's simple outfit (*left*), but Scarlett assured her sister-in-law that this was not always the case. In fact, she didn't even wear a skirt when operating the store's cash register—as long as Ernest Haller photographed her from the waist up (*below left*). For conducting lumber business on Atlanta's streets (*below* with actor Olin Howland), our heroine was provided with her nineteenth change of costume, also worn on an unfortunate trip through Shantytown.

Mrs. Kennedy had been mauled by renegades and the Atlanta menfolk were provoked enough by this to raid Shantytown in reprisal. Scarlett (*left*) waited the tense evening out with Melanie (*above*). In the excitement Miss Leigh's slate was incorrectly marked "#19" again (actually a result of shooting scenes out of sequence) and, from this point on, the Selznick costume count would remain one less than actual. Ashley (*below left*) returned with an injury but had enough foresight to bring Dr. Meade with him (*below center*). All this confusion was a little too much for Tom, the Yankee Captain, and his sergeant, who meant to catch them in the act (Ward Bond and Harry Strang, *below right*).

Impeccable Rhett Butler (*above*) had become a bit disheveled in the raid proceedings but at least Mammy (*right*) remained her fun-loving self. When the excitement died down, Melanie (*below left*) decided it would be a good time for a visit with her old friend Belle Watling (*below right*).

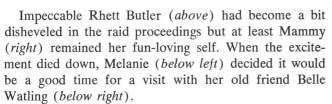

Frank Kennedy had not survived the Shantytown exploits and Rhett (*left*) was anxious to finally catch Scarlett between husbands. The lady accepted his proposal, if for no other reason than to once again set aside those boring mourning clothes ("#20," actually "#21," *above*). This new marriage provided Mrs. Butler with a marvelous wardrobe, including an ermine-trimmed robe for their honeymoon cruise, a be-doved evening gown for New Orleans dining and a divine Plunkett ensemble for everyday (*below from left*).

After Scarlett induced Rhett to buy her a twenty-fifth change of apparel, they paid a sentimental visit to Tara (*above left*) where she also persuaded him to bring Prissy and Mammy (*above right*) back to their bizarre new home in Atlanta. Hattie McDaniel, with her stand-in (*below left*), and Vivien Leigh (*below right*) awaited their cues for the "Birth of Bonnie" sequence, and although Vivien had by then probably lost track of her outfits, she possibly realized this slate should have been marked "#26" instead of "#25."

Bonnie's birth gave Scarlett some problems with her figure so she decided to have no more children. By now the wardrobe department was totally confused and catalogued Vivien's green velvet robe as change "#20" instead of "#27" (*above*). Rhett (*above right*) was so infuriated by her decision he sought comfort from Belle (*below*), who told him that Bonnie was really worth all that aggravation he received from her mother. Scarlett was indeed a trial to any man but she did agree to accompany Rhett on a walk along Peachtree Street if he would let her wear this little striped number (actual "#28," *below right*). Those clever wardrobe people arranged to have the sun reflect on Miss Leigh's slate here so no one could see how confused their efforts had become.

Cute little Bonnie (Phyllis Callow, *above left*) turned Mr. Butler (*above center*) into Atlanta's most doting father and this endeared him even to the town's sternest dowagers, Mrs. Merriwether (Jane Darwell, *above right*) and Mrs. Meade (Leona Roberts, *below left*). Within two years precious Bonnie (Cammie King, *below center*) even persuaded Rhett to give her riding lessons (*right*). He shouldn't have!

A visit to the lumber office was just an excuse for Scarlett to wear another outfit (marked here "#27" but actually "#29," *left*) and to see Ashley (*above center*). They were spied on by India and word got back to Rhett (*above right*). All this complicated the surprise birthday party planned for Ashley (*below left*) by Aunt Pitty and Melanie (*below center* and *right*).

After such a day even a leisurely cigarette couldn't help Scarlett feel comfortable about dressing for Ashley's party (*above*) until Rhett reminded her that she could wear her new burgundy velvet Plunkett (*above right*)—an opportunity no woman could resist! And that dress was so stunning, the wardrobe crew forgot to assign it any designation at all (petticoat: "#30"; party gown: "#31").

When she returned home that night, Scarlett donned a sumptuous red velvet robe (*below left*) to have a nightcap in but, instead, she encountered Rhett, (*below right*), who had a little surprise for her. (The robe was called "#29" but should have been "#32.")

The following morning Rhett asked Scarlett for a divorce, then left for London with Bonnie, and Mr. Gable (*above left*) seemed in the proper mood to play it. Miss Leigh (*above center*) had few fashion concerns since her nightgown was the one worn in the "Drunk" scene, although without the red robe (here referred to as "#29-A"). Little Bonnie (*above right*) was characteristically overdressed in a Persian lamb outfit upon her return from overseas. She was greeted by her mother in another luxurious robe (*below left*, actual "Scarlett Costume #33") and Miss Leigh here carefully held the child's new kitten under her arm. Mr. Gable (*below right*) appeared glad to see Scarlett although his ears seemed a matter of humorous concern to cinematographer Ernest Haller in the background.

Victor Fleming had no doubts that Clark Gable (both shown *above left*) could master the moment of heartbreak when Rhett cried after Scarlett's miscarriage. Meanwhile, Olivia de Havilland (*above right*) pensively prepared for that difficult sequence. Mr. Gable's ears (*left*) were again a point of amusement to all, including Vivien Leigh (*in background*), although she grew more somber (*below*) as the time for Bonnie's death scene drew nearer. (Her costume change was "#34.")

"So Bonnie had her blue velvet habit with a skirt that trailed down the pony's side and a black hat with a red plume in it." Bonnie Blue Butler's riding dress (*left*) was carefully described by author Mitchell as an example of Rhett's indulgence toward his half-spoiled daughter. Despite her mother's objections, he had granted the four-year-old's wish for this ridiculously precocious attire, as he had bowed to each of her previous whims. The pampered child, afraid of nothing but the dark, then demanded a jumping bar a foot and a half from the ground, and—even to this—Rhett reluctantly agreed. But while riding sidesaddle in this overly fancy outfit and attempting that hurdle, she fell to her death.

Mammy (*below left*) desperately feared for Rhett's sanity after the tragic accident. He was locked in his room with Bonnie's body, dissipating himself with grief and alcohol (*below center*). Only gentle Melanie (*below right*) was able to lure him back to reality. Alas, the strain was too much for her.

140

"Melanie's Death" scene was among the very saddest moments ever put on film, but Leslie Howard (*above*) took it no more seriously than any other part of his performance. Olivia de Havilland (*right*) exhibited a dedication to her craft and to this project that would soon reward her with a first Academy Award nomination. The supporting cast assembled here for the last time: (*below from left*) Alicia Rhett, Harry Davenport, Laura Hope Crews and Mickey Kuhn (as Beau).

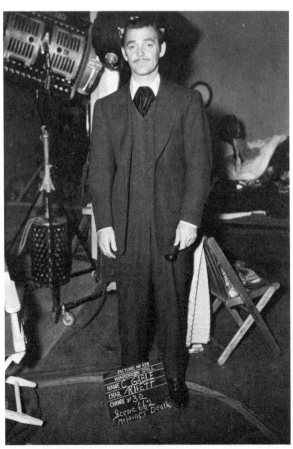

Vivien Leigh (*above*) approached "Melanie's Death" scene with some apparent levity (far from the way she played it!), but Clark Gable (*above right*) was much more in the mood. Both stars would remain so dressed until the picture's conclusion. But there had been another scene filmed and other design executed for Scarlett's return to Tara (*right*). Final editing reduced both scene and costume to a mere silhouette beneath the movie's end title. In all, Miss Leigh had changed costumes thirty-six times.

Walter Plunkett, born in 1902 in Oakland, California, had originally studied for a law career until the "acting bug" lured him to the New York theatre. After little success there, Walter returned to California and sought work as a film "extra." (One such 1925 assignment, in M-G-M's *The Merry Widow*, paralleled the early career of Clark Gable.) Turning then to design, Mr. Plunkett rose in the ranks first at the RKO studios and, by 1937, drew his first Selznick assignment with *Nothing Sacred*. In 1946 Walter became a contract designer at Metro-Goldwyn-Mayer, where he remained for two decades—achieving the reputation of "historical specialist." Although his diligent work on *Gone With the Wind* predated Academy Awards for that craft, Walter would later be one of three Oscar-winning designers for 1951's *An American in Paris*. Over the years he would receive nine other Academy Award nominations for *The Magnificent Yankee, That Forsyte Woman, Kind Lady, The Actress, Young Bess, Raintree County, Some Came Running, Pocketful of Miracles* and *How the West Was Won*. Throughout a forty-year career, until his retirement in 1966, Walter Plunkett designed costumes for more than 265 feature motion pictures.

The Sets

Among the thousands of watercolor drawings rendered by William Cameron Menzies for Gone With the Wind *was the striking one shown above, in which Scarlett walked into Tara's ravaged gardens and vowed she would overcome the miseries wrought by war. Later this beautiful color original would reside in the Herb Bridges Collection.*

Assistant director Eric G. Stacey (seated) and second assistant director Ridgeway Callow *transferred script and "call sheet" schedules to production crossboards, which kept track of the cast members and sets required for particular days of shooting—no mean feat on* Gone With the Wind.

Lyle Wheeler, who was later to become an Academy Award-winning chief art director at Twentieth Century-Fox, arranged the various set designs on "story boards" which would be juggled as often as script revisions commanded.

Intricate miniature models of the city of Atlanta were commissioned by the Selznick International Art Department for approval by David O. Selznick, William Cameron Menzies, Lyle Wheeler and Wilbur Kurtz before any actual set construction was allowed to begin.

Two other Menzies watercolor sketches later owned by Herb Bridges were the exterior (above) *and interior* (below) *of the Atlanta railroad depot for the sequence in which Scarlett searched for Dr. Meade.*

Carroll Nye's brother, Ben, was Gone With the Wind's associate makeup man, and this publicity photograph of Carroll demonstrated how actual historical Southern figures (like Jefferson Davis, shown in the framed picture) were used as models for achieving accuracy in Civil War era appearances. Ben Nye was later head make-up expert at Twentieth Century-Fox for many years.

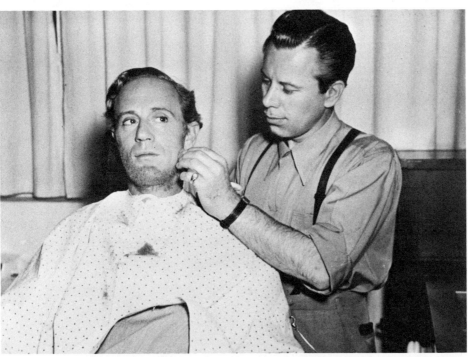

Monty Westmore created and applied a beard stubble for Leslie Howard in the "Ashley's Return from War" sequence.

In this publicity photograph, Hazel Rogers (left), associate hair stylist for the film, showed Susan Myrick actual Civil War era tintypes which the Selznick Research Department had provided for her and Mr. Westmore to consult when creating hairdos for the cast. Miss Myrick, an old friend of Margaret Mitchell's, was hired by David Selznick as a technical adviser and was referred to in Hollywood as "the Emily Post of the South."

A Chronicle of the Filming

This publicity photograph for Gone With the Wind *showed David O. Selznick* (left) *and Victor Fleming* (right) *discussing the script—their foremost problem.*

Mr. Cukor Begins

This photographic chronology of *Gone With the Wind*'s filming schedule was reconstructed from several components. Daily "call sheets" issued for cast and crew to prepare for the following day's assignments, for example, were rich in long-forgotten details. Although—like most schedules—such plans could not be strictly adhered to, the handwritten notations on these sheets brought this history into an even more precise focus. Additionally, various letters, clippings and news stories from the time supplemented that data even further. Most fascinating was a diary kept by journalist Gladys Hall in which notations of "what was being filmed when" followed the "call sheets" almost to the letter, but also provided human interest and insight into the proceedings.

After the release of *Gone With the Wind* David Selznick issued an edict whereby at no time was M-G-M to circulate enough scene "stills" for newspapers or magazines to publish a complete pictorial synopsis. Although some of the rarest scenes shown here were released for publicity purposes beforehand, many of them have never been published since the film's opening—if, indeed, ever at all. This enforced ban would later make "still" collecting highly difficult for *Gone With the Wind* followers. It seemed that the film's rarest negatives had either been misplaced through time or, perhaps, never transferred by Mr. Selznick to Metro-Goldwyn-Mayer at all. Despite the movie's various reissues, the same fairly common scenes would be circulated time and time again.

This Chronicle was prepared to serve several purposes. Most notably, it was hoped to prove that *Gone With the Wind*'s production schedule, despite a faulty beginning, was nothing short of miraculous in constructing such a vast narrative in comparatively so short a time. The completed film—three times as long as the average movie of its era and at least twice as lengthy as most "major" efforts—was in principal photography less than twenty-one weeks. In the twenty-three weeks remaining before its world premiere performance in Atlanta, David Selznick and his staff reviewed, edited and revised the components countless times. Some scenes were retaken, a few new moments added, other scenes were redubbed with new dialogue and then a few bridging titles and artistic inserts created until mid-November when the very last pictorial moment was photographed. Max Steiner's musical score was added, the film's sound track was "mixed" for varying audio levels, color processing was corrected and finalized and then, only a short time before its unveiling, mass production of prints was authorized for various cities throughout America. Within eleven months the "longest movie ever made" had progressed from a scratchy, almost scriptless beginning to multiple engagements in America's theatres.

A secondary aim of this Chronicle was to resolve the matter of directorial authorship. Contrary to popular belief, most of George Cukor's creative efforts were, unfortunately, forced into the scrap pile by a heavily revised script approach and some technical details which were corrected only after Mr. Cukor's departure. Sam Wood, on the other hand, directed some of the film's key moments and his contributions have been heretofore unappreciated.

The Chronicle was also intended to dispel rumors and legends—persistent for years—that the filming of *Gone With the Wind* was an unorganized mass of feuds, personal jealousies, firings and confusion. In actuality, it was a highly professional approach to a tediously difficult assignment that had momentarily floundered beneath script problems. Afterward, despite the sometimes daily delivery of new script pages, the filming proceeded in an orderly and precise manner. Pictorial rebuttals have been presented here also to disprove such falsehoods as: Victor Fleming directed "only a small portion" of *Gone With the Wind*; George Cukor was the "author" of the final "Paris Hat" sequence; or even that *all* of Clark Gable's scenes were directed by Victor Fleming.

But there *were* some unfortunate results from the project. The prolonged, grueling, six-days-a-week filming schedule caused temporary harm to the health of its principal director, and possibly permanent damage to the physical stamina of its leading lady. And, of course, the saddest artistic casualty of the entire project was George Cukor, who had worked along with David Selznick almost from the moment the book had been purchased for filming. In retrospect, considering Mr. Cukor's talent and experience, in contrast to a project that was not quite ready to start, it would seem almost inevitable that friction had to develop which would force his withdrawal.

George's arguments about the script proved, in time, to be well founded since the project halted after his departure and all concentration was put into making the screen treatment workable. From the first days of filming, trouble was in the air as George pursued fidelity to the book, sometimes ignoring written instructions. His filming progress was also limited by the construction of sets. While most directors (and actors) would prefer to shoot at least nearly in sequence, George Cukor and his performers found their script being altered daily and sequences jumping from early in the story to midpoint and then back again. By late January, as production

148

began, the only sets ready were the outside facade and environs of Tara (on the "Forty Acres" backlot), the lower floor of its interior, Scarlett's bedroom, Pittypat's house (interior and exterior) and the Atlanta Armory where the charity bazaar took place. Although all primary events in the story led to the Twelve Oaks barbecue and Scarlett's first marriage, Mr. Cukor was forced, in the temporary absence of a Wilkes home setting, to jump from "Scarlett as a girl" to "Scarlett as a widow," frustrating the development of her character for both himself and Vivien Leigh.

Unauthorized changes and the director's moments of inspiration angered David Selznick, who protested to George that he wanted no "projection-room surprises!" Then, David became a daily visitor and supervisor on the set—a novelty in his longtime working relationship with director Cukor. But George's eventual departure did not entirely remove his signature from *Gone With the Wind*. He continued to coach both Vivien Leigh and Olivia de Havilland secretly throughout their performances (although neither actress knew about the other for quite some time). And his more than two years of preparation certainly qualified George Cukor for permanent recognition as a major force in bringing Margaret Mitchell's book to the screen.

George Cukor called "action!" for the first time on Thursday, January 26, 1939, but the day soon evaporated in a variety of short takes, tests and press interviews. After a very brief moment between Mammy and Scarlett (in the Tara bedroom on Stage 3) was recorded as scheduled—although not the *complete* scene—good weather prompted a change, and Vivien Leigh was joined by Fred Crane and George Bessolo at Forty Acres to attempt the opening sequence on Tara's porch. The next day's "rushes" proved disastrous, however, when the curly hairdos of the Tarletons (*above*) photographed *bright orange*! Four days later the scenes were repeated, with the actors' hair styles modified to eliminate their curls and heavily darkened as well (*below*).

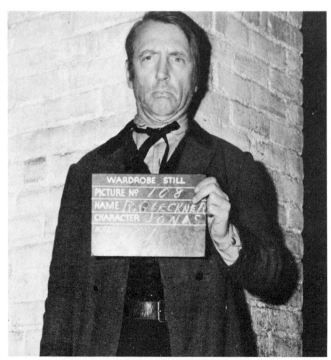

"The Arrival of Ellen" (*Scenes 19 and 20*) was filmed on Saturday, January 28, with actor Robert Gleckler portraying Jonas Wilkerson (*above* with Barbara O'Neil and in costume at *right*). Mr. Gleckler, however, would die of uremic poisoning on February 25 during a hiatus in production—forcing his early scenes to be redone later under Victor Fleming's direction. Victor Jory (*below* with Miss O'Neil, and in costume for an unused field scene, *below right*) was hired to replace Mr. Gleckler on Friday March 3.

It was also on Saturday, January 28, that the camera on Stage 3 caught *Scenes 21 through 32*, with Ellen telling Gerald about Wilkerson's illegitimate child (original version *above*—later retaken when Mr. Mitchell's hairstyle changed) and then the O'Hara family preparing for "Evening Prayer Services" (*right*). These sequences were experimentally photographed with slight illumination—new for Technicolor—and although David Selznick felt the scenes were a bit too dark, most were retained. "Still" photographs such as these were not numbered in the exact sequence in which they were taken, but done in batches. Interestingly, the one below was chosen to be first in numerical order (i.e. SIP-108-1).

Fair weather on Friday, January 27, and then again on Monday, January 30, allowed George Cukor to direct *Scenes 10 through 17*—"Gerald's Walk with Scarlett." (Mr. Cukor was photographed walking along with Vivien Leigh and Thomas Mitchell, *above.*) Upon seeing the finished results, David Selznick did not respond well to Mr. Mitchell's curly hair or to the landscaping of trees and shrubbery selected to represent the Tara plantation. The sequence was therefore scheduled for later retakes. On that same Friday *Scene 35* had also been prepared, in which Gerald, Suellen, Carreen and Pork waited for Scarlett to finish dressing for the barbecue—but it was never to be used. Neither was "The Ride to Twelve Oaks" (*Scene 38, right center*), with Pork driving the carriage as Mammy carried a box with Scarlett's gown for a ball that evening which would be canceled because of the outbreak of war. Even more disappointing was the deletion of the barbecue-pit sequences at Twelve Oaks photographed at this same time by William Cameron Menzies. These scenes personified the great detail that Wilbur Kurtz had worked tedious hours to develop from the original Sidney Howard script. They showed, for example, the separate barbecue area for the blacks (*below right*), as well as other festivities, although they did not yet include Scarlett surrounded by her beaux or any part of the Twelve Oaks mansion (which was not yet completed).

After refilming the "Tarleton Boys" scene on Monday, January 30, dull weather conditions finally forced a move back indoors to Stage 3 to pick up those scenes which had actually been planned as the initial ones. The very first Selznick "call sheet" that had been issued on Tuesday, January 24, 1939—for work to begin two days later—had blueprinted the first moments of filming to be *Scenes 33 and 34*, calling for Mammy to lace Scarlett's corset (*above left*) and then argue with her over which dress to wear to the Twelve Oaks barbeque (*above right*). They would then be joined by Prissy for *Scene 36*, in which that young scatterbrain would bring a tray of "vittles" for Scarlett's breakfast which Mammy cajoled scowling Scarlett into eating (*right*). Later that day the only other sequence shot in that bedroom was sketched out: Scarlett, as the Widow Hamilton, was to be attended by the family doctor, then would try on a "gay bonnet" to offset her mourning clothes and receive a letter inviting her to visit Pittypat and Melanie in Atlanta (*Scenes 86 through 88*). After these scenes were completed on Tuesday, January 31, only the first portion would eventually prove usable in its entirety. Script changes on the "Widow Hamilton" sequence allowed only the "trying on the gay bonnet" moment to be retained from the latter.

Maybelle Merriwether (Bebe Anderson) tried to interest a Confederate officer in a mustache cup as her mother (Jane Darwell) and Mrs. Elsing (Mary Young) looked on (later discarded).

A Patchwork Bazaar

Rehearsals and filming of dancers at the Atlanta Bazaar had been proceeding simultaneously under the guidance of dance directors Frank Floyd and Eddie Prinz. When Vivien Leigh and George Cukor were free to join them on February 1, the presence of Clark Gable, Olivia de Havilland, Laura Hope Crews, Harry Davenport, Jane Darwell and Bebe Anderson was also required for the first time. Much filming was done that week and later but—because of future script revisions—little of it would be retained. What was eventually deemed usable had to be later "patched" into Victor Fleming retakes.

Melanie comforted Scarlett after the disgrace of Rhett bidding $150 in gold for a dance with her (later discarded).

Melanie assured Pittypat that Charles would understand Scarlett's presence at the Bazaar (later discarded).

Rhett, dressed in a cape, was applauded by the crowd upon his entrance (retained).

Melanie was thrilled, Scarlett bored during the announcements (retained except for actress Betty Butcher at right).

As the book described, Rhett was initially "dressed like a dandy" at the Bazaar—complete with a very un-Gable-like cape. The actor had also been asked to assume a Southern accent and the filmed results further betrayed his image. Luckily, the script was totally changed and all Mr. Gable's original "Bazaar" scenes were discarded, except for a brief entrance (wearing that cape) and a few distant shots of his dancing with Miss Leigh. But the "stills" on this page survived through the years to present an incongruous concept of a version that was never to be! Here, Rhett (wearing that cape) greeted Melanie (*top left*), unhooked Scarlett's veil (*above*) and picked up the fan she had been toying with (*left*). After this, the trio discussed Charles' death until Dr. Meade requested a donation of jewelry.

George Cukor (seen near the camera as he filmed the "Waltz" sequence, in the photograph at *right*) evidently enjoyed creating this moment with Mr. Gable and Miss Leigh. The Cukor version proved unusable, though, since Scarlett's dialogue was far too "bitchy" and was later modified to make her a bit more sympathetic. Here, she was berating Rhett for making her conspicuous with his bid and then demanding to know why he hadn't redeemed her ring as he had just done for Melanie.

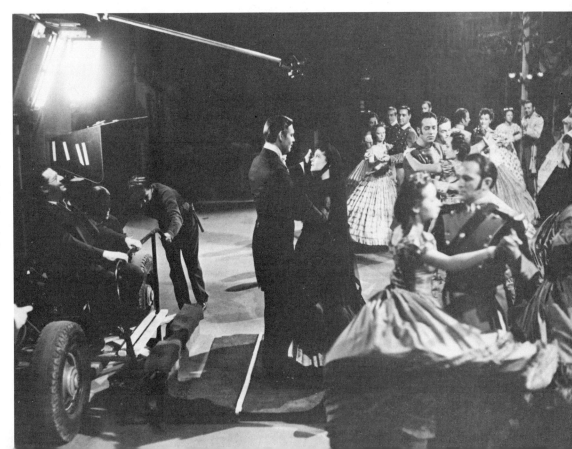

The Real "Reel"

Even the famous "Reel" sequence was later revised, although the Selznick group was able to salvage Scarlett's walking through the crowds to meet Rhett (*above left*) and Rhett's pleasure at her acceptance (*above*). But the reel photographed by George Cukor (*left*) had been designed as only a quick montage *after* the waltz and was later redone in a prolonged version by Victor Fleming to precede that crucial "Waltz" scene. In the Fleming retake (*below*) Mr. Gable and the male dancers assumed a new position placing them on the right side of the screen. Ironically, the scene "still" of the abortive reel would be the one to survive—and be used to death—for decades afterward.

Mrs. Elsing Bites the Dust

Many moviegoers would later note the absence of the Mrs. Elsing character, such an important figure in the book as Mrs. Merriwether's associate in gossip. But actress Mary Young had not only been cast for the role, she had actually filmed several scenes for the "Bazaar" sequence. *Above*: The original concept of the "Chaperon's Corner" showed her standing in horror with Pittypat and Dolly Merriwether when Scarlett accepted Rhett's dance bid. *Below*: She helped Dolly comfort Melanie who was distressed over her sister-in-law's odd behavior.

That Damned Hat

The "Paris Hat" sequence (*Scene 156*) filmed by George Cukor on Monday, February 6, was obviously a pleasant experience for all (*above*). But they might have saved their efforts! The scene's concept, following the book, had Scarlett propose dyeing the hat black to match her mourning clothes, showed Rhett momentarily taking it back until she promised not to, and later allowed him to kiss her lightly on the cheek (*below*). Additionally, Mr. Gable wore an ill-fitting cravat, the hat itself was trimmed with veiling and Miss Leigh's forehead was bare. Although "stills" from the Cukor version were perpetually circulated (*top right*—used by Macmillan on its movie edition's cover—and *right center*), the actual footage was entirely discarded. In Victor Fleming's retake the script was thoroughly changed, the veiling was removed from the hat, Miss Leigh added bangs to her hairdo and Mr. Gable traded that cravat in for a bow tie! (As shown in photograph *below right*.)

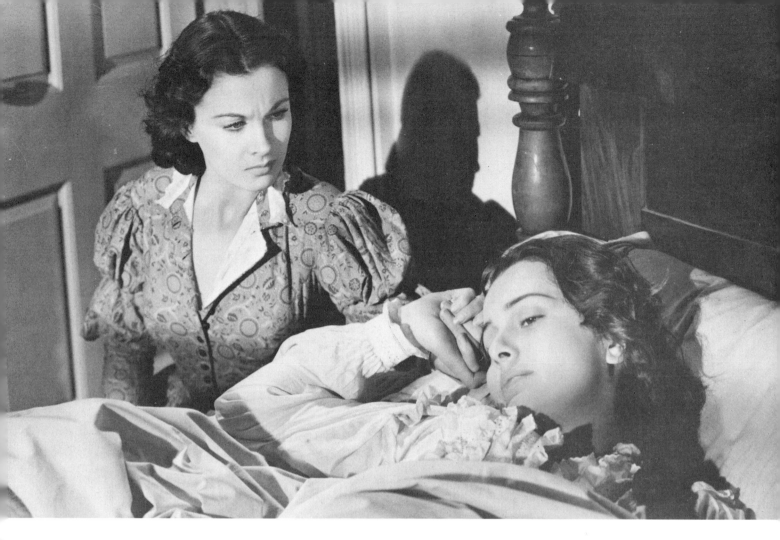

Forced to jump ahead in the script because of the unavailability of certain sets, George Cukor had been filming the events surrounding "The Birth of Melanie's Baby" (*above*) on Stage 2 for several days. But delaying script changes involving Scarlett's treatment of Prissy (*left*) constantly flowed from the front office. Then on Wednesday, February 8, the actual "Birth" moments were recorded and quite strikingly done in silhouette (*Scene 270*). In an effort to proceed in sequence, the balance of the week was devoted to Rhett's arrival (with his woebegone horse and ricketty wagon) to rescue the women and baby (*Scenes 278–280*). In intervening moments, whenever possible, Mr. Cukor, Miss Leigh, Miss de Havilland and the crew returned to the Armory set for some additional "Bazaar" takes, which did not involve Clark Gable.

But friction between George Cukor and David Selznick over script problems came to a climax that weekend and on Monday, February 13, a press statement was released announcing that George was withdrawing from the project—a mutual decision, it was said. George agreed to stay two more days, during which time he would complete those scenes presently in production involving the departure from Pittypat's on that "last night in Atlanta," and then to film his only two scenes with Leslie Howard.

159

On that "last night in Atlanta," Scarlett's lamp lit the way for Rhett to carry Melanie to the safety of his wagon.

As Melanie held her baby within the wagon, Olivia's motherly smile was considered a bit too hearty by the publicity department so this "still" was relegated to the suppressed file.

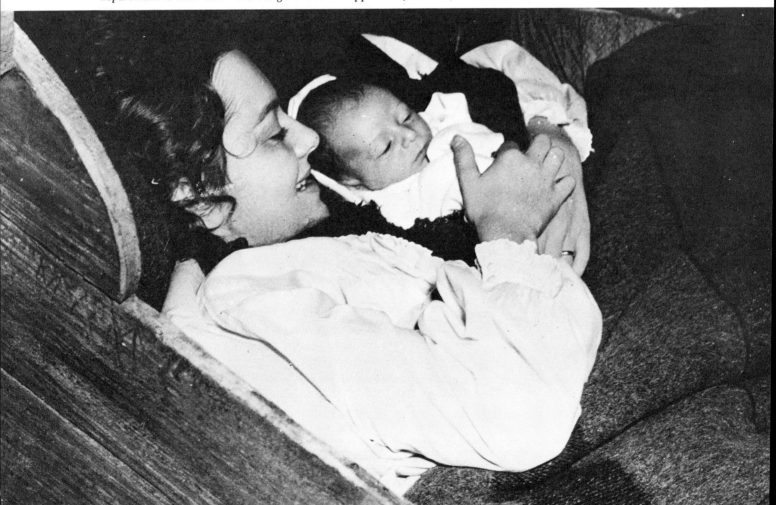

After completing Rhett's rescue (*right*), George Cukor turned to those two Ashley sequences. The first involved his walk upstairs with Melanie after Christmas dinner, as they bid Scarlett good night (*below left*). The script for this was later considered unsatisfactory and the scene was destroyed. But the second sequence, filmed on Wednesday, February 15, wherein Scarlett gave Ashley a sash and begged him for an admission of love (*Scene 194, below right*), was directly from the pages of Margaret Mitchell's book and would be retained in its entirety. After completing it, George Cukor departed from the project and production was shut down for two weeks. During that hiatus Victor Fleming was replaced on M-G-M's *The Wizard of Oz* by King Vidor and rushed into conferences with David Selznick and Ben Hecht to help devise a new script approach. David was unhappy with much already filmed and even more so with what was about to be. Principal concentration was placed on revisions in Scarlett's character—in effect to "soften" her. Since the part of Belle Watling still had not been cast, an early scene showing Belle waiting with Rhett outside the Bazaar (pointing out her customers) as well as one in which she gave Rhett a box containing the Paris hat (in view of Mrs. Merriwether and Mrs. Elsing) were deleted. Extreme changes were made in the "Bazaar" sequence so that Charles Hamilton was never mentioned, Rhett did not immediately redeem Melanie's ring and Mrs. Elsing did not appear at all. Even Maybelle Merriwether was reduced to only a quick bit as the bids for dances were offered.

Meanwhile, Margaret Mitchell had dropped some hints in letters to Susan Myrick and Wilbur Kurtz on incongruities she had spotted in the "stills" the Selznick people had sent to her. Margaret and David had *both* been unhappy with the appearance of Tara and its environs in the opening sequences, while Margaret pointed out that the Armory set was far too ornate for wartime Atlanta and that not a single wounded soldier was in view during the Bazaar. Already planning to refilm most of the dialogue scenes at the Bazaar, David had a script bit inserted wherein Harry Davenport, Jr., would portray a one-armed soldier asking for jewelry donations. Ironically, this would force later retakes of Harry, Sr.'s speech since Dr. Meade had originally made that request.

Mr. Fleming Takes Over

If Victor Fleming (*at left* with David Selznick) had realized when filming resumed on Wednesday, March 1, that none of his work for the first two days would ever reach the screen, he might not have accepted the assignment. A third version of the opening with the Tarletons (*above*) was filmed first, this time from a different angle. The two young actors were quite inexperienced and one thing was soon evident: it wouldn't be the last time this unlucky first scene was to be attempted. Jeems, groom to the Tarletons, had been helpful in the book in explaining why Scarlett might have run away. Even though actor Ben Carter went through those motions for the scene below, the film Tarletons would remain unenlightened since this sequence was cut before the first preview.

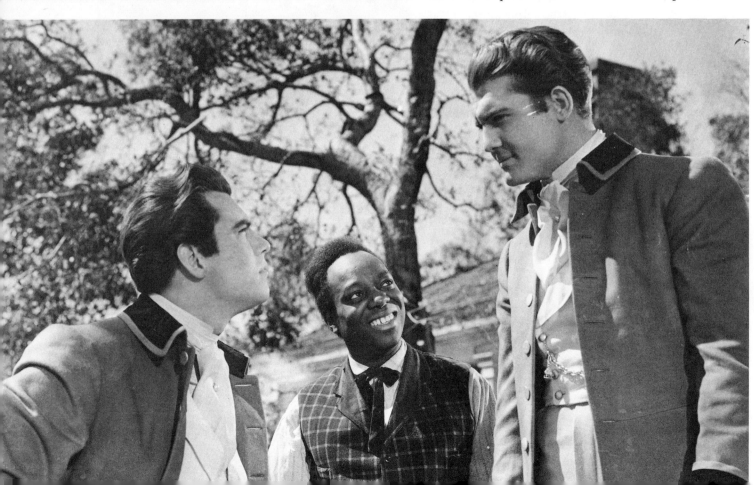

David Selznick had hoped to resume filming by Monday, February 27, but he allowed two extra days for the re-landscaping of Tara. While the different angle for the new Tarleton scene disguised those environs, a second version of "Gerald's Walk with Scarlett" proved totally unsatisfactory. After seeing the retake, David felt the plantation "looks on the screen as though it were the back yard of a suburban home." In the meantime Thomas Mitchell's hairstyle had been straightened (*right*) even though it would no longer match the tousled curls evident in his riding long shot or in the "Evening Prayer" scene. Nevertheless, the crew moved onward and on Friday, March 3, the "Wedding Reception of Scarlett and Charles Hamilton" was filmed on the interior set of Tara (*Scene 85, below left*). Later, a revised *Scene 87* picked up with Ellen now comforting Scarlett and suggesting a trip to Atlanta (*below right*).

163

The interiors of Twelve Oaks had finally been completed, and on Tuesday, March 7, Vivien Leigh and Leslie Howard began "Scarlett's Confession of Love to Ashley" (*Scene 70*). Only half of the scene was completed then, and, strangely, its conclusion would be recorded by a new cinematographer the following week. On Thursday, March 9, David Selznick announced that Ernest Haller from Warner Brothers was replacing Lee Garmes in handling the film's photographic duties. Work proceeded, though, as "The Arrival at Twelve Oaks" (*Scenes 40–48*) was filmed on Friday, March 10. In the photograph above Victor Fleming lined up the camera angle (*right*) where Cathleen Calvert (Marcella Martin) told Scarlett about Rhett Butler—Clark Gable's *actual* entrance in the film. Although Miss O'Hara would be seen greeting some of her beaux at this point in the finished film, footage showing her with Tom Seidel as Tony Fontaine, Eric Alden as Rafe Calvert and David Newell as Cade Calvert was eventually eliminated. And a line of her dialogue to the Tarleton boys—"I wore this old dress just because I thought you liked it"—was due to lose its meaning, since it would not eventually be the same dress they saw her in the previous day.

164

On Saturday, March 11, "Melanie and Ashley's Love Scene" was a gentle change from the rowdy barbecue festivities. But the "War Talk" sequence in the Twelve Oaks dining room (*above left*) brought all the excitement back into play. This was the first scene shared by Clark Gable and Leslie Howard, and the *only* scene in the film containing all three of Scarlett's future husbands. For the "Staircase Gossip about Scarlett" interlude (featuring Marjorie Reynolds, *above right*), the wardrobe crew evidently overlooked the buttons missing on the front of Alicia Rhett's gown. Luckily, they weren't noticeable on film. Later that same day Vivien Leigh became the belle of the barbecue as she sat smiling in the Twelve Oaks gardens (*Scene 57, below*), surrounded by eligible men.

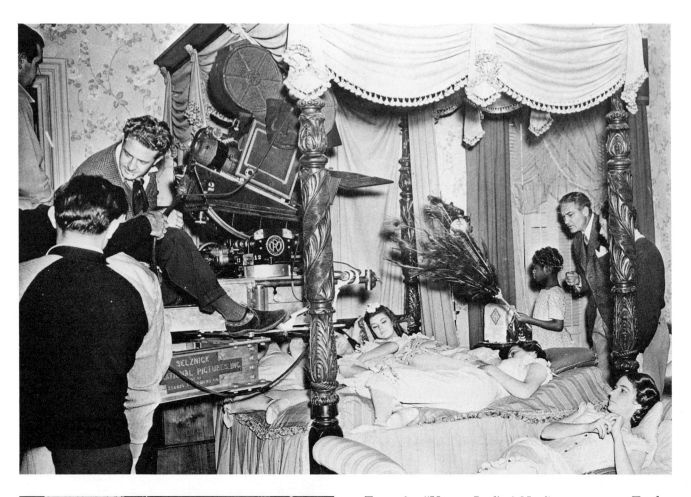

Even the "Young Ladies' Nap" sequence at Twelve Oaks (*above*) required Victor Fleming to carefully line up camera details, such as the black children who fanned the sleeping belles. Vivien Leigh and Leslie Howard relaxed on the set (*at the left*) before continuing their library scene on Monday, March 13, which would lead up to her slapping his face (*below right*) and then discovering Rhett had been in the room all along.

Various fill-in shots of Twelve Oaks continued throughout that week and, in the long run, more was recorded than it would be possible to use. Filmed but eventually deleted were "A Young Man Talks to Rhett" (*Scene 58*), "Ashley Rides Off to War" (*right*) and "Scarlett in the Garden" (*Scene 59*), in which she said, "I'd just love to drill a cavalry troop. And there's only one thing I'd expect them to know—and that's how to kill Yankees very fast!" Later, Scarlett complained, "I don't see why everybody's so excited about going to war. It's just riding horses, same as hunting." Those last two moments survived even after the first preview but were cut soon thereafter. Many of the "still" photographs taken at Twelve Oaks betrayed a stilted and artificial quality. One showed Scarlett walking upstairs right after news of the war had broken but revealed extra players in the background strolling about in total nonchalance. But the scene below unintentionally captured even more disconcerting details, from the microphone at the top to the man holding the leg of Ashley's horse at the bottom.

SIP-108-P24

167

On Monday, March 20, and Tuesday, March 21, it was Victor Fleming and Ernest Haller's turn to visit the Atlanta Bazaar. Mr. Gable shed his cape for these retakes with Vivien Leigh, Harry Davenport, Jr., and Olivia de Havilland (*above left*) and, most especially, with Miss Leigh alone (*above right*). Afterward, the newly written dance scenes between them were reperformed. After deducting the two-week production hiatus from his tenure, Lee Garmes had worked little over a month on *Gone With the Wind*, and most of his efforts, like George Cukor's, were doomed to oblivion by script rewrites. What would remain of Lee's in the final film were: "Ellen's Arrival at Tara" and "Evening Prayer," "Scarlett Dressing for the Barbecue," much of the "Twelve Oaks" sequence, "Scarlett's Wedding Reception," "Ellen Comforting Scarlett," "Scarlett's Promise to Ashley," "The Birth of Melanie's Baby," "The Flight from Aunt Pittypat's" and a few intercut scenes at the Bazaar. The Cukor/Garmes "Bazaar" scenes would remain detectable, though, through a slightly darker quality in the photography—from Scarlett tapping her feet in the booth to her look of horror as Rhett's name was announced. Later that week, "Ashley's Furlough" was recorded by Victor Fleming, from the meeting at the train depot (*Scene 168, left center*) through "Christmas Dinner" (*Scene 180*) to Scarlett watching Ashley and Melanie walk upstairs (*below left*). Meanwhile, according to Gladys Hall's journal, a rumor spread through the company that week that young Warner Brothers player Ann Sheridan would soon be joining them as Belle Watling.

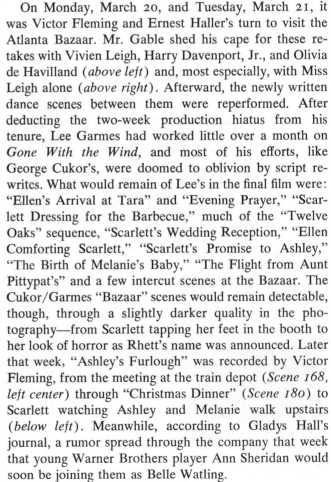

The week of Monday, March 27, brought the tragedy of Gettysburg into focus with the "Casualty Lists" sequence. As in the book, Melanie comforted Dr. Meade's family on the loss of their son Darcy (*Scene 166, above left*). But a Selznick innovation in which actress Margaret Seddon as "Grandma Tarleton" learned about the death of the two boys (*above right*) was later eliminated, as were many such "original" scenes that did not conform to the novel. (After all, Margaret Mitchell had not even created a "Grandma Tarleton"!) While William Cameron Menzies and assistant director Eric Stacey guided second-unit photography on the bulk of the crowd scenes here, Clark and Vivien—along with Butterfly McQueen (*below left*)—filmed *Scene 325,* "The Road Outside Atlanta." After Clark lifted Vivien from the wagon (*at the right*) to film one version of their goodbye, it was deemed unsatisfactory and retakes were scheduled for the following week. In the meantime, Clark spirited Carole Lombard out of town and they were married on March 29.

The "Atlanta Exodus" (*Scenes 203–208*), filmed during the week of April 3, had been carefully sketched out in advance by William Cameron Menzies so that, as disorderly as it appeared on screen, it was just that precise when Victor Fleming called "Action!" to the extras, and technicians seen preparing for it in the photograph above. Vivien Leigh refused a "double" for her run through the horses, wagons and exploding shells, and on Wednesday, April 5, according to Gladys Hall, she barely escaped a collision. Meanwhile, the "honeymooner" dropped by to hear about the excitement from Vivien and Victor (*left*).

Clark Gable was soon back in the ranks, however, and *Scenes 209–211*, "Rhett's Ride with Scarlett" (*above*—note the microphone at top and the unfinished sets), concluding with their arrival at Pittypat's (*below*), were filmed that Friday. Meanwhile, Laura Hope Crews (*right*) waited on the sidelines for her dizzy flight (*Scene 212*).

Filming in the week of April 10 took a step backward in continuity for scenes in the church that was utilized as a hospital by wartime Atlantans. The notable "Shadow" scene (*above*) was designed by William Cameron Menzies for impressive visual effect and, although it succeeded upon first glimpse, repeat viewings would indicate that the "doubles" (silhouetted by a spotlight) for Vivien Leigh and Olivia de Havilland did not move in exact unison with their counterparts. Here, in this "still" from *Scene 192*, the wounded soldier who told Melanie about his missing brother was obviously the famous entertainer Cliff Edwards. In the finished film, however, Mr. Edwards was not visible, although his "Jiminy Cricket" voice could be clearly heard.

The balance of hospital scenes (*195–202*) photographed that week followed story continuity fairly closely, with Scarlett becoming revolted at the death, lice and amputation she saw until she ran out into the "Exodus" confusion (which had been filmed the week before). "Belle Watling on the Church Steps" was temporarily postponed since the part had still not been cast, but no sooner had the company bypassed that segment than word came from the front office that New York actress Ona Munson had been signed for the role. Victor Fleming pleaded for further shooting continuity but David Selznick thought it best to concentrate on all scenes involving Clark Gable lest M-G-M need him for another picture. The schedule, therefore, jumped into Part Four of the book to the "horse jail" where Scarlett visited Rhett in her drapery dress and he discovered the calluses on her hands (*Scene 487, left*). Such frustration in filming continuity added to the long days and nights of pressured work, took its toll on Victor Fleming's nervous system. On Victor's suggestion, David Selznick began negotiations at week's end with his M-G-M partners for a substitute director should one become necessary.

Victor Fleming continued pushing all the same but by Monday, April 17 there were more front-office edicts. It had also been decided to move all of Olivia de Havilland's scenes ahead, enabling her quick return to Warner Brothers, and to complete Leslie Howard's performance so he could begin Selznick International's own *Intermezzo*. So the schedule jumped ahead even further to a long sequence at Melanie's house near the conclusion of Part Four (*Scenes 530–550*). Here, news of "The Raid on Shantytown" and of Frank Kennedy's death was learned by the ladies amidst questioning by Yankees and Rhett's bringing a wounded Ashley home. These particular scenes gave Alicia Rhett her best opportunities as she berated Scarlett for necessitating the "Raid" and then warned Melanie not to trust Rhett Butler (*above*). The sequence was completed on Friday, April 21.

With the arrival of Monday, April 24, the strain of overwork had drained Victor Fleming but he continued with the conclusion of the book's Part Four. *Scenes 556 through 570* began as Scarlett consoled herself with brandy over the death of Frank Kennedy (*right center*), and followed through the lengthy passage of Rhett's proposal (*below right*). In holding to his promise to keep the script basically "Margaret Mitchell," David Selznick had added dialogue here from two preceding book scenes between Scarlett and Rhett which were not included in the film ("The Drive to Five Points" and the "Night Porch" scene).

The next bit of business involved Ona Munson, who had joined the company that week as Belle Watling. Her first filmed scene would actually be her second appearance as she and Rhett leaned out her window to hear Prissy scream "De Yankees is comin'" (*Scene 275, above left*). Then Clark Gable, Vivien Leigh and Victor Fleming filmed the entrance to "Ashley's Birthday Party" (*above right*). That celebration itself (*Scenes 603–607*) was recorded a day later and Miss Leigh's hairstyle did not quite match from one day to the other. As a result, she would not appear as strikingly beautiful upon greeting Melanie as she did outside the house with Rhett or in the breathtaking "track" shot as she stood alone awaiting recognition. (In the photograph at the *right* Miss Leigh discussed her soon-to-be-famous velvet gown with David Selznick and Victor Fleming.)

The only remaining sequence which required the combined talents of Clark Gable, Olivia de Havilland and Leslie Howard was "Melanie's Death" (*Scene 662*). According to Gladys Hall's on-the-set journal, Sidney Howard worked all morning on Thursday, April 27, to help the overwrought Victor Fleming prepare the final shooting version of it. Those tragic moments were poignantly captured on film that day, but later in the afternoon Mr. Fleming collapsed and withdrew from *Gone With the Wind* for an indefinite rest. It was then announced to the company that veteran director Sam Wood, temporarily idle as he awaited completion of his M-G-M contract, would serve as replacement.

"Melanie's Death": Dr. Meade warned Scarlett not to make any confessions to her dying friend.

"Melanie's Death": Olivia de Havilland and Vivien Leigh created one of the cinema's most exquisitely tragic moments.

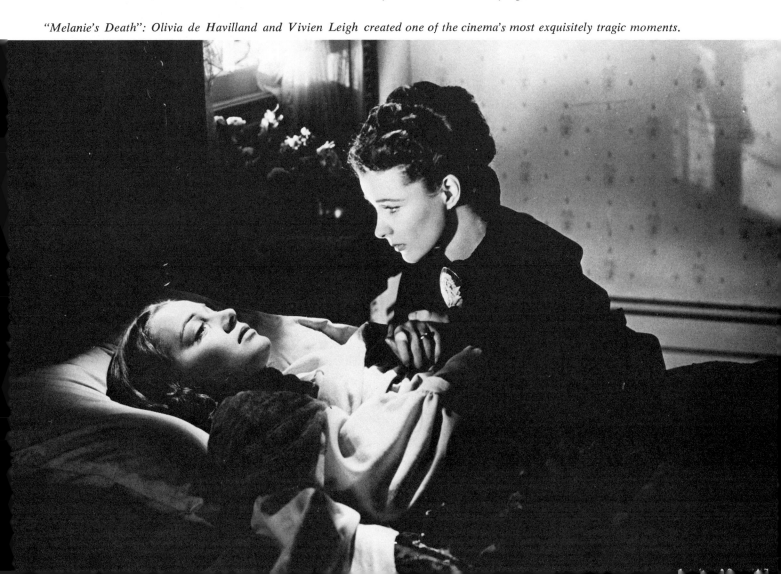

Enter Sam Wood

By Monday, May 1, Sam Wood was well in command of the *Gone With the Wind* schedule as he devoted his energies to "Scarlett and Ashley at the Lumber Mill" (*Scene 598, above*) and to "Belle Watling on the Church Steps." This last sequence became another "jinx" for the company as the first version (*Scene 193, left*) with Vivien Leigh, Olivia de Havilland and Ona Munson gave Miss Munson's heavily padded bosom far too much prominence for approval by the Hays Office. The scene was redone by Mr. Wood the following week, but again proved unusable.

In Victor Fleming's absence it was decided to give Clark Gable a short vacation as well and initial concentration was placed on sequences at Tara such as "Scarlett Tears Down the Draperies" (*Scene 486, above*—a particularly rare "still" photograph) and "Scarlett Gives Gerald's Watch to Pork" (*Scene 485, right center*). The Tara interior was used again for Scarlett as "Mrs. Frank Kennedy" with Melanie and Ashley (*Scene 514, below left*), and then Sam Wood turned his cameras to Melanie and Belle's "Carriage Scene," the most singularly touching moment of Ona Munson's performance (*Scene 565, below right*).

In that same week of May 1 Sam Wood began the "Yankee Cavalryman" sequence, with Scarlett chasing a helpful Melanie back upstairs to her sickbed (*above*). Then, as the work week ended on Saturday, May 6, Mr. Wood began the emotional "Scarlett's Return to Tara" (*left*). According to Gladys Hall, the cast and crew were moved to near alarm that day at the profound grief Vivien Leigh's acting exhibited as she collapsed with fists pressed against her face at the sight of Ellen O'Hara's body. "Scarlett's Return to Tara" (*Scenes 353–378*) resumed on Monday, May 8, as Vivien Leigh was joined by Thomas Mitchell, Hattie McDaniel and Oscar Polk for scenes that would lead to, but *not* include, her walk into the garden where she would profess her starvation oath.

Simultaneously on May 8 William Cameron Menzies filmed a montage—a series of large closeups—for the "Provost Marshal" sequence, portraying Belle Watling and her girls testifying in court to save the lives of Atlanta's men (*Scenes 552A–552I*). Those efforts of Ona Munson, Ivy Parsons (as Belle's maid), John Wray (as the provost marshal) and "the girls," Shirley Chambers and Yola D'Avril (*right*), would prove to be in vain, however. Mr. Menzies then utilized Alicia Rhett and Leona Roberts for a gossip scene and Miss Rhett again for a new sequence in which she received a letter of apology from Ellen on the morning of the Twelve Oaks barbecue. Still later that day Alicia would film her "insert" at the lumber mill where she found Scarlett with Ashley and cried out, "Are you comin' Ashley—home to your wife?" But it *really* was not Miss Rhett's day, as none of these scenes would find its way into the finished picture.

On Wednesday, May 10, Vivien Leigh and Paul Hurst went through the rather gruesome motions for Sam Wood of "Scarlett Killing the Yankee Deserter" (*Scene 431, below*). On the following day Vivien and Olivia de Havilland labored over the disposal of the soldier's body.

Victor Fleming felt well enough to return to work during the week of Monday, May 15, and was agreeable to speeding up the production schedule through any possible means. Sam Wood, with no other commitments, was equally willing to stay on and help direct scenes simultaneously. With Mr. Menzies and Eric Stacey as additional backup, it might have been possible to gain a great deal of lost time except for one highly significant detail—there was only *one* leading lady and she was in almost every scene! Vivien and Victor's primary concern that week was preparation for the complicated "Atlanta Depot" sequence to be filmed at Forty Acres, where "Scarlett Searches for Dr. Meade." Meanwhile, Sam Wood directed "Rhett and Bonnie in London" (*Scene 620*) on Tuesday, May 16, and "The Naming of Bonnie" (*Scene 585*) on the following day. This last scene required both Clark Gable and Olivia de Havilland, with only minor participation necessary from Vivien Leigh.

Mr. Fleming Returns

Weather conditions halted work at Forty Acres on Thursday, May 18, forcing Victor Fleming indoors to Stage 11, where he retrieved the megaphone from Sam Wood, who had already been preparing the "No More Babies" sequence. Cinematographer Ernest Haller lined up the angles with Vivien Leigh (*above*) for the infuriating moment when Rhett surprised Scarlett at her dressing table (in the midst of her daydreams of Ashley) and she informed him she wanted no more children (*Scenes 586–591*). The sequence, which concluded with Rhett kicking in Scarlett's bedroom door, was written (almost on the spot) by David Selznick and was hardly as romantic as the "still" at left would indicate. The striking picture of Miss Leigh—at which Rhett hurled his whiskey glass—had been painted by artist Helen Carlton, who made her living doing just such movie portraits.

Later in the day, after more last-minute script pages were delivered from David Selznick, Victor Fleming followed through with the amusing segment when "Rhett Pours Mammy a Drink" after Bonnie's birth (*Scene 583, above left*). Gladys Hall noted the crew's hilarity that day when Clark Gable surprised Hattie McDaniel by substituting real scotch for the cold tea usually used in movie decanters. Then it was back to Forty Acres for Victor and Vivien to continue work at the Atlanta depot, interspersed with a brief sequence, "Dressing for Ashley's Party" (*Scenes 600–601, above right*). While the massive depot undertaking continued that week, Sam Wood directed Clark Gable and Ona Munson in a Selznick "original," which showed Rhett seeking Belle

Watling's sympathy after Scarlett turned him out of her bed (*Scene 592, below left*). One of the few completely non-Mitchell moments to survive in the finished film, this scene served a touching purpose—with its final closeup of Belle's tearful eyes, the audience learned that she was in love with him (*below right*).

Then, on Monday, May 22, Victor Fleming concluded what was probably the single most memorable sequence in *Gone With the Wind*, in which Scarlett crossed the train depot through hundreds of wounded and dead men and the camera (mounted on a crane to rise one hundred feet in the air) pulled back to show a panorama of war's futility—highlighted by a symbolically tattered Confederate flag (*Scenes 250–262*).

In her quest for Dr. Meade, Scarlett carefully picked her way among "hundreds of wounded men . . . stretched out in endless rows."

A dummy was clearly visible at the foot of this bit player who "nursed" the wounded at the train station.

Victor Fleming and Vivien Leigh prepared for that big moment—the famous "crane" shot.

Scarlett found John Wilkes (Howard Hickman in costume, above) dying at the depot. But this non-Mitchell scene would later be eliminated.

Belle Watling giving water to the wounded (Ona Munson, above) was another "Selznick original" touch later deemed too unfaithful to the novel for retention.

Plans for "Scarlett Searches for Dr. Meade" had been formulating since the production began. When the sequence was completed on May 22, all its components lived up to David Selznick's expectations, although, as with other major sequences, more footage was shot than could be used. Much future comment would center on whether or not dummies had been interspersed among the "extra" players—a rather silly controversy since Margaret Mitchell had written, "Some lay stiff and still but many writhed under the hot sun, moaning." It would have been rather extravagant, to say the least, to pay "extra" salaries for men to "play dead" in distant shots. The Culver City telephone poles seen behind Vivien Leigh at left did not present a problem since much "matte" or process photography was utilized for the finished sequence. A dummy was also evident at Vivien's feet here. At the noon break of each day's shooting a box lunch was served to the "extra" players, as shown below. That was not Vivien Leigh waiting in line but her "double," for as Scarlett left the depot—and in all other distant shots where Vivien's face was not discernible—such "stand-ins" were used, allowing the star to complete other scenes where her facial presence was mandatory.

At 2:00 A.M. on the morning of Tuesday, May 23, Vivien Leigh left the Selznick studio with Victor Fleming and crew for location work at the Old Laskey Mesa. There, at dawn, in a setting representative of Tara's vegetable garden, she dug for a radish and proclaimed, "As God is my witness, they're not going to lick me. I'm going to live through this, and when it's all over, I'll never be hungry again." The strain of overwork had already manifested itself in Miss Leigh's appearance and this—coupled with emotional exhaustion and the ungodly hour—caused Vivien to deliver that oath (*Scene 383*) so effectively it would be remembered probably more than any other part of her performance.

With no pause for rest, it was then to "Tara's Cotton Patch," where Victor Fleming directed Vivien and the O'Hara clan in cotton-picking sequences at the destitute plantation (*Scenes 398–407, above*). Interestingly, all scenes here showing the blacks—Pork, Mammy and Prissy (with Miss Leigh, *left center*)—were deleted before the film's release on racial grounds. Scarlett's tone with these servants—in keeping with the book—was far from brotherly! A later scene would remain, however, in which confused Gerald reprimanded her for these actions.

The following day Leslie Howard took leave of rehearsals with William Wyler and Ingrid Bergman on *Intermezzo* to join Vivien for an unsuccessful attempt at the book's "Orchard Love Scene" (*Scene 467*—an unused take shown *below left*). The filmed results were not nearly as successful as Vivien's original screen test of that important moment, and Leslie Howard received a tongue-lashing from his exhausted co-star for forgetting his lines as well as a subsequent memo from David Selznick asking him to please read pages 525–535 of the book. Miss Leigh also suggested that Mr. Fleming view her test, which George Cukor had directed, and he agreed. But the next day's attempt at the scene was equally unsuccessful when Miss Leigh stumbled on her own dialogue. Mr. Howard remained sympathetically and gallantly silent.

Work began Friday, May 26, on what Selznick people candidly called the "Row and Rape" sequence (*Scenes 608–615, above*). On Saturday Mr. Gable carried Miss Leigh up the stairs of their Atlanta home half a dozen times (luckily Vivien weighed only 103 pounds) for the "ravishment"—until Victor Fleming was satisfied that they had enough footage to work with. Then, on Monday, May 29, Rhett's preceding drunken monologue (*Scene 613, right center*) was concluded. Vivien Leigh insisted on engaging her co-star in word games between camera set-ups, to compensate for the constant cruelty she displayed toward him on camera.

Meanwhile, Sam Wood was busy filming the sequence —shortly before Ashley's return from the war—where Melanie learned from a soldier that her husband had been taken prisoner (*Scene 465*). Butterfly McQueen would later relate how she objected to being seen eating watermelon in this sequence. In the "still" photograph at lower right, however, she had been inveigled into cutting one (in the background).

During the week of Monday, May 29, Clark Gable faced his greatest challenge as Rhett Butler—the moments following Scarlett's miscarriage when he was expected to cry (*Scene 639, above*). With the sympathetic help of Olivia de Havilland and the encouragement of Victor Fleming, the sequence succeeded magnificently. Even though he had previously expressed such emotions for Mr. Fleming in *Test Pilot*, the insecure Mr. Gable asked for the scene to be filmed in two versions—with and without the tears. After seeing both, he was persuaded that he had handled the tears convincingly.

Sam Wood directed Olivia de Havilland and Hattie McDaniel that week in the poignant "Staircase" scene, where Mammy told Melanie about Rhett's breakdown. The heartbreak Hattie conveyed in her recitation would later be responsible—more than any other part of her performance—for earning her an Academy Award (*Scene 659, left*). Then, on Thursday, June 1, Victor Fleming concluded that sequence with the scene in which Melanie found Rhett with Bonnie's body. At the end of that segment Mr. Gable had become so upset that he quietly left the studio.

On Friday, June 2, a final retake of "Belle Watling on the Church Steps" presented Ona Munson's bosom in a far more discreet manner (*above*), to the delight of both actress and director Fleming (*right*). Victor Fleming had finally accomplished what Sam Wood had unsuccessfully tried twice to do—please the Hays Office. After one more brief scene (outside the Atlanta jail) Miss Munson's performance was complete. At this time Olivia de Havilland was also free to return to Warner Brothers. But there was no such reprieve for Vivien Leigh since Scarlett hadn't married her second husband yet! Sam Wood began directing Vivien then in scenes of "Reconstruction Atlanta" (including that final scene with Miss Munson) and "Frank Kennedy's Store" with Carroll Nye, *below* (Scenes 500–513).

Monday, June 5, brought the news—"Rhett Wants a Divorce" (*Scenes 616–618*). That sequence began with Scarlett awakening from her "night of rapture," singing a simple verse (Miss Leigh, in singing, never sounded more British), and then listening to Mammy's miseries as that faithful old soul carried away a mysterious breakfast tray. The deletion of a scene where Bonnie brought that tray to her mother (*above*) would leave later viewers to wonder if perhaps Scarlett was in the habit of sleeping with her silver service all night. Rhett entered then (*left center*), the two argued "at cross purposes" and he departed for his London journey with Bonnie (already filmed). Meanwhile Sam Wood continued filming at "Tara" such moments as "The De-Lousing of Frank Kennedy" (*Scene 452*) and Suellen's reprimand of Mammy immediately thereafter. When Victor Fleming and Vivien Leigh were able to join them, Pork told Scarlett about the new taxes, Scarlett confronted Jonas Wilkerson and Emmy Slattery (*Scene 469*, filmed Friday, June 9) and then watched Gerald prepare for his fatal ride ("cut" scene, *below left*). Miss Leigh, Mr. Mitchell, Mr. Wood and Mr. Fleming would not stay around for that ride, however. On Saturday, June 10, William Cameron Menzies filmed it with Earl Dobbins "doubling" for Thomas Mitchell, and later that day Mr. Menzies recorded scenes of Victor Jory, Everett Brown, Earl Dobbins (as Gerald again, on horseback), and Tara's field hands for the plowing sequence at the opening of the picture—very little of which was ever used.

Vivien Leigh wasn't present for Gerald's death because she had a "fall" of her own to attend to as, on Saturday, June 10, Victor Fleming guided the events surrounding "Rhett's Return from London" (*Scenes 621–638*). Miss Leigh never looked more beautiful as she sat on her Atlanta staircase watching the arrival of her husband and daughter (*above*). Later that morning Vivien simulated a fall from the top of the staircase and then feigned unconsciousness for a camera closeup (*left center*). Gladys Hall reported that this "Fall" sequence was completed after two perfect takes.

The final moment Scarlett and Rhett shared together (*Scene 681*) was filmed over a period of several days— and in two different versions. On Thursday, June 8, Rhett had left Scarlett with the parting words, "Frankly, my dear, I don't care" (to satisfy the censors). Then, on June 10, Mr. Gable tried a version more faithful to the book, saying, "Frankly, my dear, I don't give a damn!" (The word "frankly" came courtesy of David Selznick, since it existed neither in the book nor in the Howard-Garrett shooting script.)

And still later on that June 10 Vivien Leigh joined William Cameron Menzies at a special ramp on Stage 3 to film "Scarlett Runs Through the Fog" (*Scenes 671–673*), an enlightening moment for Scarlett in the book but eventually reduced to only a few seconds on screen.

Then, on Monday, June 12, action moved to the terrace of the Butler home as Scarlett and Rhett watched "Bonnie's Last Ride" (*Scenes 646–652, below left*). However, no scenes of Bonnie on horseback or of the garden itself were filmed that day since the planned site was located at Metro-Goldwyn-Mayer.

Preparing for Rhett's exit: David O. Selznick, Victor Fleming, Vivien Leigh and Clark Gable conferred on the set.

Scarlett ran through the fog and discovered the solution to her nightmares. In the finished film that symbolism was barely hinted at.

Clark Gable returned to his alma mater, Metro-Goldwyn-Mayer, on Tuesday, June 13, where the Cohen Park location served as the Butler gardens for "Teaching Bonnie to Ride" (*Scene 595*). Although Clark and Victor Fleming worked long hours on that sequence, most of it was eventually discarded (such as the closeup, *above right*, of Rhett riding alone).

Wednesday, June 14, would be another long day for Vivien Leigh, but the actress was willing to oblige in speeding up the schedule since she planned to leave for New York (and a visit with Laurence Olivier) on June 25. She began her day by joining Victor Fleming at 8:00 A.M. for a retake of "Scarlett Curses Melanie and Her Baby" (*Scene 217*), and then filmed "Scarlett Stops a Dispatch Rider" (*Scenes 236–237*, with actor William Bakewell and director Fleming, *right center*). Upon completion (and a shampoo to get the red tile dust from Miss Leigh's hair), the crew moved to the Reuss Ranch at Malibu Lake where Vivien and Thomas Mitchell at last found a suitable location for "Gerald's Walk with Scarlett" (*Scenes 10–15, below right*). David Selznick had decided, in the meantime, that Scarlett would wear her white "Evening Prayer" dress for these retakes—meaning that none of the opening scenes previously filmed, even closeups, could be salvaged!

Still later that same Wednesday Vivien joined Clark Gable and Butterfly McQueen for *Scenes 321–322* for a new approach to the sequence on "The Road Outside Atlanta," following the escape through the burning depot. How disillusioning it would have been to later viewers if they had known that the romantic closeup of Mr. Gable asking Scarlett for a kiss had actually been filmed before —without Vivien Leigh's presence.

On Thursday, June 15, Vivien received bitter news from the front office. David Selznick had thought of a new ending for *Gone With the Wind* and she would have to postpone her New York trip for several days. Ironically, the scene she was scheduled to film that day was the one she thought would be the film's actual conclusion (*Scene 682*). In this she would collapse in tears on the Butler staircase, hear voices reminding her of Tara and vow to win Rhett back—remembering that "Tomorrow is another day!" But Vivien's personal disappointment only heightened her emotional energy and authenticated the tears she displayed. Gladys Hall reported that at the scene's conclusion Victor Fleming was biting his nails and yanking his hair in thrilled disbelief. But Olivia de Havilland, visiting the set for the first time in weeks, commented on how tired and wan Vivien was beginning to look. With very little time off, the actress had been working steadily on the project for four and a half months.

By Friday, June 16, it was time for Sam Wood to direct "Scarlett Hires Convicts" with Leslie Howard, Carroll Nye and Vivien Leigh (Scenes 515–516) on the lumber mill set.

Vivien Leigh returned to Forty Acres on Saturday, June 17, for the new David O. Selznick ending, "Scarlett's Walk to Tara." The producer hoped this would emphasize her optimism about Rhett's return. It didn't—and was never used (Scene 683).

Aware of Vivien Leigh's unhappiness with the prolonged shooting schedule, David Selznick issued an edict to the various units on Monday, June 19, to schedule all close shots and necessary retakes of Scarlett during that week. A push was also made to use doubles for Vivien as much as possible and then cut in closeups of her later on. In line with this, the Menzies unit filmed exteriors for "The Attack in Shantytown" (*Scenes 522–527*) with Yakima Canutt (*above left*), Everett Brown, Blue Washington and Aileen Goodwin ("doubling" as Scarlett) that Monday. Miss Goodwin (*above right*) was a rather unique stand-in for Vivien Leigh! Vivien's facial closeups and her moments with Big Sam were filmed four days later.

Meanwhile, Miss Leigh and Clark Gable were doing their "Walk Down Peachtree Street" for Victor Fleming and company (*Scene 593, right center*). Spirits were higher as Vivien playfully referred to Victor as "Boom Boom" (because of his penchant for "boom" shots) and he, in turn, called her "Fiddle-Dee-Dee" (one of Scarlett's pet expressions). But Clark Gable told Gladys Hall, in disgust, that he felt he'd had more costume changes than any actor in history. Even more upset was David Selznick, who agonized through many memos about the wind which had blown Vivien's hat during the scene. He finally decided against retaking it and the results, on screen, displayed a refreshing naturalness.

Meanwhile, back at the Atlanta Bazaar (of all places!) a retake of the "Chaperons' Corner" substituted Mrs. Meade (Leona Roberts) for the long-gone Mrs. Elsing in the hilarious fainting scene with Aunt Pittypat and Dolly Merriwether (*below right*).

Clark Gable next returned to the M-G-M Cohen Park location with the Menzies unit for a brief silent insert in which Rhett ran and picked up Bonnie's broken body (*Scene 656, above*).

The Selznick "call sheet" for Wednesday June 21, scheduled a group of similarly short scenes. During the day it brought Clark and Vivien to Stage 11's "Interior of New Orleans Hotel" where they filmed *Scene 573* in which Scarlett—amidst her trousseau—told Rhett that Mammy would never accept a red petticoat from him. Afterward, she awakened from a nightmare of fog (*Scene 574*) and Rhett promised to take her home to Tara. Then the company moved to Stage 14's "River Boat Cabin" for the initial moments of the honeymoon (*Scene 571*).

At 7:30 that evening Vivien donned her white "prayer" dress and met Thomas Mitchell in front of a "process" screen where he told her that "land is the only thing . . . that lasts." And at 9:15 that night she changed into her final green costume for a "process" shot to close the picture (*Scene 684*)—which would, in fact, never be used (*left*).

The following day brought the company to a New Orleans café for a brief but colorful moment with Rhett and Scarlett (*Scene 572*). This sequence in the finished film revealed a Vivien Leigh who looked particularly drawn and overtired.

The New Orleans can-can dancers (above) *had practiced for weeks in advance for their brief "pull-back" scene finally filmed on Thursday, June 22.*

Vivien Leigh wore a turquoise blue trailing skirt of net over taffeta, ornamented with nine stuffed birds, for the New Orleans café sequence. Unfortunately, the audience would barely see it, nor would they see the "Toast" scene below.

Finally in the homestretch, Vivien Leigh and Clark Gable joined a group of "bit" players on Friday, June 23, for the crucial *Scene 319* in which Rhett saw a young soldier (Junior Coghlan) collapse and decided to join the defeated army (*above left*). Miss Leigh wore a black mourning bonnet to match continuity with those fire scenes shot months before, but it would disappear in the following scene in the same strange manner in which it had appeared.

Next, Mr. Fleming took his stars to Forty Acres where they filmed "Rhett and Scarlett at Tara" (*Scene 575*), with Miss Leigh beautifully gowned but more noticeably haggard than ever. Mr. Gable was then free for the day but Vivien still had to contribute her presence to "Shantytown."

The next day, Saturday, June 24, was spent on one lengthy scene—the retake of Scarlett's love scene with Ashley (*left center*). It was now played almost entirely within Tara's paddock and Vivien's exhausted appearance actually enhanced the poignance of her performance.

On Monday, June 26, Miss Leigh began a *fourth* version of *Gone With the Wind*'s opening sequence on Tara's porch—this time dressed in white (*below*). Unfortunately, Vivien hardly looked the picture of sixteen-year-old innocence after all those draining months. Even this scene spilled over into a few hour's work the following morning. But then, on Tuesday, June 27, 1939, David O. Selznick sent a telegram to John Hay Whitney in New York, which read "Sound the siren. Scarlett O'Hara completed her performance at noon today."

Postproduction

David Selznick had realized that Vivien Leigh appeared "old" in her last few sequences and, in fact, told the actress so before she departed for a long vacation. Vivien, in turn, candidly asked him how he expected her to look after five months of unrelenting labor. The producer hoped to retake at least those early scenes one more time before the film's release but, in the meantime, instructed his staff to finish "fill-in" photography and assemblage of footage so a preview of a rough-cut version could be held for a consumer audience as soon as possible.

The Menzies unit had just filmed (without sound) a scene under a swamp bridge where Scarlett hid from unknown soldiers during a rainstorm. They utilized Joan Rodgers to "double" for Vivien Leigh while Butterfly McQueen was present to play her own Prissy. Closeups of Miss Leigh and Olivia de Havilland would, it was hoped, be filmed at a later date before sound effects were added. On the very day Vivien finished and left for New York, Joan Rodgers and Carey Harrison ("doubling" for Thomas Mitchell) traveled to the Lasky Mesa location to film the movie's first of several "pull-back" shots (*Scene 17*) with Scarlett and Gerald looking out at Tara. It was photographed in black and white, without sound, and those striking black silhouettes would be later superimposed (through laboratory processing) onto an artistic Menzies rendition of Tara in the distance. Then, Miss Rodgers changed into Scarlett's last costume for the "pull-back" finale in which Mrs. Rhett Butler returned to her family home. Again, the footage was shot in black and white for superimposure, and these would be the last frames of film used as the Selznick "end title" came into focus. It would prove to be the only time that final costume would be in view, defeating the intricate designs of Walter Plunkett's green creation (green was Margaret Mitchell's favorite color).

During the following week closeup "inserts" were photographed under the supervision of their designer, William Cameron Menzies. These included red earth in Scarlett's hand, to be thrown at Jonas, and Scarlett pulling a radish from the ground (Mozelle Miller's hand was used in both instances). Mr. Menzies then engineered the remainder of those brief pictorial interludes: Frank Kennedy's picture, the twin graves of Ellen and Gerald O'Hara, a letter reporting Charles Hamilton's death, a poster announcing the evacuation of Atlanta (later eliminated along with portions of the "Exodus" sequence), a bank draft for $300, Scarlett's (Joan Rodgers's) foot slipping out of her shoe (to surprise the deserter), an announcement of Ashley's military leave and the letter from Rhett returning the ladies' rings (with Mozelle Miller's hand doubling for Melanie's this time). Special movie "sign writer" Jack Connor was employed to pen the handwritten "inserts."

On July 5 Mr. Menzies brought Cammie King and her pony to M-G-M for the beginning of Bonnie's fatal ride, with "doubles" substituting for the backs of Rhett and Scarlett as they watched their daughter parading by. Little Miss King then returned to the Selznick studio where she was asked for closeups in her London bed. David Selznick was unhappy, though, with the child's recorded voice and already contemplated changing it through a voice "double."

Film editor Hal Kern took his turn at directing brief scenes that week which involved some special effects such as the "pull-back" shot of burned-out Twelve Oaks, showing (through a superimposed miniature) that the top of the Wilkes house had been destroyed (*Scene 345*). With the camera at a distance, Scarlett's arrival at Twelve Oaks was filmed next with Joan Rodgers and Butterfly McQueen—again, with Vivien's closeups to be cut in later. The arrival at the gate of Tara (*Scene 351*) was filmed in total darkness, making it easy for Joan Rodgers to perform the untidy task of whipping the horse one last time before it fell dead (a special effect). Then Miss Rodgers ran across the lawn of Tara, under a special moonlight effect, to match the closeup of Vivien Leigh that already existed (*Scene 352*). It was also necessary for Mr. Kern to line up Harry Davenport, a drummer and a bugler in front of a process screen for the retake of Dr. Meade's announcements at the Bazaar.

Having already viewed the "Provost Marshal" sequence, David Selznick requested that Aunt Pitty be added to the tail end and even hired actress Libby Taylor to redo the part of Belle Watling's maid, formerly portrayed by Ivy Parsons—an ironic waste of effort by all, since the entire sequence was doomed.

The next step was crucial: all existing footage was screened—day and night—and David, with Hal Kern's invaluable aid, decided on which of several alternate "takes" of each scene would be used. Decisions also had to be made as to where to insert medium shots and closeups. By mid-July the Selznick staff had assembled their "rough cut" and it was shown to M-G-M executives, who professed more enthusiasm than David had expected. But, as he wrote to Atlanta's Mayor William B. Hartsfield in explaining why he couldn't yet determine a premiere date, they were a long way from being finished. "The picture proper is completed," David wrote on July 17, "but some of the important effects including

197

Repetitive footage and the sight of too-obvious "doubles" forced the elimination of much of the original December 1938 "Fire" sequence and ended David O. Selznick's plans for a three-screen panoramic effect in theatres.

montage and battle scenes remain to be photographed. Furthermore the picture is presently four and a half hours long in its present rough assembly, and it is going to take me a considerable length of time to edit at least one hour out of the picture. . . ."

Then came the most maddening assignment of all—cutting that hour! David viewed the picture, in whole and in part, repeatedly until he knew each scene by heart. Among the first casualties was the massive footage of the fire. Heeding Wilbur Kurtz's constant reminders that "the burning of Atlanta" had occurred on November 14, 1864—not September 1 (when Scarlett fled)—David finally agreed to cut the scenes extensively and make it appear, correctly, that only Atlanta's depot area was in flames that night. As it was, much of the December 10, 1938, footage had been redone since Yakima Canutt was so obviously unlike Clark Gable on screen. The huge *King Kong* wall on fire was reused through process photography as background for the new "takes." After adding the mob scenes leading up to the depot and inserting Clark Gable's closeups with the horse as well as the miniature of an exploding boxcar, David's "fire spectacle" would remain on screen for only a few moments. And so ended forever his one-time plan of projecting this sequence for a triple-screen effect.

Such spectacle was totally unnecessary, David knew, since the drama stood exceedingly well on its own, and he then abandoned his plans for battle montages showing Ashley, Charles and the Tarletons. *Gone With the Wind* would, time would prove, remain unique among Civil War films in that it never showed any battle scenes whatsoever. Yet so successful was the illusion it presented that

later viewers would believe they had seen them—and argue accordingly.

Trimming of individual scenes—entrances, exits and pauses—brought the film down another half-hour. David attacked it again fiercely during August. To emphasize the poignancy of the depot "crane shot" (with Scarlett and the wounded), David eliminated all footage of the trains arriving with casualties when Ashley came home on leave. Only the brief scene of Ashley greeting Melanie and Scarlett would remain. Then the producer tried to eliminate any non-Margaret Mitchell footage that would not disrupt continuity—such as Belle Watling giving water to the wounded (which, in any event, might have offended pro-Mitchell Southerners). By the end of August, almost ready for a "preview," David informed M-G-M that the picture ran three hours and forty minutes and that he could cut it no further without "materially damaging it." The Selznick music department then borrowed "stock music" from Metro-Goldwyn-Mayer's library to accompany the film on its maiden outing and David made arrangements for a showing in Riverside, California, on Saturday, September 9. Just before facing that public reaction, Mr. Selznick made a statement to the press which would long be remembered: "At noon I think it's divine, at midnight I think it's lousy. Sometimes I think it's the greatest picture ever made. But if it's only a great picture, I'll be satisfied."

Before the picture started that Saturday night its "preview" audience was warned that they were about to see a long movie (in the event anyone wanted to leave or call home) but that—once the film started—no one else would be permitted to enter (lest anyone was inspired to call the press). The reaction was, according to David, a "sensational success . . . everything that we hoped for and expected." Reply cards filled out by that audience and a subsequent one in Santa Barbara ranged, in their most enthusiastic comments, from "greatest picture since *The Birth of a Nation*" to "greatest picture ever made!" David had worried in advance about two facets of the film in particular: Rhett's exit and the story's subsequent ending. Having discarded "Scarlett's Walk to Tara" beforehand, the studio went into its two previews with David's previous conclusion in which Scarlett heard the voices of Gerald, Ashley and Rhett reassuring her that Tara was the real impetus of her life. The Selznick International staff was pleasantly surprised to find no significant objections to the ending, even though it was not from the book, and imagined the audience found it faithful—at least in spirit—to Margaret Mitchell. But the omission of Rhett's "damn" had been missed and David Selznick still hoped to do something about it.

Those local California audiences could also be highly critical, since it was the habit of studios to test their films in such a manner. And even though these viewers were aware that such screenings were very "rough"—without corrected sound, color, music or titles—they did not spare vocal comments during the showing or long personal opinions on their reply cards. The Selznick contingent, especially the studio head, paid careful attention to reactions and then took *Gone With the Wind* back to Culver City for further surgery.

Guided by the audiences' responses, David began—in the first week of October—to cut several more sequences and to add newly photographed "inserts" in their place. The non-Mitchell "Death of John Wilkes" had added nothing to the depot scene of wounded and subsequently disappeared. Instead, a glimpse of his grave marker was placed into the burned-out Twelve Oaks footage and Melanie—previously seen sinking back into the wagon after a view of the desolation—now appeared to do so after looking at her father-in-law's grave. The descriptive "Ride to Twelve Oaks" gave way to a sign reading "Twelve Oaks . . . anyone disturbing the peace on this plantation will be prosecuted."

But, lest anyone think the picture's length was going to be tightened by these cuts, David had additions to make as well. Vivien Leigh had returnd to California when Laurence Olivier began filming *Rebecca* and she received instructions to stand by for some further filming. David had felt Scarlett's journey back to Tara had not captured any of the war's tragedy evident in the book nor shown how close the fighting had come to her plantation. The producer conceived a scene then to combine both factors and on Thursday, October 5, Victor Fleming was called in to direct a short sequence in which Vivien and Butterfly McQueen would drive through a battlefield strewn with dead Confederate and Union soldiers. A distant shot,

photographed from behind, was later supervised by Jack Cosgrove, with Aileen Goodwin doing the actual driving. That evening Vivien and Butterfly filmed their closeups under the swamp bridge to be inserted into the earlier Menzies footage.

During that same first week in October Jack Cosgrove began work on "The Blue and the Gray" montage to open Part Two, which used three "Yankee soldiers," four cannons firing, swirling smoke and double-printed shots of fire—all to be superimposed onto a red background. David Selznick found inspiration in the Academy Award-winning sound effects of *The Hurricane* and actually had Hal Kern "borrow" some from Samuel Goldwyn to back up that pictorial passage. Ben Hecht helped, simultaneously, to supply several "bridging" titles—holdovers from the days of silent films—to explain Gettysburg, the siege, Sherman, Carpetbaggers and the returning Confederate soldiers.

Running time of the new footage quickly surpassed what had been eliminated and, since David had promised M-G-M to keep to the three-hour-forty-minute "preview" length, further cuts were necessitated. A brief silent version of India arriving at the lumber mill, with Mrs. Meade this time, eliminated need for a gossip scene afterward. Scarlett's signing of a check as Mrs. Frank Kennedy for the $300 in tax money replaced some of Frank's footage, explanations at Tara and the previous bank draft "insert." And Ellen's letter being received by India on the morning of the barbecue disappeared then as did the entire "Provost Marshal Sequence."

By Monday, October 9, it was time for "dubbing" to begin. This was the substitution of dialogue on the sound track either because its delivery needed more emphasis or clarity or because David had been rewriting again! The most drastic victim of these revisions was Southerner Marcella Martin (as Cathleen Calvert), whose voice was entirely "dubbed" by another actress with "an authentic Southern voice." Vivien Leigh had to redo her own lines for Marcella's one scene and the greatest burden of the other "dubbing," understandably, fell into her lap—from a new, unnaturally loud rereading of her "Evening Prayer" finale to most of her script with Prissy and Mela-

An afterthought of Mr. Selznick's showed Scarlett and Prissy crossing a battlefield strewn with dead soldiers.

India lost her dialogue in a retake of the "Mill" sequence but gained a companion—Mrs. Meade.

nie before and during the birth of the baby. Additionally, Vivien "dubbed" almost all of her lines as she met Gerald on horseback (scenes filmed on location), and much later, after her return to Tara, in telling her father that she'd like to get drunk. David had even changed a line in Scarlett's honeymoon cabin, now having her say, "But you were the main one I wanted to go to the devil." There were also minor "dubbing" requirements for Melanie, Mammy, Ellen, India, Suellen and Uncle Peter, who had to record an entire scene in which he chased Aunt Pitty's last chicken for Chirstmas dinner. No less than four young girls were tested before selection was made for a voice to entirely replace Cammie King's as Bonnie Blue Butler.

Then, on Thursday, October 12, Vivien Leigh and Victor Fleming reported for their last work on *Gone With the Wind*—and (of course!) it was a *fifth* version of that interminably recurring opening scene. But the idea was a good one. Vivien was now well rested, with all her beauty restored. She joined Fred Crane and George Bessolo—now called George Reeves—to say one more time, "Fiddle-dee-dee! War, war, war! This war talk's spoiling all the fun at every party this spring."

David Selznick continued, amidst other pressing matters, to view his creation again and again. Unfortunately, most of the "Casualty List" sequence had proved unusable, so the producer instructed Jack Cosgrove to film an "Anxiety Montage" with Harry Davenport, Bebe Anderson and forty-four "extras." Then, as an artist would add a few last dabs of paint to a portrait, David added a retake of a black boy on Tara's "quittin' bell," another "process" retake of Dr. Meade speaking at the Bazaar and, finally, a sleeping cat beneath a sundial with the carved message "Do not squander time . . . that is the stuff life is made of."

Those other pressing matters burdening David at the same time included release plans for *Intermezzo,* supervision of *Rebecca*'s production, and the musical score for

Gone With the Wind. Through his relationship with Warner Brothers, Mr. Selznick had been able to borrow Max Steiner's services for both *Intermezzo* and *Gone With the Wind.* Although David had been Max's champion at RKO in creating original film scores he afterward worked at M-G-M with Herbert Stothart, a composer noted for his learnings on classical music. Mr. Steiner was already at work on *Gone With the Wind*'s music in early October when he received word that the film's producer felt a classical approach would be preferable—with themes from the Old South dominating whenever possible. Max blithely ignored that request but did fear, by early November, that because of the picture's extraordinary length he could not complete the entire score in time for a December premiere. David then commissioned *Rebecca*'s composer, Franz Waxman, to write an "insurance" score and even approached M-G-M about using Herbert Stothart as a possible replacement. None of those measures proved necessary, however, and David later commented that Max Steiner's finished score was "quite beautiful."

There was also the confusion regarding credits for *Gone With the Wind*'s main title and advertising. While admitting that "I myself did the last half or two-thirds of the script without anybody's help . . . of the comparatively small amount of material in the picture which is not from the book, most is my own personally," David decided to give sole writing credit to the recently deceased Sidney Howard. Mr. Selznick felt that he did not want to deprive Mr. Howard or his widow of a final moment of glory. Then, knowing that neither George Cukor nor Sam Wood wanted any directorial credit, David considered inserting a special screen panel thanking both those men as well as Oliver H. P. Garrett, Ben Hecht and Katharine Brown for their contributions. A brief discussion on

David O. Selznick presented Vivien Leigh with Scarlett's flowers for the fifth and final version of the film's opening sequence—photographed on October 13, 1939.

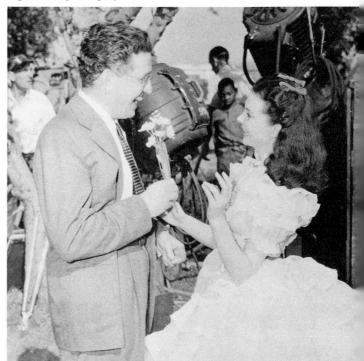

```
SELZNICK INTERNATIONAL PICTURES, INC.
                    CALL SHEET
                                    DATE  Friday,Oct. 13,1939.
        "GONE WITH THE WIND"           46-826
PICTURE ------------------------------ PROD. NO. -------- DIRECTOR  Victor Fleming
SET     EXT. TARA
LOCATION    FORTY ACRES         SET NO. -------- SCENES (Woather Permitting)

       N A M E          |  TIME CALLED  |  CHARACTER, DESC., WARDROBE
                        | ON SET | MAKE-UP |
     Vivien Leigh       | 8:00 am| 6:45 am | Scarlett       #1
     George Reeves      | 7:30 am| 5:30 am | Stuart Tarleton #1
     Fred Crane         | 7:30 am| 5:30 am | Brent Tarleton  #1

     1 Colored Boy      | 7:30 am| 7:00 am | As before
     Welfare Worker     | 7:00 am|         |
     Joan Rogers        | 7:00 am| 6:30 am | Double for Scarlett #1



                         LATER
                         INT. EXAMINER OFFICE (PROCESS) STAGE #3
```

The "call sheet" for that last version on Tara's porch showed Victor Fleming was the final "author" and that actor George Bessolo had been given a new name—George Reeves.

this point with Victor Fleming changed the producer's mind and also, unfortunately, cooled the relationship between the two men permanently. M-G-M offered a more severe stumbling block when they insisted that Clark Gable's name be presented before the film's title, as had been contractually agreed to. Contracts with the other three stars specified equal billing with Mr. Gable, which complicated the matter even further. David won that issue, however, and was able to fulfill his original plan: there would be only *one* person's name preceding *Gone With the Wind*—the only name, he felt, which belonged there.

And there was one more battle to fight! In approaching Will H. Hays of the Motion Picture Association of America about the inclusion of the word "damn" in Rhett Butler's final speech, David armed himself with appropriate ammunition. He quoted the *Oxford English Dictionary* and popular magazines of the day, related the disappointment of the "preview" audiences at its absence and called Margaret Mitchell's book "an American Bible" which required extreme fidelity. That final battle was also won, and *Gone With the Wind* was granted "Approval Certificate Number 5729."

With the billing problems solved—the film's title to be presented in "a unique manner"—and a censor's seal

granted, the lettering of the screen credits could be completed. Bebe Anderson's name was changed to Mary Anderson just in time (although her part was reduced to a Bazaar glimpse) but, in the rush, Barbara O'Neil's last name was misspelled. The negative was ready for the laboratories but Mr. Selznick took one last look and afterward trimmed the new "Casualty List" footage to make way for one last scene.

On Saturday, November 11, assistant director Eric Stacey guided Louise Carter, as a bandleader's wife, in approaching Luke Cosgrove, as her husband—her tearful eyes telling him they had lost a loved one at Gettysburg. The camera then panned to a boy in the band, probably their other son or grandson, who played courageously as tears rolled down his cheeks. Miss Carter and Mr. Cosgrove had won the honor of being featured in *Gone With the Wind*'s very last filmed scene. It was then up to laboratory technicians to blend all those many components together. At last, on Monday, December 11, 1939—only four days before its opening in Atlanta—prints were ready for shipment. David thoughtfully remembered Kay Brown, the lady in New York who had started it all three and a half years before, and sent her the message, "Have just finished *Gone With the Wind*. God bless us one and all."

The Credits

BASED ON THE 1939 SOUVENIR THEATRE PROGRAM

PRODUCED BY DAVID O. SELZNICK • DIRECTED BY VICTOR FLEMING
BASED ON MARGARET MITCHELL'S NOVEL "GONE WITH THE WIND"
SCREEN PLAY BY SIDNEY HOWARD

The Production Designed By	**William Cameron Menzies**
Art Direction By	**Lyle Wheeler**
Photographed By	**Ernest Haller, A.S.C.**
Technicolor Associates	**Ray Rennahan, A.S.C.**
	Wilfrid M. Cline, A.S.C.
Musical Score By	**Max Steiner**
Associate	**Lou Forbes**
Special Photographic Effects By	**Jack Cosgrove**
Associate: (Fire Effects)	**Lee Zavitz**
Costumes Designed By	**Walter Plunkett**
Scarlett's Hats By	**John Frederics**
Interiors By	**Joseph B. Platt**
Interior Decoration By	**Edward G. Boyle**
Supervising Film Editor	**Hal C. Kern**
Associate Film Editor	**James E. Newcom**
Scenario Assistant	**Barbara Keon**
Recorder	**Frank Maher**
Makeup and Hair Styling	**Monty Westmore**
Associates	**Hazel Rogers**
	Ben Nye
Dance Directors	**Frank Floyd**
	Eddie Prinz
Historian	**Wilbur G. Kurtz**
Technical Advisers	**Susan Myrick**
	Will Price
Research	**Lillian K. Deighton**
Production Manager	**Raymond A. Klune**
Technicolor Co. Supervisor	**Natalie Kalmus**

Associate	**Henri Jaffa**
Assistant Director	**Eric G. Stacey**
Second Assistant Director	**Ridgeway Callow**
Production Continuity	**Lydia Schiller**
	Connie Earle
Mechanical Engineer	**R. D. Musgrave**
Construction Superintendent	**Harold Fenton**
Chief Grip	**Fred Williams**
In Charge of Wardrobe	**Edward P. Lambert**
Associates	**Marian Dabney**
	Elmer Ellsworth
Casting Managers	**Charles Richards**
	Fred Schuessler
Location Manager	**Mason Litson**
Scenic Department Superintendent	**Henry J. Stahl**
Electrical Superintendent	**Wally Oettel**
Chief Electrician	**James Potevin**
Properties:	
Manager	**Harold Coles**
On the Set	**Arden Cripe**
Greens	**Roy A. McLaughlin**
Drapes	**James Forney**
Special Properties Made By	**Ross B. Jackman**
Tara Landscaped By	**Florence Yoch**
Still Photographer	**Fred Parrish**
Camera Operators	**Arthur Arling**
	Vincent Farrar
Assistant Film Editors	**Richard Van Enger**
	Ernest Leadley

Perhaps the most outrageously stupid promotion for the film was this lobby card, which read, " 'Tighter, Mammy! Mr. Butler will be at the ball! I must be beautiful!'—the prelude to a fateful meeting!" What ball? If Scarlett knew Rhett would be at the bazaar she never would have attended, much less wanted to look beautiful in her mourning clothes. And Mammy wasn't even in Atlanta then. Adding insult to inaccuracy, M-G-M illustrated that inventive dialogue with a scene in which Scarlett decided to deny Rhett his marital rights lest she become pregnant again.

Film editor Hal Kern met the most demanding challenge of all in assembling the film. This publicity photograph, however, showed him with several more than the actual thirteen "double reels" the film was finally reduced to.

One of the original advertisements for Gone With the Wind's premiere engagements which showed Miss Leigh receiving fourth billing but with the special notation "and presenting Vivien Leigh as Scarlett O'Hara."

203

The Differences

More than twenty-three years after completing *Gone With the Wind* David O. Selznick told interviewers from the publication *Films in Review*, "The trick in adapting novels is to give the *illusion* of photographing the entire book. This is more difficult than creating an original." Such was the self-admitted secret of success for the screen version of Margaret Mitchell's huge and almost overpowering novel, which the author herself had not thought filmable. But it was filmed! And many millions would feel the transition from print to celluloid was a remarkable success. Even though it was called, in its time, "the longest movie ever made," the reduction of those 1,037 pages to three and three-quarter theatrical hours involved a massive purging of primary material, secondary characters and subplots. How to do it without creating adverse audience reaction was a problem attacked from the very earliest of Sidney Howard's drafts. Any book material that could be deemed "superfluous" was automatically to be excluded. But who would make such important decisions? In comparing the book to the film's finished form, it would seem that "author" David O. Selznick made the correct choices.

The change fated to provoke the most discussion among *Gone With the Wind*'s followers was the elimination of Scarlett O'Hara's first two children. But the book's Scarlett was far from an ideal mother and, in fact, Rhett stated (in print and on film), "A cat's a better mother than you." By presenting Bonnie Blue Butler as Scarlett's only child, the tragedy of her death was significantly magnified and made Rhett's subsequent departure easier to understand. In the book Rhett had been almost as devoted to Wade Hamilton, even reassuring the boy that he was like a real son to him. With Wade in the film, could Rhett have walked out so easily? Even with Bonnie, the book's Scarlett was unable, through her immaturity, to realize the full potential of mother love but at least, in this child's case, she was aware of that and felt guilty. Little Bonnie Blue reminded Scarlett of Gerald and herself, whereas the other two children seemed to her merely spineless or silly. Yet with her total neglect of Wade and Ella, it was amazing these offspring developed as normally as they did.

The historical scope of the novel pushed the first two children into the background, so readers could easily overlook their mother's shocking neglect. On film, however, the presentation of such callous treatment would have made a vast difference (especially to women) in yielding the sympathy so necessary to bear with Scarlett through her many travails. And Melanie, who loved children, would have seemed rather unrealistic, dramatically, in loving an unfit mother all those years. The elimination of Wade Hampton Hamilton and Ella Lorena Kennedy from the cinematic treatment was, therefore, not a whim or a mere script decision—it was a necessity!

Movie censors forbade any use of "God's nightgown!" as a pet expression but Scarlett certainly had enough alternatives with "Fiddle-dee-dee," "Great balls of fire!" and her "tomorrow" slogan. Margaret Mitchell had carefully progressed that "tomorrow" motto until Scarlett finally said, "I'll think about it tomorrow," and then used it, with variations, continually. "Tomorrow is another day" was also utilized in the book on several occasions. But on screen Vivien Leigh uttered the former only three times (at the opening, after killing the deserter and after Rhett left) and saved the latter for one unforgettable reading as the movie ended.

The film cited few actual locations, with only Atlanta, Savannah, London, New Orleans and Charleston (as Rhett's home) being mentioned. Jonesboro was never alluded to nor was any idea given of Tara's proximity to Atlanta. Time elements were similarly ignored, such as the story's opening being two days after the firing on Fort Sumter or Scarlett's birth having been in the year Atlanta was named. All of Miss Mitchell's comparisons between Scarlett and Atlanta had, in fact, remained behind in the novel's pages. No ages of the characters were specified—probably for the best—so viewers never knew Scarlett was sixteen, Melanie seventeen, Gerald sixty, Ellen thirty-two or Rhett thirty-three when the story began. Proper names would only have complicated the filmed proceedings, so there were no movie reminders that Suellen was really Susan Elinor, Carreen was born Caroline Irene, Ashley's first name was George or Rhett's middle initial was "K."

Even the casting of Vivien Leigh, one of the century's most indisputably beautiful actresses, was a violation in concept of the book's opening line: "Scarlett O'Hara was not beautiful, but men seldom realized it when caught by her charms as the Tarleton twins were." But would it have been possible to convey the character's magnetism on screen if a plainer woman had played the role?

The three unsuccessful attempts at filming Scarlett in her green-sprigged muslin dress on Tara's steps had been faithful to the book. But the final decision to have her wear white was far better visually—considering the sumptuous green backgrounds of Tara on the walk she took with Gerald. And, concerning the story's other early moments, all O'Hara family history was rejected as unnecessary. There remained no explanations of Gerald's immigration from Ireland, his acquisition of Tara, Ellen's unhappy love affair, the three O'Hara sons who had died in infancy, Scarlett's brief education or her early half-successful training by Mammy. The movie's Tarleton "boys" lost their relationship as twins as well as the balance of their family—two older brothers, four sisters and parents. Beatrice Tarleton, mother of the brood, was an especially colorful character in print. Her love for her horses, it seemed, exceeded that for her family, and she appeared to regret their loss in the war even more than the deaths of all four of her sons.

Only a very late movie reference (to Rhett after Bonnie's birth) hinted to viewers that Mammy had also raised Ellen Robillard O'Hara or that she had come to Tara with Ellen after that lady's marriage to Gerald. Ellen's brief sequence with Jonas Wilkerson on screen indicated the strong role of supervision she played at Tara. But the fact that she had actually galvanized the plantation workers and made Tara successful was avoided. To have alluded to that factor would have meant explaining the "caste" system among the slaves which, for racial reasons, was better ignored (except for references by the house servants). The vast difference in age between Gerald and Ellen was also unexplored but Thomas Mitchell's makeup contrasted nicely with the casting of the youthful Barbara O'Neil and produced the correct illusion. In the matter of casting, even Margaret Mitchell was pleased by the similarity in appearance between Miss O'Neil and Ann Rutherford as her youngest daughter. But Carreen, fated to become a minor character on film, was deprived of her deep love for Brent Tarleton which would, after his death, eventually lead her to a convent.

The O'Hara neighbors—the Fontaines, the Munroes and the Calverts (except, very briefly, for Cathleen)—did not make the journey from book to film and the Tarletons' groom, Jeems, likewise disappeared (although originally filmed). Dilcey, Pork's new wife, who was purchased by Gerald along with her daughter Prissy, was also evicted, and no reference was therefore needed that Pork was Prissy's stepfather. But some non-book viewers did get the impression that Mammy might have been the mother Prissy constantly quoted. The fact that Dilcey was a midwife made Scarlett's belief, in the book, that Prissy could deliver Melanie's baby plausible. In the movie it was rather a childlike act of faith to put such trust in a whining scatterbrain.

The Selznick forces evidently felt no history was needed to explain Scarlett's two-year infatuation with Ashley or that she had known him previously since her childhood without any romantic inclination. Ashley's passion for books, music and poetry, and similar interests on Melanie's part, were implied by only one vague script line in which Ashley said, "She's like me, Scarlett. She's part of my blood and we understand each other." Scar-

lett's lack of understanding of Ashley's interests made it impossible, in the book, for her to accept his love for Melanie, and that tied in well with her willfully sketchy education. But the Selznick Scarlett appeared no less versed than those two, or even Charles or Rhett. In so presenting her, much of author Mitchell's humor at Scarlett's expense was lost, such as when she overheard Ashley mention history's infamous Borgias and said to Charles, "I don't know them. Is he kin to them?"

From his first film appearance Ashley seemed an unwilling victim of Scarlett's verbal advances. No references were made to his yearning looks at or frustrated sadness over the zesty and attractive Miss O'Hara. But the fact that ethereal Ashley had a suppressed lust in his nature was far too candid an idea for those censorable movie days. In consideration of this, Leslie Howard's often-criticized performance was therefore more artful than a non-Mitchell filmgoer might have realized, since he was forced to create a completely one-dimensional character. In the book what Scarlett interpreted as Ashley's love for her was, in reality, only repressed sexual desire, but he *did*, meanwhile, lead her on. In the movie no such thing occurred—at least not until the "paddock scene," and there it appeared, again, to be all the lady's doing.

Ashley's sister, Honey Wilkes, was another victim of the Selznick red pencil but the scenario ingeniously "combined" her with the other Wilkes daughter, India. Charles Hamilton had been Honey's beau (not India's) and it was Stuart Tarleton who had captured India's heart in the Mitchell version. In the Selznick variation Scarlett's marriage to Charles inspired India's hatred of her to be even more dramatically pronounced thanks to this clever combination of sisters.

Margaret Mitchell's book contained no entrance scene for Ashley and Melanie—Scarlett merely remembered meeting them later on in her recollections. This was particularly frustrating to David Selznick, who had even pleaded (in vain) with Miss Mitchell to write a special

In the book Charles Hamilton proposed to Scarlett in the Twelve Oaks gardens, as in the unused film scene.

"bridge" to cover the crucial introduction of two leading characters (and two of the film's stars). The eventual "meeting," which defined Melanie's nature, Ashley's devotion and Scarlett's disdain, was a Selznick creation, as was Ashley and Melanie's love scene shortly afterward.

Although Rhett Butler's movie entrance was patterned very closely on the novel, the presence of such a disreputable man at the barbecue was rather impolitely ignored (in the book he had cotton business pending with Frank Kennedy). And in print Mammy had stayed behind with Ellen at Tara to settle accounts with Jonas, whereas the film brought her to Twelve Oaks to help the O'Hara girls prepare for their naps. On screen the ladies

were not present during the war debate as Miss Mitchell had imagined, and the author had also placed that heated discussion in the garden—not in the dining room. The challenging words to Rhett had been delivered by Stuart Tarleton in the original, not shy Charles Hamilton. Charles was far too busy at that point proposing to Scarlett—*before* the outbreak of war was learned. But Scarlett did not accept him until later, as in the film, after her confrontation with Ashley. It was John Wilkes, not Ashley, who complied with Rhett's request to be shown the Twelve Oaks library (not the garden where he already was), enabling some readers to guess that he might be there when the fireworks between Ashley and Scar-

A waltz at the Atlanta Bazaar: David Selznick found an early means for Rhett to express his feelings to Scarlett.

lett started. Rhett's movie quip, "Has the war started?" after Scarlett threw the vase was another Selznick touch.

Scarlett's motivation for accepting Charles was, on screen, limited to frustration over Ashley's rebuttal. In the book she was equally anxious to get even with Honey for gossiping about her, to hurt Melanie and to escape the mortification of Rhett's having overheard her with Ashley. Scarlett married Charles (*before* Ashley married Melanie) at a Tara ceremony where she met Mrs. Merriwether and Mrs. Elsing and at which Aunt Pittypat fainted. Two of these ladies would not make their celluloid entrance until the Atlanta Bazaar, while Mrs. Elsing was exiled completely. Charles Hamilton's pathetic honeymoon was, understandably, ignored, although his death announcement was pure Mitchell. While the film jumped from Charles' proposal and a brief wedding scene to Ellen suggesting the widow Scarlett visit Atlanta, the Selznick forces had not faced a great challenge, since that wedding, Scarlett's entire pregnancy, her widowhood and the birth of Wade had been compressed by Miss Mitchell into only nine pages! Ellen did not originate the idea of sending her daughter to Atlanta since, in the book, Pittypat had made that request by letter. Mammy was not involved either and her ominous warnings to Scarlett were Selznick inventiveness. Naturally, the book's Scarlett took Wade along with her when she made that trip.

By racing ahead directly to the Bazaar, the film excluded all descriptions of wartime Atlanta, Uncle Peter meeting Scarlett at the station, family history of Charles, Melanie, Pittypat and Uncle Henry (who was weeded out), Scarlett's entrapment by the dowagers into hospital work and her clever scheming to get to that Bazaar. The fact that Scarlett and Melanie were co-owners of the Atlanta home called "Aunt Pitty's" (and that the flighty lady was merely a guest there) was discarded in the scenario. Equally absent was the irony that the warehouses near the depot—seen later in flames—were also part of Scarlett's legacy from Charles.

Scarlett had heard reports of the famous blockader Captain Butler beforehand (in the book), but did not associate the name with that man at Twelve Oaks until she began flirting with a strangely familiar face at the charity event. Vivien Leigh's horrified expression left moviegoers with no doubt that Scarlett remembered that man all too well, however. Rhett's candid confessions of his blockade activities were minimized by Hollywood and all his references to Yankee cooperation had been quickly smothered. It was Miss Mitchell's Scarlett who first surrendered her wedding ring, with Melanie gaining courage to follow suit. The movie made Melanie's the noble sacrifice and Scarlett's donation an afterthought (and Rhett, in the book, redeemed only Melanie's ring, not Scarlett's as well, as the movie presented).

The first filmed version of the "Paris Hat" sequence was more faithful to Margaret Mitchell than was its replacement.

Rhett Butler's sarcastic banter at the booth and during his dance with Scarlett was replaced on film by Selznick dialogue which maneuvered to "soften" Scarlett and put Rhett's attraction into early evidence. The Selznick "Waltz" scene showed Scarlett as a coquette instead of a frightened complainer and also invented a speech for Rhett which propelled his motivation for the three hours yet to come. "Someday," Mr. Gable said to Miss Leigh, "I want you to say to me the words I heard you say to Ashley Wilkes—'I love you.'" Presented without undue fanfare, this became on screen one of the most revealing moments in the entire first half. Where Margaret Mitchell had hundreds of pages to allow readers the luxury of slowly guessing Rhett's feelings, David Selznick had compressed them successfully into one line of dialogue.

From the Bazaar, Hollywood's interpretation skipped along (after Rhett's letter with the rings) to the "Paris Hat" sequence, leaving untouched Gerald's trip to Atlanta after he learned Scarlett had danced publicly while in mourning. Also gone with the wind were Scarlett's secret reading of Melanie's letters, her flirtations in the hospital, the devaluation of Confederate money and soaring Southern prices. In the Selznick treatment Scarlett made no trips home to Tara, as Miss Mitchell thought she should, and evidently never saw her mother alive after that initial journey to Atlanta. Hostility toward profiteers like Rhett Butler never materialized on film nor did the many visits he made to Aunt Pitty's before bringing that hat. The Cukor-Howard-Garrett version of that scene had mirrored the book, with Rhett snatching back the bonnet when Scarlett mentioned dyeing it black, and

207

then stealing a kiss on her cheek. The Fleming-Selznick variation again "softened" Scarlett into coquettishly putting the hat on backward. It then got down to brass tacks with Rhett saying he was tempting her with something that didn't include marriage, as in the book, but provided Rhett with a "new" exit line, enabling the footage to jump to the anxiety of crowds awaiting the Gettysburg casualty lists.

This last innovation meant transposing Belle's secret donation of money (in Rhett's handkerchief) to Melanie to a later movie scene, which would also involve Scarlett and Mrs. Meade. It also required the elimination of good Confederate news from Fredericksburg and Chancellorsville. Laura Hope Crews was not required to faint while awaiting news of Gettysburg (since she wasn't there) nor was it necessary to kill so many of Scarlett's old friends on those lists (since they didn't exist).

Ashley had received a week's furlough in the book, but Hollywood thought three days would be sufficient. The movie people brought the ladies to the station to meet him but they forbade Ashley's family from traveling in from Twelve Oaks. Uncle Peter chased "the last chicken in Atlanta" and Aunt Pitty served it for Christmas only on commands of the film script. (Margaret Mitchell had also written about Pitty's last chicken, but that was for a completely different dinner party later in the book.) Ashley's subsequent departure, however, was extremely close to Miss Mitchell's comprehension of it.

After the hospital "Shadow" scene and Belle's donation, the movie sped right on to a mass exodus in the midst of the Battle of Atlanta. The Hollywood compression there—into one day—of Scarlett's hospital revulsion, exploding shells, her ride with Rhett, Pitty's departure, Prissy's promise to help deliver the baby and Dr. Meade's warning not to move Melanie, covered about a quarter of the pages in the book's Part Three. Missing,

Ellen O'Hara's body lay in state at Tara—but only in the movie!

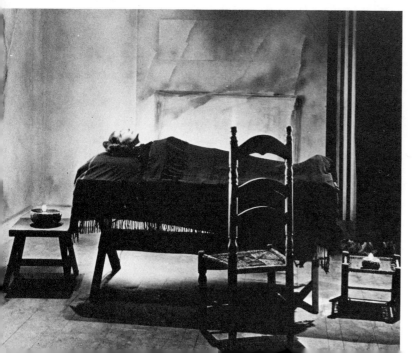

however, were the tragic march of the Home Guard, talk of "plow furloughs," Scarlett's longings for Tara, John Wilkes leaving for battle and his subsequent death, arrival of the wounded at Pitty's front lawn, the defeated army's return to Atlanta, Rhett's offer to Scarlett to become his mistress and news from Tara that Ellen, Carreen and Suellen had contracted typhoid.

Melanie's pregnancy and confinement were a bit too delicate for the Selznick pens, and news that Ashley was a prisoner was kept from movie viewers until after the war, while conditions of wartime prisons—North and South—remained the book's secret. Olivia de Havilland's Melanie did not know (as Miss Mitchell's heroine did) that Scarlett had promised Ashley to care for her and the book's Melanie had also told Scarlett, "If it's a girl, dear, I'd like her to be like you" (perish the thought!).

The film's striking panorama of wounded as Scarlett searched for Dr. Meade gracefully avoided author Mitchell's delineation of a horrendous composite of stench, blood and grisly death through which Scarlett could barely maneuver without treading on pitiful humanity as she struggled not to vomit. The doctor's gruff rebuttal to Scarlett's pleas, which then shifted to fatherly concern, was far more poignant in print because of his unawareness that his son, Phil, was just then near death and Scarlett's realization that Dr. Meade probably would not have left those dying charges even if he did know. Meanwhile, the book's drunken Belle Watling, staggering on the arm of a soldier, was hardly ready to dispense water to the wounded as the film "almost" showed.

The book had contained no scene, as the film did, of Prissy fetching Rhett at Belle's and it was to Scarlett (not Rhett and Belle) that she bragged about her help in the birth (her major contribution had been dropping the newborn baby). It was the book's Scarlett, not the film's Prissy, who dropped the china and silver in a vain attempt to pack and it was Ashley's picture (not Charles') that Melanie requested on screen. Rhett's rescue of the women and baby was similar in both versions but the movie's drive through the fire district was far more melodramatic since, in the book, the last explosion had occurred before they got there. As Miss Mitchell wrote it, the scene of retreating soldiers (with a young boy collapsing) took place *before* the race through the fiery depot. Its placement afterward in the film made a better lead-in to Rhett's departure for the army, while it also allowed uninterrupted suspense in the "Fire" sequence.

Compression was never better employed than in the movie's "Return to Tara" sequence wherein—on the same night—Scarlett found Twelve Oaks a burned shell but her own moonlit home standing, whipped the horse (which then died) at Tara's gate, was greeted by a feeble Gerald and a comforting Mammy and discovered—by seeing Ellen's body—that typhoid had ravaged the O'Hara family. At dawn, the film presented her venturing into the Tara vegetable garden where she gagged on a radish and then vowed never to be hungry again—a triumphant moment for the end of Part One and insertion of an intermission. In the book Scarlett already knew that Ellen and the girls were ill and on her homeward struggle had feared she would find her mother dead. She had stopped at the burnt MacIntosh home (not Twelve Oaks), no moon appeared to show Tara was safe, the horse did not die that night and Gerald's mental state was not immediately apparent when he calmly related Ellen's passing. Hattie McDaniel's Mammy proved far more reassuring than the book's tired and heartbroken lady, left desolate by Mrs. O'Hara's death. And Ellen had been quickly buried the day before—preventing Scarlett from ever seeing her body!

It was not until the following day that the book's Scarlett realized her father's mind was dangerously affected, learned that Rhett's horse had died, and visited the ruins of Twelve Oaks, passing Ellen's new grave along the way. It was there, not at Tara, in daytime rather than at sunrise, that Scarlett scrounged a radish from the earth, quickly devoured it and then vomited. Her oath—never to be hungry again—was uttered only as much from hunger as it was from comprehension that her world was gone, while she stood in the remnants of a plantation she had once hoped to become mistress of.

All references to the kindnesses of Yankee soldiers in sparing Tara because of the sick O'Hara women and even their supplying of a doctor (responsible for saving Suellen's life) were avoided on film, but tales of the Union forces occupying Tara as a headquarters and stealing or burning food and possessions remained intact. Producer Selznick later stated, "We have actually toned down considerably Miss Mitchell's portrait of the depredations of the invaders." While this was true as far as the barbarian Yankee treatment of Atlanta was concerned, there was little doubt left in the minds of Southern audiences as to who the villains were (dared it have been otherwise?). Not one of Margaret Mitchell's defenses of at least *some* of the Yankees appeared in the film.

The beginning of the film's Part Two compressed extreme changes in Scarlett's nature into a slapping of Suellen, after which Scarlett shot a Yankee deserter. In the book both Suellen and Carreen were still recuperating in bed at the time that murder occurred and none of the others (except Melanie) heard the shot, since they were hunting a sow in the nearby swamp. The return of the Yankee troop which set fire to Tara was totally discarded, as was the hiding of the deserter's wallet in baby Beau's diaper. But a line of dialogue from that scene—"Your army has been here before"—was changed slightly and interpolated into Scarlett's earlier confrontation with the deserter.

Melanie's help in putting out Tara's fire had emphasized the girl's "thin-steel, spun-silk courage" in the book

and that episode began to change Scarlett's opinion of her. The Selznick adapters evidently believed enough of this was shown in her help with disposal of the deserter's body. Miss Mitchell foresaw the deserter's horse as a means for Scarlett to finally visit her neighbors, who gave her some much-needed food. Since there were no neighbors in the film, the trip was unnecessary, although how the family survived was anybody's guess. The film deserter had tried to steal Ellen's earbobs (which came in handy for a barter offer to Rhett later on), but in the book Scarlett discovered those valuable trinkets on the man's body.

Scarlett's nightmares of fog began in those troubled days at Tara but Hollywood saved any hint of them until a later honeymoon scene with Rhett. Frank Kennedy's Christmas visit and request for Suellen's hand became a rerepresentative "Delousing" sequence on film, and Jonas Wilkerson was brought in by Hollywood for a brief moment in which the plight of returning soldiers and the scourge of Carpetbaggers were described. Uncle Peter's book visit with news of Ashley might have spoiled the visual drama of his return to Melanie's arms, so it understandably stayed behind. But the dismissal of Will Benteen did strain the credulity of some viewers, since it was Will who (in the book) pulled Tara together, married Suellen and took charge of the plantation when Scarlett wore her drapes on that long visit to Atlanta. It had been the book's Will, not the film's Mammy, who held Scarlett back from running with Melanie to greet the returning Ashley.

Since the film's Suellen was left no one to marry, she complained of becoming an old maid (an earlier line of book dialogue) and the film's Carreen did not enter the convent but stayed at Tara to keep Suellen company. Gerald's death was conveniently moved up from June of 1866 to November 1865 so the film's Scarlett would not have to return from Atlanta for his funeral and his confused presence was not necessary when Scarlett made her velvet curtain outfit. The movie's Pork got Gerald's watch that much earlier as well. The "Orchard Love Scene" had become considerably toned down on film, although Selznick's Ashley *did* place a ball of Tara's red earth into Scarlett's hand. What happened to that red earth had been an early mystery even for Sidney Howard, but the finished film eventually found a destination for it —Jonas Wilkerson's face!

David Selznick's completed picture successfully compressed 330 pages of *Gone with the Wind*'s Part Four into ten rather lengthy sequences (from news that new taxes were imposed on Tara through Rhett's proposal of marriage). In addition to the exclusion of Ella Lorena Kennedy, major movie digressions—even from hearsay sources—concerned subjects considered too controversial for the Hays censors or for racial sensitivities. The purged material included Rhett's murder charge, the dishonest

The cast of characters changed at Melanie's sewing circle, and so did the reading material.

means Frank had used to set up business, political abuses and racial terrors of Reconstruction days, the murder of Jonas Wilkerson and all mentions of the Ku Klux Klan. Although Scarlett did not immediately return to Tara as in the film, Miss Mitchell had imagined Suellen's bitter denunciation coming in the form of a letter. On the other hand, the movie's Suellen was absolved of her indirect responsibility for Gerald's death and near censure by Tara neighbors.

The new Mrs. Kennedy's financial pressures on Old Guard Atlantans were presented as part of a filmed gossip montage, although nothing was shown of her actual social ostracism. Naturally, Rhett wasn't needed to accompany a pregnant Scarlett on her lumber rounds nor was her early drinking trait detailed. Since Selznick "inventiveness" brought Scarlett to Tara after marrying Frank, it was then (not when Gerald died) that she and Melanie persuaded Ashley to work at the lumber mill in Altanta. The hiring of convicts had posed a problem for Hollywood until Margaret Mitchell clarified, in a letter, that they most certainly were *not* black. Scarlett was fond of blacks and would not have allowed their mistreatment by Johnnie Gallegher.

The film had no time to detail Melanie's appeal as social nucleus for the Atlanta Old Guard or Scarlett's knowledge of earlier "political meetings" attended by Frank and Ashley before the night of the Shantytown raid. Rhett did not secretly finance Scarlett in the screen treatment nor withdraw future support because of Ashley. In fact, Rhett's contempt for Ashley was never pictured on film as more than mere romantic jealousy.

By masking the story's terrors of Reconstruction, it not only seemed acceptable for the movie Scarlett to conduct business alone, but eliminated the need for Archie as a protector on her rides or at Melanie's sewing circle

on the night on the raid on Shantytown. While Mammy substituted for him there, it seemed Aunt Pitty could stay safely home with Uncle Peter—so Mrs. Meade replaced her in turn. Rhett's bringing of Dr. Meade instead of Hugh Elsing (along with Ashley) to the Wilkes house saved India the trouble of running out to find Dr. Dean. It also allowed for the film's telescoping there of an amusing little moment in which Mrs. Meade questioned her husband about Belle's—which, in the book, happened later that night in the Meade's own home. During that same sequence David Selznick added a sentimental touch of his own: instead of reading Victor Hugo's *Les Misérables* (which actually had deeper meaning for Confederates, who called it "Lee's Miserables"), Olivia de Havilland read from Charles Dickens' *David Copperfield*, the classic which that producer had so successfully presented while at M-G-M several years earlier.

The attack on Scarlett in Shantytown had been more predictable in print than it appeared on film, since the reader had been prepared for something which was not an isolated instance in those days. The incident, in the book, had occurred at nightfall (not in late afternoon) and Scarlett had been delayed first by meeting Big Sam and then by an argument with Gallegher over cheating on supply money and starving the convicts (not in the film). Scarlett had prearranged a meeting with Big Sam in the novel, so his appearance as her savior had a much less "cavalry to the rescue" flavor than it did in the picture. Sam's presence in that wretched place was also explained by Miss Mitchell (he was hiding from the Yankees), but since Shantytown's true meaning was not explored in the film, the adapters were able to spare him the humiliation of being a murderer.

Clark Gable never told Vivien Leigh about the young boy in New Orleans who was his ward but Ona Munson *did* mention to Olivia de Havilland that she had a son whom she hadn't seen in years. The book's readers had often wondered if these two mysterious children were the same person and if a tie-in had not been eliminated by the author in final editing. The movie, by discharging one of them, did not have to answer that question either.

No length of time was indicated in the cinematic version as to how long Scarlett and Rhett waited to marry after Frank Kennedy's death, whereas in the book it had been almost a year. Their New Orleans honeymoon became a rather solitary affair in the movie, which was to be prophetic of the entire screen treatment of the book's Part Five. In the novel those 190 pages provided readers with their closest insight into the character of Rhett Butler, although Scarlett still dominated the story. In deference to the star status of Clark Gable, the movie script closed in on Rhett and Scarlett at that point with very little further intrusion from outsiders. This succeeded in giving the illusion that Mr. Gable's role was larger than it actually was. Eliminated along with the fascinating people in New Orleans were all of Scarlett's "new" friends in Atlanta. Hollywood forbade Scarlett to entertain at her Atlanta home and she did not throw a large gala affair for Governor Bullock and the Republicans.

Actually, the filmed narrative jumped from New Orleans to the birth of Bonnie with one crucial new "Selznick scene" interspersed. In the book Rhett never visited Tara, but David Selznick thought he should, so an "original" moment was inserted. Actually, it served a very important purpose since it gave Mr. Gable a line of dialogue necessary to the producer's own version of the finale: "You get your strength from this red earth of Tara." And since the film skipped Scarlett's pregnancy, any mention that she thought of aborting the child was nicely avoided.

In the Mitchell work it had been a new servant, Lou (not Mammy), who laced Scarlett into an unwelcome twenty-inch waistline, causing Mrs. Butler's vow to have no more children. But she did not confront Rhett with that decision then and there (as on film) but waited until after a visit to Ashley, which the film bypassed. Her decision was reinforced by realization that Ashley did not sleep with Melanie, lest she be endangered by a new pregnancy, and Scarlett fancied some sort of romantic fidelity to him if she carried through her plans. Ashley's condemnations of Rhett for having brutalized Scarlett were also missing in the film, even though this insult was probably the deciding factor in Scarlett's plan.

When she did finally broach the subject to Rhett, the book's Scarlett asked him for separate bedrooms. Vivien Leigh did not have to make that request of Clark Gable since they appeared to already have their own rooms. She also did not miss sleeping in his arms (the way her book counterpart did) since the Hays Office had obviously never allowed her to. Mr. Gable did not take the news as calmly as Miss Mitchell's Rhett did, and, in a very famous "original" Selznick action, kicked in the door between their rooms. Immediately thereafter the movie invented another sequence in which he visited Belle Watling for sympathy and that gold-hearted "hostess" set him back home for his daughter's sake (with a tear in her eye, of course). The book's implication that Rhett began living with Belle from that point on was never even hinted at.

Rhett's awareness of little Wade's social ostracism—and fear that Bonnie would encounter the same—resulted, in the book, in a series of actions which successfully won the Old Guard over to his side. In the picture this was represented by a walk down Peachtree Street in which he and Scarlett wheeled Bonnie's carriage and cultivated "every fat old cat" they passed. A following scene in which Rhett sought Mrs. Merriwether's advice concluded with the suggestion that Mr. Butler was no longer considered a villain. All of this saved him the trouble of working at the bank, attending political meetings and donating his gold to restore Southerners to power.

Scarlett's visit to the mill to see Ashley was similar in book and film, although Leslie Howard's poetic dialogue was actually borrowed from Scarlett's thoughts in the book. And the film appointed Mrs. Meade (rather than the nonexistent Archie and Mrs. Elsing) to accompany India when she caught them in a friendly embrace.

Vivien Leigh's most memorable movie costume (apart, possibly, from the drapery dress) was that worn to Ashley's birthday party, designed in a deep red velvet and often described by viewers as being "scarlet" in color. Miss Mitchell, however, had described that gown as "her new jade-green watered-silk dress." (Had Walter Plunkett followed the author's color schemes to the letter, Vivien Leigh might have been seen in nothing but green!) In the film Rhett sent Scarlett into the "arena" of Ashley's party guests alone—leaving her at the porch door. Not so in the book, where his unexplained absence might have adversely affected his new social efforts for Bonnie.

After that party the book's drunken Rhett admitted to Scarlett that he always knew she had dreamed it was Ashley, not him, in bed with her. She then ran swiftly from the dining room and Rhett ran after her in pursuit. He grabbed her violently and carried her up to the bedroom to her night of rapture. In the film Clark Gable was

Rhett Butler kicked in Scarlett's door at David Selznick's insistence, not at Margaret Mitchell's.

not allowed to make any such mention of Ashley or their bed. Vivien Leigh strolled rather casually from the dining room until Mr. Gable picked her up—rather sedately by comparison. In the Selznick version Clark Gable's dialogue was quite subdued at that point ("This is one night you're not turning me out") from the book's fairly explicit "By God, this is one night when there are only going to be two in my bed." And, of course, Scarlett's thoughts of "surrender" had to be surmised by movie viewers only from a happy look on Miss Leigh's face the next morning. Nevertheless, it was considered a fairly daring movie scene in 1939.

It was the very next day, on film, that Rhett left for London with Bonnie. Their stay there was not too happy since Bonnie missed her mother and had nightmares in the dark. An English nurse's suggestion to just let Bonnie scream for a night or two infuriated Rhett and they returned to Atlanta. In the book Rhett didn't even come home for two days after that drunken night and it was Charleston and New Orleans—not London—that he visited with Bonnie *and Prissy!* Bonnie's nightmares had actually occurred earlier in the book and that helpful suggestion to let her scream had come from ever-thoughtful Scarlett. (Again, the movie folk softened her image by avoiding that little gem of nonmotherly understanding.) No first-person detailings of Rhett's trip existed in the book and Scarlett merely heard about it through letters.

A trip to London for Rhett and Bonnie was a movie inspiration not in keeping with the book.

Scarlett's contrite attempt to tell Melanie about her feelings for Ashley were discarded by the adapters, as was the estrangement between Melanie and India over Scarlett. Then, although the events surrounding Scarlett's miscarriage were similar in both versions, Rhett's drunken confession to Melanie was much modified on screen. Mr. Gable, in fact, seemed only heartbroken with nary a whiskey bottle in sight. From that point on the Selznick picture telescoped the remaining tragedies of the book together in quick sequence, whereas much time elapsed, in the book, between the miscarriage, Bonnie's fatal accident and Melanie's death. For this innovation—more than any other portion of the screenplay—the film would earn the unjust terminology of "soap opera." Scarlett's recuperation at Tara, Rhett's secret lumber mill deal with Ashley, the emotional gap that developed between the Butlers, the return of Southern rule, Rhett's drunken despair over Bonnie, Scarlett's trip to Marietta and Mammy's permanent return to Tara were intervening events which the film dropped along the way.

After Melanie's death the framework between novel and movie was basically the same, although Scarlett's revealing run through the misty fog was an unexplained symbolism wasted on some viewers unfamiliar with the book. Rhett did not actually *leave* Scarlett with his famous exit line, as Miss Mitchell saw it, but merely walked upstairs (perhaps to pack). And he offered to return to see her from time to time for appearances' sake— an optimistic promise avoided completely by the movie. Scarlett remembered Tara then but did *not* hear the voices of Gerald, Ashley and Rhett as she did courtesy of David Selznick. But, of course, the book's last line of dialogue remained the same.

Margaret Mitchell's greatest fear had been that the film version would alter the historical facts she had researched so diligently. With the possible exception of overemphasizing the depot fire so it would be perpetually —and incorrectly—referred to as "the burning of Atlanta," her fears proved groundless. The filmmakers did not change the author's history, although, by and large, they did ignore it! Moviegoers were expected to approach *Gone With the Wind* for its story values and to *see* the effects of the Civil War on the Southern civilization and on Scarlett O'Hara. They were fated to learn very little actual historical detail from the screen version—unlike the fascinating and enlightening panorama portrayed in Miss Mitchell's text. Whenever the term "moonlight and magnolias" was used as a description of *Gone with the Wind*, it was less arguable in terms of the motion picture.

The differences between the book and movie were vast. Yet—for years after—viewers would argue as to what they had or had not seen. David Selznick did not film a completely faithful version of Margaret Mitchell's novel—but he successfully gave the *illusion* that he had!

The Music

Possibly the most famous of all film composers, Maximilian Raoul Walter Steiner was born in Vienna, Austria, on May 10, 1888. Max was the godson of composer Richard Strauss, while the noted Johann Strauss, Jr. was another family friend. Surrounded by the inspiration of musical genius, the boy's own interests surfaced quite early. He had composed an operetta, *The Beautiful Greek Girl*, by age sixteen. Even before that Max had completed a four-year course at the Imperial Academy of Music in one year and mastered, at that time, the piano, violin, trumpet and organ.

After the successful premiere of that operetta and its year-long run, Max traveled to England where he accepted a series of offers to conduct orchestras at such notable locations as the Hippodrome and the London Opera House. At the end of 1914 he came to America, almost penniless, but two years later had risen to the rank of conductor for Broadway shows including the *Ziegfeld Follies*, and remained in New York thereafter. One of Florenz Ziegfeld's most successful stage presentations, *Rio Rita*, was purchased by RKO for a 1929 "early sound" film and Max Steiner went to Hollywood to supervise its music. As a result, a seven-year relationship began

with that studio, during which Executive Producer David O. Selznick encouraged Max to initiate original background scores throughout some of his feature pictures. In 1936 the composer began a prolific thirty-year career at Warner Brothers, during which time he was occasionally "borrowed" by other studios such as Selznick International.

Mr. Steiner's music for *Gone With the Wind* was to be the most ambitious film score yet undertaken when he accepted the assignment in 1939. In all, he composed over three hours of music for it, of which two hours and thirty-six minutes survived the final "cut." As was Max's style, the score consisted primarily of themes for many of the major characters such as Rhett, Melanie, Mammy, Gerald, Bonnie and Belle. Although the Ashley character was not assigned an individual melody, he was surrounded by the film's two love themes, "Scarlett and Ashley" and "Ashley and Melanie," befitting the fact that even in the book Ashley Wilkes, by himself, was not of major story importance. An airy, almost flighty, establishment theme was used for Scarlett O'Hara (played only in the opening sequence and at her arrival at Twelve Oaks) but this was actually based on a Stephen Foster

A Selznick International publicity photograph: Max Steiner conducting the musical score for Gone With the Wind.

composition "Katie Bell." It was no longer needed after the lady began involving herself in her various travails. More represetative of the heroine was the "Scarlett and Ashley" motif, which, at least for the first three-quarters of the film, was a subliminal reminder of exactly where Scarlett's heart was at. "Rhett's Theme," another passing subtlety, was heard briefly as the cast credits listed Clark Gable as "a visitor from Charleston." It recurred more dominantly as he watched Scarlett ascend the Twelve Oaks staircase and once again as he left her in the finale.

An Irish motif was more than suitable for Gerald O'Hara and arrived in sprightly fashion for his entrance, jumping the fence of Tara on horseback. Later, it returned in a slow, tragic tempo for "Scarlett's Return to Tara." "Mammy's Theme"—the very first heard in the picture (under the tie-in credit for M-G-M and Technicolor)—expressed the warmth and considerable humor of that noble lady. This theme was slowed to a saddened pace as she comforted the returning Scarlett just before her awareness of Ellen's death. Belle Watling had inspired a simple, lushly beautiful composition played during her carriage meeting with Melanie (to heartrending effect) and in her goodbye to Rhett. It was also subtly interpolated, very briefly and effectively, as Mrs. Meade questioned her husband about the Watling establishment. The film's most truly beautiful theme, "Melanie," was, ironically, "borrowed" by Mr. Steiner from the score of his 1934 RKO film *The Fountain*. The melody, as warm and compassionate as the character herself, was introduced at the same time she was—at Twelve Oaks—and returned throughout the film: during the war and hard times at Tara and even when she gave sympathy to heartbroken Rhett. Its most effective—and unforgettable—use came at Melanie's death, accompanied by a "heavenly choir" and successfully designed to break every heart in the audience.

For those few scenes in which Melanie and Ashley were permitted by Scarlett to be alone, and upon Ashley's return from war, the stirringly romantic "Ashley and Melanie" love theme arose. However, it bore a confusing kinship to all the music utilized in the film's final quarter, which (no matter what scene it scored) was generally referred to as "Bonnie's Theme." Of course, the most absolutely dominant, most famous and most recorded motif of all was "Tara's Theme." From the main title and prologue (complete with "heavenly choir"), it recurred whenever Scarlett needed hope and, naturally, was heard on her various returns home. "Tara's Theme" was also employed for all three major "pull-back" shots, during the last of which it was rejoined by the choir to bring the film to its conclusion.

Such a superfluous breakdown of Max Steiner's *Gone With the Wind* themes could, in itself, prove nothing. The masterful interpolations of them all, throughout the film, had to be *heard* to be appreciated. Additionally, Max wrote minor themes for scenes like Frank Kennedy's proposal, a rousing dance for the Bazaar, a touching waltz for Rhett's suggestion of love to Scarlett, a New Orleans can-can and incidental music wherever needed. His wartime musical montage for Scarlett walking through the wounded was tragic and yet truly inspirational. In addition to generous helpings of "Dixie" throughout his score, Mr. Steiner also treated his listeners to quick snatches from several Stephen Foster melodies, often used for humorous effect (such as "Massa's in de Cold, Cold Ground" just as the Widow Hamilton tried on a gay bonnet).

The incredible pressures of the *Gone With the Wind* assignment did require Max Steiner to seek some help from his associates and a few brief passages were scored by Franz Waxman, Adolph Deutsch and Hugo Friedhofer, who adapted their work to the thematic style of the major composer. Additionally, though often disputed by Steiner purists, Heinz Roemheld composed all the music for the escape from Atlanta and the burning depot scenes. None of this music would ever be included in any Steiner-authorized *Gone With the Wind* recording, although it would find its way into a sound-track album many years later.

Strangest of all were the few remnants of M-G-M "stock music" that remained in the film after its initial previews. Rarely realized by viewers, these totally "foreign" bits of music fit some particular scenes well enough for Producer Selznick to request their retention. They included the "Approach of the Yankee Deserter," "Shantytown" and, most surprisingly, "Rhett Carries Scarlett Upstairs."

It was a historical disappointment that *Gone With the Wind*'s original film score did not win an Academy Award and a miscarriage of justice that it lost to a musical film (*The Wizard of Oz*) whose adapter, not its songwriters, received the trophy. But Max Steiner was the recipient of nineteen nominations (including *GWTW*) for Academy Awards and he won the Oscar on three separate occasions.

David Selznick was impressed enough with the completed score for his Civil War epic to suggest to record companies the issuance of an album reproduced directly from Max Steiner's sound-track recordings. He found no interest, however, and even though symphonic re-recordings were issued afterward, the sound-track idea was ignored through many of the film's reissues. Finally, twenty-eight years after the score was written, the idea became a reality. Unfortunately, for most of the original Steiner recordings it was far too late.

Max Steiner died on December 28, 1971, at the age of eighty-three. He left behind an art form which he had been most instrumental in furthering, and film scores for several hundred motion pictures.

The Unveilings

A later American President would describe it as "the biggest event to happen in the South in my lifetime," and, indeed, the excitement had begun as early as mid-November, when plans for *Gone With the Wind*'s initial theatrical engagement were finalized. Courtesy of M-G-M, the forty-six-year-old Loew's Grand Theatre on Peachtree Street was the honored site and, as Atlanta newspapers announced to their readers on November 18 (when seats went on sale), tickets for the world premiere performance would cost $10 apiece—"believed to be the highest in cinema history." That same day it was related that David Selznick, Clark Gable, Vivien Leigh, Ona Munson, Laura Hope Crews, Ann Rutherford and Evelyn Keyes would be in attendance for the opening and for day-before festivities. All proceeds from the gala first showing were to benefit local Atlanta charities as administered by the Atlanta Community Fund.

However, there was one fly in the ointment. Loew's Grand could seat only 2,051 persons and a certain large number of tickets had to be reserved for the Hollywood folk and invited visiting dignitaries. Within days every available ticket for the benefit showing had been sold out and "scalpers" began charging up to ten times face value for reservations to those whose lives wouldn't be complete if they didn't attend. For those satisfied to see the film afterward, advance tickets had gone on sale simultaneously for the "indefinite run" of twice-daily performances. The four-hour (with overtures and intermission) show would begin at 1:30 each afternoon (with ticket prices ranging from 75 cents in the orchestra and balcony to $1.10 for loge seats) and at 8:30 each evening (at $1.10 to $1.50 for seats). Reservations were accepted for performances up to four weeks in advance.

Within a few weeks Atlanta learned that the premiere contingent had grown to include the presence of John Hay Whitney, Russell Birdwell, Howard Dietz (M-G-M advertising director), Howard Strickling (M-G-M publicity director), Olivia de Havilland, Laurence Olivier, Carole Lombard, the South's own Alicia Rhett and the totally unrelated Claudette Colbert. "Poor deluded Claudette," David Selznick commented, "is coming under the notion that she is going to have a good time." Such was the trepidation the producer felt as his big moment approached. He feared a circus atmosphere which could embarrass one and all and certainly detract from the artistic merits of his picture. He wanted these appreciated far more than he desired any massive publicity sendoff. "After all, we have only made a motion picture," he wrote to Kay Brown, ". . . and the idea of a town receiving us as though we had just licked the Germans is

something that I will not go through with . . . for God's sake, don't let us in for any nonsense that makes us ridiculous. . . . I want to be present to enjoy (hopefully) the first opening of the picture, but not to make a horse's ass of myself."

David's terror would have been soothed somewhat if he had known the well-organized plans under way with Atlanta's Mayor William B. Hartsfield in command. Although nothing of such scope had been planned for modern-day Atlanta before, the mayor was well aware that the premiere would come right in the middle of downtown Atlanta's crucial Christmas shopping season and promised retailers that the entire proceedings would be mapped out in advance to conflict as little as possible with that necessary commerce. As a bonus to those store-owners, the mayor proclaimed Thursday, December 14, as a municipal half-holiday, providing all of Atlanta's workers with the opportunity to come downtown to see the planned "parade of stars" and simultaneously do a little holiday buying. Partly from civic pride and partly from common sense, businessmen decorated their win-

Crowds and spotlights surrounded the world premiere at Atlanta's Loew's Grand Theatre on December 15, 1939.

215

Irene and David Selznick accompanied John Marsh (back-ground) and Margaret Mitchell into the Loew's Grand auditorium.

dows with tie-in displays featuring various *Gone With the Wind* motifs, Confederate flags and photographs of the film stars. They also distributed premium souvenirs which ranged from handbills to discount "wooden nickels."

The celebration theme spread even to private homes and by premiere week the town was bedecked with thousands of those Confederate flags, acres of bunting, innumerable new neon lights and false fronts (for stores and homes) representing old Southern mansions—all of which were interspersed with traditional Christmas decorations. And the double holiday atmosphere was even further heightened when Georgia's Governor Eurith D. Rivers proclaimed Friday, December 15, a holiday throughout the state—a move unprecedented even in movie-conscious America. The city soon swarmed with out-of-town visitors, and by Wednesday, December 13, the anticipation and suspense had brought a thorough resurgence of "Scarlett fever" to Atlanta—and even the entire South by proxy.

Through her status as an M-G-M contractee, Ann Rutherford was the first celebrity thrown to the lions and was named, on Thursday the 14th, "Honorary Mayor of Atlanta." Afterward she joined her supporting co-stars, Ona Munson, Evelyn Keyes, and Laura Hope Crews, for a luncheon sponsored by Atlanta's Better Films Council. While most of the *Gone With the Wind* personnel had chosen to fly to Georgia, Miss Crews decided to make the trip by rail. She wondered at her decision when her train was involved in an accident along the way.

Finally, after Clark Gable's arrival (with Carole Lombard) on an M-G-M chartered plane at 3:30 on Thursday afternoon, the parade was set to begin. David Selznick, his wife Irene, Vivien Leigh, Laurence Olivier, Olivia de Havilland and other movie people were already in Atlanta, but remained out of sight until Clark's arrival to make their first public appearance in that parade. The open cars containing the Hollywood royalty proceeded slowly up Peachtree Street through crowds of 300,000 onlookers until they arrived at the Georgian Terrace Hotel where the governors of five Southern states waited to greet them as each was separately introduced. Mr. Gable was, of course, the last brought before the spectators, whose cheers, applause and Rebel yells were almost deafening. The entire affair, meanwhile, was being broadcast to radio audiences across the nation.

Margaret Mitchell had decided long beforehand to stay away from the festivities, indicating that they were in honor of Mr. Selznick's film and its cast, but not related to her. Mrs. Marsh had agreed, however, to attend the premiere and two afternoon receptions. The first of these, held Thursday, was given by Rich's department store and Peggy mingled there with her Macmillan friends—Lois Cole, Harold Latham and George P. Brett—as well as two other Pulitzer Prize winners, Julia Peterkin and Marjorie Kinnan Rawlings. Meanwhile, the author had issued a press statement saying how much she was looking forward to seeing the film.

Thursday night brought the long-planned costume ball sponsored by the Junior League and held at Atlanta's Municipal Auditorium, itself a flag-covered replica of *Gone With the Wind*'s "Bazaar." The movie's stars made appearances and, again, were introduced to the five thousand guests, and all then danced to the music of Kay Kyser's orchestra. It had been the Junior League which excluded Margaret Mitchell from membership eighteen years earlier following her apache dance and, although Stephens Mitchell was among the celebrants, his author sister sent her regrets.

Finally, on Friday afternoon, Margaret Mitchell met the actors who had personified her characters on film, as well as the picture's producer, at a tea given by the Atlanta Women's Press Club. Held at the Piedmont Driving Club, across the street from Margaret's home, these proceedings were closely guarded and—aside from the club's members—only the visting politicians, Macmillan contingent and Selznick people were granted entrance. There the author chatted and posed for photographs with the Hollywood visitors—taking Clark Gable into an anteroom for a short private conversation. The actor afterward volunteered that Margaret was "the most fascinating woman I've ever met." Although the premiere that evening was the nominal cause for the entire ongoing carnival, the following day's *Atlanta Constitution* gave it only secondary prominence to an eight-column banner headline which read, "Gable and Miss Mitchell talk alone after he begs audience with author." Underneath that page-one news break a huge photo of Clark, Margaret and Vivien Leigh dominated readers' attention as it showed the diminutive Atlanta lady looking up into her Rhett Butler's face.

Since the excitement of the premiere had been building for over a month, by Friday night the city's mood was something near ecstatic frenzy. Mayor Hartsfield had promised to make Atlanta the "best lighted city in the world" and the nine searchlights in front of Loew's Grand Theatre did indeed give the winter night a stark, otherworldly effect. The theatre itself had been fronted

with porch columns several stories high over which hung a huge medallion of Mr. Gable embracing Miss Leigh. A lawn of artificial grass extended across Peachtree Street to form an impressive walkway for the arriving celebrities, most of whom were announced, some of whom spoke a few words of greeting. The arrival of Clark Gable and Carole Lombard caused a sensation among the twelve thousand overjoyed spectators, but the grateful actor made a gracious request over the microphones: "Tonight I am here just as a spectator. I want to see *Gone With the Wind* the same as you do. This is Margaret Mitchell's night and the people of Atlanta's night." (Mr. Gable's entrance was broadcast on all radio stations and filmed by several newsreel companies.)

Then the real "star" of the evening arrived on the arm of her proud husband and accompanied by David and Irene Selznick. Dressed like a movie star herself in a formal pink tulle gown, with a girlish pink ribbon in her hair, Margaret Mitchell waved to the crowds and quickly hurried into the theatre. As the newsreel cameras captured her entrance, it was entirely possible that this was the only occasion in her lifetime when the author was recorded on motion picture film. Mr. and Mrs. John

A big night for Broadway: The Astor Theatre on December 19, 1939.

New York City's Capitol Theatre exhibited huge portraits of Clark Gable . . .

Marsh were seated between the Gables and John Hay Whitney with Olivia de Havilland.

The house lights dimmed, voices quickly hushed and the bells of Selznick International's trademark rang through the theatre. But the hush did not last! For after an obligatory acknowledgment of M-G-M's participation, the audience saw whose name Hollywood had chosen for first screen honors and loudly cheered the first frames of film, which read, "Margaret Mitchell's Story of the Old South." The spontaneous reaction increased as each of the title's fifteen letters swept proudly across the screen —from right to life—in a presentation quite unique and sentimentally impressive. There was further applause for the names of the four stars (the only players to receive official screen "billing") as they rolled upward from screen bottom and then, finally, for the name of David O. Selznick. An "original" prologue introduced the story:

"There was a land of Cavaliers and Cotton Fields
called the Old South . . .
Here in this pretty world Gallantry took its last bow . . .
Here was the last ever to be seen of Knights and their

Ladies Fair, of Master and of Slave . . .
Look for it only in books, for it is no more than
a dream remembered . . .
A Civilization gone with the wind . . ."

As those last bittersweet words faded from the screen, not a eye in the theatre was left dry. For the following four hours the etiquette of that dignified audience reverted to that of a Saturday children's matinee. Rebel yells greeted news of war, applause shook the walls as Scarlett shot the deserter and hisses carried like a quick-burning fuse through the Sherman montage. In the fourth row four invited Confederate veterans who had fought in the Battle of Atlanta sat entranced as they relived a tragedy they alone—of all those there—had seen first-hand.

An earthquake of sincere applause followed Scarlett's final promise that "Tomorrow is another day," and David Selznick, overcome by emotion, quietly walked out of the auditorium. It was left to Margaret Mitchell to make the evening's final speech after Clark Gable led her to the stage. "It was a tremendous emotional experience for

. . . and Vivien Leigh in its inner lobby for the engagement of Gone With the Wind.

me," Margaret told the spellbound audience. "I cried again and again, just as did all of you. . . . It's not up to me to speak of the grand things these actors have done . . . but I just want to speak for one moment about Mr. David Selznick. He's the man that every one of you cracked the joke about, 'Oh, well, we'll wait till Shirley Temple grows up and she'll play Scarlett.' I want to commend Mr. Selznick's courage and his obstinacy and his determination in just keeping his mouth shut until he got exactly the cast he wanted."

Bnt Margaret did not forget those from her beloved Atlanta who had helped her either. She remembered librarians, storekeepers who had participated in the holiday extravaganza and even taxi drivers. "You know," she said, "everybody thinks it's just when you are dead broke and you are out of luck that you need friends. But really, when you've had as incredible success as I have had, that's really when you need friends. And, thank heaven, I've had them. And I've appreciated everything people have done for me, to be kind to me and my Scarlett."

From Atlanta *the Wind* blew to New York where four days later—on Tuesday, December 19—it faced "premieres" at two major Broadway showcases. The Astor, known as a haven for top-drawer Hollywood films, was often selected by M-G-M for its two-a-day reserved-seat attractions like *The Good Earth* or *Captains Courageous*. The Selznick "magnum opus" was elected to play there "indefinitely," while it would also begin a limited continuous engagement at the Capitol, Broadway flagship for M-G-M's more popular entertainments (and part of the Loew's chain). The Capitol was the site of the more exciting premiere and television had its first rendezvous with *Gone With the Wind* on opening night in that theatre's lobby. The arrival of celebrities was broadcast to the area's affluent few hundred who could afford an expensive novelty which carried only occasional special programs.

Although neither Clark Gable nor Vivien Leigh was present, the spectators were not disappointed with the arrivals of Olivia de Havilland and James Stewart, Joan Bennett, Alice Faye with Tony Martin, Barbara O'Neil with Joshua Logan, Ann Rutherford and columnist Walter Winchell. But the night's enthusiasm did not ex-

219

tend to all of the town's movie critics, whose crucial notices often determined a film's financial success. The next morning's reception was decidely mixed, although *The New York Times* liked it enough to select it as one of their "ten best" of 1939. "Understatement has its uses too," that paper's critic wrote on December 20, "so this morning's report on the event of last night will begin with the casual notation that it was a great show . . . although we still feel that color is hard on the eyes for so long a picture . . . anyway, 'it' has arrived at last, and we cannot get over the shock of not being disappointed."

The New York Daily News's publisher sent two reviewers to the separate "premieres" in hopes their differing opinions would make for interesting reading. That paper, famous for its "star" ratings on pictures, published both reviews the next morning and both critics had separately decided to grant *Gone With the Wind* the paper's highest rating—"four stars." Kate Cameron, having viewed it at the Capitol, found, "There has never been a picture like David O. Selznick's *Gone With the Wind* . . . one must be feeling hale and hearty to stand the strain of the long sitting . . . but for those who can bear it, *GWTW* is worth every moment of that time." Wanda Hale's critique from the Astor said, *"Gone With the Wind* is the most magnificent motion picture of all time. And the longest. Yet I feel that I am one of the privileged to have been able to see it before one foot is cut for general distribution."

Not all the reviewers were as quick to praise the film, however, and the issue came to a head on December 27 when the New York Film Critics argued over selection of their "bests" until late into the night. While several of their awards drew strongly divided voting, the bitterest balloting come in selection of the year's "Best Picture." The *Gone With the Wind* supporters were as vehement as those who chose *Mr. Smith Goes to Washington*, many of whom were so opposed to the Selznick film that they refused to budge in their decisions. Finally, just before the *fourteenth* ballot, a compromise was reached in which all critics were asked to select their *second* choice, and *Wuthering Heights* was declared the winner. Unfortunately, this deadlock would be forgotten by history and a film actually deserving of the critics' third place mention was recorded forever as the prestigious group's first choice for 1939. (Ironically, twenty-one years later, another "Best Picture" deadlock would result in a tie vote between *The Apartment* and *Sons and Lovers*.) Vivien Leigh was the group's popular winner for "Best Actress" on the second ballot (over Greta Garbo). And while John Ford was named "Best Director" for *Stagecoach*, Victor Fleming placed third in that category's final ballot.

M-G-M allowed America's theatres to choose between playing *Gone With the Wind* on an unreserved three-times-daily basis, or twice a day with reserved seats. After opening in Boston *the Wind* blew westward in late 1939.

Loew's Colonial in Reading, Pennsylvania, selected reserved-seat shows, while the Loew's Regent in Harrisburg, Pennsylvania, and the RKO Capitol in Cincinnati, Ohio, both chose the unreserved performances. (Aside from these cities and the major bookings in Atlanta, New York and Los Angeles, there were no other openings of the film until early 1940.)

The Wind blew into Los Angeles on Thursday, December 28, with its most massive "premiere" of all. The Fox Carthay Circle, once darkened by the Depression but recently the site of Hollywood's most prestigious openings (*Romeo and Juliet, Marie Antoinette, Snow White and the Seven Dwarfs*), was the theatre selected. Just three days within the boundaries set by the Academy of Motion Picture Arts and Sciences for Award-qualifying films, David Selznick faced his most truly critical audience—his peers. Who from that cynical town would come to lend support to an effort many thought already overblown with advance publicity?

But they all came—the Selznick forces, the final cast, the contenders, the competitors, those who had sneered or laughed for three and a half years, and those who had wished him well all along. The "premiere" guest list read like a "Who's Who in 1939 Hollywood" as it included: Jean Arthur, Freddie Bartholomew, Joan Bennett, Busby Berkeley, Russell Birdwell, Charles Boyer, Fanny Brice, Rand Brooks, George Burns and Gracie Allen, Frank Capra, Richard Carlson, Claudette Colbert, Ronald Colman, Gary Cooper, Merian C. Cooper (with Dorothy Jordan), Fred Crane, Joan Crawford, George Cukor, Marion Davies, Dolores Del Rio, Cecil B. DeMille, Irene Dunne, Deanna Durbin, Victor Fleming, Arthur Freed, Clark Gable, Paulette Goddard, Samuel Goldwyn, Cary Grant, Harry Ham (Vivien Leigh's agent from London who had helped her win the part), Leland Hayward, William Randolph Hearst, Alfred Hitchcock, Miriam Hopkins, Herbert and Natalie Kalmus, Evelyn Keyes, Hedy Lamarr, Vivien Leigh, Mitchell Leisen, Mervyn LeRoy, Harold Lloyd, Carole Lombard, Ernst Lubitsch, Jeffrey Lynn, Fred MacMurray, Joseph Mankiewicz, Alan Marshal, Harpo Marx, Louis B. Mayer, Hattie McDaniel, William Cameron Menzies, Ona Munson, Carroll Nye, Laurence Olivier, Mary Pickford, Walter Pidgeon, Walter Plunkett, William Powell, Tyrone Power, Basil Rathbone, George Reeves, Edward G. Robinson, May Robson, Ginger Rogers, Mickey Rooney, Rosalind Russell, Victor Saville, Randolph Scott, Myron Selznick, Norma Shearer, Ann Sheridan, Ann Sothern, Eric Stacey, Max Steiner, Margaret Sullavan, Shirley Temple, King Vidor, Josef von Sternberg, Jack L. Warner, Franz Waxman, Orson Welles, Lyle Wheeler, John Hay Whitney and William Wyler.

Probably never again would so many contributors to or friends of *Gone With the Wind* be together under the same roof. The saga seemed complete.

1939: Hollywood's Golden Year

Of Mice and Men, a Hal Roach production directed by Lewis Milestone, premiered only in Hollywood in 1939, to compete for Academy Awards. The compassionate John Steinbeck 1937 best seller arrived on screen after a prize-winning dramatization had fascinated play-goers and, despite the delay, none of the Steinbeck art had been lost along the way. Walter D. Edmonds's novel of Revolutionary America, *Drums Along the Mohawk*, had provided readers with historical fiction at its best, and John Ford's film version for Twentieth Century-Fox was an exciting, basically faithful one, substantially aided by the contributions of Claudette Colbert, Henry Fonda, Edna May Oliver and Technicolor. Far less faithful to its source was Fox's version of Louis Bromfield's *The Rains Came*, which ignored the author's primary sociology of India in favor of the doomed romance between Myrna Loy and Tyrone Power. But the movie was more than noteworthy for its visually thrilling special effects of earthquake and flood.

Hollywood had reached even further back in its 1939 literary quest—to renowned authors of the past. A large portion of Emily Brontë's *Wuthering Heights* inspired adapters Ben Hecht and Charles MacArthur to create a liberally modified treatment for Samuel Goldwyn's pro-

Vivien Leigh and Leslie Howard in Gone With the Wind, *the innocent object of Hollywood's objections.*

Robert Donat and Greer Garson in Sam Wood's Goodbye, Mr. Chips.

It was not without cause that several journalists and many citizens of the movie colony objected when David Selznick squeezed *Gone With the Wind* in just under the wire to compete for the various film awards of 1939. For that year had already been acknowledged by authorities as an unusually prolific one in the number of quality motion pictures released. But no one could have realized then that, even decades later, 1939 would be looked upon as the milestone year in cinema history. It was, many would say later, "Hollywood's Golden Year"— filled with illuminating combinations of all screen genres.

Very possibly the *Gone With the Wind* phenomenon had encouraged 1939 filmmakers to rely more than ever on recent best-selling fiction, and works of James Hilton were the source of two extraordinarily fine screen translations. Sam Wood's *Goodbye, Mr. Chips*, the first of these, was an M-G-M British production which solicited unabashed emotions from its audiences through the poignant performances of Robert Donat and the debuting Greer Garson. And Mr. Hilton's *We Are Not Alone* became a Warner production of rare tenderness and beauty, largely through the performance of Paul Muni.

Laurence Olivier and Merle Oberon added a new dimension to William Wyler's production of Wuthering Heights.

duction. They also endowed the classic love story with an added romantic dimension which was then vividly brought to screen life by Laurence Olivier, Merle Oberon, David Niven, newcomer Geraldine Fitzgerald and, especially, by director William Wyler. Mr. Hecht and Mr. MacArthur found a greater challenge in adapting a Rudyard Kipling poem for the cinema but George Stevens directed Cary Grant and company with enough skill to make *Gunga Din* an adventurous delight. Mr. Kipling proved equally serviceable for Paramount Pictures and director William Wellman, who helped Ronald Colman and Ida Lupino revive the author's first novel, *The Light That Failed*, for a third and most successful screen version.

That same studio and director also resurrected Percival Wren's old chestnut *Beau Geste* for another cinema go-round. But the ensemble of Gary Cooper, Ray Milland, Robert Preston, Brian Donlevy and Susan Hayward played the by then overdone themes of brotherly sacrifice in the French Foreign Legion as a stirring visual symphony of adventure for moviegoers. The same result was evident in Alexander Korda's remake of *Four Feathers*, A. E. W. Mason's novel that had been filmed twice previously but this time with the considerable benefit of Technicolor. Meanwhile, as Charles Laughton portrayed a new *Hunchback of Notre Dame* and Mickey Rooney was the latest *Huckleberry Finn*, Basil Rathbone (as Sherlock Holmes) searched out Arthur Conan Doyle's secrets in *The Hound of the Baskervilles*.

The Broadway stage was no less important for 1939 filmmaking inspiration, most notably in Warner's version of *Dark Victory*. Bette Davis was never more spirited, poignant or superbly convincing than in this film of a play that had been only mildly successful on stage when essayed by Tallulah Bankhead. Director Edmund Gould-

ing orchestrated a delicate tragedy without maudlin overtones, a task helpfully abetted by George Brent, Humphrey Bogart and Geraldine Fitzgerald. M-G-M's *Idiot's Delight* was a fine lead-in for Clark Gable to his upcoming Rhett Butler and another personal achievement for Norma Shearer. The Robert E. Sherwood political comedy had served as a stage vehicle for no less than Alfred Lunt and Lynne Fontanne, but *The New York Times* greeted Clarence Brown's screen version "with boundless enthusiasm" and found it "as timely as tomorrow's front page."

George Cukor's *The Women* with those "disappointed Scarletts" brought—to the surprise of many—most of the delightful nastiness of Clare Boothe's gossipy play to the screen intact. It also treated the men in its audience to an inside look at females dissecting each other's private lives with relish, venom and outrageous humor. Maxwell Anderson's 1930 play *Elizabeth, the Queen* reached the screen nine years afterward with an impressive cast—Bette Davis, Errol Flynn and Olivia de Havilland—and had been photographed in Technicolor. It had also gained a rather elongated title (which Warners changed back to the original after disappointing initial business), namely *The Private Lives of Elizabeth and Essex*. Miss Davis also joined Miriam Hopkins that year for a faithful rendition of Zoe Atkins' Pulitzer Prize-winning play *The Old Maid*, directed by Edmund Goulding for Warner Brothers. And Clifford Odets' *Golden Boy* was another basically faithful stage-to-screen translation in which Columbia Pictures and director Rouben Mamoulian nicely employed the talented Barbara Stanwyck and a young actor in his film debut, William Holden.

Bette Davis and George Brent treated a delicate theme beautifully in Warner Brothers' Dark Victory.

James Stewart and Jean Arthur had fun with the Senate in Frank Capra's Mr. Smith Goes to Washington.

There was another notable American film debut in 1939—Sweden's Ingrid Bergman, who entranced Leslie Howard and moviegoers in *Intermezzo, A Love Story*. A remake of the Swedish film which had brought Miss Bergman international recognition, directed by Gregory Ratoff, the Selznick International/United Artists picture handled the age-old "eternal triangle" ploy in a sensitive and mature fashion. And that triangle, believe it or not, was equally serviceable and adult for Carole Lombard, Cary Grant and Kay Francis in RKO's *In Name Only*, directed by John Cromwell. And, on the subject of love stories, *The New York Times* found Mr. Cromwell's *Made for Each Other* interpreted warmly and sympathetically enough by Miss Lombard and James Stewart to include it as one of the "ten best pictures" of 1939. The domestic drama was an original screenplay written by Jo Swerling for Selznick International. Another original screen drama blended the talents of director Leo McCarey with the appealing personalities of Irene Dunne and Charles Boyer into a glowing concoction called *Love Affair*, a bittersweet romance release by RKO.

Original screen writing was at its peak in 1939 Hollywood, especially in the field of comedy. *Bachelor Mother* was a brilliant farce devised by Norman Krasna and Felix Jackson and directed by Garson Kanin, which fit the comedic talents of Ginger Rogers and David Niven perfectly. Charles Brackett and Billy Wilder adapted an original story idea into a lively and witty comedy to which Paramount added Claudette Colbert, Don Ameche, John Barrymore and director Mitchell Leisen, and then called it *Midnight*. Writers Lewis R. Foster and Sidney Buchman provided director Frank Capra with the ammunition to give the United States Senate a deflating kick in the rear in *Mr. Smith Goes to Washington*, a skillful interweaving of high comedy and light romance. Mr. Capra owed much of his picture's success to the bravura performance of James Stewart, whose work was gracefully and humorously supplemented by that of Jean Arthur, Claude Rains, Thomas Mitchell and Harry Carey.

But the most anticipated comedy news of 1939 had been the promise "Garbo Laughs!" And American moviegoers did too—extensively—at the original screen story for M-G-M's *Ninotchka*, adapted by Charles Brackett, Billy Wilder and Walter Reisch, which poked merciless fun at the Communist ideal. The brilliant director Ernst Lubitsch was ringmaster for the droll proceedings, with Melvyn Douglas and Ina Claire as his principal clowns in support of the newly realized comedic talents of the previously tragic Greta Garbo.

The offbeat casting of another Hollywood goddess, Marlene Dietrich, with James Stewart in Universal's *Destry Rides Again* gave 1939 moviegoers another delightful surprise, although the film, adapted from Max Brand's novel, fell somewhere between the categories of comedy and western adventure. But there was was no mistaking the genre of *Stagecoach*, which was destined to be among the finest western films ever made. John Ford's United Artists vehicle, which carried John Wayne, Claire Trevor and Thomas Mitchell, was, according to *The New York Times*, "a motion picture that sings a song of cameras . . . a beautiful sight to see."

If Fox's Technicolored *Jesse James*, with Tyrone Power and Henry Fonda, was a western, it also fit into the mold of "Hollywood biography," a genre in which resemblance between the life story depicted and reality was often coincidental. *Juarez* was partially "biography" and mostly historical drama, convincingly played by

Garbo laughed in Ninotchka *while Melvyn Douglas and all America laughed along with her.*

Claire Trevor and Thomas Mitchell rode John Ford's memorable Stagecoach *to personal glory.*

Paul Muni, Bette Davis, Brian Aherne, Claude Rains and John Garfield in Warners' recounting of the Mexican upheaval in the 1860's. *Union Pacific* was "collective biography" in a way, as showman Cecil B. DeMille led Barbara Stanwyck, Joel McCrea and Evelyn Keyes in paying tribute to railroad pioneers of the last century. John Ford and Henry Fonda commendably recreated events in the life of *Young Mr. Lincoln*, Don Ameche and Loretta Young attempted to tell *The Story of Alexander Graham Bell* and Spencer Tracy unraveled some of the mystery surrounding *Stanley and Livingstone*, all under the auspices of Twentieth Century-Fox. Then there was Anna Neagle as *Nurse Edith Cavell*, and also Don Ameche as Stephen Foster in one of the more "inventive" biographies, a Technicolored epic called *Swanee River*.

Another musical biography, *The Story of Vernon and Irene Castle*, would later be referred to as the "final" pairing of Fred Astaire and Ginger Rogers. Moviegoers didn't know it but that ninth teaming almost never came to be, since the real-life Mrs. Castle had originally demanded a "Scarlett O'Hara-type search for an unknown" to portray her. And the slightly overbearing lady also shared costume design credit on the film with Walter Plunkett. That "talent search" idea was far from exhausted. Universal also had conducted one to find a new Prince Charming, Robert Stack, to give Deanna Durbin her initial screen kiss in *First Love*, an updated and musicalized Cinderella tale. Strangest of all along those lines was the film *about* such a search—Fox's *Second Fiddle*. This one related the hard times a Hollywood producer experienced in finding a leading lady for his long-delayed epic until—miraculously—Sonja Henie skated into view (inspired by guess what?).

Hollywood's musicals were then in a period of transition but Busby Berkeley's *Babes in Arms*, for M-G-M, at least gave Mickey Rooney and Judy Garland an opportunity to display their considerable talents. Another field somewhat neglected in 1939 was entertainment for children. Shirley Temple was still active—though growing noticeably older—in *The Little Princess*, her first all-Technicolor feature, and Paramount tried, with moderate success, to enter the Technicolor cartoon feature field with Max Fleischer's *Gulliver's Travels*. But the charm of the previous year's Walt Disney children's classic had been its equal appeal to adults. Mr. Disney did not have a new feature in 1939, but M-G-M released a real-life fantasy which proved to have just such unanimous acceptance by young and old alike.

Author L. Frank Baum had once produced *The Wizard of Oz* himself as a silent film. M-G-M's decision to remake it, and in Technicolor, reflected a costly effort that remained in production almost as long as *Gone With the Wind*. Entire books could have been—and would be—written about that fascinating undertaking. This fantasy for all ages was also directed by Victor Fleming and was destined to travel through time, along with *Gone With the Wind*, forever refreshing its appeal, as few examples of motion picture Americana could. The incredibly talented Judy Garland, as the story's young Kansas heroine, had a message of hope as perpetual as Scarlett O'Hara's "tomorrow"—although hers lay somewhere "Over the Rainbow."

Judy Garland as Dorothy in Victor Fleming's The Wizard of Oz *with her co-stars Ray Bolger, Bert Lahr and Jack Haley.*

THE PHENOMENON
The Fever Rages

"Hollywood itself is practically dead, But <u>Gone With the Wind</u> goes on forever."

—Time, May 5, 1961

The Academy Awards

Spencer Tracy, the previous year's "Best Actor," presented Vivien Leigh with the Academy Award for "Best Actress."

"To offer me an award of this sort is an insult!" George Bernard Shaw said the previous year when informed he had won an Academy Award for *Pygmalion*'s screenplay. Fortunately Hollywood's 1940 population felt exactly the opposite way (although there were fated to be dissenters in the future). The controversial annual event became even more so in the wake of *Gone With the Wind*. Even before nominations were announced, the press was kept busy making predictions. Press stories reported bitterness on all sides that in such a triumphant year—overflowing with productions of merit—David O. Selznick had produced a trump card at the last minute which seemed destined to dominate Hollywood's night of honor.

Then the nominations were made public and most of the dire predictions had come true. *Gone With the Wind* was nominated in twelve categories, with a double nomi-

nation in one of them (supporting actress) bringing the total nomination honors to an unprecedented *thirteen!* Some advance predictions had not been realized and there were disappointments for Leslie Howard (if he cared!) and Ona Munson. Mr. Howard had been touted as a "Best Supporting Actor" contender, which would have been a loss of some prestige after being nominated the previous year in the "Best Actor" category for *Pygmalion*. Perhaps it was just as well that he was overlooked, but, unfortunately, Mr. Howard was fated never to be nominated again.

Producer Selznick had not deemed Leslie's role dominant enough to compete in the major 1939 race and final competition there was indeed formidable. Clark Gable was in the running for the third (and last) time for his Rhett Butler performance, and Robert Donat, another 1938 "loser" (for *The Citadel*), was contending (also for the last time) for his poignant schoolteacher, "Mr. Chips." The other three "Best Actor" nominees were all first-time entrants (all of whom would receive plural nominations in the future). Laurence Olivier's "Heathcliffe" in *Wuthering Heights* was an ample match for James Stewart's marathon *Mr. Smith Goes to Washington*. But young Mickey Rooney's honor was singular in that his astounding versatility in *Babes in Arms* far outweighed the vehicle which contained it. Insiders hinted that Mr. Gable's former win for *It Happened One Night* tipped the scales a bit away from chances of a repeat trophy, although Bette Davis, Luise Rainer, Spencer Tracy and Walter Brennan were already two-time winners in the Awards eleven-year history.

Ona Munson's touching performance as Belle Watling had been thought by many as a sure bet for a nomination and there were those who predicted *the Wind* would sweep the "Best Supporting Actress" category to include Hattie McDaniel, Laura Hope Crews and Butterfly McQueen. This did not prove so although two *GWTW* performances were contained in that contest. Those in support of Miss McQueen must not have realized that *no* black performer had yet been nominated in *any* acting category, and the final inclusion of Hattie McDaniel was considered a remarkable breakthrough, as it was. And Mammy was competing not with Belle, Prissy or Aunt Pitty—but with Melanie, of all people. Olivia de Havilland had been left to wonder forever why David Selznick had promoted her in that lesser category when her performance was just about as long as Rhett Butler's. And her role was, without doubt, larger than Greer Garson's in *Goodbye, Mr. Chips*, and Miss Garson *was* named a "Best Actress" nominee! *The Wind*'s two ladies marched into combat against three worthy opponents: young Geraldine Fitzgerald for *Wuthering Heights* and veterans Edna May Oliver for *Drums Along the Mohawk* and Maria Ouspenskaya in *Love Affair*. Madame Ouspenskaya had formerly been nominated for 1936's *Dodsworth* but the other four were new to the contest (and only Olivia would compete again).

The "Best Supporting Actor" race offered Brian Aherne for *Juarez*, Brian Donlevy for *Beau Geste* and two gentlemen from *Mr. Smith Goes to Washington*, Claude Rains and Harry Carey. But, insiders whispered, fifth nominee Thomas Mitchell (nominated once before for *The Hurricane*) in *Stagecoach* had both *Mr. Smith* and *Gone With the Wind* in his corner. (Claude Rains would be nominated three times in the future without ever winning; none of the others would be nominated again.) Another possible factor in Mr. Mitchell's favor, it was said, was the "split vote" anticipated by the two *Mr. Smith* contenders.

Such divisions had occurred previously when performers from the same film—nominated in the same category—lost to another party, since studio support was indecisive. It had been precisely that factor which inspired David Selznick to place Olivia de Havilland in the "supporting" division—even if it meant losing that Award entirely. He dared no chance of conflict with Vivien Leigh, already predicted by many as the sure-fire "Best Actress" winner. But Vivien's competition was far from simple, for, in addition to Miss Garson, she was opposing Bette Davis for *Dark Victory*, Irene Dunne in *Love Affair* and Greta Garbo for *Ninotchka*. (Only Miss Garbo was never to be nominated again, although Miss Dunne would never win an Oscar either. Fifteen years later the Academy would vote Greta Garbo a "Special" Oscar for her "unforgettable screen performances.")

David Selznick's own competition for the "Best Picture" derby was overwhelming—nine of the finest films ever produced in Hollywood! Fully conscious of what had happened in New York, David regarded *Mr. Smith Goes to Washington* and *Wuthering Heights* as his most dangerous rivals, although he knew there was strong support for *The Wizard of Oz*. (It would not be until the 1944 Awards that nominees for "Best Picture" were limited to *five* films.)

When the big night arrived—February 29, 1940—an incident occurred which was fated to change all future Academy Award presentations. Winners were made known to the press in advance, under pledge that the information would not be printed in editions *prior* to the ceremonies. *The Los Angeles Times*, however, published the winners in its early edition that evening—with *Gone With the Wind* in banner headlines! The Academy's guests were therefore well up on the results before the banquet started. From that year on, winner's names were placed in sealed envelopes by an outside tabulating firm so no one would know the results until the actual moment of presentation.

It was considered regrettable in Hollywood—not just to Walter Plunkett's allies on the *GWTW* team—that the Academy did not give recognition for costume design (such Awards would begin nine years later). There had also been some dissatisfaction that Judy Garland was not a nominee for *The Wizard of Oz*. As a consolation prize, the Academy voted the seventeen-year-old Judy a "Special Award for outstanding performance by a screen *juvenile*." Unperturbed by that rather odd misnomer, Judy sang the year's "Best Song"—"Over the Rainbow" —for the festive audience.

Even without suspense, it was exciting to see the evening's proceedings rapidly blow in the direction of Selznick International. But, contrary to predictions, *Gone With the Wind* did not win on every one of its nominations. The "Special Effects" Award—a new category that year—was voted instead to *The Rains Came*. Max Steiner's musical score lost to Herbert Stothart's efforts on *The Wizard of Oz*, and *GWTW*'s sound recording was not felt superior to that for *When Tomorrow Comes*.

But it was generally *the Wind*'s evening otherwise. Bob Hope, master of ceremonies (for the first of many times), called it a "benefit for David Selznick" as Oscars were announced for *GWTW*'s editing, interior decoration and color cinematography. The "Best Screenplay" Award, voted posthumously to Sidney Howard, was accepted by Sinclair Lewis (a man who once refused the Pulitzer Prize). Thomas Mitchell's predicted win for *Stagecoach* was welcomed wholeheartedly by his clan from Tara, and Victor Fleming, who was not present, was named the year's "Best Director." With claims to two of the "Best Picture" nominees, Mr. Fleming's win was a highly popular choice. A "Special Award" plaque was announced for William Cameron Menzies "for outstanding achievement in the use of color for the enhancement of dramatic mood in the production, *Gone With the Wind*."

While it was logical to count Mr. Menzies' honor as a *GWTW* victory, a Class III Certificate of Honorable Mention to Don Musgrave and Selznick International Pictures, Inc. "for pioneering in the use of coordinated equipment in the production, *Gone With the Wind*" was merely recognition of combined efforts for the future of the industry. And certainly a "Special Award" to the Technicolor Company could not be claimed by *GWTW*, in view of that process's widespread use by 1939.

David O. Selznick so wanted Academy recognition that it had acted as a driving force in all his film efforts. On this—his night of nights—however, he was to be honored more than once. The coveted "Irving G. Thalberg Memorial Award" was, not surprisingly, awarded to David for consistent excellence of production but, as such a composite honor, it was not specifically for *Gone With the Wind*.

The announcement of "Best Supporting Actress" provided an extremely touching moment. Hattie McDaniel, who then became the first black performer to win an Oscar, received the night's most rousing ovation and, despite a wide grin, the gracious lady was overcome by tears. Olivia de Havilland would later relate how she could barely get through the balance of the evening and finally stole away to indulge in tears of disappointment. But, Olivia said, it was only a short time later when she realized how important—and justified—Hattie's win really was. (It would be a decade before another black performer was nominated and nineteen years before a black actor would win again, although one "Special Award" was granted in the meantime.)

Clark Gable knew in advance that he had lost the "Best Actor" Award to Robert Donat, but he attended the banquet with Carole Lombard at his side. Vivien Leigh was also present, with "loser" Laurence Olivier, as Spencer Tracy read each actress nominee's name and each was followed by applause. Mr. Tracy then said, "Need I say this is a privilege and an honor to announce this winner: Miss Vivien Leigh in *Gone . . .*"—the deafening applause drowned out the actor's voice as Vivien quickly walked to the podium to accept her first Academy Award.

By then, there was only the formality of announcing *Gone With the Wind* as Academy Award-winning "Best Picture of 1939." Unfortunately, neither David nor any-

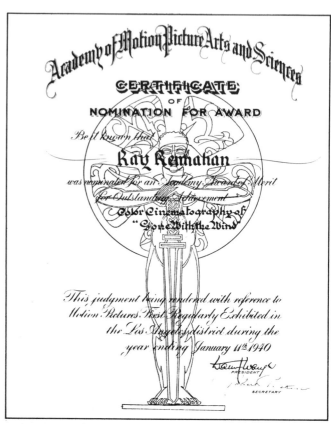

The certificate of nomination given to Ray Rennahan for his Technicolor cinematography of Gone With the Wind.

one else that evening remembered to mention the little lady from Atlanta to whom they all owed such a great debt. In all, it had been a night when both top acting Awards were given to British performers, when a black actress had made a significant breakthrough and when *Gone With the Wind* had won a record-breaking eight Academy Awards. The nominations of Vivien Leigh and Laurence Olivier had also made 1939 one of the few years in which two performers—married to each other at some point in their lives—had simultaneously contended. With the noncompetitive Menzies Award added to *GWTW*'s eight "wins," the film could legitimately claim *nine* Oscars. However, in the future, Selznick or M-G-M publicists would advertise various other totals—even up to fourteen!

As to who the "star" of the unsuspenseful evening had been, Vivien Leigh probably summed it up best in her gracious acceptance speech. "Ladies and gentlemen," Vivien said, "if I were to mention all those who have shown me such wonderful generosity through *Gone With the Wind*, I should have to entertain you with an oration as long as *Gone With the Wind* itself. So, if I may, I should like to devote my thanks on this occasion to that countermine figure of energy, courage and very great kindness, in whom all points of *Gone With the Wind* meet, Mr. David Selznick."

Hattie McDaniel, the first black performer to win an Academy Award (for Gone With the Wind*).*

Major Academy Award Nominations for 1939[†]

PICTURE

Dark Victory	Warner Brothers
*Gone With the Wind	Selznick International/ Metro-Goldwyn-Mayer
Goodbye, Mr. Chips	Metro-Goldwyn-Mayer (British Studio)
Love Affair	RKO Radio
Mr. Smith Goes to Washington	Columbia
Ninotchka	Metro-Goldwyn-Mayer
Of Mice and Men	Hal Roach Productions/ United Artists
Stagecoach	Walter Wanger Productions/ United Artists
The Wizard of Oz	Metro-Goldwyn-Mayer
Wuthering Heights	Samuel Goldwyn Productions/ United Artists

DIRECTOR

Frank Capra	Mr. Smith Goes to Washington
*Victor Fleming	Gone With the Wind
John Ford	Stagecoach
Sam Wood	Goodbye, Mr. Chips
William Wyler	Wuthering Heights

WRITING
ORIGINAL STORY

Bachelor Mother	Felix Jackson
Love Affair	Mildred Cram and Leo McCarey
*Mr. Smith Goes To Washington	Lewis R. Foster
Ninotchka	Melchoir Lengyel
Young Mr. Lincoln	Lamar Trotti

SCREENPLAY

*Gone With the Wind	Sidney Howard
Goodbye, Mr. Chips	(England) Eric Maschwitz, R. C. Sheriff, Claudine West
Mr. Smith Goes to Washington	Sidney Buchman
Ninotchka	Charles Brackett, Walter Reisch, Billy Wilder
Wuthering Heights	Ben Hecht and Charles MacArthur

CINEMATOGRAPHY
New Classifications
BLACK-AND-WHITE

Stagecoach	Bert Glennon
*Wuthering Heights	Gregg Toland

---

† Excluding the acting nominees previously mentioned.
* Asterisks denote winners.

COLOR

*Gone With the Wind	Ernest Haller, Ray Rennahan
The Private Lives of Elizabeth and Essex	Sol Polito, W. Howard Greene

INTERIOR DECORATION

Beau Geste	Hans Dreier, Robert Odell
Captain Fury	Charles D. Hall
First Love	Jack Otterson, Martin Obzina
*Gone With the Wind	Lyle Wheeler
Love Affair	Van Nest Polglase, Al Herman
Man of Conquest	John Victor Mackay
Mr. Smith Goes to Washington	Lionel Banks
The Private Lives of Elizabeth and Essex	Anton Grot
The Rains Came	William Darling, George Dudley
Stagecoach	Alexander Toluboff
The Wizard of Oz	Cedric Gibbons, William A. Horning
Wurthering Heights	James Basevi

SOUND RECORDING

Balalaika	Douglas Shearer
Gone With the Wind	Thomas T. Moulton
Goodbye, Mr. Chips	(England) A. W. Watkins
The Great Victor Herbert	Loren Ryder
The Hunchback of Notre Dame	John Aalberg
Man of Conquest	C. L. Lootens
Mr. Smith Goes to Washington	John Livadary
Of Mice and Men	Elmer Raguse
The Private Lives of Elizabeth and Essex	Nathan Levinson
The Rains Came	E. H. Hansen
*When Tomorrow Comes	Bernard B. Brown

MUSIC
SONG

Faithful Forever (Gulliver's Travels)	Ralph Rainger, Leo Robin
I Poured My Heart into a Song (Second Fiddle)	Irving Berlin
*Over the Rainbow (The Wizard of Oz)	Harold Arlen, E. Y. Harburg
Wishing (Love Affair)	Buddy de Sylva

SCORE

Babes in Arms	Roger Edens, George E. Stoll
First Love	Charles Previn
The Great Victor Herbert	Phil Boutelje, Arthur Lange

The Hunchback of Notre Dame	Alfred Newman
Intermezzo	Lou Forbes
Mr. Smith Goes to Washington	Dimitri Tiomkin
Of Mice and Men	Aaron Copland
The Private Lives of Elizabeth and Essex	
	Erich Wolfgang Korngold
She Married a Cop	Cy Feuer
*Stagecoach	Richard Hageman, Frank Harling,
	John Leipold, Leo Shuken
Swanee River	Louis Silvers
They Shall Have Music	Alfred Newman
Way Down South	Victor Young

ORIGINAL SCORE

Dark Victory	Max Steiner
Eternally Yours	Werner Janssen
Golden Boy	Victor Young
Gone With the Wind	Max Steiner
Gulliver's Travels	Victor Young
The Man in the Iron Mask	Lud Gluskin,
	Lucien Moraweck
Man of Conquest	Victor Young
Nurse Edith Cavell	Anthony Collins
Of Mice and Men	Aaron Copland
The Rains Came	Alfred Newman
*The Wizard of Oz	Herbert Stothart
Wuthering Heights	Alfred Newman

FILM EDITING

*Gone With the Wind	Hal C. Kern, James E. Newcom
Goodbye, Mr. Chips (England)	Charles Frend
Mr. Smith Goes to Washington	Gene Havlick,
	Al Clark
The Rains Came	Barbara McLean
Stagecoach	Otho Lovering, Dorothy Spencer

SPECIAL EFFECTS
New Category

Gone With the Wind	John R. Cosgrove, Fred Albin,
	Arthur Johns
Only Angels Have Wings	Roy Davidson,
	Edwin C. Hahn
The Private Lives of Elizabeth and Essex	Byron Haskin,
	Nathan Levinson
*The Rains Came	E. H. Hansen, Fred Sersen
Topper Takes a Trip	Roy Seawright
Union Pacific	Farciot Edouart, Gordon Jennings,
	Loren Ryder
The Wizard of Oz	A. Arnold Gillespie,
	Douglas Shearer

230

Other Awards and Honors

There were far fewer nationally recognized motion-picture awards in 1940 America than there were destined to be in later years. After the Oscars and New York Film Critics prizes, the most prominent laurels were those bestowed by the National Board of Review, *Photoplay* magazine and *The Film Daily*. Because of *Gone With the Wind*'s unusual release pattern, it contended for those various honors over a period of three years.

The National Board of Review Awards, instituted in 1930, were announced annually after voting by a "Committee on Exceptional Films," consisting of about 175 movie-oriented citizens. Their results often varied greatly from those of any other body for reasons never quite clear and sometimes debatable. Social and political considerations it seemed, occasionally influenced final judgment (e.g., *Confessions of a Nazi Spy* was voted "Best Picture" of 1939). The Board did not grant *Gone With the Wind* consideration until the end of 1940 and, at that time, it placed ninth on its "ten best" list of the year's films, followed by *Rebecca* in tenth position. (*The Grapes of Wrath, The Great Dictator* and *Of Mice and Men* placed first, second and third, respectively.) The National Board of Review did not single out any performances as "best" at that time but published an alphabetical list of those contributions it felt worthy of "Best Acting" accolades. Their 1940 compilation listed the names of seventeen performers, including Vivien Leigh for both *Gone With the Wind* and *Waterloo Bridge*, Jane Darwell for *The Grapes of Wrath* and Thomas Mitchell in *The Long Voyage Home*.

The *Photoplay* Gold Medal Award was the oldest in the industry (dating from 1920) and the *only* one given in response to balloting by the general public. The advent of World War II suspended that magazine's recognition for the years 1940 through 1943 but the last given before then was a 1939 medallion to David Selznick for *Gone With the Wind*. (Only one annual award, for "Best Picture," was given by *Photoplay* at that time.)

The Film Daily had conducted polls each year since 1922 of approximately five hundred movie reviewers throughout America and—through a "point" system of totaling, based on the number of mentions and the positions on individual lists—a tabulated chart of "ten best" films was announced in winning order. Since *Gone With the Wind* had not entered complete national release in 1939 (when *Goodbye, Mr. Chips* was the winner) or 1940 (when *Rebecca* won), it was postponed for inclusion until the 1941 poll. At that time five hundred forty-eight critics participated in the balloting and *Gone With the Wind* was chosen first-place winner with 452 votes. (*Sergeant York* followed closely with 413 important mentions, after which *The Philadelphia Story* and *Citizen Kane* were runners-up.)

The 1939 Photoplay *magazine Gold Medal* (front and back) *awarded to David O. Selznick for* Gone With the Wind *(from the Herb Bridges Collection).*

231

1940-1941: The Reaction

One might have thought that *Gone With the Wind*'s Academy Awards triumph finally marked its peak as a newsworthy item. In those days, a film's first-run life was a few weeks at best, after which it immediately started the complicated journey through neighborhood subruns until it eventually became the staple of a few smaller theatres specializing in revivals. Once prints were sufficently battered to be deemed unplayable, they were withdrawn and the picture became only a nostalgic memory, since there were very few reissues (and, of course, no television showings).

Not so with David Selznick's Technicolor creation. The producer had persuaded M-G-M that careful handling might keep interest in *Gone With the Wind* active for up to two years. After arguments with Metro over the initial advertising campaign were settled, even the magazine ads which appeared in January 1940 took a unique approach in motion-picture marketing. Those publications carried what amounted to an "announcement" rather than a "hard-sell" movie ad as they pictured a New Year's cherub tolling a bell inscribed "Ring in the News." A very small portion of the page was devoted to the film's credits or stars and even the reduced size of the title assumed everyone knew in advance exactly what that "news" was.

David studiously oversaw M-G-M's publicity campaign and insisted special directives be sent to all branch offices concering "forbidden" misinterpretations of his film. These warned (in part):

DON'T call this a Metro-Goldwyn-Mayer picture. It is a Selznick International picture.
DON'T publish a synopsis of any kind.
DON'T allow any publication to have so many stills at one time as to be able to tell a consistent story of the picture by stills.
DON'T ignore Victor Fleming as the director of this picture.
DON'T write publicity stories about Margaret Mitchell.
DON'T refer to the Tarletons in the cast as "the Tarleton twins." They should be called either "the Tarleton boys" or "the Tarleton brothers."
And most importantly
DON'T refer to the BURNING OF ATLANTA as such. The scene in the picture is *not* the burning of Atlanta but rather the burning of certain buildings containing war materials. *The city in general was not touched by these fires!*

Additionally, David was responsible for Loew's, Inc. issuing a sixteen-page booklet entitled "Suggestions for Presentation of *Gone With the Wind*" to theatre ex-hibitors throughout America. That brochure carefully detailed how and when showmen should start the film's overture, dim the house lights, begin intermission cues and the Part Two overture and, finally, at exactly what point the final curtain and exit music should be signaled. Diagrams were included showing how many feet of film were involved in those crucial reels along with advice as to lighting of the auditorium for least conflict with the Technicolor image and even instructions on sound levels.

Neither David nor M-G-M were experiencing any delusions of grandeur with such requests for the specialized presentations. All involved realized that word-of-mouth was their best box-office ally and that audiences who felt they had been treated to a "very special evening" would certainly relay that news to friends. Additionally, polls already showed that a great many Americans were thrilled enough by the experience to indulge in "repeat"

Vivien Leigh's GWTW prominence rewarded her with billing over Robert Taylor in ads for M-G-M's Waterloo Bridge.

Joan Fontaine and Laurence Olivier in Rebecca, *the second consecutive Selznick film to win the Academy Award.*

visits—even at the advanced prices. And if the studio men hadn't been completely aware that they were handling something extraordinary, *Variety* certainly clarified the situation when it reported that *Gone With the Wind* had grossed an unprecedented $945,000 in a single week throughout America—an accomplishment which remained without parallel for several decades.

And, unbelievably, the film was still just then opening in various key cities where it was garnering generally rave reviews. After its Chicago "premiere" on January 25, 1940 at both the Oriental and Woods theatres, that city's *Daily Tribune* (although it complained about its length) proclaimed, "It's true! *Gone With the Wind* has everything." The film debuted that same night at San Francisco's Warfield Theatre where *The Examiner* thought it "is greater than an epic film because it is perhaps the greatest indictment against war that has yet been pictured." That last comment held a clue to part of the nationwide acceptance the Selznick film was experiencing, for "isolationist" America wanted reassurance that its stand was correct when friends throughout the world were suffering through imperialistic slaughter.

Popular American magazines of the day had also seemed to turn a favorable eye upon the long-awaited event. *Time* found it "a first-rate piece of Americana," *Newsweek* ventured that "It was a titanic effort and a successful one," while *Liberty* granted it an "extraordinary, four star" rating and called it "a celluloid landmark," even though the reviewer didn't personally care for it.

But there was opposition! Although the Hays Office had been persuaded that *Gone With the Wind*'s moral content was just fine, the Catholic Church thought otherwise. Granting it a "B" rating—"morally objectionable in part for all"—that religious body's Legion of Decency found fault with: "The low moral character, principles

and behavior of the main figures as depicted in the film; suggestive implications; the attractive portrayal of the immoral character of a supporting role in the story." (Belle Watling, no doubt!)

Such a directive from an influential organization which advised America's large population of Catholics (and those of other faiths who respected its guidance) had sounded a death knell for many a previous film's success. Nevertheless, since many of the most religious citizens had already read the book and were promised that the movie had added no further "moral dangers," America's Catholics—and even some members of the clergy—trotted off with everyone else to see what little Scarlett was up to.

Meanwhile, David Selznick had granted M-G-M the services of Vivien Leigh for her first post-*GWTW* film and the actress built her hopes up since Laurence Olivier was already contracted by that studio for *Pride and Prejudice.* However, Metro felt their new star, Greer Garson, was more suitable for the Jane Austen classic and cast Vivien opposite Robert Taylor (again) in a remake of Robert E. Sherwood's *Waterloo Bridge.* Even in the wake of Scarlett O'Hara, Vivien's touching performance as a ballerina who turned prostitute when her fiancé was reported killed in the war did not disappoint.

Warner Brothers tried to recapture GWTW's elements of success with Bette Davis in All This, and Heaven Too.

GWTW's *Jane Darwell, here with Henry Fonda, won an Oscar for her performance in John Ford's* The Grapes of Wrath.

But more fascinating was that, within two years and on the basis of only one film, M-G-M now saw fit to bill Miss Leigh's name *above* the star of *A Yank at Oxford*. The studio also built its ad campaign (without saying so) around *Gone With the Wind*. "Vivien Leigh returns to you," the M-G-M ads announced, "—beautiful, tender, appealing and talented beyond description."

Two of *GWTW*'s "losers," George Cukor and his friend Katharine Hepburn, united for a 1940 version of the Philip Barry play in which Miss Hepburn had renewed her career. *The Philadelphia Story*, as a movie, brought the lady an M-G-M contract as well as Oscar nominations for herself and her director. *GWTW*'s Sam Wood would also be a 1940 Oscar contender for RKO's treatment of the best-selling novel *Kitty Foyle* and he directed its star, Ginger Rogers, in a performance which would win that elusive gold trophy. Mr. Wood, that same year, transferred Thornton Wilder's *Our Town* to a memorable screen version. In the first year after "helping" on *Gone With the Wind*, Sam Wood found these two efforts both competing for Hollywood's "Best Picture" honor and began a totally new career, destined to grow steadily in prestige.

More than ever, after the phenomenon of *Gone With the Wind*, Hollywood was seeking inspiration in best-selling novels. Just as M-G-M delivered its long-promised Technicolor version of *Northwest Passage*, David Selznick released his *Rebecca*. The excitement that had generated sales of over a million copies of Daphne du Maurier's mystery in America still lingered in March 1940, and *Rebecca*'s premiere at the Radio City Music Hall brought far more acclaim than even its producer

anticipated. The film's leading lady, Joan Fontaine, immediately soared to super-stardom and an enviable acting career. The Hollywood Academy would see fit to grant the haunting film several nominations: to performers Laurence Olivier, Miss Fontaine, Judith Anderson; to director Alfred Hitchcock, composer Franz Waxman, editor Hal Kern (of *GWTW*), art director Lyle Wheeler (of *GWTW*); and to its screenplay, its photography (for which George Barnes won), and its special effects. But—most important of all—*Rebecca* would win the Academy Award as "Best Picture" of 1940, and minute Selznick International would be honored with that impressive laurel for two consecutive years!

Not to be outdone by his rivals, Jack L. Warner had tried to put as many *Gone With the Wind* elements (except Technicolor) as possible into his production of *All This, and Heaven Too*. The success of Macmillan's best seller had prompted Mr. Warner to purchase the Rachel Field story for $100,000 (twice the fee paid to Margaret Mitchell) and produce an unusually long film (two hours and twenty minutes) with Bette Davis and Charles Boyer as his stars. The film was endowed with *GWTW*'s photographer, Ernest Haller, and composer, Max Steiner, not to mention Selznick cast members Barbara O'Neil, Harry Davenport and Mary Anderson. Even the advertisements, which displayed Miss Davis in an out-of-character lowcut gown, traded on the illusion of *Gone With the Wind*'s success as they showed characters stepping from the pages of a famous book. Warner's publicity campaign even tried to sell the film on the basis of identification through its initials—*ATAHT* (like *GWTW*)—but that ploy did not catch on with the public.

The screen treatment was only partially faithful to Miss Field's book, for which the author had reached back into her family tree (shades of Margaret Mitchell!) to recount the events surrounding a notorious French murder trial in 1847. But the Hollywood Academy still voted *ATAHT* a 1940 "Best Picture" nomination and similar honors to Mr. Haller and Mr. Steiner. The most noteworthy nomination, however, fell to Barbara O'Neil for her performance as the shrewish unbalanced wife who drove her husband to murder. It was destined to remain the most remembered role of that fine actress's screen career.

Ironically, it was one of Barbara's *GWTW* co-stars, Jane Darwell, who was to claim that gold statue for her moving portrayal of "Ma Joad" in the film version of another best seller, *The Grapes of Wrath*. John Steinbeck's 1939 American tragedy had provided Twentieth Century-Fox, director John Ford, Miss Darwell and her fellow players with an opportunity for celluloid immortality.

The *Gone With the Wind* excitement sweeping America in the spring of 1940 wasn't limited to viewings of the film. It was everyone's conversational topic and the source of many related business enterprises. One offshoot that movie patrons could enjoy free of charge was the "Traveling Tour of Costumes" dreamed up by M-G-M as advance publicity for openings of the picture. Americans in various cities were given a firsthand opportunity to inspect Clark Gable's "Bazaar" tuxedo, Vivien Leigh's green-sprigged muslin and white evening-prayer dress, Leslie Howard's uniform and Cammie King's riding habit, as well as costumes worn by Olivia de Havilland, Ona Munson and Evelyn Keyes.

Then there were the merchandising tie-ins! From the time David Selznick signed a contract with M-G-M in 1938, all such deals came under the jurisdiction of Loew's, Inc. (far better able to contend with unauthorized abuses than Margaret Mitchell). In that period immediately following *Gone With the Wind*'s premiere, American manufacturers seemed to find a way to claim it as inspiration for almost every retail product imaginable. Authorized national tie-ins (according to Loew's own published reports at the time) included: leather goods,

toiletries, cosmetics, slipcovers, brassieres and corsets, dress patterns, ladies' hats, veils, turbans, snoods, hairbows, scarves, handkerchiefs, jewelry, lamps and lighting fixtures, living room furniture, drapery valences, costumes, displays, children's cut-out books, paper dolls and games. There were Scarlett or Rhett wristwatches, *Gone With the Wind* plaques and Rhett Butler ties and bows. The "Scarlett O'Hara doll" received almost as much prominence, briefly, as the Shirley Temple doll had, and Nunnally's ("the Candy of the South") packaged a delightful box of *GWTW* sweets with pieces named after its characters. *Gone With the Wind* quilts were called "the selling sensation of 1940" and Scarlett O'Hara perfume promised enticement. Americans who purchased a tube of Pebeco toothpaste received a free copy of the *Gone With the Wind* cookbook, which included "125 treasured Southern recipes." The country's menfolk faced a serious threat from a conspiracy La Cross nail polish promulgated: "Scarlett O'Hara Danger! . . . wear it for

Macmillan's paperbound "Movie Edition" (above left) *was a brisk sixty-nine-cent seller at first. Later it was rebound by Grosset & Dunlap in hardcover* (above right) *to sell for even less.*

romance . . . a nail polish so glamorous you'll want to live up to it . . . a sirenizing deep red to add Scarlett glamour like a jewel." La Cross promoted three separate shades called Scarlett O'Hara "Night," "Morning" and "Noon."

The Southern Comfort Corporation introduced recipes for two new alcoholic drinks with the slogan "no more than two lest you be *Gone With the Wind*":

SCARLETT O'HARA COCKTAIL: Add the juice of ¼ fresh lime, one jigger of cranberry juice and one jigger of Southern Comfort to a cocktail shaker filled with cracked ice; shake well; strain into a cocktail glass.

RHETT BUTLER COCKTAIL: Add the juice of ½ lime, the juice of ⅓ lemon, ½ teaspoon of sugar, a barspoon of Curacao and one jigger of Southern Comfort to a cocktail shaker filled with cracked ice; shake well; strain into a cocktail glass.

The former drink became quite popular and remained an American staple, but the latter never quite took off. However, Van Heusen shirts found success by saluting the attire of Clark Gable as Rhett Butler in its spring 1940 ads, and a beauty salon in Washington, D.C., claimed "*Gone With the Wind* permanents sweep the town!" Then there was the Chicago restaurant which asked, "Going to see *Gone With the Wind*? Thrilling . . . long to be remembered . . . and so indeed is our new Crystal Skillet fried chicken dinner (for 90¢)."

But the long-awaited fulfillment of seeing *Gone With the Wind* on screen was tragically limited in its promised international appeal. The conflict in Europe spread that year to hideous proportions as German forces invaded Denmark, Norway, Holland, Belgium and Luxembourg. The Nazis stormed France and by June marched into Paris. Helpless French citizens were forced to sign German and Italian armistices allowing occupation of their country by Axis armies for the duration of the war with Britain, although underground resistance forces sprang up immediately. It was said that Adolf Hitler initially admired *Gone with the Wind* and that, at first, he advocated reading it in admiration of its "damn Yankees" aspect. Later, when he heard that the French looked upon the novel as an inspiration for secret resistance, he banned the book completely.

The Selznick film had, even before its release, been responsible for altogether new imitations, parodies and "inspirations." In Hollywood such cues ranged from Miriam Hopkins as a Confederate cutie in *Virginia City* to Mickey Rooney and Judy Garland singing about Scarlett and Rhett in "Our Love Affair" from *Strike Up the Band*. On Broadway, the 1940 musical revue *Keep Off the Grass* featured a skit in which Ilka Chase was Scarlett, Ray Bolger played Ashley and Jimmy Durante (of all people!) portrayed Rhett. On America's other coast, Tiny's Embassy Club in San Francisco featured *Let's Go Slap Happy*—"the dizziest, dopiest, daffiest burlesque on *Gone With the Wind*," featuring Tommy Reilly as "Rat Butler," Ben Goman as "Harlette O'Hare" and the entire company of Embassy Eyefuls. The film also provided enough material to inspire countless feature magazine articles such as *Liberty*'s "Hollywood's Colossal Crisis," which pointed out how many of *Gone With the Wind*'s scenes took place on staircases (at Tara, at Twelve Oaks, Scarlett slapping Prissy, the shooting of the deserter, the miscarriage and Melanie with Mammy).

Finally, in June of 1940, *Gone With the Wind* had completed the major portion of its advanced-price "road show" engagements. In accordance with the initial advertising promise that it would not be shown in any theatre at reduced prices until 1941, M-G-M withdrew the film from circulation. The studio estimated that twenty-five million people had paid those extra tariffs by then for the privilege of seeing it and its domestic gross at that point was an absolutely unprecedented $23,500,000—of which $13,500,000 was the distributor's share (known in the industry as "rentals"). In Atlanta, it had enjoyed a particularly fascinating six-month history, grossing a total of $240,000 on 223,366 paid admissions at three successive theatres.

Coinciding with the M-G-M withdrawal, Harold Latham of Macmillan wrote to Margaret Mitchell in early July to break the news about his company's overstock of 350,000 copies of the Movie Edition and asked permission to dispose of them cheaply (Oh ye of little faith!). Margaret agreed to whatever Macmillan thought best, and those paperback copies were subsequently sold to Grosset & Dunlap, which quickly rebound them in cloth covers and made a nice profit by selling them at fifty cents a copy when the film was placed in general release.

Although Margaret sympathized with Macmillan for the loss they took on overprinting the Movie Edition, she was secretly thrilled that America's intense interest in *GWTW* was giving indications of subsiding. But she noted from her publisher's report that, even though the original $3 edition was all that was left in print, over sixteen hundred copies of that more expensive volume had been sold in the previous month alone. And authorized foreign translations would still be bringing her revenues; permission for one to be published in Brazil had just been granted. Of course there were still those "pirates" to worry about! The German invasion of Holland had occurred only days before her piracy case was to have reached the highest Dutch Court, and Margaret realized she would hear nothing further for the duration. Chaotic world conditions also made it difficult for the author to pursue other piracy problems and, in 1940 alone, she learned that Cuba, Chile, Bulgaria and Greece were casually violating her rights with either unauthorized book editions or serializations.

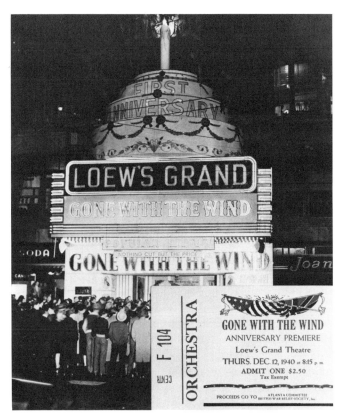

Loew's Grand in Atlanta was the site of GWTW's "First Anniversary Premiere," marking its national release (inset: actual premiere ticket).

Macmillan needed no sympathy for the comparatively small loss on their *GWTW* overstock, since the entire country had united to make its new novel *How Green Was My Valley* by Richard Llewelyn the number-one best seller of 1940. However, the eventual total of 176,280 copies that book sold was a far more normal annual championship than the *Gone with the Wind* experience had evidenced.

In the midst of the continuing world emergency Franklin D. Roosevelt was reelected for an unprecedented third Presidential term. And while burdened with constant threats to the peacetime survival of American democracy, the exhausted President unwittingly became one of *Gone With the Wind*'s severest critics when, after falling asleep during a White House screening of it, he awakened to complain, "No movie has a right to be that long!"

Italy declared war on Great Britain and France and soon afterward attacked Greece and overran Yugoslavia. Despite its isolationism, America prepared for what seemed inevitable and the first peacetime draft of eligible men went into effect. In the late summer of 1940 German raiders began continuous bombings of London with staggering losses of life and property. But England, too, had found inspiration in *Gone With the Wind* in its time of crisis. After its opening at the Ritz Theatre in London, the Selznick movie began what was to be the longest run

of any film in history. For almost four and a half years—232 consecutive weeks—despite the terrors of their air raids or the wartime deprivations which made luxury spending difficult, the English people would repeatedly flock to see the indomitable Scarlett refusing to accept defeat.

Considering the close attachment the South had always felt to Great Britain and, of course, the fact that two of *Gone With the Wind*'s stars were English, it was fitting that the film's "First Anniversary Premiere" in Atlanta was planned to benefit the British War Relief Society. Another festive night was planned to mark the beginning of *GWTW*'s "popular price" engagements and, considering the charitable cause, Vivien Leigh, Laurence Olivier and Alfred Hitchcock agreed to make personal appearances on the opening night of December 12, 1940. This time a huge replica of a birthday cake, featuring one candle, topped the Loew's Grand marquee and "premiere" tickets cost *only* $2.50.

M-G-M had conducted another "talent search," interviewing 750 of Georgia's young beauties, and finally selected Atlanta's Louella Stone as "Miss Anniversary" to help conduct the night's festivities—after which she would be given a trip to Hollywood. Unfortunately, bad weather delayed the arrival of the plane carrying Miss Leigh, Mr. Olivier and Mr. Hitchcock for a full twenty-four hours and it was left to Miss Stone alone to cut the immense cake wheeled out onto the Grand's stage. The first slice was delivered—boxed and ribboned—to an unobtrusive couple in the audience, Mr. and Mrs. John Marsh. Margaret would have preferred, again, to stay out of the spotlight, but in the absence of the Hollywood group, she had no choice but to again assume a position as the evening's guest of honor. Atlanta newspapers applauded Miss Stone's courage in acting as "pinch hitter" and published photographs of her with Vivien Leigh and Laurence Olivier after their arrival the following day.

To everyone's delight—and contrary to many predictions—M-G-M released *Gone With the Wind* at reduced prices completely intact and featuring a new slogan in its advertising—"Nothing cut but the price!" After new first-

Margaret Mitchell became the unwitting hostess of GWTW's Anniversary Party when bad weather delayed Vivien Leigh.

run engagements in major cities, *the Wind* drifted into local theatres, with tickets selling for as low as forty cents for matinees and fifty-five cents in the evenings. This second release grossed an unexpected $5,000,000, making the film 1941's top box-office attraction and a two-year triumph for M-G-M and Selznick International. As a result, after that one trip through the various Loew's chains—and then through smaller independent theatres —the two studios agreed to withdraw it once again, hoping for one more major cycle of play dates before all the prints were completely worn out.

As all-time Oscar and box-office champion, *Gone With the Wind* was inevitably fated to become—and remain for decades afterward—the criterion against which every subsequent "big" or important film would be compared. Just as it was playing out its general release in 1941, another motion picture premiered which was destined to compete with it for the rather meaningless title of "greatest American movie ever made." The Orson Welles production of *Citizen Kane*, starring, co-written and largely dominated by Mr. Welles, arrived amidst a storm of controversy and rumors of attempted suppression (due to its purported resemblance to the life of publisher William Randolph Hearst). Be that as it may, many critics found that its brilliant photographic style and strikingly effective narrative technique represented a historic and innovative cinematic breakthrough.

For those who waited, an uncut GWTW was released in 1941 at far more reasonable admission prices.

But, although it was proclaimed "Best Picture of 1941" by the New York Film Critics and nominated for nine Academy Awards, *Citizen Kane* won only one Oscar (for its screenplay). In no way did it demonstrate popular box-office appeal and, after its initial theatrical life, the film vanished—never to be reissued. Relegated almost to the status of a forgotten film for years, a future generation "rediscovered" it through television exposure and art theatre revivals. Afterward, it attained renewed prestige and an incredible reputation, and was often termed "the best motion picture of all time" by both American and international film societies.

Admittedly, *Citizen Kane* encountered distribution problems after its release, although it did not lose money. But, with all its fine critical notices, why did it not attain a living and revivable popularity with Americans of its era? It seemed that, despite its technical wizardry, its story and protagonist lacked the romanticism, identification, inspiration and pure entertainment values that audiences in the 1940's required. Film scholar Eric Rhode would later partially explain it: "Both *Citizen Kane* and its central character are like the proverbial onion: to peel away their pretensions is to peel them away to nothing. . . . Kane has no principles and by extension the self-pity in which he shrouds his defeat contains no dramatic meaning. For all his worldly power, his role in the plot is insubstantial, being no more than a foil to other characters." D. W. Griffith, the "father of the American film," was impressed with Orson Welles and his film, but for another reason. "I loved *Citizen Kane*," Mr. Griffith remarked, "and particularly the ideas he took from me." (What did Mr. Griffith think about the other film in question? "I saw *Gone With the Wind* twice," the master offered, "and thought it better than *The Birth of a Nation*—not really of course.")

By the end of its 1941 general release the phenomenon of *Gone With the Wind* seemed to have subsided. Metro-Goldwyn-Mayer, motivated by the hope for historical preservation, agreed to donate a thirty-five-millimeter, three-strip Technicolor release print of the film to the National Archives in Washington, D.C., and it thus became the *first* feature film to be so included there. Also reflecting on *GWTW*'s history, The Macmillan Company announced that, by 1941, the book's total sales in America had reached 2,868,200 in its various editions. Margaret Mitchell began to feel that she could appear publicly again without undue harassment and traveled to Kearny, New Jersey, to christen the cruiser *Atlanta* on September 6, 1941. Even when David Selznick contacted her that fall inquiring about rights to produce a musical version of *Gone With the Wind* on stage, Margaret was not disagreeable to the proposal. But when rumors reached her of a possible new "talent search," she decided to withhhold her permission permanently, lest the circus start all over again. David was not about to let go of a good thing completely, however, and asked Kay Brown to intercede in dealing with the author about other possibilities. "If we can't get a sequel," David suggested, "I would still be delighted to have a story to be called *The Daughter of Scarlett O'Hara* with Vivien playing the daughter . . ."

But the influence of *Gone With the Wind* was still very much in evidence, especially in 1941 Hollywood's films. Twentieth Century-Fox envisioned newcomer Gene Tierney as a Southern *Belle Starr* driven to lawbreaking because the "damned Yankees" had burned her plantation home. And M-G-M pictured Clark Gable breaking in another door to gain conjugal comforts from Lana Turner in *Honky Tonk*. Even *Kiss the Boys Goodbye* finally reached the screen, although much of "the search" aspect had been eliminated. Master showman Cecil B. DeMille found the best recipe of all, though, in late 1941 as he took two "disappointed Scarletts" (Paulette Goddard and Susan Hayward), flavored one of them (Paulette) with a Southern accent thick enough to cut, added a Mammy (Louise Beavers) and a dizzy, fainting aunt (Hedda Hopper, who admitted taking "swoon lessons" from Laura Hope Crews), stirred in a dash of Oscar Polk as "Salt Meat" (rather than Pork), generously spiced the mixture with Technicolor and then decorated the finished product with "Wind" in the title —and served up *Reap the Wild Wind*, bound to be a box-office delight. Dramatically? Picture Paulette in the midst of shipwrecks, tidal waves, death and disorder muttering, "This is all mah doin'," and the question was answered!

That two-year period was also one of personal tragedy or joy and professional accomplishment or disappointment for several members of the *GWTW* company. Monty Westmore, the film's makeup director, died in April 1940 of a heart attack following minor surgery at the age of thirty-seven. His doctors claimed his condition had been weakened by simultaneously working on Selznick's *Gone With the Wind*, *Intermezzo* and *Rebecca*. But Vivien Leigh and Laurence Olivier were finally free to marry, which they did in August 1940, and dialogue director Will Price married new Hollywood star Maureen O'Hara in late 1941 in his native South.

Ona Munson had hoped Belle Watling would open new doors for her often spotty film career and winning the role of Madame Gin Sling (Mother Goddam on stage) in the Josef von Sternberg screen version of *The Shanghai Gesture* seemed to fulfill that promise. But the film, unfortunately, was crucified by many critics and *The New York Times* thought Miss Munson "looks like an alabaster statue and acts like a gunman's moll." Ona's screen opportunities grew increasingly limited afterward. Olivia de Havilland's career, however, soared even further on loan to Paramount for *Hold Back the Dawn*. In the year-end New York Film Critics vote she was at one point deadlocked for the "Best Actress" Award with her own

Vivien Leigh and Laurence Olivier in That Hamilton Woman, *a film which provoked investigation by the Senate.*

sister, Joan Fontaine (for Alfred Hitchcock's *Suspicion*). A subsequent ballot gave the Award to Joan, a prophecy of exactly what would happen in the upcoming Academy Awards derby in which Olivia competed for the major acting honor for the first time.

The English production of Alexander Korda's *The Thief of Bagdad* had been interrupted by war in the fall of 1939, and, with William Cameron Menzies' active participation, it was finally completed in America and released just in time for the 1940 holiday season. The British producer decided to stay in America then, and starred his bride, Merle Oberon, in *Lydia*, a film which reunited several of *GWTW*'s family—Lee Garmes, Walter Plunkett, George Reeves and Ben Hecht. Mr. Korda also granted the wish of Vivien Leigh and Laurence Olivier to co-star on film and cast them in *The Hamilton Woman*, which recounted the story of England's heroic Lord Nelson and his notorious affair with a married noblewoman. The beautifully acted 1941 film, however, inspired hostile comments from many American isolationists and the producer found himself served with a Senate subpoena to explain his motives in producing a pro-British war effort film in America while it was still at peace with Germany. Mr. Korda's date in Washington, D.C., was scheduled for mid-December 1941 but an intervening act of fate made that appearance unnecessary.

In November the Japanese had made certain demands upon the United States to end interference with their imperialistic policies in the Pacific. But while the American government prepared counterproposals, a carrier fleet bearing war planes set sail toward Hawaii on November 25. On Sunday, December 7, 1941, a Japanese air attack on Pearl Harbor claimed the lives of twenty-four hundred Americans and devastated the Pacific naval fleet. The following day Congress declared war on Japan and, as allies of that country, Germany and Italy proclaimed war on America three days later.

Scarlett returned to help wartime morale and M-G-M adopted a new slogan for its advertising.

1942-1945: War Years Interlude

For more than three and a half years America was involved in its most serious and tragic conflict since the Civil War. Geographic names—Bataan, Midway, Guadalcanal, Salerno, Anzio, Normandy, Guam, Bastogne, Iwo Jima, Okinawa—became eternal heartbreaking reminders to millions of families of the thousands upon thousands of young men who lost their lives protecting their country from its aggressors. It was a time of unselfish patriotism, when those on the home front voluntarily sacrificed time and comforts to support their fighting forces. And, more than ever, they looked to their idols, the citizens of Hollywood, for inspiration.

When war began, the Selective Service Department announced that film production was an essential industry —necessary for morale—and its employees were indefinitely deferred from the draft. But members of the Screen Actors Guild disagreed and over fifteen hundred of them—from stars to bit players—enlisted in branches of the armed forces. They were joined by executives,

producers, directors, writers, cameramen and technicians. Some of these worked together to produce essential training films and others served as entertainers but a great many more went into actual combat. What of those who did not enlist? In the years following the Pearl Harbor attack, some thirty-five thousand morale-building appearances were made by entertainers in America and abroad. While some concentrated on visiting domestic army posts, naval stations and hospitals, over two thousand other performers joined USO tours overseas to entertain on the "foxhole circuit," and a full sixth of them were "name" Hollywood stars working without compensation.

Movie studios donated prints of their films to bases in remote locations throughout the world and the majority of new pictures they produced in that period were designed either to portray significant war issues or to provide necessary escapism for lonely soldiers, tired defense workers or worried families. Innumerable war combat stories, no matter how dramatically naive, gave Americans perpetual hope for victory while dozens of musicals relied heavily on star power and Technicolor (but often very little on plot). Two of the newer and most talented musical ladies, Betty Grable and Rita Hayworth, donated even more to the efforts as thousands of their photographs became "pin-ups"—symbols of home —for fighting men everywhere. And as the movies were so much a part of the country's life, the stars used their valuable example to stimulate even further patriotism from their fellow Americans. Charitable efforts by the stars coupled with fund raising in movie theatres raised over $30,000,000 during the war years for the Red Cross, United National Relief, and Army and Navy Emergency Relief. Then in six separate Hollywood Bond Cavalcades, conducted on tours throughout the country, several *billion* dollars in war bond sales were raised.

It was on just such a bond tour—only six weeks after war was declared—that the country sustained one of its foremost civilian casualties, Mrs. Clark Gable. Returning from a war bond rally in her native Indiana (where in Indianapolis alone she sold over $2,000,000 in bonds), Carole Lombard's plane crashed into the mountains near Las Vegas, Nevada, on January 16, 1942. Although he had previously considered enlisting, his wife's death was the convincing factor and Clark Gable joined the Army Air Corps that August. After attending Officers Candidate School, Clark graduated as a second lieutenant. Mr. Gable volunteered for overseas duty, which included several bombing missions over Germany, and remained in active service for over two years until he was discharged with the rank of major.

Clark and Carol's tragedy was not the only one experienced by the *Gone With the Wind* family during the war years. Perpetually active Laura Hope Crews was acting on Broadway in *Arsenic and Old Lace* when stricken with a kidney ailment in October 1942. After a month's illness the veteran actress died—just one month short of her sixty-third birthday. Then, Leslie Howard, who had journeyed to Portugal on a British Council lecture tour in May 1943, prepared to return to London by plane on the first of June. That was the same day on which Britain's Prime Minister Winston Churchill was due home from conferences at Gibraltar. The Germans, according to reports, were erroneously informed that Churchill was traveling on Mr. Howard's flight and dispatched a warplane which shot down the defenseless passenger craft above the Bay of Biscay, killing all aboard.

Olivia de Havilland's presence on screen was interrupted during the war era by legal problems with her Warner employers which kept her from working professionally for almost two years. But Olivia did her part to help morale with other stars at the Hollywood Canteen, although she did not quite go to the extent a 1943 *Photoplay* cover insinuated when it pictured her as an airport mechanic! Vivien Leigh would also be absent from American movie screens for the duration. Soon after Vivien and her new husband returned to England in early 1941, Laurence enlisted in the British Navy and Vivien did her part in building morale with London stage work. But as Vivien passed Leicester Square each day to see long lines circling the Ritz Theatre—even after all-night bombing attacks—to gain hope or escape from *Gone With the Wind*, she decided to become more involved. She toured British troop bases in 1943 with a revue in which—among other things— she performed a parody of Scarlett O'Hara. Afterward Vivien accepted a role in a film which, unfortunately, Americans would not see until after the war had ended.

But there were many other popular movies which helped build morale in those dark days, like *Casablanca, Yankee Doodle Dandy, Laura, Double Indemnity, Going My Way, Now Voyager* (for which Max Steiner won his second Academy Award), Sam Wood's *The Pride of the Yankees*, George Cukor's *Gaslight* and *Winged Victory*, and Victor Fleming's *A Guy Named Joe*. One patriotic musical, Irving Berlin's *This Is the Army*, had inspired its studio (Warner Brothers) to donate all its profits to the Army Emergency Relief and this patriotic ideal

There were those who felt Photoplay *magazine exaggerated Olivia de Havilland's contributions to the war effort.*

Margaret Mitchell did her part too—selling war bonds for the victory effort.

led the film to become the second-highest-grossing film in history (with $8,500,000 in grossed rentals of which over $7,000,000 went to the army charity). And there were new Oscars too (made of gold-leafed plaster for the duration) for Gary Cooper, Greer Garson, James Cagney, Ingrid Bergman, Bing Crosby and a young "unknown," Jennifer Jones, who was discovered by David O. Selznick and who would later become the producer's second wife.

The most honored film of the period, based on a 1940 best seller, served as homefront inspiration more than any other single picture and won a morale endorsement from President Roosevelt. M-G-M's *Mrs. Miniver* had actually been filmed before Pearl Harbor and dealt with England's—not America's—crisis. After its release in 1942 it earned $5,000,000 in rentals for its studio (to become Hollywood's fifth most successful film up to that time) and won six Academy Awards (on twelve nominations). Director William Wyler followed a formula which had been so effective in *Gone With the Wind*—he showed no firsthand battle scenes and contrasted prewar innocence and gaiety to the onset of sudden and tragic involvement.

The English author of *Mrs. Miniver*, Jan Struther, whose husband was a prisoner of the Germans, had been in America since 1940 and toured the country when the film was released. Upon visiting Atlanta, she was invited to a luncheon with Margaret Mitchell which Miss Struther approached with trepidation since she had never read *Gone with the Wind*. The lady was relieved to learn, however, that Margaret inscribed the names of those who made that admission upon a roll of honor.

The war had moved many people to acts which would

formerly have been contrary to their nature and the little lady from Atlanta overcame her dislike for public gatherings as she sold war bonds, worked in Civilian Defense and as a member of the Red Cross. Margaret also spent an extraordinary amount of time writing encouraging letters of reply to fighting men overseas, as well as sending food packages to the needy abroad. Margaret also expressed to intimates a sincere desire to write again. Ideas, long postponed, had germinated to the point where they needed fulfillment. But that ambition was thwarted by her volunteer work, correspondence and the lingering illness of her father, which made constant demands on her time until his death in mid-1944.

But even without a new Mitchell book, there were many new best sellers over those years to provide Americans with escape. Historical fiction was still predominant as was a newer trend toward religious or inspirational themes and, still motivated by the *GWTW* phenomenon, Hollywood bought rights to most of the new popular fiction for immediate screen translation. While few new novels dealt with American involvement in the world crisis, many of the nonfiction pacemakers of the time did, and movie men adapted quite a few from both categories. M-G-M purchased *Random Harvest, Dragon Seed, The Valley of Decision, Mrs. Parkington, The Green Years, See Here, Private Hargrove* and *They Were Expendable*; Warner's took *Saratoga Trunk* and *Kings Row* (for Sam Wood); Paramount laid claim to *And Now Tomorrow* and *For Whom the Bell Tolls* (another Sam Wood project); and Twentieth Century-Fox purchased the most of them—*The Song of Bernadette, The Moon Is Down, The Keys of the Kingdom, This Above All, A Tree Grows in Brooklyn, The Razor's Edge, Leave Her to Heaven, A Bell for Adano* and *Anna and the King of Siam*.

Two other best sellers—vastly different in theme—were also bought by the Fox studio and each set sales records impressive enough to threaten the championship of *Gone with the Wind*. Lloyd C. Douglas's *The Robe*, published in 1942, remained high on best-seller lists for a four-year period and had sold almost two million copies by late 1945. Thirty years later, the religious novel would still place third in all-time hardcover fiction sales totals. And its film version—postponed for a decade—was destined to signal a new era in motion picture presentation. *Forever Amber*, another long, historical novel published by Macmillan and written by a woman, Kathleen Winsor, became the third-largest-selling novel (next to *GWTW* and *The Call of the Wild*) in that publisher's history. Amber St. Clare's bawdy exploits in Restoration England were a far cry from Scarlett O'Hara but (helped by a Boston ban) she led her story to two years of notorious fame and over a million and a half copies in sales.

But *Gone with the Wind* was itself still very much a "living thing" both to Americans and to their allies fighting for freedom. Even soldier-cartoonist Bill Mauldin dedicated a caricature to it from Italian battlefronts. "Dear, Dear Miss Mitchell," Mr. Mauldin's cartoon was headlined as it pictured a "dogface" writing to thank the author because a thick copy of her book under his uniform had deflected a bullet and saved his life. In France and other occupied countries the inspiration carried by *GWTW* made it an expensive "black-market" item throughout that dismal period. Then, on August 25, 1942, Macmillan reissued *Gone with the Wind* in America as a contribution to domestic wartime morale. This new (still hardcover) version, slightly smaller in size and printed on lower-grade paper due to wartime priorities, retailed at $1.49 and showed amazing sales strength despite its competition. Paper shortages affected all publishers at that time, and considering *GWTW*'s great length, if it hadn't maintained a significant pace, it undoubtedly would have disappeared for the duration. But in its first year the new edition sold 23,572 copies and 42,450 more were purchased between 1943 and 1944. Then, incredibly, sales soared to 56,710 copies in the last full year of conflict—amazing for a book that was by then nearly a decade old, but Scarlett O'Hara's optimism had totally new relevance for wartime America. This time around, the book's dust jacket was decorated with a new emblem. The familiar liberty insignia (which also adorned movie titles of the period) reminded citizens to "buy United States war bonds and stamps" as it greeted readers from the back cover of *Gone with the Wind*'s "Victory" edition. Although shortages in England prevented any reprintings after 1942, *GWTW*'s international appeal spread to Turkey, which nonchalantly pirated the book in 1942, and to Spain and Rumania, where authorized editions were published in 1943. Bulgaria, which had originally been guilty of piracy, reversed its stand and published a legal edition in 1944. Meanwhile, American moviegoers had been allowed the privilege of seeing—or reseeing—the film version for the greater portion of the war years.

During the early spring months of 1942, when Americans were still mobilizing and trying to counter the shock of their involvement, M-G-M brought *Gone With the Wind* back to theatres for a revival which the studio would later term its "first reissue." Actually, the prints used for this successful "return" were those from its initial engagements, and its advertising campaign was basically the same. But a new slogan—carried in some cases on the replica of a ruler—promised "not one inch, not one thrill has been cut!" Again, the film placed among the largest money-making films of the year and M-G-M did not withdraw it after those 1942 showings. Instead, it was left in release for well over a year until, by late 1943, calls for it finally dwindled. By then, the studio announced, it had grossed in excess of $32,000,000 in its North American play dates. As battered prints were returned to M-G-M exchanges, they were destroyed, and by 1944 the organization shifted its position in their ledgers to "out of circulation." This was altogether M-G-M's prerogative, since at that time they owned the film outright.

The production hiatus which Selznick International had enforced after *Rebecca* had proven to be a permanent one. In 1942, that independent studio was liquidated (for tax purposes) and, in the course of events, David Selznick sold his entire interest in *Gone With the Wind* to John Hay Whitney. Partially motivated by gratitude for her book's influence on his professional career and partially because rumors persisted that she had been exploited, David sent Margaret Mitchell a surprise check for $50,000 upon dissolution of his studio. The lady was thrilled with the gift but little public attention was directed, in the future, to the fact that the author did receive a total of $100,000 for the sale of movie rights to her novel (albeit over a period of six years). Two years later John Hay Whitney sold his complete interest in *GWTW* to Metro-Goldwyn-Mayer for a huge profit and the picture was, from then on, the absolute property of Louis B. Mayer's domain.

But David Selznick could not remain inactive. He formed Vanguard Productions in 1943 (which would, however, carry the same screen trademark as Selznick International) and purchased rights to *Since You Went Away . . . Letters to a Soldier from His Wife* by Margaret Buell Wilder. The simple structure of the book was exactly what its subtitle implied, for it was in the form

Macmillan's 1942 "Victory" edition reminded readers to do their share in buying war bonds and stamps.

243

DAVID O. SELZNICK *presents:*

CLAUDETTE COLBERT | JENNIFER JONES | JOSEPH COTTEN

SHIRLEY TEMPLE | MONTY WOOLLEY | LIONEL BARRYMORE | ROBERT WALKER

The screen's most distinguished cast in

"Since You Went Away"

The producer's first picture since
"Gone With The Wind" and "Rebecca"

David O. Selznick called his Since You Went Away *"The four most important words since* Gone With the Wind!"

of chatty letters written by the mother of two teenage daughters to sustain the morale of her husband in service. But David Selznick visualized bringing to its screen version all the possible elements which had made his landmark production such a success. And since he had, on that former film, experienced so many adaptation difficulties, he wrote this one himself! "Screenplay by the Producer" the film's credits read and anyone ever in doubt as to the authorship of *GWTW*'s scenario needed only to view David's World War II production to solve the mystery. This presented no small feat, since the book offered no story line but only characters and day-to-day events.

David endowed his new venture with considerable length (almost three hours), employed Hattie McDaniel as the family's wise mainstay, designed a climatic "pullback shot" for a railway depot scene, envisioned a soldiers' dance in a huge airplane hangar (rather than *GWTW*'s bazaar in an armory) and presented the graphic tragedy of hospital wounded. Thematically, it was even more closely fashioned to be a latter-day replica of *Gone With the Wind* as it focused primary attention on the lives of courageous women during wartime and, like *GWTW*, resisted the temptation to ever show any scenes of that conflict—rare for serious contemporary films of the period. David cast the film carefully—and most

effectively—with Claudette Colbert, Jennifer Jones and a maturing Shirley Temple, then had it photographed by *GWTW*'s Lee Garmes (all was forgiven!). The icing on the cake was provided by a touchingly emotional score by Max Steiner, again a challenging assignment considering the film's length. Then David delivered the package to the public with a far from modest slogan: "The four most important words since *Gone With the Wind—SINCE YOU WENT AWAY!*"

And *Since You Went Away* found great favor with America's 1944 public, although several critics dismissed it or were outraged by its running time. However, James Agee in *Time* magazine found "scores of such evidences of a smart showman's eye, mind and heart. Added up, they give the picture taste, shrewdness, superiority, life"; he also commented on "David Selznick's extremely astute screen play and production." Throughout the country long lines formed wherever it played and word-of-mouth spread from those who were deeply stirred by its patriotic story and sentiment. David's $2,400,000 investment was rewarded with enormous box-office results—at $4,950,000 in rentals returned to the producer, it became the eighth most successful film in history up to that time. And the Hollywood Academy voted David a "Best Picture" nomination as it similarly honored Miss Colbert, Miss Jones, Mr. Garmes and supporting actor Monty Woolley. Even though David had persuaded Max Steiner to include a few themes from *A Star Is Born* in his score, the Academy voted Max a third (and final) Oscar for his creative efforts.

World War II ended for Americans in August of 1945 and a unique period closed suddenly. Despite the former unification of its people, America quickly reverted to a spirit of individuality. There were then new and pressing matters to contend with, like the absorption of returning veterans, reconstruction of the economy and even new national leadership—for Franklin Roosevelt had died in office on the very eve of peace, being succeeded by his Vice President, Harry S Truman. That the solidarity Americans experienced during the war years interlude had forever become anachronistic was evidenced in the unkind way history would deal with *Since You Went Away, Mrs. Miniver* or, for that matter, any of the Hollywood films reflecting the morale effort during World War II. Future generations of Americans who would witness two futile wars and could not justify their involvement were to label such efforts as "pure propaganda." This they were, although that terminology had held a different interpretation in an era when the people of a country had rallied together against unprovoked attack.

The film version of *Gone With the Wind*, however, came through that period unscathed. It had contributed its presence to the time but did not become a part of it. Nor was it to become inexorably linked with any specific era, as its future revisitations would prove.

1946-1949: Tenth Anniversary

A decade after it all began . . . the world was again at peace and Scarlett had a new message for all . . . the stars returned and so did the film . . . David O. Selznick was still trying . . . Olivia de Havilland won two Academy Awards . . . and multiple tragedies struck the Gone With the Wind *family . . .*

If any one new star had come to represent artistic and financial prestige to the movie industry during the war years it was M-G-M's Greer Garson, who, in a succession of filmed best sellers (*Mrs. Miniver, Random Harvest, Mrs. Parkington* and *The Valley of Decision*), brought a bonanza of benefits to her employers. It was, therefore, to no one's surprise when her studio announced she would co-star with "the King" upon his return to films. "Gable's Back and Garson's Got Him," the 1946 ads proclaimed, "in the Victor Fleming production of *Adventure.*" And the unconventional film indeed earned its title by casting both stars against type in a wordy and sometimes mystical screenplay based on a novel, *The Anointed*, by Clyde Brion Davis. For Mr. Gable and Mr. Fleming, it was a *GWTW* reunion as they were joined by Thomas Mitchell and Harry Davenport. The film's notices were decidedly mixed but its star power made it among the year's highest-grossing films ($4,250,000 returned to M-G-M) and a line-former from its Radio City Music Hall premiere through its subsequent engagements.

Vivien Leigh was back on screen as well in *Caesar and Cleopatra*, and that film's advertising carefully stressed that she appeared "by arrangement with David O. Selznick." Miss Leigh and Mr. Selznick would, however, never work together on a project again, despite the long-term contract she had signed when cast in *Gone With the Wind*. But the most impressive screen return of all in 1946 was made by Olivia de Havilland. With her legal problems behind her and a new precedent set for contracted screen actors, Olivia was present in *four* films that year, in one of which she played twins (*The Dark Mirror* with Thomas Mitchell) and in another of which she finally got the role destined to bring Oscar to her doorstep. Mitchell Leisen's *To Each His Own*, for Paramount Pictures, provided Olivia with an actress's dream —the heart-tugging story of an unwed mother trying to regain custody of the child inadvertently taken from her. And her nemesis in realizing that goal was none other than *GWTW*'s Mary Anderson (with *second* billing no less). Although Olivia finished a close second in 1946's year-end New York Film Critics poll, two and a half months later an Academy Award for "Best Actress"

The legendary slogan told it all.

was finally hers. She then became the sixth (and last) member of *Gone With the Wind*'s cast to enter the select Oscar-winning circle.

Americans were more movie-hungry than ever in the immediate postwar period and quite a few films (*The Bells of St. Mary's, Blue Skies, Spellbound, Notorious* and, most notably, *The Jolson Story*) achieved grosses hardly imagined before. But the film that scored the greatest critical and box-office success was one which hit home with many Americans, since its story dealt with the problems of returning veterans. William Wyler's *The Best Years of Our Lives* returned over $11,300,000 to Samuel Goldwyn Productions and came close—with seven Oscars—to tying the Academy Award record held by *GWTW*.

The *Gone With the Wind* mystique continued to haunt its producer (as indeed it would throughout his lifetime). David Selznick had begun a film in 1944 based on a small psychological western novel, *Duel in the Sun*, which had enjoyed only moderate success in hardcover book form.

It was Paramount Pictures which finally provided Olivia de Havilland with the vehicle that brought her a first Oscar.

For over two years, David reshot, expanded, inflated, changed directors, supervised all facets of production, and spent $6,000,000 on a project which hardly seemed to warrant it. Then, on December 31, 1946—the very last day to qualify for Academy Awards—he premiered his new epic in Los Angeles. The producer would win no Oscars for this rather ponderous expenditure but he did receive an unexpected bonus—condemnation by the Catholic Church! "Filming of this immoral story," said Church officials, "indicates the beginning of a new and dangerous Hollywood trend." Additionally, initial reviews were not only unenthusiastic but sometimes absolutely jeering. The Selznick showmanship overcame all, however, and David invested an additional $1,000,000 in the loudest, longest and most outrageous campaign of publicity and merchandising tie-ins since *Gone With the Wind*. Since Selznick productions were no longer obligated for United Artists release, the film was handled by David's own distribution company, Selznick Releasing Organization. After numerous cuts to satisfy religious leaders, *Duel in the Sun* was used, throughout 1947, to test an innovative approach in film marketing: in each of many major areas, it saturated numerous theatres simultaneously as if to "get the money fast before word-

of-mouth spreads." And it worked! *Duel in the Sun* became—and remained for many years—one of the ten top moneymakers in the film industry's history.

Meanwhile, *Gone with the Wind*—as a book—had quietly celebrated its tenth anniversary in May of 1946 and, at that time, Macmillan announced that upon the completion of its first decade the American public had purchased 3,713,272 copies of its various editions. Later that year Margaret Mitchell estimated that 1,250,000 copies of *authorized* foreign translations had been sold as well (its huge popularity in pirated editions, such as those in Japan and China, could only be guessed but illegal sales might easily have matched or exceeded the legal ones). With the end of wartime shortages, Macmillan withdrew its "Victory" issue and substituted a tenth-anniversary volume (published October 8, 1946) with the rather unflattering catalog terminology of "cheap edition" ($1.98 retail). Even with its slightly higher price, sales remained consistently good as it sold over 43,600 copies between 1946 and 1947. The following year sales climbed past 50,800.

While Macmillan handled her domestic business to Margaret Mitchell's complete satisfaction, foreign affairs were a mass of confusion following the war. After hostilities ceased, normal publication of *Gone with the Wind* resumed in some countries like France and Italy. But there were other areas where there was no news forthcoming for well over a year. Then new "Cold War" policies developed between America and the Soviet Union, and although publication of *GWTW* had been renewed in Czechoslovakia, Poland and Hungary—and a new Yugoslavian edition appeared for the first time in 1946—the "Iron Curtain" descended around those countries under Soviet domination and, by 1948, *Gone with the Wind* was banned there forever. Russia itself denied ever publishing *GWTW*, although through future years, citizens of that country innocently volunteered the information that they had read serialized versions of it in Russian periodicals. But free countries continued to contact Margaret for translation rights; Belgium published a French-language edition in 1947, while Switzerland issued it in German the following year.

With all those foreign transactions, it was not surprising that Margaret Mitchell had been unable to begin writing again. But something far closer to home also dominated any free time she might have found, for John Marsh was stricken with a serious heart attack in December 1945 and required maximum attention for over a year. Even upon John's subsequent recovery and his retirement in 1947 (when he was able to take much of the publishing burden from his wife), Margaret was plagued by a discouraging flock of new stories that she had actually completed a second novel. And what was the source of those annoying new rumors? It seemed *that* movie was back again!

Although M-G-M had a policy against reissues for many years, it experimented, beginning in 1944, with the revival of a few films like *Waterloo Bridge*. The studio discovered that in some markets box-office grosses exceeded those of the films' original releases. The war years had forced cutbacks in feature film production at all studios and those reductions were still significant in the years immediately afterward. Reissues, then, became standard fare on M-G-M's yearly release schedule—under the term "masterpiece reprints"—and, in early 1947, the studio announced that *Gone With the Wind* would return to theatres beginning in the spring of that year. Serious doubts were expressed in the industry, since the Selznick film had been in complete withdrawal for only a little over three years and the market had been saturated by it during the four years of its theatrical life. If M-G-M's judgment was premature, the film's future theatrical value could conceivably be permanently damaged. Metro was also known to be spending a considerable amount in furnishing new Technicolor prints and on an updated advertising campaign. When the film reopened with only modest hoopla at Loew's Grand in June, instant crowds of ticket buyers verified Margaret Mitchell's statements that hardly a day had passed when Atlantans did not inquire about the film's return.

Those heartening results were not confined to Atlanta. Reconstruction Scarlett had as much meaning to 1947 Americans as wartime Scarlett had a few years before. The picture ran for weeks after its opening on Broadway at Loew's Criterion and similarly at first-run theatres throughout the country before beginning extended subrun engagements at neighborhood houses. It was also destined to be among the top money-making films of the year— the *fifth* separate year it was so designated in the nine years of its existence. And in many countries overseas— especially France—where the movie had never been seen, its postwar premieres inspired total identification with the heroine's struggles and resulted in phenomenally long theatrical engagements. M-G-M again withdrew *Gone With the Wind* in 1948 and, by then, perennial future reissues of it were guaranteed. But what no one could have realized at that time was that it would never again be returning in its original format.

M-G-M announced that *Gone With the Wind* had, after its first *actual* reissue, been seen by 100,000,000 people and that its total boxoffice grosses then exceeded $35,000,000. The 1947 ad campaign had stressed the phrase "*Everybody* wants to see *Gone With the Wind*!" and had informed the doubtful that it was "Complete! Intact! Exactly as originally shown!" Therein lay some

Posters and lobby cards for the 1947 reissue of Gone With the Wind *(from the Herb Bridges Collection).*

Rhett and Scarlett returned to show the postwar world how to reconstruct.

running time, the phrase gained a new meaning that year and was usually avoided in future M-G-M advertising.

That same year had also brought a picturization of the works of Atlanta's other foremost author, Joel Chandler Harris, and Walt Disney had the good sense to employ Wilbur Kurtz as technical adviser for his *Song of the South*. Hattie McDaniel received another opportunity to sing on screen in the film, while black actor James Baskett as "Uncle Remus" was later granted a "Special" Academy Award for his inspired performance. That picture was destined for strict racial censure in the future, as was *Gone With the Wind*.

James A. Michener, who had worked as a Macmillan editor when the *GWTW* phenonmenon first began, published his first book, *Tales of the South Pacific*, in 1947, to begin a career as one of America's foremost authors of best-selling fiction. That initial volume of related sketches, based on his wartime experiences, brought Mr. Michener a Pulitzer Prize and became a 1949 Broadway musical landmark. And, a decade later Twentieth Century-Fox would transfer that classic Rodgers and Hammerstein version to the screen.

The Fox studio had, meanwhile, continued its romance with best sellers over that four-year period, acquiring *The Snake Pit*, *Prince of Foxes*, *Gentlemen's Agreement* (which became 1947's Academy Award winner), *The Black Rose*, *Lydia Bailey*, *The Egyptian*, *The Wayward Bus* and *The Young Lions*. With various changes just beginning to run rampant through the film industry, some of those properties would not be produced for up to ten years. One purchase which was immediately transferred to film was Frank Yerby's first novel, *The Foxes of Harrow*, which as a book and a movie bore a striking resemblance in characters and incidents to those of Margaret Mitchell. M-G-M bought rights to a few succesful novels like *The Hucksters* (for Clark Gable) but had found its own method for securing premium fiction for the screen by sponsoring a contest with large cash prizes ($125,000–$150,000) for winning selections. *Green Dolphin Street*, its 1944 winner, proved a 1947 screen gold mine with Lana Turner as its star. The studio's prize in 1947 was granted to Ross Lockridge, a young Indiana teacher, for his *Raintree County* and M-G-M announced that Miss Turner would again star in the film version—budgeted at $5,000,000—to be the "biggest epic since *Gone With the Wind*." Soon after the book's publication in early 1948, when it had become a huge best seller, Mr. Lockridge—who had never written another book—committed suicide. Shortly thereafter the film version was indefinitely postponed.

Portrait of Jennie, a beautiful fantasy released a generation before its time, spelled the temporary end of David Selznick's producing career in America. He traveled abroad afterward to become involved in several foreign co-productions. But Olivia de Havilland enhanced

irony for a film that had once inspired mild censorship controversies, since it played throughout that year side by side with its producer's *Duel in the Sun*, which had undergone many cuts just to secure play dates. And even the storm the Selznick western briefly inspired was mild compared to the condemnations, picketing and local censor actions taken in 1947 against Howard Hughes' *The Outlaw* and Fox's *Forever Amber*, both of which were forced to undergo scissored dilutions before general release. Whereas *GWTW*'s "intact" referred to its her professional stature even further in 1948 in Fox's *The Snake Pit*, for which she won the New York Film Critics Award and a fourth Oscar nomination for her compelling enactment of a confined mental patient. Olivia's disappointment at losing the 1948 Oscar, she would later admit, was tempered by knowledge that she had just finished a film for William Wyler which she hoped would give her another opportunity. Her crystal ball proved correct and Olivia's remarkable performance in 1949's *The Heiress* resulted in her second consecutive New York Critics honor and her second Academy Award. That brilliant film would be the high point of her career, remaining just as noteworthy for future generations. *All the King's Men*, also released in 1949, became only the second Pulitzer Prize-winning novel to be turned into an Academy Award-winning "Best Picture," although Robert Penn Warren's novel had not enjoyed hardcover best-seller status as *Gone With the Wind* had.

That little entertainment novelty for the home which had been threatening to make its presence known for two decades finally became a popular reality on the postwar scene. Although there were only 175,000 television sets in American homes in early 1948, that number increased to dominate 5,000,000 households—or about 12 percent of the country's total—by the end of 1949. Names of successful entertainers in the television medium, like Milton Berle or Sid Caesar, were suddenly part of everyday American conversations in a way formerly reserved only for movie stars. And Hollywood studios noticed significant differences in revenue. While a number of films were still successful in luring people away from their homes and sets, other expensive items, like Victor Fleming's $5,000,000 1948 production *Joan of Arc*, failed to recoup their costs. For director Fleming, that was to be his last screen opportunity; while visiting a Cottonwood, Arizona, ranch on January 6, 1949, he was stricken with a fatal heart attack. Coronaries also claimed the lives of veteran actor Harry Davenport on August 9 of that year and of Sam Wood on September 22. And there was another tragedy in 1949 which took its aim right at the heart of the *Gone With the Wind* family.

Margaret Mitchell had always loved the movies, even though one of them had brought years of havoc into her life. After John Marsh's heart attack, Margaret bought a sixteen-millimeter movie projector and ran rented films for their enjoyment at home. She hadn't felt well all day on that hot August 11, and, by evening, thought going out to a movie with John might be a comfortable diversion. She parked their car across the street from Atlanta's Peachtree Arts Theatre and the Marshes began to cross Peachtree Street at a curved point where it was impossible to see approaching northbound traffic. Suddenly the headlights of a car—speeding between forty or fifty miles an hour—bore down upon the couple. John stepped quickly forward but, to his horror, Margaret didn't go with him and hastily moved in the other direction, trying to reach the curb. With each step she took, the car swerved further and further toward her, almost as if in a chase, until a moment of unavoidable, possibly predestined, impact. At the wheel of the careening auto was an off-duty taxicab driver who had been drinking and who had a record of twenty-three arrests for traffic violations in the past five years.

For five days the world anxiously waited for news or plagued Atlanta's Grady Hospital with concerned calls. News broadcasts gave constant bulletins on Margaret's comatose condition. Then, just before noon on the morning of August 16, it was all over. Many radio broadcasters followed their sad announcement by playing "Tara's Theme." John Marsh carried on bravely, assuming all of Margaret's business affairs until, three years later, he joined her.

The tributes and sincere condolences that poured into Atlanta or were printed in publications throughout the world could easily have filled several volumes (and undoubtedly would have embarrassed Margaret no end). Probably the most noteworthy was a wire which President Harry S Truman sent to John Marsh on August 17, 1949: "The nation to which she brought international fame through a creative work of lasting merit shares the sorrow which has come to you with such sudden and tragic force. Great as an artist who gave the world an eternal book, the author of *Gone with the Wind* will also be remembered as a great soul who exemplified in her all-too-brief span of years the highest ideals of American womanhood."

After thirteen maddening years, Peggy Mitchell Marsh finally found the peace which had eluded her so long. She was forty-eight years old.

Ralph Richardson, Olivia de Havilland and Montgomery Clift in The Heiress, *which provided Olivia with a second Academy Award.*

1950-1953: Scarlett Takes a Streetcar

England's Vivien Leigh won an Academy Award for the second time by playing another American Southern woman.

It was Irene Mayer Selznick, David's first wife, who had produced *A Streetcar Named Desire* when it opened on Broadway December 3, 1947. The South's Tennessee Williams had conceived a hauntingly poetic masterpiece which was then superbly directed by Elia Kazan. The production featured Jessica Tandy, Marlon Brando, Kim Hunter and Karl Malden and won the year's Pulitzer Prize for drama. In October 1949 an English version was directed by Laurence Olivier and starred his wife, Vivien Leigh, in a production that played to capacity London audiences for eight months. Then, in the summer of 1950, the British couple traveled to America: she to replace Miss Tandy in the otherwise original Broadway cast of a *Streetcar* to be filmed at Warner Brothers, he to work with William Wyler in *Carrie*, a film co-starring— to make the circle complete—the second Mrs. Selznick, Jennifer Jones.

For the second time in her limited film appearances, Vivien Leigh played an American Southern woman. And she created what would later be judged by many as the most brilliant screen performance of all time. When the film debuted in the fall of 1951, *The New York*

Times commented about Vivien: "Her mental confusions, her self-deceptions, the agonies of her lacerated nerves and her final, unbearable madness . . . are clearly conveyed by the actress with a tremendous concentration and economy of power. . . . And since Miss Leigh is present in virtually every scene or sequence of the film, the demands upon her vitality and her flexibility are great."

It had been feared in advance that gentle Vivien might be overshadowed by the dynamic presence of young Marlon Brando and, in popular appeal to American audiences of its day, that proved to be true. But it was Vivien's performance and the film which won the New York Critics' prizes. She, Miss Hunter and Mr. Malden also predictably won Academy Awards and, even though Mr. Brando did *not* win, the film was nevertheless the first picture ever to win *three* Oscars for acting.

To those who loved Vivien Leigh as Scarlett, *A Streetcar Named Desire* had even deeper poignancy, for here was an aging Southern belle left without her defenses, still acting the coquette to no avail. Where Scarlett's Tara was always there to protect her and to rely on, Blanche DuBois had lost her one-time plantation home, Belle Reve, and disintegrated without it in a world

Broadway's Marlon Brando was assured of a successful movie career with his performance opposite Vivien Leigh in Warner's film version of A Streetcar Named Desire.

where gentility was left no opportunity to survive. Unobserved by many, there was also a touching reunion in *Streetcar*'s opening sequence: the young sailor who gave Blanche assistance was played by *GWTW*'s Mickey Kuhn (little Beau grown up).

Hollywood had never recovered from the *GWTW* phenomenon and another attempt to match its success, *Quo Vadis*, finally reached movie screens, also in late 1951. The long-heralded project had been delayed seven years by World War II, and M-G-M injected much of the *GWTW* formula into its production to safeguard their $7,000,000 investment. First there was three hours of (excessive) running time; there was a "Burning of Rome" sequence which even excelled the Atlanta depot fire in technical expertise; and finally there were simultaneous major Broadway premieres at the Astor and Capitol Theatres. Dramatically *Quo Vadis* left much to be desired, but its spectacle and promotion quickly propelled it into fifth position of the screen's all-time money makers (of course, at a top price of $2 a ticket on first run, it had a distinct advantage).

Another M-G-M drama, directed by Vincente Minnelli and released in late 1952, raised quite a few eyebrows in the movie colony. *The Bad and the Beautiful*, judged by many to be among the best "inside" glimpses at film people, related the tale of a ruthless filmmaker (played by Kirk Douglas) who vowed to succeed in Hollywood, the town which had treated his movie-pioneer father badly. Stepping on everyone along the way, the producer formed an independent studio carrying his name and reached his apex in filming a Civil War epic—from which he fired the director to complete it himself. Any resemblance to David O. Selznick was "purely coincidental."

But M-G-M and other Hollywood studios felt ever-growing pressures from television in the early Fifties. The home medium had gained in prestige by giving firsthand reports on America's futile three-year war involvement in Korea and even providing armchair viewers with a seat at the inauguration of President Dwight D. Eisenhower in January 1953. Ironically, a higher audience rating than that ceremony (record breaking, in fact, for years to come) was gained by one-time Scarlett contender Lucille Ball's phenomenally popular *I Love Lucy* television series—for a program devoted to the birth of her son (in real and "reel" life). Evidently, while television was invaluable for current affairs, what Americans really wanted was entertainment, and they gladly substituted this home variety for their former trips to movie theatres. And throughout the nation, those establishments began to go bankrupt and close by the thousands. Film studios were rampant with panic. Management changes deposed even the powerful Louis B. Mayer from his throne at Metro, partially due to disagreements over another Civil War film, *The Red Badge of Courage*.

Television—the new American vogue—presented some excellent comedy and dramatic innovations and even a limited supply of old Hollywood movies (including Selznick's *A Star Is Born*, rights to which David relinquished in liquidating his studio). It also granted employment to many performers who would otherwise have found it difficult with cutbacks in movie production. Among those visible—for free—at home were *GWTW*'s Thomas Mitchell, Eddie Anderson, Ward Bond, Victor Jory, Cliff Edwards, Marjorie Reynolds and, especially, George Reeves. Mr. Reeves assumed a new professional identity in 1951 and, as "Superman," enjoyed a popularity with youngsters comparable to the amazing phenomenon created by the televising of old "Hopalong Cassidy" films. The latter, some of which featured George Reeves and many more of which co-starred Rand Brooks, inspired merchandising tie-ins which put the Shirley Temple, *GWTW* and *Duel in the Sun* campaigns to shame. Hollywood—with all its publicity gimmicks—was hard pressed to overcome its new rival.

Sadly, Hattie McDaniel, who had triumphed on radio as "Beulah," benefitted only briefly from the new medium. That grand lady of the screen succumbed to

M-G-M invested its expensive Quo Vadis *with many GWTW elements, including a massive fire sequence.*

cancer in October 1952. Other losses to the *GWTW* family in those years included Robert Elliott in 1951, John Marsh in 1952, Paul Hurst, Lee Phelps and Everett Brown in 1953 and Leona Roberts, Tom Tyler and Ernest Whitman in 1954.

Significant economic changes in the Fifties were not limited to Hollywood. America's publishing companies had feared that television's intrusion into America's leisure time would also adversely affect book sales. While this did prove true, to some degree, in the hardcover market, the "orphans" of the industry—paperback publishers—felt a sudden upswing in their direction. While those little "throwaways" had been steadily growing in sales momentum in postwar years, they experienced a boom in the early Fifties, spearheaded by the remarkable acceptance of Mickey Spillane's paperback mystery stories. Where a 100,000-copy sale of a hardcover novel had always been extraordinary, million-plus sales of paperback reprints or originals at twenty-five to fifty cents became standard fare within the decade.

Meanwhile, The Macmillan Company, which broke ties with its British forebears and became a wholly American-owned company in 1951, continued to rely on *Gone with the Wind* as a revenue staple. The changing economy forced the book's price to creep from $1.98 in 1949 (its sixty-fifth printing) to $4 for the sixty-seventh edition in 1953, but sales acceptance continued amazingly well nevertheless. The book's appeal continued to spread "south of the border" too as Mexico nonchalantly decided to pirate it for an edition published there in 1953.

While the film industry looked to its newer players like Marlon Brando, Marilyn Monroe, Audrey Hepburn and former juvenile Elizabeth Taylor to relieve those television doldrums, some of the "older" crowd proved they could still pull their own weight at the box office. M-G-M discovered this when Clark Gable enjoyed his biggest postwar success in John Ford's 1953 production of *Mogambo* (a remake of Victor Fleming's *Red Dust*), with Clark being given two exciting leading ladies in that jungle epic, Ava Gardner and newcomer Grace Kelly. Vivien Leigh, however, was stricken with an emotional collapse in March 1953 while filming Paramount's *Elephant Walk* in Ceylon with Peter Finch. Because of the great resemblance between Miss Leigh and Elizabeth Taylor, Paramount secured the younger actress's services from M-G-M—hoping to retain all distant location footage in which Vivien appeared. But, by the time the movie was released, enlarged theatre screens made the discrepancy all too apparent.

There was still some reliance by Hollywood on best-selling fiction, like Daphne du Maurier's *My Cousin Rachel*, which became a Fox film starring Olivia de Havilland and introducing Richard Burton to American audiences. But changing literary tastes in the Fifties made the transitions more difficult. James Jones was 1951's newly famous author and his *From Here to Eternity* topped best-seller charts with a total of 240,000 copies purchased. Mr. Jones was credited with helping make four-letter words and explicit sex the new standards for fiction writers, and Columbia Pictures faced quite an ordeal in bringing his novel to the screen. Yet the highly laundered film version of *From Here to Eternity*, released in 1953, was considered an adult, precedent-setting and thoroughly successful cinematic treatment. It won eight Academy Awards (on twelve nominations), including "Best Picture," finally tying the thirteen-year record of *Gone With the Wind*. And, within a year, it was fourth on *Variety*'s list of all-time large-grossing films.

But the picture which, at the end of 1953, was *second* most financially successful—after only a few months in release—had also been adapted from a best seller, and signaled the beginning of a new theatrical era which, it was hoped, would save the movie industry from the treacheries of television. In the fall of 1952, the premiere of *This Is Cinerama* had introduced a unique type of wide-screen theatre projection which, with a side-by-side triple image, was not ideally suited for dramatic presentation. Then, for a large portion of 1953, movie patrons slid down into their seats as a cavalcade of three-dimensional (or "3-D") films gave the illusion of hurling everything in sight out into the audience. The necessity of wearing polarized eyeglasses to view those gimmick films and the fact that Hollywood utilized extremely turgid scripts in their earliest "3-D" efforts killed that novelty fairly quickly. But, in September 1953, Twentieth Century-Fox seemed to have found the answer, with its introduction of Cinemascope in a long-postponed production of *The Robe*.

An image two and a half times normal length was projected through special lenses, necessitating expensive theatre refurbishing to accommodate Cinemascope screens and, in some cases, new sound systems as well. Stereophonic—or directional—sound was an optional by-product of that wide-screen revolution in which the film's sound track was apportioned to several different speakers throughout a theatre's auditorium. The vast financial success of *The Robe*, which starred Richard Burton, convinced Hollywood that Cinemascope was the weapon needed to conquer television, and most other studios followed Fox's lead in converting their important projects to the process. But the most significant problem with the wide-screen era (which had actually preceded *The Robe* by several months in America's theatres) was in the projection of older movies photographed in a standard ratio. Whereas these films were not elongated to the Cinemascope size, they were still exaggerated to a rectangular shape which sometimes cut off actors' feet or, even worse, decapitated them.

1954-1960: Wide Screen and Stereophonic Sound

Metro-Goldwyn-Mayer and the city of Atlanta decided to alter history a bit and, rather than wait until December 1954, they celebrated the fifteenth anniversary of *Gone With the Wind* on May 20 of that year with a lavish new "premiere" at Loew's Grand. Actual surviving celebrities of the film's cast seemed rather hard to find but M-G-M dispatched reliable Ann Rutherford and Cammie King— by then a five-foot-nine-and-a-half-inch college sophomore—to the proceedings, along with their own George Murphy as master of ceremonies. To tie in with the festive occasion, Rich's department store featured a display of the late author's memorabilia—on loan from friends—including forty-five volumes of the book printed in twenty-three languages. Then, a pre-opening party was

hosted by M-G-M in collaboration with Atlanta's Smith College Club, where it was announced that a Margaret Mitchell Scholarship to that institution was being initiated through sales of "premiere" tickets. As far as the movie itself was concerned, *The Atlanta Journal* reported: "The impact on more than 2,000 Atlantans who filled Loew's Grand Theatre for another look was tremendous . . . on a screen almost twice as large as that used for the original premiere here on December 15, 1939."

Yes, even *Gone With the Wind* had undergone some changes in the seven years since its last reissue, but lasting benefits of those alterations were debatable. While viewers throughout America appreciated the film's new panoramic scope that year, many wondered why the color

Loew's State Theatre on Broadway proclaimed the news—the Wind had blown back in a new format.

had faded so drastically in certain segments. The cause was simple: in projecting the 1939 image onto a wide screen, crucial portions of some scenes were cut off and, to compensate, M-G-M had actually rephotographed those sequences with a black mask at screen bottom to raise the affected footage. In so doing, the original color was significantly drained from those moments and their new appearance was limited to a near tintlike quality.

Something else had occurred in the manufacture of motion-picture film in the years since *GWTW*'s last release which, luckily, would be preserving older films for the future. Movie negatives and release prints were, until 1952, on a nitrate-based stock which could in time disintegrate, shrink or even explode. Old nitrate film was dangerous to store and almost impossible to preserve. But at the time of *GWTW*'s 1954 reissue, acetate safety film—which *did* survive—was in common use. While M-G-M was able to preserve *GWTW*'s future by transferring it to the new type of film stock, the studio (influenced by wide-screen popularity) thought to do so only with its newer "masked" version, and the priceless original was inadvertently left behind to rot.

But the 1954 presentation also offered a novelty that was a distinct advantage for those theatres equipped with the latest sound systems. Despite its original one-channel, optical (or monaural) sound track, M-G-M technicians did a difficult and splendid job of dividing it onto a new multiple-channel magnetic tape which broadcast the film in "Perspecta stereophonic sound." The effect was brilliant: conversations were actually divided line by line (only in certain scenes) and the voice of a character out of camera range could be heard over a viewer's shoulder—from the back of the theatre. This was particularly well used for Ashley's reminiscences at the lumber mill and in the finale. Stereophonic sound lost its popularity fairly quickly in the following years and this particular divided sound track *was never employed again.*

New York City's daily press devoted a fair amount of editorial space to *Gone With the Wind*'s 1954 reissue, but the film opened quietly on Broadway at Loew's State Theatre on Saturday, May 29. Nevertheless, New Yorkers were still tremendously responsive to the old film and it remained in that engagement for most of the summer. Just as it was packing its bags to leave Broadway, the

Hollywood honored David O. Selznick in August 1954 with a new "premiere" and Academy Awards on view to remind spectators of Gone With the Wind's *championship.*

A host of celebrities attended the 1954 Hollywood opening, including Ona Munson (left—only six months before her tragic suicide) and a grown-up Cammie King (right).

vintage movie was given its most impressive 1954 honor by Hollywood on the night of August 10 at the Egyptian Theatre, with a massive celebrity ceremonial. In February of that year fireworks had exploded after a televised tribute to M-G-M's Thirtieth Anniversary. It seemed that, on "The Ed Sullivan Show," a film clip of *GWTW* had been shown along with some from M-G-M films produced over the previous three decades, and David O. Selznick was enraged by the studio's taking credit for his production. By August—after apologies all around—the Hollywood "premiere" actually became a personal testimonial to the producer as Oscars representing the film's Academy Award triumph were on display in the Egyptian's lobby along with David's own Thalberg Award. M-G-M publicists, meanwhile, informed the press that "the gala event marked the first time in history that any picture ever had been given a second Hollywood permiere."

The 125 stars who held reservations for that big night included most of M-G-M's remaining contract players, a selection of the town's Old Guard (Joan Bennett, Gary Cooper, Joan Crawford, Merle Oberon, Tyrone Power, Edward G. Robinson, Barbara Stanwyck, Norma Shearer, Shirley Temple and Spencer Tracy) and several surviving members of *Gone With the Wind*'s cast (Mary Anderson, Jane Darwell, Clark Gable, Cammie King, Thomas Mitchell and Ona Munson).

Selznick International's masterpiece was again shown in its original uncut running time in 1954. However, the movie industry had hardly accepted long pictures even

then, as witnessed by the sad fate of Warner Brothers' musical remake that year of *A Star Is Born*, which starred Judy Garland (in probably her finest performance) and was directed by George Cukor. That project had been extraordinarily costly and its three-hour running time limited the number of performances which could be scheduled each day. When box-office returns in its first few weeks did not guarantee a quick enough cash return, the Warners took drastic action and slashed a half-hour from the film—destroying its dramatic quality and, many said, depriving Miss Garland of the Academy Award. When, a decade later, film historians appealed for an opportunity to see *A Star Is Born* in its original state, Warners regretfully admitted that the missing scenes appeared to have been lost. Had *Gone With the Wind* been similarly cut in any of its revivals (to make more money in per-day performances), there was every reason to believe its deleted footage could have met the same fate.

A Star Is Born kept *Gone With the Wind* company on The Catholic Legion of Decency's "B"—"Morally Objectionable in Part for All"—list. Despite the vast changes the world had undergone in those past fifteen years, the Church remained constant as it found similar objections to such other films of the period as *Sabrina, Carmen Jones, Deep in My Heart* and *The Egyptian*. But nothing kept *GWTW*'s popularity back even in the wide-screen, Eisenhower Fifties. By the end of its 1954 release *the Wind* blew on, leaving M-G-M with a new total worldwide gross of almost $50,000,000. *Variety* reported that the reissue had earned $7,000,000 in returned rentals

The first recording of Gone With the Wind's *film score was issued by RCA Victor in the summer of 1954.*

from M-G-M's United States and Canadian playdates as it updated its annual list of the "golden ten" all-time moneymakers. *Gone With the Wind* was still in first position with $35,500,000 (again for rental returns in America and Canada only) and was followed by *The Robe* (with $17,500,000), *The Greatest Show on Earth* ($12,800,000), *From Here to Eternity* ($12,500,000), *This Is Cinerama* ($12,500,000), *White Christmas* ($12,000,000), *Duel in the Sun* ($11,300,000), *The Best Years of Our Lives* ($11,200,000), *Quo Vadis* ($10,500,000) and *Samson and Delilah* ($9,000,000).

The success of the 1954 reissue prompted another *Gone With the Wind* milestone as RCA Victor issued a ten-inch, long-playing recording of Max Steiner's musical score for the first time (RCA catalog # LPM-3227). This was not a "sound track" transference but a symphonic treatment of most of the film's individual themes, specially arranged for best listening and conducted by Mr. Steiner himself.

Ironically, *Gone With the Wind*'s 1954 return coincided with Clark Gable's departure from M-G-M after twenty-four years, upon completion of his last film for them, *Betrayed* with Lana Turner. The actor candidly admitted what the Rhett Butler role had done for him when he said, "Every time they begin to forget me, out comes *GWTW* again." And he implied it again when he received the *Woman's Home Companion* award as most popular actor of 1954 and muttered, "You can be sure as hell I didn't get this for *Betrayed*." Clark quickly shifted operations to free-lancing with percentages of profits as he began that new—and last—phase of his career in *Soldier of Fortune* with Susan Hayward at Twentieth Century-Fox. Mr. Gable had also never gotten over the fact that M-G-M had not given him a percentage

of *GWTW*'s profits, even though they never would have owned it without him. When informed of its latest grosses, Vivien Leigh also commented—in her ladylike way—"I wouldn't have minded a little percentage."

The popularity of the Macmillan book did not diminish either, and its sixty-eighth printing in July 1954 carried a new price tag of $4.50 (a "cheap edition" at $2.95 was still available). And, in April of that year, Doubleday—which had purchased subsidiary rights—published a Permabook edition and *GWTW* finally joined the new trend toward paperbacks. The company called it "the longest modern pocket-sized book ever to be published. It has 864 pages." And that little edition (too thick for any pocket) simulated the original novel's Confederate typeface on its plain cover and retailed at seventy-five cents. Where M-G-M's 1954 advertising campaign for the film's revival had less than modestly progressed to "the greatest motion picture ever made!", Permabooks employed the catchline "the greatest American novel of the century" on its cover. Meanwhile, Garden City Books, book-club subsidiary of Doubleday, secured rights to a $1.98 hardcover premium edition for its members, which was also available that year in bookstores.

Gone With the Wind was just then playing in West Berlin in what would eventually prove to be a marathon run of two and a half years, during which it was seen by 600,000 viewers and in which four prints of the film were worn out. During that same reissue period, it also reached Holland for the first time, to astounding results. For *GWTW*'s most avid American movie followers, that release had also provided an additional bonus: 1954 "trailers" (previews of coming attractions) included scenes from *GWTW* for the very first time. Previous releases had advertised the film in theatres with a more dignified approach by showing only artistically lettered panels and sketches.

Atlanta celebrated the 1954 revival of interest in various reverential ways. On December 12 of that year, the Atlanta Board of Education dedicated a new elementary institution as the Margaret Mitchell School. Then, on December 15, the Margaret Mitchell Room was opened in the Atlanta Public Library to exhibit various mementos (changing from time to time) which had been bequeathed by John Marsh. Margaret's husband had left to the library the most complete collection in existence of editions of *Gone with the Wind*, Margaret's reference books on the Civil War, some of her other books and souvenirs from her career as an author. Among the editions of the book were nine different versions published by Macmillan, including a first edition specially autographed by Macmillan officials and presented in a special leather case, and the millionth copy with a specially printed presentation page—given to Margaret on December 15, 1936—also in a special binding. It was the same fall of 1954 when the Atlanta Council named a street in Peggy Marsh's favorite town Margaret Mitchell Drive.

Atlanta was indelibly linked to that little lady who wrote *the* book, as evidenced by the dedication of radio and television stations WSB and WSB-TV in a building called "White Columns" on Peachtree Street on April 7, 1956. The media organization wanted something memorable as a souvenir of that occasion and arranged with Macmillan for five hundred specially bound copies of *Gone with the Wind* with a specially printed dedication page showing a picture of the new edifice. This very special and very limited edition had been prepared by Macmillan especially for the occasion and, since it was never available for sale, soon became an extremely rare collector's item.

Right on schedule at the end of June 1956, Macmillan issued press releases marking *Gone with the Wind*'s twentieth anniversary and announcing that worldwide sales had reached almost eight million. These published listings included editions issued (legally) in twenty-five countries and in twenty-eight different languages. Macmillan also reminded all that the motion-picture version had been on view somewhere in the world almost every day since its first release and was believed to have been seen by 100,000,000 people.

The long romance between Hollywood and best-selling fiction finally began to lessen in the late Fifties as many of the most profitable books of the decade inspired remarkably undistinguished films (*The Silver Chalice, The View from Pompey's Head, Bonjour Tristesse, A Certain Smile*). One major exception, however, was the sexually "hot" book of the Fifties, *Peyton Place*, published in 1956, which sold half a million copies in hardcover and eventually—through a Pocket Books paperback version—soared stratospherically past *Gone with the Wind* to become the best-selling novel in America's history. (By 1965 it still led the fiction field in America with combined sales of 9,317,483; by 1975, although no longer first, it had sold 10,672,302 copies in the United States.) A year after its publication it was on screen, courtesy of Twentieth Century-Fox, in a critically acclaimed film version which contained much of author Grace Metalious's drama but none of her explicit sexuality, and still made a box-office fortune.

Two other notable exceptions were John Steinbeck's *East of Eden* and Edna Ferber's *Giant*, both of which starred the gifted young actor James Dean, who made but three films before his death in an automobile accident. Although Mr. Dean lived only six months after the premiere of his first film, his popularity would continue for decades afterward. This was largely due to a decision reached by the major film studios in 1956 which guaranteed immortality to its players but eventually placed the final nail in Hollywood's coffin. Warner

Brothers and M-G-M led the field in 1956 when they leased their pre-1948 film libraries for television viewing. Within five years, even newer films would be sold, until a point arrived where a motion picture was often available for television within a year after its theatrical exposure. Although M-G-M included virtually all its older films (except a few which had legal restrictions or had disintegrated) in the television sale, it made two noteworthy exceptions. *The Wizard of Oz* would be sold on a "special" basis of one showing each year and *Gone With the Wind* would not be sold at all. This was made quite clear to stockholders at a meeting in March 1957, when Loew's president Joseph R. Vogel countered objections that the film should have been sold rather than "kept in mothballs." Mr. Vogel claimed that the film was not in mothballs but that M-G-M "kept it in a safe" and would continue to reissue it theatrically at seven-year intervals. The official also reminded those stockholders that *Gone With the Wind* did more for the company on each reissue than most new pictures. Nevertheless, within a few years, as television watchers became accustomed to seeing old films at home, disputes arose with many swearing they had already seen telecasts of *GWTW*. For the same reason, few films ever proved successful in theatrical reissue since patrons were sure that any "old" film was television bait.

The late Fifties would later be judged as quite dull and uneventful even though it was the period when a movie star, Grace Kelly, became Princess of Monaco; when the Soviet Union led the world toward exploration of space; when America added two new states; and when phenomenons ranged from the short-lived Davy Crockett excitement, inspired by television, to the lasting Elvis Presley cult, begun through recordings but magnified through television and movies. It was an era which

Macmillan prepared a special presentation edition of GWTW for the dedication of Atlanta's WSB and WSB-TV in 1956.

Elizabeth Taylor gave a fine performance in M-G-M's Raintree County—but she wasn't Scarlett O'Hara.

saw television set ownership spread to 32,000,000 American homes (about 67 percent of the total) by 1955 and yet one in which the studios of Hollywood enjoyed their last period of rather erratic prosperity. Despite the fact that those organizations had begun terminating contract arrangements with all their players, they concentrated on making mammoth films which were bigger, more expensive, primarily in color and *certainly* longer—although no commercially released American film passed *GWTW*'s running time (*The Ten Commandments* came close, at three hours and thirty-nine minutes, with *Ben-Hur*, *War and Peace* and *Giant* not far behind).

Without best-seller inspiration, the more noteworthy films of the time relied on other books which had not enjoyed immense hardcover success (*Sayonara*, *The Bridge on the River Kwai*), on older books (*War and Peace*, *Around the World in 80 Days*, *Ben-Hur*, *Elmer Gantry*), on Broadway (*Picnic*, *Mister Roberts*, *The King and I*, *South Pacific*) or even, ironically, on television plays (*Marty*, *Twelve Angry Men*). The apathy toward tremendously successful books showed in the fact that *Andersonville* never reached the screen, although plans were announced for it several times. MacKinlay Kantor's Civil War novel, which won the Pulitzer Prize in 1956, recounted the horrors of the Confederate prison which Margaret Mitchell had touched upon. But even though the *Gone With the Wind* mystique did not inspire film translation of *Andersonville*, it was still much in evidence with a trio of expensive films released in 1957.

Warners' *Band of Angels*, based on a Robert Penn Warren novel, asked Clark Gable to revisit the antebellum South in the guise of a New Orleans cotton baron.

The only thing memorable about Mr. Gable's trip was Max Steiner's evocative musical score. And music, this time by John Green, was also the key point of interest in M-G-M's eventual realization of *Raintree County*, which pictured Elizabeth Taylor as a half-demented daughter of the Deep South. Studio executives were forced into panic after a lukewarm premiere engagement and immediately cut almost half an hour from their $5,000,000 film. The resulting version, despite a Civil War panorama, its inspired score, Walter Plunkett's masterful costumes and Miss Taylor's Oscar-nominated performance, was confusing and difficult to follow. *Gone With the Wind* it wasn't! And the same could unhappily be said about David O. Selznick's return to moviemaking with a new version of Hemingway's *A Farewell to Arms*. Filmed under the usual Selznick pressures and presented in epic fashion with even a side-sweeping title (in imitation of *GWTW*), the picture was not well received critically and was also destined for later "shortening," although it returned $5,000,000 to its backers.

Ten-inch disks were discontinued by record manufacturers in 1956 with the twelve-inch size becoming standard thereafter. RCA Victor therefore dropped the original issue of Max Steiner's *GWTW* score that year but simultaneously reissued it as a twelve-inch item, supplemented with themes from some of Max's other films (RCA catalog # LPM-1287). That recording would itself be out of print only a few years later. Then, in 1959, the newly formed Warner Bros. Records, Inc. issued a totally new version: "Commemorating the twentieth anniversary of the world's most popular motion picture *Gone With the Wind*—a new stereophonic recording by Muir Mathieson conducting the Sinfonia of London." Max Steiner had personally authorized this arrangement and traveled to England to supervise its recording in the new stereo process which was just then finding popularity with America's record buyers. The cover art for that 1959 issue (WB Catalog #WS-1322) was a representative Southern scene, bearing no relation to any portion of the film, but it was soon discontinued and replaced by one which carried an actual "still" of Clark Gable and Vivien Leigh (same catalog number).

Coincidentally, Macmillan felt the need for a change also in *Gone with the Wind*'s original dust jacket. Under the publishing terminology of "New Format, Reissue" the novel was granted another publishing date—September 19, 1960—and reappeared with a mustard-yellow, solid color jacket and a brand-new promotional campaign (and a slightly lower price of $3.95). The "new format" line was misleading, however, since this seventieth printing was exactly the same as always inside. Macmillan cautiously ordered only 15,500 copies for that printing, but within eight months almost all of them had been sold.

In the late Fifties *Gone With the Wind*—the movie—

finally lost two of its leading championships: top Academy winner and all-time box-office leader. Although 1953's *From Here to Eternity* and 1954's *On the Waterfront* had tied *GWTW*'s eight actual Oscar wins, defenders still pointed to the additional Special Academy Awards *GWTW* was granted in 1940. But 1958's *Gigi*, directed by Vincente Minnelli, ended some of the arguments when it won *nine* Academy Awards, including "Best Picture," in early 1959. The M-G-M musical had also proved a total victor by winning for every category it was nominated in. A tenth honor could possibly be added to *Gigi*'s total, since a Special Oscar was voted to its veteran star Maurice Chevalier (which would be at least as ethical as counting David Selznick's Thalberg Award in *GWTW*'s total). But *GWTW* purists still disputed the fairness of ceding the championship, since *Gigi* won an Oscar for a category—costume design—which had not existed two decades earlier. A year later there was no longer any doubt. *Ben-Hur*, a last moment of glory for the M-G-M that was, thundered across movie screens in the late fall of 1959, bringing critical acclaim unusual for any such religious spectacular and powerful box-office support from the public. In early 1960 the William Wyler production won a total of eleven Oscars, including one to the $15,000,000 production itself. Even though there were still some who criticized a new era of Academy Award "bandwagon" wins, *Gone With the Wind*'s Oscar championship was indeed lost forever. Almost predictably in an era of televised films, *Ben-Hur* did poorly when reissued ten years later and its three-and-a-half-hour running time was at that time unmercifully butchered.

And by the end of 1960, when *Variety* published its annual list of all-time box-office grossers, significant changes showed *Gone With the Wind* no longer first there either. The late Cecil B. DeMille's *The Ten Commandments* was the new champion with total rentals of $34,200,000 while *Gone With the Wind* had fallen to second place with its constant $33,500,000. The other members of that select "top ten" were, in descending order: *Ben-Hur* (with *projected* rentals of $33,000,000), *Around the World in 80 Days* ($22,000,000), *The Robe* ($17,500,000), *South Pacific* ($16,300,000), *The Bridge on the River Kwai* ($15,000,000), *The Greatest Show on Earth* ($12,800,000), *From Here to Eternity* ($12,500,000) and *This Is Cinerama* ($12,500,000).

The intervening years had not dealt kindly with the *GWTW* family. The once idyllic marriage of Vivien Leigh and Laurence Olivier ended in divorce in 1960, while suicide had claimed Ona Munson in 1955 and George Reeves in 1959. Other notable *GWTW* deaths included William Cameron Menzies and Louis B. Mayer in 1957, Zack Williams in 1958, Olin Howland in 1959 and Louis Jean Heydt in 1960. In November of 1960, at the height of his fame on television, Ward Bond died of a heart attack, and only eleven days later "the King" himself was similarly stricken.

Clark Gable had accepted the leading role in John Huston's *The Misfits* opposite Marilyn Monroe, the actress who had gained worldwide popular, if not critical, acceptance in the Fifties. Unfortunately, Miss Monroe was also plagued with instability, insecurity and a total inability to work on schedule. The highly disciplined Mr. Gable had become increasingly aggravated by the unprofessional working approach Miss Monroe and others in the cast and crew exhibited on production of the film on its Nevada location during the hot summer months of 1960. He also foolishly volunteered to undertake his own strenuous stunt work in a horse-roping sequence for the film's conclusion. Within two days after his final retake on November 4, 1960, Clark was stricken with a serious heart attack and on November 16, while he was still hospitalized, a second heart attack took his life—exactly one month short of the twenty-first anniversary of *GWTW*'s premiere in Atlanta. With Clark at the time of his death was his fifth wife, the former Kay Williams, who was then expecting their child. *The Misfits*, albeit an uneven film, proved a fine farewell for the actor and many thought it his best performance since Rhett Butler. For the tragic Marilyn Monroe, it would also be a final film. Almost two years later, in early August 1962, shortly after being discharged by Fox for erratic attendance while filming a comedy with George Cukor, the actress was found dead from an overdose of barbiturates.

On March 20, 1961, John Clark Gable—the son his famous father never saw—was born in California. Eleven days earlier *Gone With the Wind* had returned to Atlanta with its most festive "premiere" celebration since 1939.

Marilyn Monroe and Clark Gable bid farewell to movie audiences in the United Artists film The Misfits.

1961: Civil War Centennial

While to many "Yankees" it seemed a strange idea for the South to be celebrating the hundredth anniversary of the Civil War, the actual inspiration behind it was historically admirable. The chartered purposes of the Civil War Centennial in 1961—little publicized in the North—included (of course) honoring and perpetuating the memory of Southerners who had fought and died for their principles. But it was also intended to actively locate and preserve monuments, graves, documents, diaries, manuscripts, photographs and other relics which could contribute accurate knowledge of the conflict to future generations.

Metro-Goldwyn-Mayer had arranged, long in advance, to tie-in a new Southern "premiere" of *Gone With the Wind* on March 10, 1961, with that noble endeavor, while the city of Atlanta prepared a Centennial Benefit Costume Ball to be held the night before at the Biltmore Hotel in an attempt to rival its gala 1939 predecessor. Honor guests at the ball included the governors of Alabama, Arkansas, Florida, Kentucky, Louisiana, Maryland, Virginia, North Carolina, Mississippi, Oklahoma, South Carolina, Tennessee, Texas and, naturally, Georgia. A movieland contingent was invited which included Vivien Leigh, Olivia de Havilland, David O. Selznick, Wilbur Kurtz and two unrelated Hollywood visitors, Douglas Fairbanks, Jr., and George Murphy. The master of ceremonies for the ball was William B. Hartsfield, still Mayor of Atlanta even though twenty-one years had elapsed.

Preliminary events, it was hoped, would duplicate as closely as possible those of the original in December 1939. The film's personnel were greeted at the airport with much ado and driven once again down a thronged Peachtree Street in separate open cars. Next came a visit to the Atlanta Cyclorama where Olivia de Havilland and Vivien Leigh, who had not seen each other in many years, engaged in a moving and nostalgic reunion. Olivia sensed then and through that night's ball, however, that the newly divorced Vivien was not well and, in fact, had problems remembering the original occasion.

At the following night's "premiere," Olivia later recalled, after entering Loew's Grand (decorated as it was in 1939) and viewing the film, both she and Vivien shivered at how many of the *GWTW* family were al-

Stephens Mitchell, Vivien Leigh, Douglas Fairbanks, Jr., George Murphy, David O. Selznick and Olivia de Havilland posed for photographers during the nostalgic 1961 pre-"premiere" ball in Atlanta.

ready dead. But Miss de Havilland found the picture's optimism unchanged and recalled how it had inspired the entire group of film workers. "We all believed in this picture," she said. "These were real people with weaknesses and strength, with happiness and unhappiness and tenderness and cruelty. Margaret Mitchell held a mirror to life: 'I'll think about it tomorrow' became a national catch line."

After Atlanta the reissued movie debuted—without such trimmings—in Los Angeles on March 24 at the Hollywood Paramount, and in New York City on April 26 at Broadway's Loew's State. Then, after similar first-run engagements throughout America and Canada, it journeyed downward through smaller theatres for the balance of the year. Amazingly, that 1961 reissue eventually returned $7,700,000 in rentals to M-G-M, and at the end of 1961 Gone With the Wind was the ninth-highest-grossing film of the year according to Variety's annual compilations (in a year when only ten films had earned $5,000,000 or more). Variety also noted that Gone With the Wind had recaptured its all-time box-office leadership as it listed the five champions (in order): Gone With the Wind (total rentals of $41,200,000), Ben-Hur ($40,000,000), The Ten Commandments ($34,200,000), Around the World in 80 Days ($22,000,000) and The Robe ($17,500,000).

By then the unfairness of such comparisons was obvious, since the second, third and fourth-place winners all shared the advantage of year-long (in some areas) advance-price first-run engagements. But such was the new concentration of movie marketing in the Sixties. Studios invested huge sums in "big" productions with the hope of reaping large rewards through these reserved-seat ("hard ticket" or "road show") bookings. This was a decided gamble that paid off handsomely in some cases (1960's Spartacus and 1961's West Side Story) but in many other instances failed miserably. Yet Hollywood needed a "gimmick" to lure television viewers from their homes and hoped it had found it in the hoopla surrounding reserved-seat films.

The condition of the American film industry in 1961 was documented by Time magazine with a "revisitation" review of Gone With the Wind (published in May 1961) in which the periodical stated, "Hollywood itself is practically dead but Gone With the Wind goes on forever." Time's commentary stirred heated controversy among the Wind's followers since, although intended as praise, it gave the film several rather backhanded compliments. After reporting current "block-long ticket lines and the weeping, cheering customers," the magazine dubbed GWTW "the greatest soap opera ever written." Time felt moved to use such phrases as "grand, simple-minded, 19th century story" and "splendid theatrical caricatures" in its description. Then, while suggesting that "Hattie McDaniel as Scarlett's hammy old mammy just about

waddles off with the show," it also noted, "The Jim Crow humor, acceptable to most audiences in 1939, will embarrass the average moviegoer today." Time also felt impelled to bring latter-day attention to "Producer David Selznick's rather tacky preference for gnarled trees silhouetted against flaming sunsets. The spectator sometimes gets a peculiar sensation that the picture has not really begun—he's still watching the travelogue." Although that notable publication's article enraged many of the picture's most devoted supporters, its intent was well-meaning in detailing the unique success of a 1939 film in a 1961 marketplace.

Time's feature story concluded with an observation which had already been noted by many of Gone With the Wind's repeat viewers. "Why," Time asked, "has the print been darkened? Every color has been tainted with sepia." It was suggested that this was merely the result of the aging of the original Technicolor, and the feature's writer described in detail the lengths to which M-G-M reportedly went in preserving the master negative and a master print called "the platinum yardstick" against which the colors on all subsequent prints were measured. But neither Time nor the public realized at that time what the color difficulties with Gone With the Wind really were. The expensive and technically exacting three-strip Technicolor photography process had been quickly abandoned by Hollywood filmmakers between 1952 and 1954 after the introduction of "monopack" techniques which employed Eastman stock film. Even the Technicolor Company was itself eventually forced to readapt to a "mono-pack"—or single-strip—process, which was clearly not comparable in results to its original technique, although some preferred it as "more realistic." In any case, the newer process was more economical in that it used only one-third as much film for negative production. Shortly after the one-strip innovation was introduced, many studios drifted away from Technicolor entirely and adapted Eastman film to be processed by their own laboratories with individual names like Metrocolor (for M-G-M), Warnercolor (for Warner Brothers) or DeLuxe Color (for Twentieth Century-Fox).

Those sepia tones observed in 1961 first-run engagements of GWTW had actually been caused by the Eastmancolor (Metrocolor) process used in new prints prepared by M-G-M for prestige bookings. The problem was not apparent to all that year, since many still-serviceable 1954 Tehnicolor prints were used for subsequent engagements which, despite the maskings and sporadic fadings, were still quite faithful to the original concept. And since there was such a mixture of prints in use in 1961, M-G-M was still able to use the term "Technicolor" in its advertising for that reissue. Of course, the master negative and "platinum yardstick" which Time reported on were of only the 1954 "masked" variety—not the 1939–1947 original.

Macmillan's 25th Anniversary Edition of Gone with the Wind *tied in nicely with the Civil War Centennial. Pictured here is an original 1961 deluxe offering surrounded by reproductions of artwork (included for the first time within the book) by artist Ben Stahl. Also included in the slipcased edition was an informative booklet about the book and its author (top center).*

1962-1975: Other Highlights

Vivien Leigh had been filming *The Roman Spring of Mrs. Stone* (with newcomer Warren Beatty) when she took a brief leave to attend the 1961 Atlanta festivities. The Tennessee Williams tragedy, released theatrically late that year, presented Vivien in another neurotic role and she was once again seen portraying an American woman. Miss Leigh embarked on a world tour with the Old Vic company in 1962 and shortly afterward returned to Broadway in a musical version of *Tovarich*. She received the Antoinette Perry ("Tony") Award for "Best Actress in a Musical" in the spring of 1963, but collapsed from exhaustion a few months later and withdrew from the play.

Vivien was top-billed in the all-star screen version of Katherine Anne Porter's 1962 best seller *Ship of Fools*, which was released by Columbia Pictures in 1965. Again the actress won critical acclaim for playing an American Southerner. In the spring of 1966, Miss Leigh made her last appearance on the New York stage in a revival of *Ivanov*.

Tuberculosis had intermittently plagued Vivien Leigh since 1945, and in mid-1967 a recurrence of it had confined her for several weeks. On July 7 she sent a birthday telegram to George Cukor, the man who had guided the screen tests which won her the role of Scarlett O'Hara. The next day she was found dead in her London home. In a gesture more fitting than any words that might have been written, London's theatres darkened their lights for an hour that night in silent tribute.

The motion-picture version of *Gone With the Wind* returned again in 1967 in a presentation that was advertised months in advance in major cities. The picture opened in the fall as part of the current "reserved-seat phenomenon," but unfortunately, in an effort to present it as something "new," M-G-M had felt inclined to magnify the film's image on seventy-millimeter film—regardless of which portions of the tops or bottoms of the frames were resultingly eliminated. As an added "bonus," the studio's technicians added an "electronically enhanced" stereophonic soundtrack (bearing no relation to the careful audio divisions made in 1954) which blared the music and amplified such incidental sounds as the rustle of hoopskirts but often drowned out important moments of dialogue. The total effect was often aesthetically offensive but—in a year when many other "hard ticket" films failed—the new version of *GWTW* was received with such enthusiasm that it was listed among *Variety*'s box-office leaders week after week and remained in some of its first-run engagements for a year or longer. Even though none of those debuts occurred until late in 1967, by the end of that year its all-time rentals had soared to $47,400,000 (an increase of $6,200,000 since the 1961 release). At the close of 1968, when first-run engagements had just about ended, *Variety* reported *GWTW* had reaped total rentals of $70,400,000. Nevertheless, *Gone With the Wind* had intermittently lost its championship (which it would not regain) to Twentieth Century-Fox's *The Sound of Music*. That popular Rodgers and Hammerstein musical film, which won the Academy Award as "Best Picture of 1965," had the benefit of those higher-priced reserved tickets, and was undisputed victor by the end of 1968 with a total of $72,000,000 in rentals.

The producer of *Gone With the Wind* had not lived to see its triumph in the late Sixties. David O. Selznick had died in Hollywood on June 22, 1965—only an hour after being stricken by a heart attack. Mr. Selznick had devoted much of his later life to supervising the career of his actress-wife Jennifer Jones and had been fairly inactive in the film industry since producing *A Farewell to Arms* in 1957. But when he died, at age sixty-three, David was in the midst of plans for a return to an active producing career. Among the titles he had registered for the future with the Motion Picture Association of America (all of which were revealed shortly after his death) was *Scarlett O'Hara*—for his long-planned musical version of his most famous film.

David Selznick had also expressed interest through the years in bringing *GWTW* to the stage. Little more than a year after his death, on November 3, 1966, the Margaret Mitchell story finally did reach the stage—in Japan! Rights for the five-hour production had been licensed from and sanctioned by Stephens Mitchell, who wrote an introduction for the Japanese souvenir program. The play, despite its length and its twenty-one scenes, covered only the first half of the novel. The following summer, a second play—covering the novel's second half—opened at the same Imperial Theatre in Tokyo where its predecessor had run for five months and had played one hundred ninety-seven performances to a total attendance of 380,000. The second play, which ran four hours, also achieved huge commercial success in Japan and ran for four months. A combined version of both plays opened there in the fall of 1967 and was slightly condensed to run a total of six hours.

Then on January 2, 1970, a musical version called *Scarlett*, with music and lyrics by America's Harold

Rome and book by Kazuo Kikuta, premiered at the Imperial in Tokyo. This production, which was directed and choreographed by Broadway's Joe Layton, had encountered so many difficulties in its inception that Florence Rome, wife of the composer, wrote a humorous account of it in a book called *The Scarlett Letters*.

A little more than two years later, on May 3, 1972, an English translation of the Harold Rome musical version premiered at London's Drury Lane Theatre and local newspapers reported that it was the costliest show ever produced on the London stage, with an estimated budget of $450,000. But the magic formula seemed to have left *Gone with the Wind* at that point, for the British production received many poor critical notices. A slightly altered adaptation opened in Los Angeles on August 28, 1973, and in San Francisco on October 23, 1973, but its reception was even more unkind. June Ritchie and Harve Presnell had portrayed Scarlett and Rhett in England while Lesley Ann Warren and Pernell Roberts inherited those roles for the American version.

America's once-staid values underwent drastic changes throughout the Sixties and the resulting "new morality" swept in a wave of permissiveness in motion pictures. The Hollywood film industry—struggling harder than ever to survive—hoped that more mature themes would lure Americans back to a moviegoing habit. The Motion Picture Association of America relaxed its former restrictions and introduced a rating system in 1968 by which audiences could judge in advance whether a film was suitable for individual or family viewing. *Gone With the Wind*—in the midst of its most lucrative reissue—was granted the most acceptable rating of all: "G"—approved for general (or all) audiences. And even the Catholic Church felt impelled by then to change its mind on the film. The National Catholic Office for Motion Pictures (formerly the Legion of Decency) reclassified *GWTW* as "morally unobjectionable for adults and adolescents." The Church body issued a laudatory and lengthy review of the reissued film which stated: "The social changes following World War II have made what once appeared

Olivia de Havilland, Mayor Allen of Atlanta, Susan Myrick, Stephens Mitchell, Evelyn Keyes, Victor Jory and Ann Rutherford at the festive premiere of the 70-millimeter version of GWTW *held at Loew's Grand on October 4, 1967.*

The technical process used by M-G-M to enlarge GWTW *to 70 millimeter obviously eliminated a portion of the original screen image.*

as daring scenes seem almost innocent on the screen today."

With the new permissiveness in America came a wave of "nostalgia" as Americans looked longingly—and often humorously—toward more naive eras. In the late Sixties and early Seventies more books on movies were published than in almost all previous years put together. *Gone With the Wind*, its players and creative forces were, quite naturally, included in a great many of these. Bosley Crowther selected it as one of *The Great Films*, his 1967 tribute to the international history of cinema—which was comprised of his choices of the fifty most important films ever made. Mr. Crowther wrote of it: "Of all the American motion pictures entitled to be designated great on the basis of *all* their qualifications, including the extent of the excitement they have caused, one towers above all

the rest. . . . there has never been one more effective than *Gone With the Wind*. There may never be." Unfortunately, Mr. Crowther erroneously informed his readers that Victor Fleming had died during *GWTW*'s production.

Bosley Crowther was not alone in making such a mistake. Despite the entertainment values of the new movie books, many of them were filled with just such gross errors—leaving a dubious heritage for future historians. While some of these came from faulty scholarship, there were other contributing factors—most notably that Hollywood people themselves often remembered things incorrectly. To a great many of them filmmaking in the "golden era" had been just a job. They rarely kept notes or diaries and relied on distant memories (which were often confused) when recalling the past for author-interviewers.

Gavin Lambert seemed to have been a victim of this in preparing *GWTW: The Making of Gone With the Wind*, which was published in 1973. Mr. Lambert, a successful novelist (*Inside Daisy Clover*), had touched upon *GWTW* previously in his book *On Cukor* in 1970. But he had interviewed many of the film's survivors for his later book and came to such dubious conclusions as that no entire scene was ever cut from *GWTW*, and that the final retake of the opening scene was filmed in August 1939 and that Sam Wood had directed it. The author also attributed a passage from the movieola script to the pen of David Selznick (when the words belonged to Margaret Mitchell) and claimed that dialogue was cut from the film when it actually had been retained.

Metro-Goldwyn-Mayer had undergone several management changes in that era and the quality of its film production had slipped noticeably. On May 3, 1970, the studio put its historic sets, props and costumes up for public auction—signaling what many regarded as the end of an empire. Although *Gone With the Wind* ended its fourth official reissue in 1969, the studio kept it in constant circulation for the next six years to bring in much-needed theatrical revenue. In the fall of 1973 an even more significant change occurred when M-G-M bowed out of the distribution business and signed an agreement with United Artists to distribute its new and older films. Had it not been for the popularity of Clark Gable, United Artists might have distributed *GWTW* upon its first release. Twenty-four years later the film finally came into its domain.

Had *Gone With the Wind* been a United Artists release it might have played the Radio City Music Hall, as all the other Selznick International pictures had. (Its extreme length had always made that seem doubtful, however.) By 1975 the Music Hall itself had undergone significant changes and at times booked revivals when no

M-G-M's ads for the 1967 reissue evoked an eroticism the studio felt was in keeping with America's new morality.

suitable new films were available. So it was—on April 24, 1975—that history's most famous film finally played at the world's most famous movie theatre. The one-week engagement was a financially rewarding one for the Music Hall, as it drew crowds of primarily younger patrons.

Alice Payne Hackett's *70 Years of Best Sellers 1895–1965* listed *GWTW* as all-time hardcover fiction leader with reported sales of 5,170,004 copies. In the combined hardcover and paperback fields the Margaret Mitchell novel finished fourth (to *Peyton Place*, *In His Steps* and *God's Little Acre*) with sales of 6,978,211 copies. In the next decade several other novels broke existing sales records and, as in former days, most of them became financially successful movies. *Valley of the Dolls*, *Airport* and *Love Story* became box-office victors and they also broke television rating records when subsequently unveiled on the home medium. Three other books—*The Godfather*, *The Exorcist* and *Jaws*—served as bases for films so successful in accruing revenues that they eventually joined *The Sound of Music* in topping *Gone With the Wind* on *Variety*'s all-time list of champions.

A poster for the Japanese stage version of Gone With the Wind *which opened in Toyko in 1966 (from the Herb Bridges Collection).*

The Herb Bridges Collection

Herb Bridges posed here with a few of the many foreign editions included in his collection.

An original "neighborhood" poster from the 1939 release.

Original lobby posters—handmade of wood—were rescued by Mr. Bridges from Loew's Grand shortly before they were due for destruction.

Various Japanese editions, especially in later years, employed movie scenes on their covers.

Autant en Emporte le Vent *was the title of the many French editions published through the years.*

269

*Among other interesting covers of foreign editions
in the Bridges collection were those from Italy (above
left in hardcover and above right in a four-volume
paperback edition), Spain (below left in paperback),
Portugal (a two-volume paperback edition below
center) and Germany (hardcover, below right).*

Other interesting editions from the Bridges collection included Finland (above left), Belgium (a rare World War II edition, above center), Vietnam (above right), Sweden (slipcased edition, center/center), Norway (center right), Poland (below left), Lebanon (below center) and Latvia (below right).

Denmark was another country which published many interestingly adorned editions of Gone with the Wind.

China

Yugoslavia

Typical foreign editions of the novel: Israel (top left), Finland (top right), Yugoslavia (bottom right), Egypt (bottom left).

It was many years before Gone with the Wind *became a paperback, but from 1954 through 1969 it was issued by Pocket Books in six different cover versions* (top and center rows, *chronologically arranged) and later by Avon Books* (below left) *and its subsidiary Flare imprint (larger edition,* below right).

Throughout her life as an author, Margaret Mitchell was plagued by pirated foreign editions, such as those pictured above.

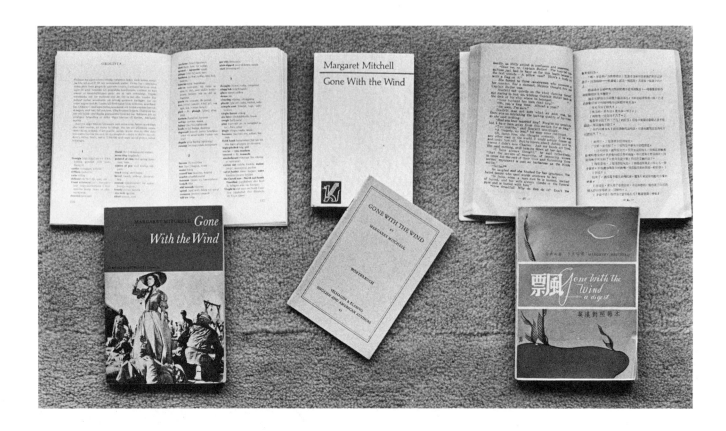

Gone with the Wind was so well thought of by countries like China and Sweden that it was used in schools to teach English as a second language (above). Below, *two of the limited editions issued by the R. H. Macy Company which achieved significant sales after their American Book Club two-volume sets were released in 1968 (with a piece of representative artwork pictured).*

The "RHETT BUTLER" BOW OF TODAY
INSPIRED BY
"RHETT BUTLER"
PORTRAYED BY CLARK GABLE IN
GONE WITH THE WIND

A SELZNICK INTERNATIONAL PICTURE • PRODUCED BY DAVID O. SELZNICK • A METRO-GOLDWYN-MAYER RELEASE

Herb Bridges always tried to find those collectibles which related to the book rather than to the movie. He didn't have too much luck. But pictured here, find a few of each. Above left: *A dress tag used for the GWTW garments, which were highly popular in the late Thirties.* Above right: *An advertisement for the "Rhett Butler" bowtie.* Below left: GWTW *bookends, which were inspired by the book.* Below right: *Bookends which copied the likenesses of Clark Gable and Vivien Leigh and were inspired, of course, by the movie version.*

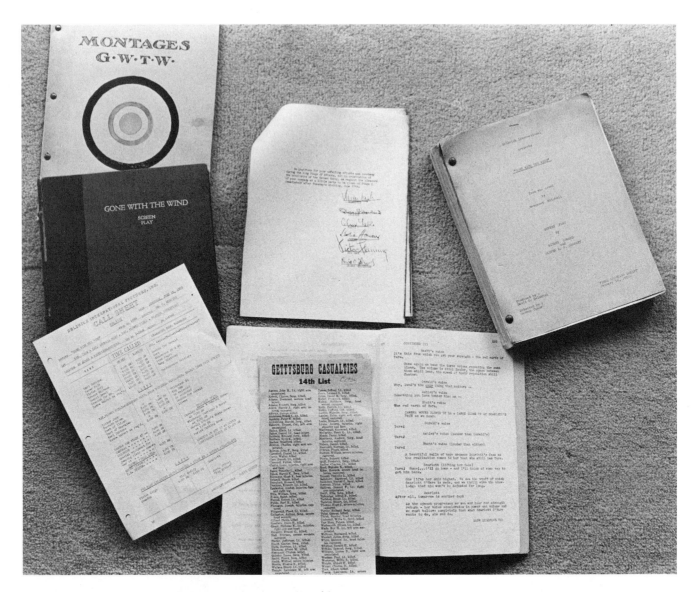

The filming of the movie yielded many individual collectibles which were, by their very nature, exceedingly rare. Pictured above (counterclockwise from top left): A "montage" script for battle sequences which were never actually produced; a leatherbound presentation copy of the final script given to cast and crew members; a daily "call sheet" issued to the company during production, listing the following day's agenda; a "Gettysburg casualty list" with the "W" names repeated throughout so Miss Leigh could spot them easily; (underneath) an original shooting script; a Sidney Howard/ Oliver H. P. Garrett script which listed George Cukor as director; an invitation to the cast party.

At right: The miniature train used by Selznick's special effects department for the closeup of an about-to-explode munitions boxcar in the depot-burning sequence.

Above: *The seven different pressbooks sent to theatre exhibitors suggesting advertising ideas and merchandising tie-in publicity gimmicks for the film's initial engagements and its various "returns" and reissues.*

At right: *The Gone With the Wind Cook Book, which was offered as a "premium" for several tie-in products from the film's original release until 1954.*

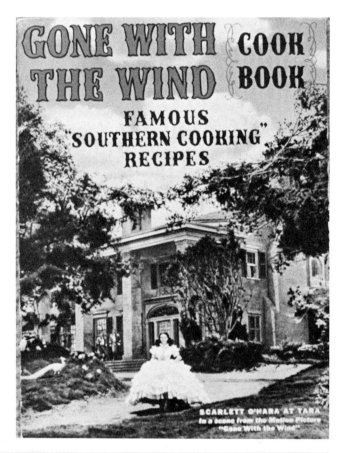

Pictured below: *Some of the famous Scarlett O'Hara dolls dressed in a variety of costumes which represented different scenes in the film, together with a GWTW paper doll book, a folio of paper doll costumes, a paintbook and an original 1939 ad for the first two dolls available.*

From top left (counterclockwise): *A Scarlett O'Hara game which was, inside, merely called "Bet Chu Can't"; Nunnally's package of chocolates designed to resemble a book (with a photograph of Vivien Leigh on its cover) and the color photo which came inside; a Rhett Butler statuette; a Scarlett O'Hara perfume decanter; an advertisement and sample product which claimed "Margaret Mitchell rolled her own" (meaning cigarettes then)—although the lady in the ad was clearly not the famous Atlanta author; an ad, and sample premium, for the Scarlett cameo brooch; GWTW handkerchiefs and scarf laid across a GWTW dress pattern.*

Above: *The Herb Bridges collection yielded an extremely valuable representation of the theatrical posters and lobby cards from the motion picture's first release.*

Below: *But there were also fascinating and magnificently printed four-color movie posters from Norway* (top left), *Sweden* (center), *Finland* (top right), *a Finland/Sweden combination* (below left) *and one from the 1961 reissue in Denmark.*

Above: *Exquisite full-color posters were distributed for later reissues of* Gone With the Wind *in Japan.*

Below (top row, left to right): *A poster from Argentina, one from Belgium (in French), one from Spain and another from Germany; (bottom row, left to right): A 1954 poster from Holland, one from Belgium (in Dutch), another from Italy and (bottom center) a rare lobby card from Poland.*

Miscellaneous memorabilia from the Japanese musical production in 1970, above, and from the British musical production in 1972, below.

1976 AND THE FUTURE
Will the Fever Subside?

"Look for it only in books, for it is no more than a dream remembered . . . A civilization gone with the wind . . ."

—From the prologue to
David O. Selznick's
1939 motion picture

A Sequel

Nineteen hundred and seventy-six . . . a presidential election year, an Olympiad and the celebration of a very important American anniversary . . . the technology of the United States soared to unbelievable new heights and the monarchy of England was much in the country's thoughts . . . there were news items about Margaret Mitchell, Rudolph Valentino, Shirley Temple, the Book-of-the-Month Club, silent movies and the National Broadcasting Company . . . amid criticism of the Academy Awards structure, one motion picture won all five of Hollywood's top honors . . . King Kong *and* A Star Is Born *were the year's most eagerly awaited films . . . and speculation was rampant as to who would portray Scarlett O'Hara and Rhett Butler on the screen . . .*

In the words of oldtime moviegoers, "Wasn't this where we came in?" No, fifty years had passed since Margaret Mitchell began writing her novel and a full forty years since Macmillan published its most famous book. Commercial aviation, just a hope half a century before, had advanced to a stage where regular flights circled the world in a mode of travel which provided every comfort for passengers from enjoying a cocktail to watching an old Clark Gable movie. The triumph of Richard Byrd's 1926 voyage to the North Pole faded in the light of America's Viking spacecraft, which made a perfect landing on planet Mars in mid-July, seven years to the day after the country's first arrival on the moon. Television, also a dream in 1926, brought spectacular photographs of that mysterious vista before the eyes of the world immediately thereafter. However, the United States was even more troubled by problems of alienated youth, drug addiction and alcoholism and had not yet come to terms with its racial differences.

As 1976 began, almost all of the country's focus was on America's two-hundredth Birthday Party scheduled for the Fourth of July. Ironically, in the midst of that mighty and progressive year, *Gone with the Wind* was experiencing its largest popularity since the premiere of the Selznick film.

The Macmillan Publishing Company found focus on *Gone with the Wind* required its primary efforts for pur-

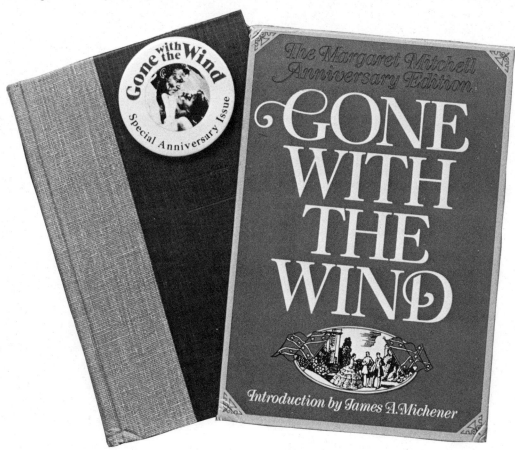

The anniversary edition of the novel published by Macmillan in 1975.

Life-sized poster used by the Macmillan sales force at the 1976 American Booksellers Association Convention in Chicago.

poses of both business and sentiment from the very beginning of 1976, as it prepared a printing of its history-making novel's eighty-fifth regular edition. When later challenged that this new issue retailed at $9.95, more than three times the 1936 price, Macmillan people liked to point out that Atlanta's other leading national contribution, Coca-Cola, had multiplied in price to a far greater degree in that time span. Since the company was also preparing publication of a book concerning the movie and another devoted to Margaret Mitchell's *GWTW* correspondence, Macmillan decided the fortieth anniversary of the novel's publication was a milestone important enough to be celebrated at the American Booksellers Association convention and trade exhibit that spring.

Scarlett, Rhett, and a Cast of Thousands, published early in Macmillan's busy year, was a collection of anecdotes surrounding the filming of David Selznick's movie version. Author Roland Flamini, a Los Angeles correspondent for *Time* magazine, had expanded on the

subject already described by Gavin Lambert in 1973 by incorporating additional published and unpublished material and leaning heavily on the Louella Parsons columns of the 1936–1939 period. His account traveled from attempts to sell the film rights through the Atlanta world premiere and discussed such legendary themes as "The Search for Scarlett," which climaxed in "the burning of Atlanta" in December 1938. Along the way there were "confidential" revelations, gossip, power struggles, feuds and scandals, all falling together in an entertaining, easily read fable. The volume was heavily illustrated with photos of casting candidates, behind-the-camera shots and many of the most beloved scenes from the film itself.

Reader's Digest was impressed enough with Roland Flamini's research to arrange a condensation for their October 1976 issue, which was published under the heading "The Greatest Movie Ever Made" and featured a full-color reproduction of the 1967 poster art. Mr. Flamini's book was an exceptionally well-received item for

Macmillan, being reprinted three times during the first half of the year. The New York publisher had every reason then to be optimistic about its upcoming *Margaret Mitchell's GONE WITH THE WIND Letters*, edited by Richard Harwell, and to anticipate renewed success for its forty-year-old novel in general.

Chicago was the city selected for the seventy-sixth annual American Booksellers Association convention in early June, where a gathering of five hundred exhibitors represented virtually every publisher and many other related industries. The estimated eight thousand visitors to the four-day event milled through the huge McCormick Place meeting center and gave optimistic proof of increased activity in book sales. This, of course, delighted those who had outdone each other in arranging booth displays to impress the book buyers from America's retail stores. Macmillan had selected a show-business motif with an impressive marquee billboard whereon the slogan "*GWTW*: Success Every Step of the Way" adorned a massive blowup of the movie's "Bazaar" sequence. The proud announcement was accompanied by enlarged covers of a standard *GWTW*, its 1975 Anniversary Edition, Mr. Flamini's account of the filming, and the upcoming collection of *Letters*, which was among the company's more predictable successes for the fall 1976 season.

The upsurge in paperback sales was a much-discussed trend among ABA attendees, and New American Library did not miss the opportunity to arrange a "sneak preview" of Twentieth Century-Fox's *The Omen* to publicize its upcoming Signet novelization. Avon Books devoted booth and catalog space to its new paperback issue of *GWTW*, slated for September release, with appropriate references to the movie's upcoming telecast. Poster displays showed their fall printing would be carrying a new cover design, as would a similarly released "trade" volume under the publisher's Equinox imprint.

America's massive two hundredth Birthday Party began in northeastern Maine when the first dawn of July 4, 1976, was experienced at 4:31 A.M. It continued with a symbolic lighting—by converted starlight—of Paul Revere lantern replicas in Boston, and lasted, from coast to coast, almost until the next dawn's early light. In Philadelphia—site of the country's original decision to pursue freedom—to the delight of over a million celebrants, President Gerald Ford initiated festivities which included a reenactment of signing the Declaration of Independence and a careful striking of the cracked Liberty Bell. The President—and the country's attention via television—was then taken to the U.S.S. *Forrestal* on New York's Hudson River where he, Prince Rainier and Princess Grace of Monaco along with three thousand guests accompanied the carrier, which acted as host ship for the day's most heralded event. On this panoramic stage of water 212 sailing crafts from 34 nations,

including 16 of the world's tallest ships, journeyed northward and were joined by an estimated thirty thousand smaller boats filled with uninvited patriots.

Throughout the country celebrations continued, in places like New Orleans, where a statue of great black American jazz musician Louis Armstrong was unveiled, and Miami, Chicago and Detroit, where many thousands who had chosen that day to attain citizenship enlisted in mass naturalization ceremonies. For more than two hours flower-laden floats paraded down Atlanta's Peachtree Street where, had fate ruled differently, John and Peggy Marsh might have been avid spectators as they celebrated their fifty-first wedding anniversary. It was an emotion-filled day of marches, music, parties, flags and sentiment. Through the convenience of television, the patriotic and the curious could sample all the highlights without leaving the cool comfort of their homes and armchairs. As the unique event concluded with a Boston concert and spectacular fireworks at the Statue of Liberty, it seemed the infant home medium had never been more happily welcome as it personally included and collectively united the entire American nation.

The Bicentennial gala, unfortunately, brought with it an inundation of merchandising tie-ins that far outweighed any entertainment phenomenon of the past and ranged from the inspiring to the amusing to the downright insulting. The American public was defenseless before a commercial deluge that began long before 1976 and continued many months after the July celebration. Almost every manufacturer found a way to work his product into this Bicentennial bonanza as stars, stripes, red, white and blue were everywhere. In addition to free local reminders like tricolor fire hydrants, window or in-store displays, and an unprecedented coverage by the media, there were T-shirts, caskets, posters, bumper stickers, dolls, plates, food boxes, beer cans, window curtains, candy, toys, beach towels, recordings, even paper towels and trash cans. One hoped many of the more offensive items would not become collectors' items but —at some later date—they undoubtedly would (even the caskets?).

Among the more highly regarded enterprises connected with the Bicentennial was the American Freedom Train, which had begun a twenty-one-month tour in April 1975. The half-mile-long caravan journeyed by rail from coast to coast, stopping for a few days in smaller cities in each of the states, where the public was invited, for a relatively small fee, to tour ten railroad cars on a moving walkway and see 750 artifacts representing America's origin, growth, arts and innovations. Historical memorabilia on display ranged from George Washington's copy of the Constitution and the original Archibald M. Willard painting *The Spirit of '76* to Hank Aaron's homerun baseball and bat. Car number eight was devoted to "The Performing Arts" and its almost fifty featured items inspired

memories of America's vast entertainment history: Shirley Temple's teddy bear, Fred Astaire's top hat, Alfred Hitchcock's director's chair, Judy Garland's *Wizard of Oz* dress and Robert Redford's suit from *The Sting*. There, too, along with vintage movie cameras, "Oscar," "Emmy" and *Look* magazine awards, were Clark Gable's bound presentation script of *Gone With the Wind* and a brooch worn by Vivien Leigh in the role of Scarlett O'Hara.

Only a few days after the July 4th spectacle, while "Bicentennial Fever" was still raging, Queen Elizabeth II and Prince Philip paid America a courtesy visit. The royal couple engaged in protocol and sightseeing tours through Philadelphia, New York City, Washington, D.C., Boston and Newport, being honored by a White House state dinner along the way. England's gracious monarch gifted the United States with a second "Liberty Bell" from her country, which, she said, had learned a valuable lesson from her former colonies' fight for independence. It seemed, humorously, that perhaps—200 years after the fact—the British had finally forgiven the upstarts who separated from them.

Also proving that time had brought forgiveness, Olivia de Havilland flew from her Paris home in July to officiate at the opening of a Warner Brothers retrospective at New York's Regency Theatre. Forgetting her former legal problems with that studio, Olivia told the first-night audience of the ten-week, thirty-four-film revival that little did Hollywoodites in the Thirties think their films would someday become classics or that they would indeed be remembered for more than a year or two.

These revivals were by no means unusual in a year which witnessed the temporary closing of six of New York City's major theatres from sheer lack of new films. There were collective tributes to stars like Humphrey Bogart, Bette Davis and Katharine Hepburn, to musicals and comedies and to California studios such as M-G-M, Twentieth Century-Fox and even Selznick International. Some theatres in various cities devoted themselves entirely to vintage Hollywood movies. The Walt Disney organization, which had always reissued its cartoon classics on a periodic basis, suddenly seemed to have most of them in circulation at the same time. And even though television rights had already been sold to *Gone With the Wind* and *2001: A Space Odyssey*, M-G-M kept these perennial moneymarkers in theatrical circulation until immediately before their premiere broadcasts. Unfortunately, the constantly lucrative position of *GWTW* had prevented it from being part of those festivals honoring Mr. Selznick's work, even though they now included the once lost *Nothing Sacred* and *A Star Is Born*. Nostalgia was in evidence everywhere, not only in revivals of past productions but as a direct influence, perhaps out of necessity, on the films that were currently being made.

Having destroyed virtually everything in sight during their "disaster" cycle, film producers leaned more heavily on the past than ever before. The two most heralded ventures of the year were reinterpreted classics whose originals had long been associated with David O. Selznick's name and were much beloved by theatrical and television audiences. Both also carried echoes of Mr. Selznick's 1939 travails, entering production as the year began and racing through completion to meet December premieres for Academy Award consideration—and gathering a great deal of publicity along the way.

The third version of *A Star Is Born* featured an updated background of the rock music world, with Barbra Streisand and Kris Kristofferson essaying roles created in the 1937 Selznick original by Janet Gaynor and Fredric March and in the 1954 Warner remake by Judy Garland and James Mason. Forced by legal restrictions to begin filming before a finished script, cast or songs had been established, the new Warner Brothers musical had been in planning stages for over a year prior to its January 1976 starting point. Actual production was peppered with rumors of feuds, temperament and misunderstandings—all duly noted in magazine features and newspaper columns. Nevertheless, reports indicated that the project had finally finished on schedule and within its budget. It was also fated to reap a box-office fortune.

King Kong, however, was an ape of quite a different color. Italian producer Dino de Laurentiis had, during his career, managed many fine films from *La Strada* through *Serpico*, but was also responsible for *Mandingo*.

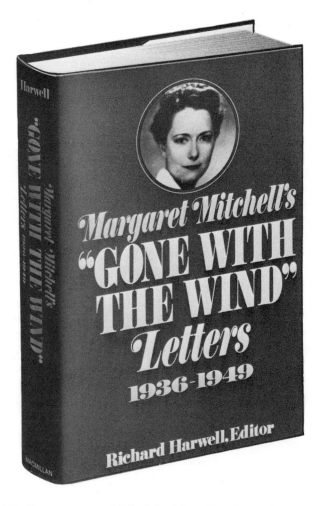

The Letters *were published by Macmillan in 1976.*

This movie mogul personally envisioned a mammoth new version of RKO's 1933 masterpiece only after seeing a poster of the original in his daughter's bedroom. While it is true that many works of art have been engendered from even more trivial whims, this 1976 venture involved $24,000,000 for a film two hours and fifteen minutes in length, rather short for the cost involved.

Mr. de Laurentiis and his studio, Paramount, optimistically looked for domestic grosses of between $50,000,000 and $100,000,000 and hoped to have the most profitable film in history. (Despite a huge promotion and advertising campaign, *King Kong* would fall far short of that goal.) The production, it seemed, had been beset by more difficulties than any such prior endeavor. *Gone With the Wind* seemed like child's play compared to the reports emanating from the Hollywood locations. This comparison was ironically fascinating since Merian C. Cooper and Ernest B. Schoedsack's 1933 *King Kong* had financially (though not creatively) fallen under David O. Selznick's supervision at RKO.

First, a competition with Universal Studios, which planned a simultaneous version (remember *Jezebel*?), forced filming to begin before the mechanical ape was ready to perform (Universal eventually withdrew for a monetary consideration). Then, of course, there was the mandatory "search for an unknown" to play the lady whose charms enticed *Kong* and led to his destruction. It was reported about then that Fay Wray, star of the original *King Kong*, had been offered a small part in the remake but refused on the grounds that such a classic should *not* be redone. Useful publicity was generated by the construction of a forty-foot mechanical gorilla costing almost $2,000,000—which would be used in some sequences. However, this good was almost counteracted by the reactions of civil rights leaders to an ad placed by the moviemakers for a tall, well-built black man to play the monkey in the balance of Kong's scenes. Finally, mechanical breakdowns of the gorilla's hand, so crucially needed for closeups, added further to a delay caused by flea infestation in the huge ape model's horsetail hair covering.

The original *King Kong* had been a phenomenon of the Depression era when Americans desperately sought escapism in the movies. Yet its mythology continued to mesmerize audiences forty-three years later. While *Jaws* had been similarly themed—terror attacks by a beast of nature—it contained more than a thread of reality, since great white sharks have always existed. Whether a forty-foot ape would be accepted by sophisticated America in a wide-screen version where the special effects were discernible seemed comparatively unimportant to a Paramount publicist who, in midyear, far from modestly declared, "This film has already generated more audience excitement than any film since *Gone With the Wind.*"

A new trend that hopefuly would not last, inspired by

the deluge of Hollywood nostalgia books in the past few years, concerned some rather curious biographies of movie immortals. *W.C. Fields and Me* was based on Carlotta Monti's book of remembrances and succeeded principally through the creative efforts of Rod Steiger as the famed comedian. *Gable and Lombard*, however, had only the title in common with Warren G. Harris's 1974 dual biography as it strangely twisted facts for the screenplay's own convenience. Earnest performances in the title roles by James Brolin and Jill Clayburgh could not overcome such distortions as placing their legendary first meeting in 1935—three years after they had co-starred in *No Man of Her Own.*

In a *New York Times* feature piece entitled "Gable Never Made a Turkey Like This," critic Vincent Canby suggested it was "one of the dumbest big-budget movies of 1976." Mr. Canby further described a rather startling re-creation: "The film takes us onto the set of *Gone With the Wind* during the shooting of the scene in which Rhett Butler accompanies Scarlett out of the flaming Atlanta. If *Gable and Lombard* were just a tiny bit better, the effect of this curious piracy—featuring a sort of dumpy 'Vivien Leigh'—would be to diminish one's fond memories of *GWTW*. It doesn't do anything to memories though." (For actress Morgan Brittany, who as Scarlett had drawn Mr. Canby's rather graphic displeasure, it was charitable to realize that she had an awfully tough act to follow.) The film was awarded a "Restricted" (for adults) rating by the Motion Picture Code Administration because of the producers' inspiration to recreate Miss Lombard's fabled fondness for spicy epithets. They were not inspired, however, to convey her artistry which in the movies' "Age of Innocence," was in no way influenced by her private vocabulary.

The film industry honored Rudolph Valentino on the fiftieth anniversary of his death in August with a tributary film showing, while, at Hollywood's Memorial Park Cemetery, over one thousand still-devoted fans gathered in silent homage to an actor whose voice had never been heard on screen. Director Ken Russell simultaneously began a motion-picture biography of the legendary performer in England with the ballet world's Rudolf Nureyev in the title role. The James Dean legend lived on twenty-one years after the actor's death, first in an ABC television movie and later in the production of a theatrical film entitled *9/30/55*, detailing the after-effects Mr. Dean's early death had on young Americans of his time. It was also evidence of the curious 1976 phenomenon when Bantam's paperback edition of *East of Eden*, then in its forty-second printing, featured James Dean's image on its cover even more prominently than author John Steinbeck's name. But, again, whether in trying to recapture the starlight of its former personalities or in remaking older films, Bicentennial Hollywood was indeed getting most of its inspiration from the past.

Actor-producer-director Tom Laughlin, who had recently shown remarkable acumen in marketing a series of "Billy Jack" films, took the same trip Frank Capra had taken in 1939 through the updated *Billy Jack Goes to Washington.* Meanwhile, a resurrection of 1932's Oscar-winning *Grand Hotel* was planned by M-G-M as a handy commercial for its Las Vegas enterprise, with the remake budgeted at between $8,000,000 and $10,000,000. Other producers showed a leaning toward the literary classics with planned fresh interpretations of *Gulliver's Travels, The Prince and the Pauper* and *The Prisoner of Zenda.* Radio City Music Hall's Christmas present was *The Slipper and the Rose*, a British retelling of *Cinderella*, and—a world away in taste—different breeds of moviemakers decided *Cinderella* and *The Wizard of Oz* would be delightful bases for pornographic films.

Even producers Richard Zanuck and David Brown, riding high on the tail of *Jaws*, realized the potentials of the past with a proposed expensive remake of H. G. Wells' *The War of the Worlds* as a future Universal Studios–Paramount Pictures collaboration. The Zanuck-Brown team was also zealously involved in another preeminent 1976 phenomenon "The Sequel!" Their future schedule listed productions of both *The Sting II* and *Jaws II* although "shark fever" had by then prompted so many theatrical and television imitations that the public had begun to think it had already seen the latter.

The old theory that "nothing succeeds like success" had become proven fact with the monetary returns of *The Godfather, Part II, Airport 1975* and *That's Entertainment, Part 2*, thereby driving movie executives into a frenzy of "sequelizations" never before witnessed to such extremes even in trend-conscious Hollywood. Box-office success of a film seemed to automatically generate a movie follow-up announcement. Within six months of its debut Paramount reported an upcoming sequel to *The Bad News Bears*, a Walter Matthau and Tatum O'Neal romp that had scored a financial home run with its light account of little league baseball. Not to be outdone, Olivia de Havilland joined the sequel trail with Jack Lemmon, James Stewart and Lee Grant in Universal's third go-round of Arthur Hailey's original concept entitled *Airport 1977.* And Richard Burton gained two new leading ladies, Oscar-winner Louise Fletcher and once-possessed Linda Blair, in *Exorcist II: The Heretic.*

Still more 1976 continuations included *Part 2 Sounder, The Pink Panther Strikes Again, The Return of a Man Called Horse*, a new "James Bond" epic, a further "Dirty Harry" episode, *Futureworld* and the inelegantly titled *Poor White Trash, Part 2*. Other plans were under way for additional chapters to *The Guns of Navarone, The Poseidon Adventure, The Happy Hooker* and even further exploits of "Rooster Cogburn." Erich Segal, who had novelized his screenplay *Love Story* into the book-movie combination of all time, promised to pursue it in *Oliver's Story*.

Inspired by 1973's bonanza *The Exorcist*, Twentieth Century-Fox's chilling *The Omen* was a triumph for them and inspired the studio's announcement of *three* separate sequels following the anti-Christ child to manhood, with the fourth film eventually depicting "the end of the world." Meanwhile, New American Library's Signet version of *The Omen*, which had been novelized by the original screenwriter, David Seltzer, and published simultaneously with release of the film, became the best-selling paperback in America at the same time the film was the nation's ultimate attraction. One publishing executive publicly declared that these "movies-into-books" were the surest thing for paperback success next to a best-seller reprint. However, the past's most successful "novelizations," from *The Human Comedy* down through *Love Story* and *Summer of '42*, had begun their careers in hardcover. *The Omen* gave every indication of becoming history's biggest such success in a book prepared directly for the paperback market, an important milestone in light of the year's most surprising *Gone With the Wind* event.

In view of these trends, it should not have come as such momentous news—but it did—that *Gone With the Wind* was to be "sequelized." For official records, the first announcement appeared in morning newspapers on June 9, 1976, and the initial reports were, to understate the case, rather confusing. All that was certain at first was that Richard Zanuck and David Brown, producers of the phenomenal *Jaws*, had acquired necessary rights from the estate of Margaret Mitchell and from Metro-Goldwyn-Mayer. M-G-M would be a co-equal in the new motion picture with Universal Pictures, Zanuck-Brown's home studio, and a novel was to be written for publication concurrent with release of the movie.

The New York Times quoted a spokesman for the producers saying, "We don't want to be known as spenders but as filmmakers. Also we don't have to burn down Atlanta. It's already in ashes when we start." Reports in various other papers disclosed that the sequel's turn of events would take Scarlett and Rhett through the South's Reconstruction period. Quite obviously, the press agent selected was not familiar with either the book or the movie, since Atlanta had already been rebuilt and the Reconstruction Era virtually completed at the conclusions of both the Mitchell and Selznick versions. Nevertheless, it was exciting to see the large amount of media coverage devoted to this announcement under such headings as "*Gone With the Wind* Is Not Quite Gone," "Will Rhett Give a Damn After All?," "Back With the Wind" and "Tomorrow Is Another Movie."

Variety offered some welcome clarity to the proceedings with a large feature article detailing a three-month negotiation period that had climaxed with the surprise press announcement. These dealings, it seemed, had been going on since early in the year with the Margaret Mitchell Estate, represented by a firm called International Creative Management. The paper went on to explain that the "unusual aspect to the sequel project is that M-G-M already held such rights outside the U.S. to *GWTW* so nobody could make a second film without Metro (unless for the domestic market alone; a business absurdity, of course). Metro's lingering rights derived from its eventual total acquisition of *Wind* from the interests of Selznick and his onetime indie [independent] production backer, Jock Whitney. . . . But when the U.S. film copyright was up for renewal about 10 years ago [actually nine years before, in 1967], Metro re-negotiated a deal [presumably with the Mitchell Estate] in which it surrendered sequel rights in return for extended releasing rights to *GWTW*. Not a bad move, considering that M-G-M's continuing rights abroad effectively foreclosed anybody else's maneuvers in the U.S. As a result of the current sequel agreements, Universal has acquired domestic sequel filmmaking rights, and Metro has contributed the other territorial rights which it still owns."

Variety's story continued with a diagnosis of the distribution agreement which M-G-M had entered into with United Artists in 1973. That pact had evidently contained a provision whereby UA did not automatically hold exclusive releasing rights to any project not totally controlled by the Metro-Goldwyn-Mayer studios, and therefore the M-G-M/Universal partnership would face no legal obstacles. The same story stated that there was no proposed timetable yet in the minds of the principals but that M-G-M was to be the lead (or managing) studio partner in the joint venture and that eventual filming would take place on location as well as at Metro's Culver City facilities. There was also a reminder that no part of the original had been photographed at M-G-M's own establishment, but only at David O. Selznick's independent organization. *Variety* could not help comparing the Richard Zanuck/David Brown rise to fame with Mr. Selznick's own ascent from RKO production chief to major-unit M-G-M producer and eventual studio mogul. The two younger men had started at Twentieth Century-Fox, and moved to Warner Brothers and finally to Universal with their own independent wing. *The Sting* and *Jaws*, which had catapulted them to national prominence, were by then already heading for a cumulative $300,000,000 in worldwide theatrical film rentals.

The enlightening *Variety* article did include a hint of mystery in its opening sentence with the statement that "a tentative agreement has been reached on a projected theatrical film sequel to *Gone With the Wind*." No other report at that time had given any inkling that the new venture was anything but definite in all its aspects. The trade paper inadvertently perpetuated one famous myth concerning the original version as well as repeating that "the characters and plot would be rooted in the Reconstruction period following the pre- and Civil War environs of the basic *GWTW*." On the myth side, while discussing casting of the original, *Variety* said, "Hardly anybody ever saw an actor except Gable for the part. It's legend that author Mitchell herself wrote the book with him in mind when developing the Rhett Butler character." Well, Margaret had often proven that she possessed some extrasensory powers, so perhaps she did envision Clark as Rhett five years before his film debut after all.

To more than compensate for this one forgivable lapse into fairy tales, *Variety* offered a recomputation that was long overdue in view of the *Jaws* box-office publicity. "Domestic theatrical film rentals on the original David O. Selznick production of *GWTW* are currently near $75,000,000," the publication stated, "and foreign tally is approximately $49,000,000. While these numbers trail *Jaws, The Godfather* and *The Sound of Music,* latter three pix are all within the last decade. . . . On the other hand, *Wind* has undergone several theatrical swings since its December, 1939, hardticket preem [reserved seat premiere]. In particular, about half the domestic rentals were generated before the successful 1967-to-date widescreen and stereo-enhanced reframing of the film, and in those earlier release periods, ticket prices were on the order of one-seventh to one-half of current prices, and rental percentages were lower. Hence, if earlier data were translated to today's dollar, *Wind* would lead the feature film rental pack; thus, the conclusion that it remains the most widely seen film yet made."

A few weeks later, when the dust had settled, Richard Zanuck and David Brown personally commented on their plans. Mr. Zanuck explained that the opportunity had been brought to them eight months before by representatives of the Margaret Mitchell Estate. Although sequel offers had been withstood for many years, Mr. Brown guessed the Estate had felt 1976's telecast would end a theatrical era for the original film and that this had changed the minds of those concerned. He revealed that the new story would not be shown in theatres for at least three years.

Mr. Zanuck admitted the project was "a bit scary" but he optimistically believed the new picture would be just as big and well made as the first or, he confided, they wouldn't be attempting it. The gentlemen conceded that Mr. Selznick's 1939 classic, which had cost almost $4,000,000, could not be duplicated for ten times that amount. However, they had budgeted their tentatively-titled *Gone With the Wind, Part II* at about $12,000,000, to be jointly financed by M-G-M and Universal.

Both producers agreed that no attempt would be made to find performers resembling Clark Gable or Vivien Leigh and concurred that it had not yet been determined whether the story would pick up Rhett and Scarlett a few

Campaign button given out at the 1976 Democratic National Convention in New York.

days or a few years after the final scene of the original.

Newspaper reporters immediately realized that much publicity would be generated in a "search" to cast the leading roles and that it would not be helpful, in light of this, for the producers to assign anyone to the roles too soon. So, in summing up that day's interview, the wire service reports solicited public suggestions, which should be sent to Zanuck and Brown—but barred Barbra Streisand and Al Pacino from the contest. (In view of the credits and awards these two performers had accrued in the past, it seemed Miss Streisand and Mr. Pacino would have had good reason for objecting to this exclusion.)

The proposed sequel also prompted a great number of humorous journalistic columns and feature stories on the outcome, with some of the most outrageously funny proposals any film project had offered since the 1939 original. *The New York Times* found the whole idea worthy of not one but two stories on the opening page of its August 1st Sunday entertainment section. "Who Will Play Rhett and Scarlett in *GWTW, Continued?*" was writer Joseph Morgenstern's honest query placed above a movie photo in which Mr. Gable's and Miss Leigh's faces had been obliterated. Mr. Morgenstern's feature piece began with the statement that, even in this age of Roman-numeraled continuations, "the news of a sequel to *Gone With the Wind* still comes as a shock." A new interview followed with Mr. Zanuck and Mr. Brown wherein they reiterated that they would never have been presumptuous enough to have originated the idea but had indeed been approached by the Margaret Mitchell Estate. The article quoted the producers as saying they "very seriously discussed the notion. While

293

we were immensely flattered to be approached initially, we did, after taking a couple of breaths, ask ourselves, you know, really, do we want to do this, or is it maybe an impossible challenge? And after a great deal of soul-searching we thought that we could do it and do it properly."

The movie men declined to comment any further as to who really initiated the idea but suggested an interview with Kay Brown—yes, the same industrious lady who had brought the original book to David O. Selznick's attention in 1936. Miss Brown, still working, was then an agent for International Creative Management—the firm previously mentioned by *Variety*—in New York City. The lady would have liked to clarify the reasons for the sequel permission, but she also declined. Yet everyone in literary and film circles realized that "the Margaret Mitchell Estate" was a terminology which really represented the late author's brother, Stephens Mitchell. Respect for Mr. Mitchell, his family and his late sister's memory was great enough for all those involved to remain publicly silent on any matter concerning *Gone With the Wind*.

The Times' article then veered to casting possibilities and broadly mentioned such unlikely candidates as Donny and Marie Osmond, the teenaged brother and sister then highly popular in television and recordings. Still, it did quote producer Brown as saying, "We're tabulating the letters as they come in. So far there's been a very strong Robert Redford poll." Then, finally, there came what in 1976 terms would be called the interview's "zinger." While stating that the original was "the most revered piece of filmmaking in the history of the entertainment business," Mr. Zanuck admitted that "it's not that we want to make a racy film out of it but we have to have our characters not only say but do things that are more in keeping with what audiences expect."

This particular quote hit the sensitivities of readers and movie fans who immediately remembered the crystal-pure *Funny Girl* in 1968 and the reprised Barbra Streisand *Funny Lady* in 1975, in which biographed Fanny Brice had, in the intervening years, acquired a decidedly foul mouth. However, those who did the wondering were, most probably, the same theatre audiences who, unbeknownst to Mr. Zanuck, had been driven back to their television sets by the movies' newfound explicitness.

The second story in *The New York Times* that Sunday provided amusement for readers but not too much respect for the two sincere Hollywood filmmakers. In questioning fifteen prominent authors of the day, the *Times*'s survey resulted in some unexpected quips. One even suggested an updating in which Rhett could re-meet Scarlett in a New York singles bar. James Jones proposed that she would get him back only to lose him again when he became bored, while Peter Benchley suggested

Scarlett might turn to selling Southern fried chicken. But, of all those quoted, Edward Albee's remarks were the most devastating and possibly the most closely linked to popular opinion. Mr. Albee's suggestion was that if the producers could not get either Margaret Mitchell or William Makepiece Thackeray to write the sequel, they shouldn't do it at all since "they're just after a buck anyway."

The San Francisco Chronicle was among the first to resurrect the forty-year-old legend by printing a rumor that Macmillan was in possession of "two final chapters" written by Margaret Mitchell for her book, which the publisher had elected not to include back in 1936. Macmillan itself was not too amused by that reported nonsense, or by the proposed new venture at all, although it made no public statement. It seemed the publisher had learned of the sequel like everyone else—in the newspaper announcements. And this was in spite of the fact that there would also be a published book involved and the company had been the careful guardian of the original for forty years.

To Olivia de Havilland, the proposed sequel was highly personal. Bob Thomas reported that her first reaction upon hearing the announcement was, "Oh dear, do you realize that poor Melanie will not be in it?" When asked if she felt the continuation was a good idea, Olivia replied, "Let's put it this way: It is extremely important that it succeed. I believe that strongly, really I do. It is absolutely imperative that they do not fail with the sequel. Because if they do, they will be damaging something that is very dear to a great many people." Miss de Havilland contributed some ideas which she had discussed with others at the 1967 Atlanta "re-premiere." "We all agreed," she said, "that Scarlett waited about six weeks and went to Charleston where she was the house guest of a distinguished family. Then she managed to appear at the same dinner party with Rhett and won him back." The actress further thought that Mr. and Mrs. Butler emigrated to San Francisco "since they were both adventurers." Olivia also hinted that Scarlett would arrange a new marriage for Ashley by quoting Melanie's dying words, "Take care of Ashley, but never let him know."

Shortly afterward, the supremely challenging task of writing the sequel became the responsibility of Anne Edwards, author of *Judy Garland* and a then-unpublished biography of Vivien Leigh. Miss Edwards was instructed to write a "deep, rich and complex novel" from which the screenplay would be adapted. The book, it was decided, would be published in paperback at the time of the film's release. Zanuck and Brown requested an outline in the fall of 1976 and the finished novel within a year. The producers, at this point, used Hollywood ingenuity and changed the proposed title to *The Continuation of Gone With the Wind*.

Time magazine reported on the sequel preparations and selection of its author by explaining that Anne Edwards felt difficult moments in her early life gave her a true affinity for Scarlett's art of survival. Miss Edwards, who once worked as a junior writer at M-G-M and had produced seven other books, toured the South for seven weeks in the summer of 1976, returning to her New York apartment with five cartons of photocopied newspaper clippings. These files concentrated on published reports from Atlanta, Charleston, Savannah, New Orleans and Jonesboro between 1872 and 1882. Her thorough research material included historical maps, century-old financial reports, references to that period's fashions, government proceedings of the time and even lists of medicines for the yellow fever epidemic. Anne Edwards was hesitant, as the project began, to discuss the directions it might take, but did reveal that Scarlett would gain wisdom and Rhett would *not* be going to San Francisco.

Although *The Continuation of Gone With the Wind* could not exactly be described as a "novelization" (like *The Omen*), since Anne Edwards had been employed to write a book first, it posed an interesting problem. Many major motion pictures undergo drastic changes from their original concept to the completely edited film. Would the paperback book Miss Edwards wrote be revised before publication to reflect any possible changes that occurred during movie production, and become, in fact, a "novelization"? Or would it see print exactly as written despite such possible variations?

In summarizing Stephens Mitchell's change of heart that led him to sell the rights to the *Jaws* producers, *Time* quoted the eighty-year-old Atlanta attorney as saying, "I figured I might as well let them have a go at it. Nobody can write like Margaret could anyway."

The vogue for nostalgia had made an equally heavy impression on Bicentennial Broadway, center of America's theatrical life. Although the New York stage had always gloried in periodic revivals, in 1976 echoes of yesterday seemed to dominate. A triumphant twentieth-anniversary production of *My Fair Lady* led a parade of reactivated musicals during the year: *Porgy and Bess*, *Fiddler on the Roof*, *The Threepenny Opera* and *Pal Joey*. Returning dramas like *Who's Afraid of Virginia Woolf*, *The Heiress*, *The Royal Family* and *The Night of the Iguana* closely followed recent reprises of *Cat on a Hot Tin Roof* and *A Streetcar Named Desire*. An all-black cast encored *Guys and Dolls* with the same acclaim accorded 1975's *The Wiz*, a prize-winning black version of *The Wizard of Oz*.

Meanwhile, Harold Rome's musical play *Gone with the Wind*, which had not yet reached Broadway after its 1973 debut in California, was also being heard from again—this time in the South. Television's David Canary was the new "Rhett Butler" and Broadway's Sherry Mathis portrayed "Scarlett" in a touring version that entertained audiences in Dallas, Kansas City, Miami Beach and other Southern cities during the spring and summer. The production was by then in two acts and nine scenes with twenty-two songs and a company of forty-four players. This still-changing edition had incorporated four new numbers since its West Coast premiere, but had eliminated about a dozen others—mostly chorus

The 1976 publicity for Gone With the Wind *inspired new and amusing merchandising tie-ins including puzzles, ties, checkbooks, paper dolls, "Passion Peanuts" candy, a paperback book entitled* Tara Revisited, *another book* Gone With the Ape *(linking Scarlett O'Hara with King Kong) and a GWTW beachtowel (in the background).*

tunes used for scene establishment. However, Rhett Butler lost three of his ballads and surrendered another to Frank Kennedy, whose previous solo moment had also vanished. Belle Watling first lost her song and a duet with Rhett, then found her character deleted entirely in this somewhat shorter renovation.

Creator Harold Rome referred to his epic as "the world's longest out-of-town tryout" as he expressed hopes that it would eventually find a home in New York. Reviewing it from Kansas City, *Variety* found the most recently revised *GWTW* "an entertaining evening" and reported it was doing respectable—although not record-breaking—business. The paper felt the fire at Atlanta's depot was, technically, the high point of the production. "Respectable" was the kindest term that could be used to describe its mid-July reception in the city of *GWTW*'s birth, where it played for one week at the magnificently modern Atlanta Civic Center. Atlanta, it seemed, had more to think about in 1976 than *Gone with the Wind*. But if *GWTW* did not reach the Broadway stage in the near future, Southerners could at least take consolation that one of their famous had provided inspiration for a planned million-dollar musical, *Kentucky Lucky*, based on Colonel Harland Sanders of the fried chicken empire.

Atlanta, Georgia, had come a long way since it received its name in the year Scarlett O'Hara was born. Peggy Marsh might have had difficulty recognizing the amazingly modern convention center her beloved hometown had become. So important was that convention business to the state's economy, in fact, that "blue laws" had been recently repealed to allow liquor service on Sundays for frolicking out-of-towners. "The Crossroads of the South" was never more prominent nationally than when the Atlanta Disease Control Center was relied upon by the whole country to solve the mystery of a serious illness that struck a Philadelphia convention in the summer of 1976. Atlanta, and all of Georgia, benefitted even further from the political publicity generated that year by the state's former governor, Jimmy Carter, in his bid for the Presidency.

When asked, Atlanta citizens expressed belief that their library display and the Margaret Mitchell Square were living proof that they had not forgotten the author and book that had once brought that city worldwide attention. However, the memory of *Gone with the Wind* was actually far better preserved by other locations in America and throughout the world. And, tragically, the Loew's Grand Theatre, site of all those famed premieres, had fallen upon sad times, turning, by economic necessity, into a haven for exploitation films.

Those engrossed by the mystifying world of book publishing detected a renewed *GWTW* influence in the Bicentennial year. In addition to Mr. Flamini's concept of the filming, Macmillan proudly issued *Margaret Mitchell's GONE WITH THE WIND Letters, 1936–1949* in October. Compiler Richard Harwell had previously written or edited fifty other books and had been a friend of Miss Mitchell's from his student days, when he worked at the Emory University Library. *Gone with the Wind* was the first of over one thousand books the gentleman would review in his lifetime. Through the years Margaret had referred pursuers of Civil War facts to Mr. Harwell and had made a unique exception and read the manuscript of his *Confederate Music* shortly before her death. That book, when published in 1950, was fittingly dedicated to the late Atlanta lady. Richard Harwell also had scholastic affinity for *GWTW* and its author, since most of the books he had written or edited concerned the Confederacy or American literary figures. And he had brought to this new project the experience of his own library career, which included work with rare materials in Southern literature and history at Duke, Emory, Bowdoin and other libraries.

While director of libraries at Georgia Southern College, Richard Harwell was asked to appraise a donation of the Margaret Mitchell Marsh Papers that had been made in 1970 to the University of Georgia libraries. He at once realized their publishing potential if permission could be received from Stephens Mitchell. Aware that the *GWTW* author had insisted that none of her letters was ever to appear in print, Mr. Harwell felt that her importance was now a matter belonging to history and that Margaret would hardly have kept these thousands of carbons if the notion of their historical significance had not at some time occurred to her.

He approached Mr. Mitchell with the argument that someone would do such a book eventually and it could more accurately be produced by a person who had known the lady and was familiar with Atlanta and those people referred to in the correspondence. Stephens Mitchell agreed—hesitantly and reluctantly—and the challenge to Mr. Harwell began with his having to select those letters to be used from among twelve thousand in the collection. Richard Harwell took extreme care to extract only material directly involving the novel and movie, honoring Miss Mitchell's desire for privacy in her personal affairs.

The 333 letters finally used by Mr. Harwell were among a 57,000-piece collection—which included the other correspondence, photographs, news clippings and miscellaneous papers—that had been a gift from Stephens Mitchell to his alma mater. The Mitchell memorabilia, however, remained restricted from use without permission in order to protect the rights of the Estate and in respect for the author's wishes.

Although all of Margaret Mitchell's private letters had been destroyed after her death, the sampling of business correspondence culled for the new Macmillan book did succeed in revealing much of the intelligence, sociability and wit the lady was noted for in her lifetime. But, as Mr. Harwell mentioned in his Preface, "she wrote full and charming letters, personalizing them while seldom revealing her private self." Still, through them readers were permitted to witness the momentous change *GWTW*'s publication brought to her world. It was quite sad, then, to realize that Margaret was never again able to resume the "quiet peaceful life" she had cared so much for. The historical importance of the *Letters* publication was gratefully acknowledged as Richard Harwell explained: "I was privileged to range as widely as I wished in choosing which letters would most thoroughly and most truly record Margaret Mitchell in what comes as close as anything ever will to being her autobiography."

This volume of *Letters*, only the second book whose authorship could be credited to Margaret Mitchell, was far more engrossing and entertaining than its concept might have implied. A fascinating scope of subject matter included expressions of gratitude to book reviewers, congratulations to the actors on their casting, and answers to queries from interested strangers. *Margaret Mitchell's GONE WITH THE WIND Letters, 1936–1949* was designated a Book-of-the-Month Club Alternate (the eighth book club selection in Richard Harwell's literary career) and its public acceptance was greater than Macmillan had anticipated. Critical reviews were respectful and full of praise, with probably the most delightful observation coming from Granville Hicks in *The New York Times Book Review*. Mr. Hicks commented that, as a Yankee, he had felt no enthusiasm for *Gone with the Wind* when it was published nor had he ever seen the film version. But the *Letters*, he claimed, enhanced his opinion of Margaret Mitchell as a diligent worker and a generous, modest woman. As a result, he looked forward to finally seeing the movie.

Hollywood Costume—Glamour! Glitter! Romance! by fashion authorities Dale McConathy and Diana Vreeland, a rather expensive Abrams deluxe issue, paid long-overdue homage to some of filmland's designers. Essentially inspired by the New York Metropolitan Museum of Art's highly successful 1975 show, the book's interesting text-history was supplemented with 127 photographs of actual costumes—including 79 in full color—and 200 other movie and television scenes. Highlighted among a parade of movie gowns from 1912 through 1975 were seven exhibited examples of Walter Plunkett's artful creations for *Gone With the Wind*, including Bonnie's riding habit, Scarlett's wedding gown, her New Orleans honeymoon dress and two sumptuous peignoirs. A magnificent color photograph of the low-cut gown Scarlett wore to Ashley's birthday party was referred to by the authors as "a claret velvet ballgown that sums up her affluence as Mrs. Rhett Butler."

The writers noted, in fact, that "few American movies used costumes so effectively to chronicle the fortunes of characters . . . with Scarlett's passage from innocence to disillusionment charted in her gowns." A major point of interest which some 1976 booksellers utilized for open-book window displays was a full page showing the green "drapery dress" in all its colorful grandeur. "Probably no other costume," the authors stated, "has symbolized so well the experience of a period as Scarlett O'Hara's dress made from her mother's portières. It became an emblem of survival for the generation that lived through the Great Depression."

In addition to a brief biography of Walter Plunkett (and ones for twenty-two other film designers), there was a quote from Mr. Plunkett which observed that, although David Selznick wasn't interested in accuracy, he himself had felt research in the South was necessary for the *GWTW* assignment. Amid the descriptive credits of the costumes, readers also learned that the seven *GWTW* pieces appeared by permission of either the David O. Selznick or Helen Larson Collections and, sadly, that the "drapery dress" was only "a reproduction of the original."

David Chierichetti's *Hollywood Costume Design* approached the same subject in a more comprehensive and less grandiose manner, but still utilized more than 160 illustrations. Filmographies of ninety-nine designers, including Walter Plunkett, were a valuable inclusion, as was a photograph of Mr. Plunkett's original sketch for that notable "drapery dress." Author Chierichetti also quoted Walter Plunkett on his *GWTW* experience: "I don't think it was my best work or even the biggest thing I ever did. There were more designs for *Singin' in the Rain*, *Raintree County* and *How the West Was Won*. After all, Olivia de Havilland had only two changes before Melanie went into mourning! But that picture, of course, will go on forever, and that green dress, because it makes a story point, is probably the most famous costume in the history of motion pictures. So I am very glad I did it."

Black literature took a giant step forward with the fall publication of Alex Haley's *Roots*, which traced the author's own family history back seven generations from 1750 Africa through kidnapping for slavery to the struggle for survival in America afterward. Doubleday thought enough of the "non-fiction novel" to schedule a 200,000-copy first printing and was rewarded with an instant best seller. Mr. Haley, who had spent twelve years on the project he described as "faction," saw it as a Bicentennial gift to his country and a legacy to all black Americans. And television had not missed the entertainment potential of *Roots*. Even as the book was being officially published, producer David Wolper was in Savannah, Georgia, busily filming a six-million-dollar, 12-hour serialization for ABC to be presented as "A Novel for Television" in January 1977.

Television

Television! It had never before seemed such an integral part of American life. Whether joining in Bicentennial celebrations, participating in Queen Elizabeth's visit or showing the first pictures from Mars, television included everyone in all facets of the fascinating 1976. It had also become something of a political necessity and the three competing networks spent a cumulative $25,000,000 to bring the national conventions to viewers' attention. July's Democratic pageant, that party's first in New York City in fifty-two years, was a highpoint of summer viewing for all those deeply involved in the upcoming election. However, there was a hint from sampled ratings that a great many indifferent Americans found old movies more worthy of their attention than the future government of their country. Georgia's James Earl "Jimmy" Carter was an almost uncontested victor for the Presidential nomination and it was thought his good luck might actually have been helped by the campaign buttons distributed in Madison Square Garden which bragged "Scarlett O'Hara Loves Jimmy Carter!"

August's Republican Convention in Kansas City was less predictable as Gerald Ford entered the arena facing popular one-time actor and former California Governor, Ronald Reagan. (It was interesting to note the number of times President Ford was referred to by journalists as seeking "reelection" to the office he had never been elected to at all.) Gerald Ford's eventual nomination gave promise of a closely contested race, which would be made all the more personal to voters by the televised debates promised between the candidates in the preelection weeks.

One of the most amazing aspects of the modern television age was the reliance the motion-picture industry had on its once feared and hated rival. Television was essential in 1976 to promote new films, generate income from the reshowings of vintage productions and even to bring the film industry's own image into closer focus with the American public. This last factor was never more evident than in the broadcasts of two of Hollywood's most respected affairs: The American Film Institute's Achievement banquet and the Motion Picture Academy of Arts and Sciences Awards.

"Oscar" had gotten himself into quite a bit of mischief since that night in 1940 when everyone knew beforehand that *Gone With the Wind* was the evening's champion. Not only had George C. Scott and Marlon Brando refused their awards, but other prominent players had let their sentiments about this "contest" be publicly known even when they were nominees themselves. Nevertheless, the event—despite perennial criticism of its staging—was always among the highest-rated television programs of any given year. Shortly after bestowing the forty-eighth annual awards, the Hollywood Academy of Motion Picture Arts and Sciences began plans for the half-century anniversary year festivities that would begin May 4, 1977 and were to include educational and cultural activities.

Yet there had been celebration already in March 1976 when Jack Nicholson and Louise Fletcher became the first team since Clark Gable and Claudette Colbert in 1935 to win the leading acting Oscars for the same picture. *One Flew Over the Cuckoo's Nest* had also won the other three most prestigious honors of "Best Picture," Director and Screenplay.

The original 1962 Ken Kesey novel upon which the play and film, *One Flew Over the Cuckoo's Nest,* had been based finally became a best seller thanks to the movie version. New American Library's Signet paperback edition grew to a total of forty-four printings with more than five million copies distributed during the picture's first theatrical voyage. The film had finally brought Jack Nicholson long-overdue Academy Award recognition after four previous defeats. Louise Fletcher, who delivered masterfully in her first major film assignment, contributed the single most touching moment in the televised Awards' history when she thanked her deaf parents through sign language for teaching her to have a dream that they were then seeing come true. Home viewers might have been deprived of this poignant scene if the Academy had heeded the pleas of some to abolish the "Best Actress" Award in protest of the significant lack of roles for women in current films. Luckily for Miss Fletcher, they didn't consider it.

There were no such barriers for actresses working in the television medium. In fact, by mid-1976 twelve leading shows featured women as their central figures. There were challenging dramatic roles of the type once offered by filmmakers to Vivien Leigh, Olivia de Havilland and Greer Garson. Most of these opportunities came in the nature of movies made directly for television consumption. Jane Alexander magnificently captured the spirit of America's former first lady in *Eleanor and Franklin*, Elizabeth Montgomery brought skill to an updated *Dark Victory* and Susan Clark, 1976 "Emmy" winner for *Babe*, encored as *Amelia Earhart*, the pioneer aviatrix and early "women's libber." Just as leading movies of the day teamed two male stars, television films like *Sybil* and *The Disappearance of Aimee* matched brilliant performances by females.

The "novel for television" innovation gave worthy employment to many women in *Rich Man, Poor Man* and *Captains and the Kings*, while Helen Hayes was even called upon to essay a role that had been male in the book *The Moneychangers*. Maureen Stapleton, Patricia Neal, Cloris Leachman, Sada Thompson and Michael Learned were actresses regularly on view in dramatic programs, while Carol Burnett, Mary Tyler Moore, Beatrice Arthur, Nancy Walker, Jean Stapleton, Valerie Harper, Suzanne Pleshette and Esther Rolle often raised television comedy to the status of art. Their forerunner in this profession, Lucille Ball, was feted by the CBS network in the fall of 1976 with an "all-star special" tribute honoring her twenty-fifth anniversary as the "Queen of Television." That madcap lady had come a long way since she had auditioned on her knees for the part of Scarlett O'Hara in David O. Selznick's office.

The social effects of the home medium were far more widely reaching than its mere entertainment aspect would have implied. Leading sports events often turned American wives into part-time "widows," while the timeliness of television journalism seriously affected the publication of magazines and newspapers. Television's preoccupation with women, even in news broadcasting, garnered much 1976 publicity when ABC lured Barbara Walters, with an unprecedented opportunity and a lucrative contract, to leave NBC and join its ranks. Issues of the day were often incorporated even into TV's situation comedies, wherein Mary Tyler Moore could detail the encounters of a single career woman, or *All in the Family* and *Maude* cleverly reminded viewers of bigotry and racial hatred. Significantly, black performers also found their talents had recently come much into demand as 1976 evidenced the programming of four regular series featuring all-black casts. Still, television's greatest bonus was that it allowed every American to become a participant in events of rare and special interest.

Director William Wyler, whose long career so often paralleled *GWTW*'s, became the fourth honoree of the American Film Institute's annual tribute, which was televised in March 1976. Paying special homage that night to the man who had guided some of their finest performances were Greer Garson, Walter Pidgeon, Myrna Loy, Jennifer Jones, Henry Fonda, Audrey Hepburn, Charlton Heston, Merle Oberon, Barbra Streisand and once-blacklisted author Jessamyn West. Highlights were shown from Mr. Wyler's Academy Award-winning *Mrs. Miniver, The Best Years of Our Lives* and *Ben-Hur*, and a special appearance was made by the First Lady, Mrs. Betty Ford.

Mrs. Ford, seated at the table of honor with Mr. and Mrs. Wyler and Fred Astaire, told the gathering: "When I was a girl in high school growing up, I never dreamed of being married to a President. In fact, in those days, I was dreaming—as most high school girls my age were—of perhaps going to Hollywood and having the oppor-

Cover of the November 6-12, 1976, edition of TV Guide.

tunity to glide across a beautifully glazed floor with Fred Astaire. But because of the magic of movies, I've danced and I've laughed, I've cried my way through several lifetimes. . . . Like millions of people, the President and I love the movies. Movies light the candle of imagination, they enrich our dreams and expand our understandings. May we always be a land that loves make-believe and storytellers like the man we honor tonight." In his acceptance speech, Mr. Wyler reminisced about meeting his wife: "When I met Talli [Margaret Tallichet], she was a young actress under contract to David Selznick and was one of those testing hopefully for the part of Scarlett O'Hara in *Gone With the Wind*. But I was lucky, she didn't get the part—she got me instead."

Non-network or "syndicated" television shows were highly popular in both daytime and early evening broadcasting and they relied heavily on the quiz, game or panel format. While many were harmless fun in which contestants played for relatively low stakes, some purposely deceived their audiences and others gave evidence of the more unpleasant sides of human nature. One in the latter category was an amateur talent audition whose very premise was so shockingly cruel as to defy belief—

yet it was highly popular with viewers in totally sophisticated America. But one of the nicer panel-show "old-timers," *To Tell the Truth*, provided a sentimental moment for Herb Bridges when he appeared on it in the fall of 1976. Although most of the experts guessed that he, among three possible candidates, was indeed the real Sharpsburg collector of *GWTW* material, the producers surprised Herb with a guest appearance by Butterfly McQueen. The gracious actress seemed genuinely delighted to finally meet the man she had corresponded with over the years and then told the studio audience about her current one-woman show. Before leaving, Miss McQueen recited the line from *Gone With the Wind* about "birthing babies" as no one else ever had or could.

Daytime television serials (also known as "soap operas"), an American tradition dating back to 1926 radio days, reached new heights in 1976. Some of the fourteen regularly scheduled presentations featured former film performers, but largely, they created stars of their own. George Reinholdt, Marie Masters or K. T. Stevens (daughter of *GWTW*'s Sam Wood) might be names fairly unknown to evening viewers but their popularity and that of scores of other daytime players was enough to justify the existence of more than twenty magazines following their lives and careers. Entire digest publications and valuable newspaper space were devoted to capsulized plot outlines for followers who missed espisodes. Those never-ending sagas were also capable of involving some audience members to such an extent that their players received mail instructing them how to solve the situations dramatists had placed them in.

Proof that "soap operas" had been accepted as a lasting American entertainment form was a television parody of them that appeared in early 1976 and—despite lack of adoption by the three major networks—briefly mesmerized millions of the country's televiewers. *Mary Hartman, Mary Hartman* became such a phenomenon in its first few months on the air that *The New York Times* devoted a feature article to its impact on America. Fan clubs had sprung up, T-shirts appeared, posters posed "Mary Hartman for President," bumper stickers proclaimed love for the series' heroine, daily synopses were carried by newspapers and a near prison riot erupted when inmates were deprived of the show. *MH²* (as it was affectionately nicknamed) had some serious shortcomings but its brainwashed heroine, in responding to all of life's problems with the language of TV commercials, did justifiably comment on the dangerous intrusion—sometimes even subliminal dominance—that television's consumer messages had on the innocent viewing public. And it seemed Mary had also caught "*GWTW* fever" when, on the first show of her fall season, she announced that she was not Scarlett O'Hara and frankly she didn't give a damn!

Mary Hartman was not alone in voicing objections to television's plethora of commercial messages—often insulting, tasteless or sexist. These uninvited nuisances were generally deplored by the public and occasionally attacked in print, but they still dominated programming. It was a bitter fact of life that these very same disturbing sponsorships were what made free television possible. Educational television stations, subsidized by grants and donations, escaped these annoying interruptions and, in most cases, displayed intellectual taste in their choices. However, much of the former output of the motion-picture industry was financially beyond their reach. For those who desired more balance in their entertainment but still wanted to avoid commercials, there was another alternative, a system commonly called "pay TV."

"Pay television" was a method of bringing select programming to home audiences by means of a cable system installed in one's home and usually broadcast along the neighborhood phone wires. A monthly fee was charged, which varied from one area to another but in 1976 averaged (if all-inclusive) from $16 to $19 per month. One such system incorporated under the name Home Box Office had made arrangements with all the major film companies except Walt Disney by which almost all new films would be broadcast soon after their theatrical cycle was completed. During 1976 Home Box Office subscribers could choose such recent film fare as *The Exorcist, Nashville, Shampoo, Mandingo, Young Frankenstein, Funny Lady, The Blue Bird, Murder on the Orient Express, The Day of the Locust* and *The Missouri Breaks*. Those who preferred vintage films could see a festival of Alexander Korda's finest efforts and, for a limited time, *Gone With the Wind*.

Almost two years after selling broadcast rights to NBC Metro-Goldwyn-Mayer made a surprise commitment with Home Box Office for fourteen performances of the 1939 Selznick film during June 1976 before the picture had to be contractully surrendered to the National Broadcasting Company for its one-time showing. NBC, which at that very moment was soliciting commercial time from prospective sponsors for a record $234,000 per minute, said little publicly about these cable viewings, but one could easily guess the network's private sentiments.

These commercial-free broadcasts of *GWTW* brought with them a future problem for M-G-M but a boon to some of the film's devotees. Film "piracy," or the selling of prints of copyrighted movies to private collectors or to foreign exhibitors, was an offense under investigation by both the FBI and the motion-picture industry, especially when it affected the loss of foreign revenue. A "bootleg" print of *Gone With the Wind*, according to underground rumors, might sell for well over $1,000. Ironically, home video-tape duplicating machines were at that very time being advertised for sale on the commercial networks. So, while it was illegal to own a print of *GWTW*, there was nothing to prevent owners of such equipment from making video copies of it for their private use.

Gone With the Wind, through the auspices of the Home Box Office system, made its actual world television debut on Friday, June 11, 1976, at 2:30 P.M. and was repeated at 8:00 that evening. The film was thereafter broadcast twice a day on six other dates throughout the remainder of June for a total of fourteen performances. Dick Cavett was the pleasant host selected for an introductory session in which he repeated for audiences some of the more popular "legends" surrounding the casting and filming of the epic. (Some of his script, however, like the misconstrued nonsense about twenty-seven copies of the calico dress or the revelation that dummies were used in the depot sequence, may actually have detracted from some viewers' pleasure.) The print exhibited was shown in its original 1939 ratio—as all televised films are—but it was of the 1954/1961 genre, displaying black maskings on the lower portions of several scenes. The color was more faded than had ever been apparent before and the print had certainly not been processed in Technicolor. The sound seemed curiously mixed, with the rustle of hoopskirts often louder than spoken dialogue—a result of the rechanneling of the film's original track for its 1967 reissue. Luckily, it was not a seventy-millimeter version, which would have deprived viewers of more than half of every scene. But despite these technical failings, the Home Box Office exposures were enthusiastically received.

A survey published in *Variety* claimed that more than 85 percent of Home Box Office's 450,000 subscribers—or a minimum of 382,500 viewers—watched at least one of these showings. But as with all *GWTW* figures, these were disputed. Another newspaper reported that HBO boasted 500,000 subscribers, and a third listed the number at 700,000—all of which rendered the survey's facts virtually meaningless. And they actually didn't account for much since reports of *GWTW* "parties" with families and neighbors crowding around television sets complemented other home viewers' claims of having seen numerous repeat performances. But then did it really matter historically how many pairs of eyes viewed the film or how many times they did?

The New York Times captured the significance of the event succinctly in a feature story detailing pros and cons of the pay-cable system. "The potential of pay TV," said *The Times*, "is grasped for several hours, and it is apparent that commercial television has every reason to dislike, if not hate, the pay system. The main attraction on Friday was *Gone With the Wind*, shown both in the afternoon and in the evening. Vivien Leigh and Clark Gable, Scarlett and Rhett, have survived magnificently on celluloid. The Margaret Mitchell story retains its epic-sentimental magic. All the performances—by Olivia de Havilland, Leslie Howard, Thomas Mitchell, just to skim the top—are memorable. The magnificent film made splendid television. As it happens, a commercial network, NBC-TV, has acquired, at great expense, *Gone With the Wind* for presentation this fall. In the commercial instance, though, the film will be offered in two installments on different evenings (a Sunday and Monday). And, of course, the movie will be riddled with interruptions for commercials. Given the typical trappings of commercial TV, Tara will not, indeed cannot, be the same."

The New York Times also listed in the cable television plus column a Home Box Office special featuring popular entertainer Bette Midler which had also been presented that June, and the *Variety* survey showed that Miss Midler had captured 57 percent of the potential audience, considered an excellent showing, yet still 28 percent points behind the vintage film. *The Times* did point out that not very much of the film fare regularly broadcast by HBO measured up to *GWTW*'s standards, but even a casual observer realized this was the ultimate result of the quality of recent theatrical movies made available rather than any deliberate preselection by the cable company.

But even commercial-free cable television could not solve the problems inherent in the home entertainment medium. The movie theatre, with its large projection and sophisticated sound system, still offered a rich concept of detail impossible to grasp on the smaller screen. Panoramic film processes were still not adaptable to televising, and a film photographed in such a manner would be missing a large portion of its artistic concept when airwaved to homes. Even if larger or wider television sets could be developed in the future, they would still never match the fabled "magic" of movie theatres, which forced people to temporarily leave their homes filled with life's inherent challenges and seek "escapism" in the comfortable shelter of a darkened auditorium.

It was often reported that three decades of the home medium had severely damaged the viewing etiquette of theatrical audiences. Younger moviegoers often spoke out loud, smoked marijuana or ate pungent meals throughout a film performance in the manner they might in their own living rooms. The integrity of film projectionists had also sadly slipped. Misframed and out-of-focus images, along with faulty sound adjustment, were commonplace in 1976, even in the expensive first-run theatres, whereas technical perfection had once been a matter of great employee pride in the smallest of neighborhood movie houses.

As a bonus, film distributors supplemented sloppy projection with worn and tattered prints of the very newest pictures. Either faulty processing or poor quality of the film used resulted in distracting scratches or abrasions, and movies still in their initial engagements more than likely had been damaged and poorly patched together with little regard for missing dialogue or continuity. Even more alarming, final work by the studios themselves showed faulty techniques in editing, sound mixing and special effects, leading one to surmise that there existed a climate of apathy by all concerned. Many reviewers thought that poor postproduction technique contributed to the artistic failure of *The Blue Bird* and *A Matter of Time*. Color processing in 1976 was often so crude that film historians regarded it as a blessing that the colors would soon completely fade away.

To those who had followed the career of *Gone With the Wind* and cared about the movie, the greatest relief was that the television sale would finally free theatres of the horrendous prints that M-G-M had in continuous circulation for nine years since the 1967 reissue. What remained of the Metrocolor reprocessing in these relics was far closer to black and white or sepia. Patchwork was so vast that often an entire scene or two was missing in the midst of spliced jumps. In its "Golden Era," Metro-Goldwyn-Mayer had treated its treasure with infinitely more respect.

Despite this tragic lack of preservation, audiences, incredibly, still filled theatres to see *Gone With the Wind* wherever it played and fully enjoyed it. The enthusiastic applause from principally younger viewers at the main title and finale was quite touching, although they often cried out in shocked disbelief when, in the midst of an integral scene, a splice destroyed its impact. The main title varied in prints, sometimes sweeping across the screen as in 1939 through 1961, but occasionally being the stationary substitute introduced in 1967—even in standard ratio prints. Audience reactions could also be anticipated when Scarlett shot the Yankee deserter, after her oath to never starve again, and, of course, when Clark Gable said, "Frankly, my dear . . ."

The thunderous applause which greeted Mr. Gable's entrance—looking up at Scarlett on the Twelve Oaks staircase—was especially heartwarming since these ovations did not occur in reissues during the actor's lifetime. It seemed the younger generation was fated to keep Clark Gable's memory alive. Newer patrons, however, seemed determined to find racial slurs in *GWTW*'s dialogue and sometimes reacted a bit too quickly in their criticisms. For example, when Ashley challenged Scarlett about hiring convicts in the lumber mill she countered that he hadn't objected to once having slaves. "That was different," Ashley would begin to reply, but hoots of derision from the audience usually drowned out the balance of his explanation that he intended to free them anyway after his father's death.

Gone With the Wind had, over the past few years, been a frequent visitor to revival houses in the larger cities. In New York City in 1976, for instance, it played at both the well-known Elgin Theatre and the Carnegie Hall Cinema. The latter thought well enough of the vintage film to book it as its July 4th Bicentennial attraction. But it was far from restricted to such nostalgic engagements, since it returned to New York's prestigious Rivoli Theatre on Broadway for the fourth time in September 1976—only two months before its scheduled network television unveiling. That same city's Cinema Studio then played it in late October, preceding its broadcast by only a matter of days.

Poignantly, many famed theatres which had once played the 1939 Academy Award-winning film were literally gone with the wind by then. Hollywood's Carthay Circle and New York City's Capitol were only memories by 1976 and the once-proud Astor had—on its way to oblivion—become a "flea market." The most renowned of them all, Radio City Music Hall, had fought a difficult battle for survival that year when labor disputes almost forced its permanent closing. Even though this near tragedy was averted, the movie palace no longer held its former illustrious prestige. Film selections became non-exclusive and "sneak previews" and giveaways were initiated to encourage attendance. In a continuing effort to present "family" programming, the theatre was forced at one point to exhibit a film already shown on cable TV, and also to engage the year's two most regrettable disappointments—Vincente Minnelli's *A Matter of Time* and George Cukor's *The Blue Bird*. Perhaps, like so many other remnants of America's recent past, it was for "the showplace of the nation" really just a matter of time.

But while America's theatres might be closing, television was gaining in popularity—if not prestige—as the country's leading source of entertainment. And *Gone With the Wind*, the story of a woman—and called the "ultimate soap opera" by some—was coming to America's 71,400,000 television homes, to a medium in which women were appreciated and where "soap operas" thrived. The film was also making its home debut in the most bitterly fought ratings season in television's history.

That year, for the first time, the former underdog American Broadcasting Company (ABC) had surpassed both the Columbia Broadcasting System (CBS) and the National Broadcasting Company (NBC) to become the new ratings champion. ABC's victories ranged from telecasts of the Olympics to situation comedies, which featured some of the most phenomenally popular young players of the day. For NBC, which was just then marking its fiftieth anniversary, it proved a rather disappointing time for celebration. The network placed great hopes in *Gone With the Wind* to recapture some of its former ratings prestige.

In the week preceding the *GWTW* telecast, America's thoughts were dominated by the Presidential election while the three television networks competed for viewers' attention in election returns on November 2 as actively as they did with their regular programming. And from early that evening it was apparent that this was one of the closest such contests of the century. For those who watched the coverage on NBC there was a humorous bonus. The network had decided to employ its station breaks for "trailers" of *Gone With the Wind*, and in the midst of a suspenseful evening, Scarlett O'Hara was shown vowing never to be hungry again. Perhaps Scarlett brought some luck to her fellow Southerners for, in the early morning hours of November 3, it became evident that Jimmy Carter had won and had become the first man from the Deep South to be elected President since Zachary Taylor in 1849. Some observers commented that—110 years after the Civil War had ended—the South had finally "rejoined" the Union.

Mr. Carter publicly acknowledged the power of the home medium when he expressed the feeling that he might have lost the election had it not been for his televised debates with Gerald Ford. (Later in the year President-elect Carter would discuss *GWTW* with Barbara Walters in a nationally telecast ABC interview "special" and would describe the 1939 premiere of the film as "the biggest event to happen in the South in my lifetime.")

With a Georgian elected President, the country's focus shifted to some other famous "citizens" of that state. For those who were not yet aware, *TV Guide* devoted its cover that week to Scarlett and Rhett—an unprecedented move in the telecasting of an "old" movie. And the magazine's movie reviewer, Judith Crist, summed up the apprehensions of many when she wrote: "This is *Gone With the Wind*'s week, and television, via NBC, will be on trial with its presentation of the 1939 classic." Its first portion was to premiere on Sunday, November 7, 1976, under an NBC programming umbrella called *The Big Event*, and the remainder would be broadcast the following night—on what would have been Margaret Mitchell's seventy-sixth birthday.

Quite a few of that weekend's newspapers devoted space to feature stories recapping the history of *GWTW*, and several regularly inserted television booklets highlighted movie scenes on their covers. The New York *Sunday News* included a "*GWTW* puzzle" in its amusement section, and thought the telecast was timely enough to call attention to it (and that crossword game) in a heading on the first page of its news section as well. Unfortunately, several writers who had innocently referred to previously published articles or books to research the subject recounted some of those devilishly persistent falsehoods surrounding *GWTW*'s legendary beginnings.

Readers were thereby erroneously informed that: Selznick bought the book from galley proofs in 1935; George Cukor directed the "Twelve Oaks" sequence; Victor Fleming "walked off the set" and was replaced by Sam Wood; the South had resented Vivien Leigh's casting; the

depot fire represented "the burning of Atlanta"; and that Max Steiner's score had won an Academy Award. Of course, the total number of Oscars varied from story to story. Still, enough common sense prevailed for a few writers to realize that the "search for Scarlett" had been merely a publicity disguise. A few pre-reviewers felt obliged to describe the film's second half as "high-class soap opera" but urged viewers to watch anyway since the telecast promised a restoration of the original framing and color. *The Philadelphia Inquirer* intelligently explained that in the past two decades of televising films from the major studios, other films like *Casablanca* and *The Wizard of Oz* had graduated into a status of "American Folk Movies," a position once held—through its constant revivals—only by *GWTW*. Repeated television exposure of those two films, as well as *Citizen Kane, King Kong, All About Eve, Sunset Boulevard, The Maltese Falcon* and scores of others, had indeed challenged *Gone With the Wind*'s once undisputed hold on national folklore.

It was simultaneously revealed by several sources during the weekend that Olivia de Havilland had originally been asked by NBC to introduce the film, but had refused when she learned of the numerous interruptions and the plan to divide it beyond the normal intermission point. "For this film to be shown in such a crude manner in this Bicentennial year is, I think, most insensitive and very foolish," the actress commented. "I'm quite sure that Clark Gable, Vivien Leigh and Leslie Howard are up there somewhere right now incensed over the proceedings." NBC officials countered Olivia's statement by reminding that FCC regulations permitted the network seven minutes of commercial time each hour. Naturally, mathematically minded viewers wondered how those allowable minutes (a total of 35 for the five-hour broadcast), when added to the film's running time (of 222 minutes), accounted for the 300 minutes scheduled over both nights. NBC hadn't bothered to explain that, in addition to a thirteen-minute reprise of Part One to be shown Monday evening, quite a bit of the additional thirty minutes would be utilized to promote the network's own current or upcoming shows. Then there would be additional time devoted to station break announcements, local messages and news bulletins.

Writer Dan Lewis quoted Olivia even further: "I was appalled to learn that they planned to give so much time to commercials . . . a break in the showing every 20 minutes. I object to that. I don't blame NBC. They undoubtedly paid a great deal for the rights to televise the picture. I blame M-G-M for making that kind of an agreement. They should have laid down regulations." At the same time, Olivia expressed her approval of the Home Box Office airings the previous June: "It was beautifully done. I had a good reaction seeing myself. I forgot it's me." When asked if she would make any alterations in acting style if she were called upon to play Melanie in 1976, Miss de Havilland replied, "I wouldn't change a thing. In retrospect, the woman I played in *Gone With the Wind* was the wisest woman I ever played."

Finally it came: Sunday evening November 7, 1976, with an NBC announcer's voice proclaiming "the most eagerly awaited event in television history." A good start! But from then on it became quite evident that for the first time in *Gone With the Wind*'s thirty-seven-year movie history, something new had been added. "We"— the collective television audience of America—viewed the night's proceedings and saw an "old friend" presented in a somewhat unusual manner. First, actress Candice Bergen materialized to say a few words about Polaroid cameras, then a healthy group of men tried to squeeze into a Volkswagen car. Robert Young, proclaiming he was not really a doctor, sanctioned Sanka and an emporium called Shakey's introduced the latest innovation in pizza. Next Selznick International's trademark heralded familiar panels crediting M-G-M, Technicolor and Margaret Mitchell just before an original main title swept gallantly across the home screen looking more richly colorful than it had in many a year.

The balance of the credits were reinstated originals with one surprising change (more on that later), and we then joined Scarlett O'Hara on the steps of Tara with the Tarleton boys. Scarlett ran to meet her father, Gerald, and they returned for evening prayer with the entire clan. The following morning Mammy helped Scarlett prepare for the day's barbecue and we learned there was a new generation of Volkswagens, saw Candice Bergen study photos with a magnifiying glass and witnessed the undressing of a glass of cola. Scarlett professed her love for Ashley at Twelve Oaks, met Rhett Butler and accepted Charles Hamilton's marriage proposal just in time for a supermarket interview to show us that more people preferred Stovetop Stuffing to potatoes. After another visit to Shakey's pizza palace and hearing evidence that a new car would cost $6,000, we went to a wedding where the groom was wearing a New York Life sweatshirt. Local news bulletins caught up with Jimmy Carter and murders of the day while Karl Malden advised us not to carry cash on vacations and some scenes of Robert Redford illustrated *The Great Waldo Pepper*. The news that plastic bottles were a convenient novelty for Coke buyers broke just as we went off to another wedding, and this time it was Scarlett's. Charles Hamilton's hasty death sent his widow off to Atlanta where she danced with Rhett at the Bazaar, got a Paris hat and first heard about Gettysburg. It was then back to Shakey's, after which a canoe ride for Polaroid and a peek at an auto showroom carried us through to knowledge that Musk Oil after-shave cologne would act as a romantic enticer. *Sybil*, in the guise of Sally Field, screamed for Joanne

Woodward just before the Gettysburg casualty lists informed Melanie and Scarlett that Ashley was safe. After Ashley's brief Christmas leave, the girls went nursing at the hospital where they met Belle Watling and Candice Bergen showed us another camera. Raisin Bran, we learned, was more practical than plain old cereal with bananas as we traveled to a racetrack with Volkswagen and stopped by a McDonald's hamburger establishment. Possibilities were revealed for seeing a fashion show when flying Air Jamaica or for saving money on brandname products at a local discount chain. General Sherman's first shells hit Atlanta and soon thereafter Melanie went into labor. Scarlett searched for Dr. Meade, finally finding him and hundreds of wounded Confederates along with a new Volkswagen scene and Miss Bergen with still another camera. An Ohio housewife then demonstrated a new gelatin dessert just before some leading authorities extolled Gallo wine.

After a glimpse of *The Moneychangers* informed us of multimillion-dollar deals sweetened by sex, Scarlett and Prissy delivered Melanie's baby and Rhett took all safely out of Atlanta, leaving them on the road to Tara. Scarlett bravely continued the journey, hiding under a bridge to avoid rain and soldiers while Ultra Brite revealed the secret of white teeth and Dynamo promised savings on laundry bills. A very-slow-running catsup looked tasty on a hot dog, the Volkswagen Rabbit passed by and a montage of scenes promoted NBC's upcoming fiftieth-anniversary show. Scarlett got back to Tara and found her mother dead, then went into her yard where she proclaimed her famous oath and Candice Bergen took us on a Polaroid hayride.

A pair of dismembered white gloves demonstrated microwave ovens, after which a dog food for older pets made way for the Excedrin headache, which by now was a distinctly possible ailment. *Waldo Pepper* Redford returned, Datsun promised to save money on gas mileage and several people over one hundred years old testified to the benefits of eating yogurt. Following some more "news updates," a title card told us of Sherman's devastation and the *Wind* which swept through Georgia. Tara had survived but the O'Hara family had to labor in the cotton fields and Scarlett was forced to shoot a looting Yankee deserter. Ashley returned to Melanie's arms and rice pudding, cough drops, Flare pens and more aftershave lotion paved the way for a return visit from *Sybil*'s many personalities.

Scarlett heard that carpetbaggers were raising the taxes on Tara and asked Ashley for advice. He was no help, and Gerald's death was a further complication so she ripped down her mother's draperies for a new dress and prepared to travel to Atlanta. Instead we went to Florida's space center where Anita Bryant endorsed orange juice and scenes of mascara, sinus pills and bath oil passed before our eyes. Previews of *Baa, Baa Black*

Sheep and other NBC shows drifted into the laughter of movie-fan passengers on National Airlines and two automobiles were pitted against each other. Scarlett visited Rhett in jail but found no luck in obtaining tax money, so she married Frank Kennedy for it. As she started her lumber business with Ashley managing, the scene suddenly froze and we were promised some highlights from the following night's concluding installment. But not before there was further enlightenment on wine, vitamins and *The Moneychangers*. The promised scenes then peeked into the futures of Rhett and Scarlett, concluding with his sweeping her up their Atlanta staircase—but audiences were forced to wait twenty-one more hours to get the full details.

In all, the first night's viewing had encompassed 150 minutes of *Gone With the Wind*, and these were intact except for one brief but memorable moment. The final glimpse of wounded soldiers at the Atlanta depot had always before depicted a panorama which (in the original) was front action superimposed onto a "matte" painting. The artwork had, in point of fact, always seemed a bit unrealistic, since the painted Confederate flag was all too stationary in contrast to the windblown effect in the preceding "movie crane shot." This specific moment had been drastically reframed in 1954 so that soldiers on the ground (meant to be seen at the bottom of the screen) would not be cut off in wide-screen projection. This view had been plainly visible in Home Box Office's presentations, where the lower quarter of the picture was merely black masking. Since NBC was evidently unable to restore the original framing of that momentary longshot, it eliminated it entirely and repeated a brief visual moment from the former "crane shot." This substitution was a bit jarring to sharp-eyed viewers who could see Scarlett walking again toward the car barn she had supposedly just left.

The motion picture's many devotees were pleased at the care taken to present *Gone With the Wind* on television as closely as possible to its original concept. Scenes underneath title panels for cast and technicians were once again filled with the movement of water rippling or flags and trees blowing. (Home Box Office's print had been of the 1967 genre with all these backgrounds stationary, as if they were paintings.) But when the famous prologue ("There was a land of Cavaliers and Cotton Fields . . .") appeared, many of *GWTW*'s faithful repeat viewers were momentarily stunned to see something entirely unfamiliar to them.

Mr. Selznick's movieola scripts described the background of the prologue as follows: "Field, sunset sky with clouds. Horsemen ride across horizon in silhouettes right to left." As the last six words rose from the bottom of the screen, the background changed to "Slaves driving oxen to the camera . . . silhouetted against a sunset sky." *This* was the scenic backdrop remembered most clearly through the decades by the film's most ardent followers.

But NBC's print suddenly projected the prologue against a strikingly beautiful blue sky with moving clouds—not a slave or rider in sight! Where did this substitute come from? Why were there two variables? Another *Gone With the Wind* mystery began, and would remain an arguable point until original prints of various vintages could be found and examined. (Some rumors cropped up that the television print had come from Europe when no acceptable one could be found in America.)

As mentioned, the color of the titles was richer than it had been in some time, and throughout the viewing, it was apparent that steps had been taken to render the best hues possible. It was still, sadly, not quite up to the color which 1939 audiences had been treated to. But the sound was consistently good (a great improvement over the Home Box Office showings) with dialogue crisp and audible. Even the musical scoring benefited from the reversion and a theme for Charles Hamilton's proposal—almost inaudible in 1967's stereophonic madness—seemed a welcome rediscovery.

The continuation of the "*GWTW*-Big Event" on November 8 rather incongruously fell under a different programming banner called "Monday Night at the Movies." After an unnecessary announcement of what film we were about to see, there were reprises of the previous night's three initial commercials and a full re-running of the movie's trademark and titles up through the prologue. Next we saw thirteen narrated minutes highlighting the hours of film unspooled the night before, in which NBC had taken some amusing minor liberties in continuity. In the midst of this capsulized *GWTW* we were told that Scarlett and Rhett had been trapped "as the stately city of Atlanta burns around them."

But before we were allowed to rejoin the film, there was a painful return visit to Shakey's, more of those men squeezing into that car, some nonsense about Musk Oil, and a reindeer walking the streets in both 1810 and 1976 to advertise the Hartford Insurance Company. Only then were we permitted to pick up the story where we had left it—with Scarlett O'Hara Hamilton Kennedy, the businesswoman.

Scarlett drove her buggy through Shantytown where an attack on her provoked a reprisal raid by Frank, Ashley and the Old Guard Southern men. Rhett saved Ashley's life but brought Scarlett the news that her second husband had been killed. Then Jim McKay told some cute children they could furnish their schools with sports equipment by saving cereal boxtops. Polaroid caught even cuter children playing football and the $6,000 car price was reprised until we saw more pizza at Shakey's and Carol Burnett promoted *The Dick Van Dyke Show*. After a moment or two from *Captains and the Kings*, we were offered a maintenance-free car battery and Belle Watling paid a visit to Melanie. Rhett proposed marriage to Scarlett and Vivian Vance poured instant Maxwell House coffee for an office staff, Kevin McCarthy demonstrated General Electric's pot-scrubbing dishwasher, we breezed again into the auto showroom and Neil Sedaka's singing voice accompanied some dancing cats.

NBC warned that in *Flood!* "a town learns the meaning of panic," after which the newly married Butlers sailed to New Orleans on their honeymoon. Soon, little Bonnie Blue Butler was born but Scarlett decided to have no more children. In a rage Rhett sought comfort from Belle but Volkswagen took us, in the meantime, back to the racetrack from which we dashed to Shakey's and then once again to that sweatshirt wedding. After a little wine and a few news items about the President-elect, Petula Clark and a girlie chorus danced and sang the joys of one-piece pantyhose.

A "survey" proved that one airline was most popular, after which Rhett and Scarlett wheeled Bonnie's carriage down Peachtree Street. Tormented by Scarlett's continued thoughts of Ashley, Rhett drank too much one night and carried her up their stairs for a few moments of romance. Gaines then told us puppies should have a special diet, the Hartford reindeer pranced through a forest and some moistured lipstick was termed refreshing. Alka Seltzer Plus looked very helpful as we traveled through a moment of *The Red Hot Scandals of 1926* and heard Sergio Franchi sing about a different brand of car.

Children got a hot school lunch on snowy days, someone told us just before Scarlett awoke, happily remembering her night with Rhett. The Butlers quarreled and he left for London with Bonnie, and, upon his return, discovered Scarlett was pregnant. However, she suffered a miscarriage, Bonnie was killed in a fall shortly afterward and the Polaroid hayride returned. Some more wine, bath oil and dog food were a prelude to another snatch of *Sybil*, from which we returned to *Gone With the Wind*, which followed through then to its conclusion.

In all fairness, the National Broadcasting Company had displayed superb programming judgment in the insertion of commercial messages. Each interruption was preceded and followed by a special title card that informed audience members when they could run for a beer or gave them warning to return to their seats. There were thoughtful pauses after important scenes even before the intermission cards appeared and there was a long, respecful moment of silence after the finale. The camera and automobile sponsors, at least, had displayed tasteful advertisements that did not jar one's concentration too greatly. Nevertheless, absorbed viewers were forced to spend seventy-eight unnecessary minutes in front of their television sets and, even if they thought otherwise, their concentration was unduly broken on fifteen separate occasions. The division into two nightly installments did definite harm to a full appreciation of *GWTW*'s carefully

contructed narrative, especially since NBC ignored the official intermission point and substituted its own rather senseless one. The fact that *Gone With the Wind* easily could have been broadcast in its entirety within one night was proved all too well only two weeks afterward when NBC devoted four and a half successive hours to its own "50th Anniversary Tribute."

How big was the audience? Never had so many been forced to wait so long for something that was usually immediate. But it seemed the Neilsen Company, guardian and executioners of those all-important ratings, had developed computer problems and the nationwide results of the *GWTW* telecast would be slightly delayed.

But meanwhile something of a phenomenon had occurred among motion-picture attendees. A *Variety* headline reported (in covering New York City's theatrical business): "Current Alibi: '*Wind*' on TV." The article stated, "Scarlett O'Hara may never go hungry again, but she saw to it that exhibs [exhibitors] starved a bit on Sunday and Monday when *Gone With the Wind* had its two-part NBC television airing. With exhibs struggling to recover from the Election Week pay window blues, the *Wind* clout was the week's alibi for generally soft biz around town." Philadelphia, the same paper reported, also suffered on Sunday and "several downtown houses scratched [canceled] their regular 10 P.M. shows." Los Angeles had encountered a "rather bleak" week at that same time.

Conversely, Macmillan noticed an immediate sales upsurge in *GWTW* hardcovers, along with other related titles, and Avon Books rapidly ordered three more printings of the novel's paperbound version. But the Bowie Theatre in Fort Worth, Texas, recorded a perhaps unique achievement. *Gone With the Wind* had been its film selection for the weekend of the telecast and the management reported that on the evening of Sunday, November 7, it had a full theatre of five hundred patrons. It also told of "lines around the block" awaiting admittance the previous night to a movie that might have been seen "free" at home only twenty-four hours later.

The aftermath of the telecast also provided a period of unexpected but good-natured television parody. Joanne Woodward appeared on a John Denver "special" in a Scarlett O'Hara-style costume and was astonished when a great white shark suddenly devoured her boating beau (Mr. Denver). Carol Burnett and friends almost accomplished the impossible when they compressed the entire *GWTW* scenario into a reverently hilarious thirty minutes called *Went With the Wind*. In it, Dinah Shore portrayed a complacent "Melody" who eventually pushed "Starlett O'Hara" down a staircase, and Vicki Lawrence was a White "Sissy," who proudly returned a face slap to her mistress. The program's most successfully satiric moment presented "Starlett" greeting "Rat Butler" in a gown made from draperies with their holding rods intact.

Suspense generated by the *GWTW* telecast results vanished when national Neilson ratings were finally published showing that Sunday, November 7's "Part One" segment had earned a 47.6 rating and a 65 percent share of the audience during its three-hour span. Monday's follow-up was slightly lower with a 47.4 estimate and a 64 percent share. The overall average of both nights totaled 47.5 rating points and a 65 percent portion of total viewers. The National Broadcasting Company quickly proclaimed it "the highest-rated television program ever presented on a single network." It further declared that *GWTW* was the first program ever viewed in more than thirty million homes per average minute. NBC chiefs believed that 33,890,000 homes had tuned in the film on Sunday and that it had reached 33,750,000 residences on the following evening. The network seemed to have made good its original prediction that 110,000,000 people would see some part of the film. NBC, thanks to *GWTW*, had also been victorious for the first time in that season's weekly ratings battle, having momentarily dethroned ABC.

Metro-Goldwyn-Mayer was not about to forgo its share of the glory and purchased two facing pages in *Variety* to proclaim, "The greatest motion picture in history is now the greatest television show in history." The studio did not lose the opportunity to remind readers of the future either. "There's going to be another one," the advertisement concluded as it footnoted, "Now in development *The Continuation of Gone With the Wind* to be produced by Richard D. Zanuck and David Brown as a co-production of Metro-Goldwyn-Mayer and Universal Pictures."

Variety estimated that NBC's showing of *Gone With the Wind*, in addition to breaking all previous viewing records for any single television program, had "probably grossed in the neighborhood of $8,420,000 on the five-hour, two-night movie" (this was based on simple multiplication of the reported per-minute price by the commercial minutes involved). It had therefore earned more—as well as cost more—than any other television show in history. The medium's previous high-score champion had been "Bob Hope's Christmas Show" in January 1970, with a 46.6 rating. (*Airport* and *Love Story* had tied at 42.3 points, followed by *The Godfather*'s 39.4 rating, as the three feature films that had posted highest scores up until that time.)

An honest footnote to those ratings that required reporting paralleled the box-office totals of *GWTW*, which had never been updated to modern dollar values in the wake of the films which seemed to have surpassed it. *Variety* pointed out that the "modern" era of ratings had been initiated by the Neilsen organization in 1960. Under Neilsen's previous system, the *I Love Lucy* "maternity show" had scored a 71.7 total, based on far fewer total homes with television sets.

However, *Gone With the Wind* indisputably held fast as television's highest-rated "movie" showing of all time and the greatest money maker in the medium's history. It had conquered in still another field—the most modern one—and there was then bittersweet speculation as to whether this would eventually prove to be its last important victory. It was by then mid-autumn, twilight for the Bicentennial year. A cycle of life had ended but another would eventually begin. The leaves had fallen and *the Wind* blew on.

So there it was: fifty years of an author, her novel and its movie—of other books and films, Presidents and movie stars, studios and publishers, phenomenons, awards, merchandise and memories, of life and of death—all concluding in one dizzying year of celebration. Now, what would the future hold? *Gone with the Wind*, which had in its time survived depression, war, disillusionment, assassinations and political upheaval, suddenly faced its greatest challenge. Could it survive itself?

Television exposure and a planned sequel within the same year brought the unavoidable danger of overexposure to something whose value had once been so preciously guarded. Any commodity that seemed so readily available easily lost its elusive magic with the paying public. The telecast, despite its success, had saddened many of the faithful, for they feared the film's theatrical life was ended forever. Already they envisioned more home viewings and, eventually, the day when program listings for a local late, late showing would read, "GONE WITH THE WIND—Southern belle fights to save plantation. Long. Beware of cuts!"

Loyal followers also had that impossible-to-imagine sequel to contend with and a simultaneously published "paperback" book—how ignominious for the original novel's forty-year hardcover life! There were those, too, who seriously questioned Stephens Mitchell's motives, as guardian of his late sister's estate, in selling continuation rights to her only novel in direct opposition to her wishes. But Mr. Mitchell, a shrewd lawyer, realized that in giving this permission to film producers whose care for artistry had already been established, he was only a few decades away from the inevitable.

Mr. Mitchell had decided to secure for his descendants the benefits of financial gain from this sequel, under his guidance, since he knew that even under revised copyright laws *Gone With the Wind* would enter public domain in thirty-five more years and thereafter become fair game for any film adapter, publisher or television producer to do with as he felt inclined. There could then be abridgments, distortions, soap operas, pornographies, miniseries, maxiseries and sequels galore. The O'Hara/Butler families might be immortalized with countless *Son of* or *Daughter of* versions, or future liaisons might be arranged between Scarlett and Ashley, Rhett and Belle, even Prissy and Beau. Since Rhett Butler was a generation older than Scarlett O'Hara, she probably outlived him and went on to other adventures. Scarlett would have been free then to travel to all sorts of exotic or romantic locales, meeting every manner of interesting character from Jesse James to the great white shark or, possibly, King Kong.

Although all this promised pain for those who had known, loved and reverently treasured the original from its beginnings, the faithful would, by then, be ending life's journey themselves. The deepest concern—if considered important at all—was for the future. Here was a beautiful heritage that had thrilled millions of people for many years and which, one might hope, could be left intact for those who would come after—for far more generations than the few which had passed. Certainly there would *have* to be just such a preservation movement for *Gone With the Wind*, and its many illustrious contemporaries, which had represented culture, history and inspiration throughout the great part of a troubled yet excitingly unique era.

But Bicentennial America was a country disenchanted even with the political foundations of its government. It was an extremely mature nation that demanded realism in place of romance and often found it necessary to ridicule nostalgia. The existence of an idea like "Hollywood"—which once personified the dreams of everyone—had indeed taken its last bow. Idols of the day were more transitory, their popularity divided among age and taste groups. Mass entertainment desires were seemingly satisfied only by what was graphically sexual or chronically violent. The forgotten innocence of a country which once thrived on romantic historical novels and motion pictures could be found only in social histories—if anyone cared enough about that former time to look. But what, amid all of this, would become of *that* book and *that* movie?

Did the fact that 110,000,000 individuals had retreated for a few hours in 1976 to another threatened era in pursuit of "survival" have any definite meaning? Not necessarily. Eventually, there might no longer be a need for a tremendously long novel with embarrassing reminders of America's bleakest moment or of a time when its racial problems might have been solved but were instead exploited. Least of all in that ever-increasing sophistication might there be a place for the gradual romance between a middle-aged rogue and a feisty opportunist who shrugged worries into the future. If so, perhaps it was destined for only a brief mention that once there had been a book of great popularity and a film which earned a great deal of money. After all those years Margaret Mitchell's work might become nothing more than a legend unclearly remembered.

But there remained a more hopeful alternative. It was still possible for that relatively young nation to solve its internal discord and represent a people united in the cause of justice and equality as, two hundred years before, it had hoped to. Then America could find a reason, with its social conscience satisfied, to turn again toward idealism, beauty and art—or, in the words of Betty Ford, to "light the candle of imagination . . . enrich our dreams and expand our understandings."

Would *Gone with the Wind* survive? Only "tomorrow" will tell.

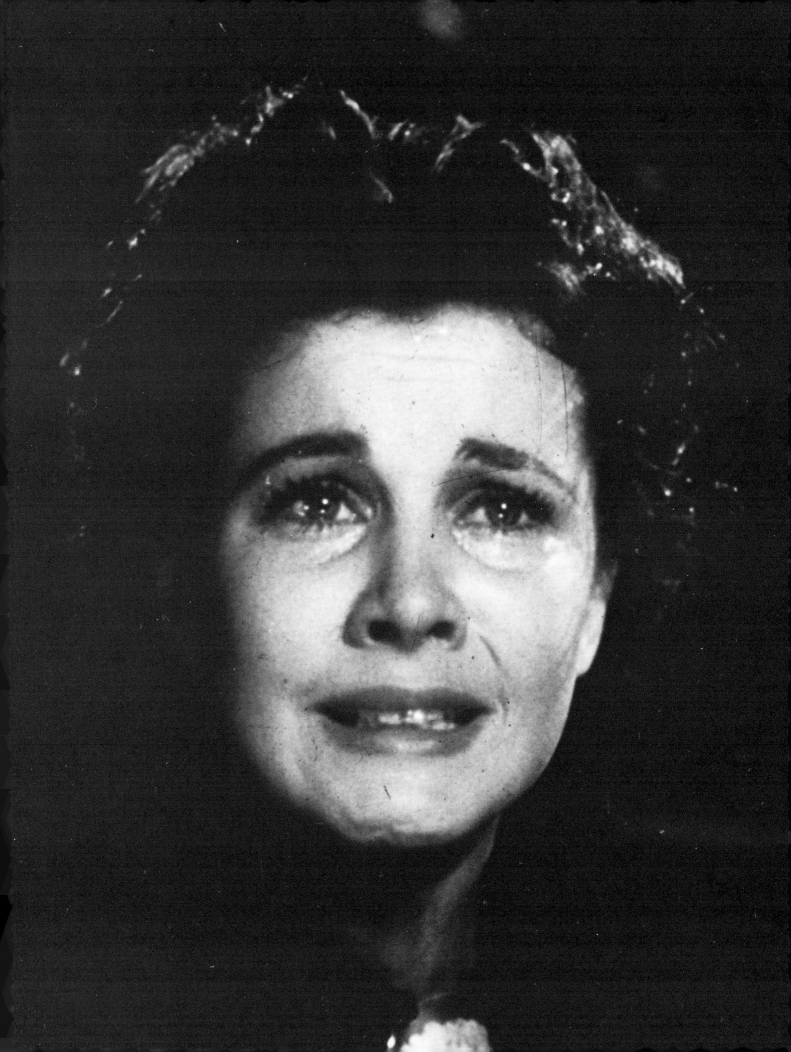

Epilogue: Did She Get Him Back?

At the start of 1977 *Variety* listed *Gone With the Wind* in *fifth* position on its annual "All-Time Rental Champs" chart (following *Jaws*, *The Godfather*, *The Exorcist* and *The Sound of Music*) with a cumulative $76,700,000 yielded to its distributor. Within six months another film, Twentieth Century-Fox's *Star Wars*, began a stratospheric climb to box-office heights which threatened all five of those champions.

Bowker's *80 Years of Best Sellers 1895–1975*, published early in 1977, still proclaimed the novel *Gone with the Wind* as the largest-selling hardcover fiction title in the history of such compilations with total sales in America of 5,190,004 copies. After combining that figure with sales of 3,440,000 *GWTW* paperbacks, the Bowker publication also listed Margaret Mitchell's book in ninth position on its cumulative tally of all-time best-selling fiction titles (following *The Godfather*, *The Exorcist*, *To Kill a Mockingbird*, *Peyton Place*, *Love Story*, *Valley of the Dolls, Jaws* and *Jonathan Livingston Seagull*).

Alex Haley's *Roots* had become the country's leading best seller shortly after its 1976 publication and remained in that position for the first quarter of 1977 with more than a million and a half copies in print. And the "Novel for Television" film version, broadcast by ABC on eight successive nights (January 23 through January 30, 1977), broke ratings records throughout America. Seven of the eight episodes captured positions on television's all-time "top ten" roll of honor (aided to a degree by a nationwide cold wave that made outside activities difficult). The final installment of *Roots* exceeded the ratings of *Gone With the Wind* to become the new champion. But while the two portions of *GWTW* broadcast by NBC fell to second and third positions, there were those who argued that the Selznick classic *in its entirety* still held the record for viewers' attention of any *complete* televised program.

Had Alex Haley's book posed a serious threat to the hardcover fiction championship held by Margaret Mitchell? Even the Pulitzer Prize committee had difficulty deciding the proper category for *Roots* as it voted it a "special" award that spring. *Roots* had also created its own phenomenon when—during its sales surge—bookstore windows were broken, stolen copies were sold on street corners, and disappointed potential buyers learned that most dealers were sold out shortly after shipments arrived. And Americans were inspired to trace the "roots" of their own ancestries, sometimes to rather surprising results.

Roots crossed *GWTW*'s path in a far more humorous way when a bindery mixup at a plant preparing copies of both books resulted in the delivery of Scarlett's saga within the covers of *Roots* to stores in both Connecticut and Wisconsin. No one was quite sure how many such copies escaped plant detection but one thing was certain —a new and valuable collector's item had been created.

The Thorn Birds by Colleen McCullough—promoted by Harper & Row as another *Gone with the Wind*—made history even before its May 1977 publication when paperback rights to the Australian family saga were sold to Avon Books for an unprecedented $1,900,000. As it soared to the position of number-one best seller, *The Thorn Birds* proved that even in the sophisticated Seventies there was a market for good historical fiction. And Warner Brothers, the studio that ignored another epic forty-one years before, quickly purchased film rights.

Metro-Goldwyn-Mayer celebrated its first major Academy Award victory in a decade when *Network* became the first film since *A Streetcar Named Desire* to win three Oscars for acting (in March 1977). The film—a sardonic comment on the television industry—helped demonstrate the perversity of the times when it was sold for broadcast to CBS only a few months after its Academy triumph (for $5,000,000—the same price NBC paid for *GWTW* in 1974). At the same time, M-G-M refused an offer from NBC for a second telecast of *Gone With the Wind*, deciding instead to hold back the film for future theatrical reissues. If these plans materialized, the studio would be forced to find a new "premiere" site, however, since Atlanta's Loew's Grand Theatre announced in July 1977 that it was closing its doors forever.

United Artists, distributors of *Network*, shared the movie's Oscar glory with M-G-M and also captured the year's most enviable film honor—"Best Picture of 1976" —with *Rocky*, a low-budget production which gave audiences promise for a hopeful tomorrow.

The Academy of Motion Picture Arts and Sciences lent its participation to a 1977 television "special" that featured scenes from all forty-nine "Best Picture" winners. For those who may have wondered how the Hollywood Academy regarded it, *GWTW* was honored with a unique spotlight in the final and longest segment of that program and was introduced by Olivia de Havilland.

On June 18, 1977, NBC televised a "live" broadcast of the Fifty-Sixth Annual *Photoplay* Gold Medal Awards. While *A Star Is Born* was named "Favorite Motion Picture of 1976," *Gone With the Wind* was the choice of *Photoplay*'s readers in another category, "All-Time Favorite Movie" (*The Sound of Music* and *Jaws* were runners-up. Olivia de Havilland was on hand to accept the medallion and she expressed thanks, as she said David O. Selznick would have, to Margaret Mitchell and individual members of the film's cast and technical staff. "We did hope that it might survive," Olivia said, "but none of us ever dreamed that almost forty years later it would still be receiving awards as this one tonight."

By mid-1977 *The New York Times* reported Anne Edwards was "putting the finishing touches on a film sequel to *Gone With the Wind*." And at that same time, the author's newest biography, *Vivien Leigh*, was enjoying best-seller status. Meanwhile, *Variety* quoted a spokesman for M-G-M on the production plans for that sequel: "We aren't rushing. . . . There's no chance the film will be made in 1977. We hope it might be rolling in 1978. But if it's 1979, 1980 or 1981, it will still be right to do it."

Talk of the sequel continued among *GWTW*'s followers in early 1977. Would Robert Redford, Paul Newman, Warren Beatty or Jack Nicholson play Rhett? Would Elizabeth Taylor, Natalie Wood or Jacqueline Bisset be the new, maturing Scarlett? Finally the controversy and excitement dwindled. But knowledge of the proposed sequel had presented an encouraging new gift. Thanks to Stephens Mitchell, Richard Zanuck, David Brown and Anne Edwards, *Gone With the Wind*'s faithful supporters had finally won the right to voice an answer to that forty-year-old burning question. The answer which, in their hearts, they had known all along.

Did she get him back? Of course she did!

Bibliography

The author of *Scarlett Fever* owes a great debt for research origins to the following publications:

Atlanta Historical Society. *The Atlanta Historical Bulletin, Volume IX, Number 34, May 1950, the Margaret Mitchell Memorial Issue.* Atlanta, Ga.: 1950.

Behlmer, Rudy, ed. *Memo from David O. Selznick.* New York: Viking Press, 1972.

Farr, Finis. *Margaret Mitchell of Atlanta: The Author of* Gone with the Wind. New York: William Morrow & Company, 1965. (Copyright Finis Farr and Stephens Mitchell.)

Harwell, Richard, ed. *Margaret Mitchell's GONE WITH THE WIND Letters 1936–1949.* New York: Macmillan Publishing Co., Inc., 1976 (Copyright Stephens Mitchell and Richard Harwell).

Mitchell, Margaret. *Gone with the Wind.* New York: Macmillan Publishing Co., Inc., 1936.

Osborne, Robert. *Academy Awards Illustrated.* Calif.: Ernest E. Schworck, 1969.

Selznick, David O., et al. *The Screenplay for* Gone With the Wind. Unpublished. Culver City, Calif.: 1939.

Atlanta Constitution, Atlanta Georgian, Atlanta Journal, The Boston Herald, The Chicago Daily News, The Chicago Daily Tribune, Cinema Arts, Collier's, Hollywood, Liberty, Life, Look, The Los Angeles Times, Modern Screen, Motion Picture, Newsweek, New York, The New York Daily News, The New York Herald-Tribune, The New Yorker, The New York Post, The New York Times, The Philadelphia Inquirer, Photoplay, Pictorial Review, Publisher's Weekly, Reader's Digest, The Record (Bergen County, New Jersey), *The San Francisco Chronicle, The San Francisco Examiner, The San Francisco News, The Saturday Evening Post, Screen Guide, Screen Stories, Scribner's, Time, TV Guide, Variety, The Washington Post* and *Women's Wear Daily.*

Very special recognition is given to *Films in Review*, its editors, contributors and correspondents, for keeping cinema history alive.

OTHER PRINTED SOURCES

Balio, Tino. *United Artists: The Company Built by the Stars.* Madison, Wis.: University of Wisconsin Press, 1976.

Barker, Felix. *The Oliviers.* Philadelphia and New York: J. B. Lippincott Company, 1953 (*Vivien Leigh*).

Bennett, Joan, and Kibbee, Lois. *The Bennett Playbill,* New York, Chicago and San Francisco: Holt Rinehart and Winston, 1970.

Block, Maxine, ed. *Current Biographies* (various editions). (*Hattie McDaniel and Victor Fleming*).

Burdick, Loraine. *The Shirley Temple Scrapbook.* New York: Jonathan David Publishers, 1975 (*memorabilia and collectibles*).

Chierichetti, David. *Hollywood Costume Design.* New York: Harmony Books, 1976 (*Walter Plunkett*).

Croce, Arlene. *The Fred Astaire and Ginger Rogers Book.* New York: Outerbridge & Lazard, Inc., distributed by E. P. Dutton, 1972 (*the Irene Castle "talent search"*).

Crowther, Bosley. *The Great Films: Fifty Golden Years of Motion Pictures,* New York: G. P. Putnam's Sons, 1967.

———. *The Lion's Share.* New York: E. P. Dutton & Company, Inc., 1957.

Denton, Clive. *The Hollywood Professionals,* vol. 5. New York: A. S. Barnes & Co., 1976 (*King Vidor*).

Eells, George. *Hedda and Louella.* New York: G. P. Putnam's Sons, 1972.

Funke, Lewis, and Booth, John E. *Actors Talk About Acting.* New York: Random House, 1961 (*Vivien Leigh*).

Goldner, Orville, and Turner, George E. *The Making of King Kong.* New York: A. S. Barnes & Co., Inc., 1975 (*the Atlanta depot fire*).

Goodman, Ezra. *The Fifty-Year Decline and Fall of Hollywood.* New York: Simon and Schuster, 1961 (*D. W. Griffith*).

Grossman, Gary H. *Superman: Serial to Cereal.* New York: Popular Library, 1976 (*George Reeves*).

Hackett, Alice Payne. *70 Years of Best Sellers 1895–1965.* New York and London: R. R. Bowker Company, 1967.

Hackett, Alice Payne, and Burke, James Henry. *80 Years of Best Sellers 1895–1975.* New York and London: R. R. Bowker Company, 1977.

Hart, James D. *The Oxford Companion to American Literature,* 4th ed. New York: Oxford University Press, 1965.

———. *The Popular Book: A History of America's Literary Taste.* New York: Oxford University Press, 1950.

Howard, Leslie Ruth. *A Quite Remarkable Father.* New York: Harcourt, Brace and Company, 1959 (*Leslie Howard*).

Jacobs, Jack, and Braum, Myron. *The Films of Norma Shearer.* New York: A. S. Barnes and Company, 1976.

Kulik, Karol. *Alexander Korda: the Man Who Could Work Miracles.* New York: Arlington House, 1975.

Lambert, Gavin. *On Cukor.* New York: G. P. Putnam's Sons, 1972.

Leggett, John. *Ross and Tom.* New York: Simon and Schuster, 1974 (*Raintree County*).

Look Magazine Editors. *Movie Lot to Beachhead.* New York: Doubleday, Doran and Co., 1945 (*World War II*).

McClelland, Doug. *Down the Yellow Brick Road: The Making of* The Wizard of Oz. New York: Pyramid Books, 1976.

McConathy, Dale, and Vreeland, Diana. *Hollywood Costume: Glamour! Glitter! Romance!* New York: Harry N. Abrams, Inc., 1976 (*Walter Plunkett*).

Madsen, Axel. *William Wyler.* New York: Thomas Y. Crowell Company, 1973.

Martin, Pete. *Pete Martin Calls On.* New York: Simon and Schuster, 1962 (*Clark Gable*).

Myers, David, ed. *Hollywood Life Stories, Number Four.* New York: Dell Publishing Company, 1954 (*Susan Hayward*).

Notable American Women 1607–1950, Volume I. Cambridge, Mass.: Belknap Press, Harvard University Press (*Laura Hope Crews*).

Ragan, David. *Who's Who in Hollywood 1900–1976.* New York: Arlington House, 1976 (*various GWTW cast members*).

Rhode, Eric. *A History of the Cinema.* New York: Hill and Wang, 1976 (Citizen Kane).

Schemmer, Benjamin F., and the Editors of Armed Forces Journal. *Almanac of Liberty: A Chronology of American Military Anniversaries from 1775 to the Present.* New York: Macmillan Publishing Co., Inc., 1974.

Symons, Arthur. *The Religion of Beauty: Selections from the Aesthetes.* London: William Heinemann Ltd., 1950 (*Ernest Dowson*).

Thomas, Bob. *Selznick.* New York: Doubleday & Company, Inc., 1950.

Thomas, Tony. *The Hollywood Professionals*, vol. 2. New York: A. S. Barnes & Co., 1974 (*Sam Wood*).

Tornabene, Lyn. *Long Live the King: A Biography of Clark Gable.* New York: G. P. Putnam's Sons, 1976.

Valentino, Lou. *The Films of Lana Turner.* Secaucus, N.J.: Citadel Press, 1976.

Vidor, King. *On Film Making.* New York: David McKay Company, Inc., 1972.

Wagenknecht, Edward. *Cavalcade of the American Novel.* New York: Henry Holt and Company, 1952.

Wagner, Walter. *You Must Remember This.* New York: G. P. Putnam's Sons, 1975.

Westmore, Frank, and Davidson, Muriel. *The Westmores of Hollywood.* Philadelphia and New York: J. B. Lippincott, 1976.

Index

316